D0330773

VERTICAL

VERTICAL

The City from Satellites to Bunkers

Stephen Graham

VERSO
London • New York

To my friends

This edition first published by Verso 2016
© Stephen Graham 2016

Every effort has been made to contact the copyright holders for the images used herein. Verso and the author would like to extend their gratitude, and to apologise for any omissions, which, should we be notified of their existence, we will seek to rectify in the next edition of this work.

For permission to reproduce images we would like to thank the following in particular: David Coulthard's car on the Burj Al Arab's helipad, courtesy of the Jumeirah Group (p. xii); 'City of Volume' image, courtesy of Pierre Bélanger (p. xvi); the flat map courtesy of Neil Brenner, from Brenner's 'Introducing the Urban Theory Lab' (p. 8); Lightful by Buckminster Fuller, from *Operating Manual for Spaceship Earth* (2008), courtesy of the Buckminster Fuller Institute (p. 24); Menwith Hill NSA Base photograph courtesy of Steve Rowell (p. 35); São Paulan executive's helipad illustration, courtesy of Eduardo Martino (p. 101); designs for Cairo skyscrapers, courtesy of Reese Campbell and Demetrios Comodromos at Method Design (p. 128); Kingdom Tower image, courtesy of Malec (p. 150); London skyscrapers image, courtesy of Darjole (p. 165); Sky Tower billboard in Mumbai, courtesy of Andrew Harris (p. 207); Skybridge in Minneapolis, courtesy of Thunerchild5 (p. 226); Bangkok's Skytrain, courtesy of Moaksey (p. 231); Fake skyline in Hong Kong, courtesy of Drew; *Underneath New York* by Harry Granick, book cover (1991), courtesy of Fordham University (p. 280); 'Sacrifice Zone', courtesy of Kaitlin Donnally (p. 290); Awaaz Foundation poster, courtesy of the Awaaz Foundation (p. 299); Photograph of Devi Lal, courtesy of Beena Sarwar (p. 338); 'Palestinian tunneller', courtesy of Getty Images (p. 351); 'urban cave' project, courtesy of Andrea Star Reese (p. 353); 'Urban Explorer', courtesy of Bradley Garrett (p. 361)

1 3 5 7 9 10 8 6 4 2

Verso
UK: 6 Meard Street, London W1F 0EG
US: 20 Jay Street, Suite 1010, Brooklyn, NY 11201
versobooks.com

Verso is the imprint of New Left Books

ISBN-13: 978-1-78168-793-2
ISBN-13: 978-1-78168-996-7 (US EBK)
ISBN-13: 978-1-78168-995-0 (UK EBK)

British Library Cataloguing in Publication Data
A catalogue record for this book is available from the British Library

Library of Congress Cataloging-in-Publication Data

Names: Graham, Stephen, 1965– author.
Title: Vertical : the city from satellites to bunkers / Stephen Graham.
Description: Brooklyn : Verso, 2016.
Identifiers: LCCN 2016033169 | ISBN 9781781687932 (hardback)
Subjects: LCSH: Cities and towns – Growth. | Land use, Urban. | Space (Architecture) – Social aspects. | BISAC: SOCIAL SCIENCE / Sociology / Urban. | POLITICAL SCIENCE / Public Policy / City Planning & Urban Development. | ARCHITECTURE / General.
Classification: LCC HT371 .G69 2016 | DDC 307.76–dc23
LC record available at https://lccn.loc.gov/2016033169

Typeset in Minion Pro by MJ & N Gavan, Truro, Cornwall
Printed and bound by CPI Group (UK) Ltd, Croydon, CR0 4YY

Contents

Vertical city: a 1928 image of the future by city planner Harvey Wiley Corbett published in the US magazine *Popular Mechanics*

Preface: Dubai, January 2010

> What would happen if you took geographic thinking and instead of
> putting it on a horizontal axis, you added a vertical axis?
>
> Trevor Paglen

My brain simply could not process what I saw. That tiny grey smudge, just visible far below to my right through the ice-specked Perspex, was *Baghdad*! As 200 travellers and holidaymakers around me sipped gin and tonics, delved into familiar episodes of *Friends* and *The Simpsons*, or played classic 1980s arcade games like *Missile Command* or *Battlezone* on in-flight entertainment systems, we were flying high above a full-on war zone.[1]

Between us and the ground, complex military air operations were under way, coordinated from a bunker in our destination country linked, since the previous August, to newly established air traffic controllers in their own fortified complexes in Baghdad itself. Each day, around sixty commercial flights were being routed either over or around combat operations; these command centres were simultaneously organizing war and tourism within the same airspace.

The circuits of global capitalism and tourism – and in the case of

---

1 After the Malaysian Airlines flight MH17 was shot down by a Russian-made surface-to-air missile, killing all 298 passengers and crew on board on 17 July 2014, many expressed astonishment on finding out that commercial airlines routinely overflew war zones. Tony Wheeler, founder of travel publisher Lonely Planet, immediately blogged about a Qantas flight from Dubai to Heathrow that crossed northern Iraq. 'Azwya, and Mosul, which we flew close by, have both been flashpoints for the ISIS takeover of parts of Iraq in recent weeks. It's remarkable how peaceful everything looks from 40,000 feet.' In July 2014, escalating conflicts in Iraq involving ISIS led Emirates to stop overflying Iraq; other major airlines continue to do so but at increased heights. Wheeler, cited in *Sunshine Coast Daily*, 18 July 2014, sunshinecoastdaily.com.

my colleague and myself, travel for academic research – were not to be interrupted by a mere full-scale counterinsurgency war. Such violence could, since the airspace was 'liberalised' in 2008, simply be bypassed, the aircraft icon hovering on a digital map on a small screen, a banal signifier for passage over contested territory riven by violence.[2]

And so to our stopover: Dubai. By chance, we were in town during the ultimate stage-managed urban spectacle: the opening of the world's tallest building, the 830-metre Burj Khalifa. Here, rather unexpectedly, was a place that, like few others, hammered home the growing need to appreciate the vertical aspects of geography and urbanism: a centre of extraordinary vertical politics and vertical geographies.

Jet-lagged and dazed, we walked among excited crowds. We also enjoyed the vast fireworks display and lightshows emanating from the tower itself and the 30-metre, $225 million 'dancing' fountains (the world's tallest, needless to say). The fountains seemed especially lavish in a desert country with no real rivers, a collapsing or totally nonexistent ground water supply and the highest per-capita water consumption on Earth. As the towers and fountains have risen, so Dubai's ground water level has plummeted by over a metre in the last twenty years. It would take centuries for this drop to be reversed, even with a complete cessation of usage.

We looked in awe at the most verticalised of cityscapes, ratcheted into the sky in a mere decade, rearing up from hundreds of miles of pancake-flat desert.[3] It felt as though we'd arrived on some vast stage set for a highly sanitised sequel to *Blade Runner* made by Disney. Everywhere we looked there were exalted proclamations that the Burj Khalifa, which snaked ever upward like a sci-fi icon, heralded, along with the many other new skyscrapers in the city, Dubai's arrival as a 'world-class' or 'global' city.

---

2   Political theorist Mark Neocleous, remarking on the importance of the no-fly zone in contemporary policing and counter-insurgency war, observes that 'one of the remarkable features of contemporary official discourse concerning air power is that it openly looks back and seeks to learn from the use of air power in colonial pacification campaigns of the 1920s.' Mark Neocleous, 'Police Power, All the Way to Heaven', *Radical Philosophy* 182, November/December 2013, p. 5.

3   In 2011, fully 24 per cent of the world's 125,000 construction cranes were in the Gulf region.

No longer, it seemed, are the world's tallest skyscrapers erected merely to house the headquarters of corporations competing for prestigious space in the centres of tightly packed financial districts. Nor are they the products of utopian and visionary thinking about housing future urban populations. Now they emerge, isolated in deserts, as visual symbols constructed to demonstrate a location's global clout. 'Not since 1311, when the spire of Lincoln Cathedral first topped the Great Pyramid of Giza', novelist Geraldine Bedell reminds us, 'has the tallest structure in the world been located in the Arab world'.[4]

Such towers are ultra-vain – and some would say suspiciously phallic – embodiments of the hubris of the super-rich. Despite the claim that high-rise construction is necessary to accommodate a burgeoning humanity, between 15 per cent and 30 per cent of their height – the highest part, the so-called vanity height – is so slim as to be capable of housing only lift shafts and services.

Such super-tall towers are catalysts designed to add value to vast malls and real-estate projects. And they are stage sets for media stunts designed to lubricate the worlds of tourism or hyperconsumption. 'Burj Khalifa is more the spike of luxury, than anything accessible … the condominium level [rents] for $2,000 per square foot.'[5] Startlingly, the top 244 metres of the tower fall into the vanity height category – the sole purpose of this part of the tower is to get the place into the record books.

Meanwhile, the sculpted, *Thunderbirds*-style helipad atop Dubai's other famous new structure, the super-expensive, sail-shaped Burj Al Arab Hotel – count those seven stars! – is as much a global stage of bling as a place for the super-rich to land and take off. It has been used to stage-manage launches of Aston Martins and Formula 1 racing car teams, to play host to superstar tennis matches, and to accommodate Tiger Woods's golf demonstrations and product launches.

Also central to the spectacular vertical rise of places like Dubai are global flows of speculative investment as the cash-rich super-elite who profit most from global neoliberalism seek iconic vertical buildings in low-tax, unregulated enclaves as investment vehicles. In

---

4 Geraldine Bedell, 'Burj Khalifa: A Bleak Symbol of Dubai's Era of Bling', *Observer*, 10 January 2010.

5 Ibid.

David Coulthard's Formula One car on the helipad of the Burj Al Arab, where it had been lifted in a 2013 media stunt

Dubai, as elsewhere, this process raises towers that are often not even fully occupied by people: while projecting their symbolic value to the world, they often house capital rather than humans. 'Brand Dubai' is thus all about linking the rising forest of steel, concrete, aluminium and glass to a collective architectural fantasy, a phantasmagoria of 'supreme lifestyles',[6] for consumers, tourists, speculators and elites orchestrated through the complex machinations of global finance, global airline systems and global geopolitics (as well as, less visibly, organized crime, money laundering, financing of terrorism and sex and people trafficking). Vertical metaphors saturate – indeed *constitute* – these narratives.

Critics also invoke vertical metaphors to come to grips with Dubai. Mike Davis lambasts the city as a surreal world apparently drawn from the imaginations of Margaret Atwood or Phillip K. Dick: a world where fantasy itself is 'levitated'.[7]

---

6   Like most words describing status, quality, power or achievement, 'supreme' is itself a vertical metaphor. Its origins are late fifteenth century (in the sense of 'highest'): from Latin *supremus*, superlative of *superus,* 'that which is above'.

7   Mike Davis, 'Fear and Money in Dubai', *New Left Review* 2:41, 2006, pp. 47–68.

The opening of the extreme verticality of the Burj Khalifa was loaded with multiple myths, symbols and messages of progress, arrival, success, centrality and future prosperity. For one, the tower's height and strength were over-coded with ubiquitous images of Dubai's apparently benevolent and patriarchal ruler, the tall bearded figure of Mohammed bin Rashid Al Maktoum. Combining the roles of monarch, prime minister and president, Al Maktoum and his family rule Dubai as a quasi-medieval fiefdom: he must always be called 'His Highness' (HH). With absolute power, Al Maktoum and his family 'own every lucrative grain of sand in the sheikhdom';[8] he is even able to personally dictate criminal sentences.

Dripping with endless bling and cordoned-off, hyper-luxury enclaves, Dubai and its architectural rise have been matched, crucially, by its location at the heart of the most aggressive airline and airport expansion project of the early twenty-first century. By June 2014, Dubai's 'ascendency', following the economic collapse of 2007–8, meant that it had become the world's largest hub for international air travel. Within two short decades a humble refuelling and duty-free stop for airliners travelling between Europe, Asia and Australia was re-engineered to replace London Heathrow as the largest international hub airport on the planet – the aerial 'crossroads of the world'.[9] By 2020, the Dubai government estimates that the airport and its related industries and services will generate fully 22 per cent of Dubai's employment and 32 per cent of its GDP.

The United Arab Emirates (UAE) – itself the world's fifth largest gas and oil producer – also houses one of the greatest concentrations of US military power on the planet, with more US Navy ship dockings than any other nation outside the United States. (Jebel Ali is the only Gulf port capable of taking US aircraft carriers.) Meanwhile, Al Dhafra Air Base in Abu Dhabi, the next emirate to the west of Dubai, which the US Air Force took over during the First Gulf War in 1990, is one of the US Air Force's most important drone and spy plane bases. Al Dhafra is only a hundred miles as the drone flies from Iran.

---

8 *Socialist Review*, 'Evil Paradise: An Artist's Vision of Dubai in the Future', September 2005.

9 Jad Mouwawad, 'Dubai, Once a Humble Refueling Stop, is Crossroads to the Globe', *New York Times,* 18 June 2014.

A short distance along the coast to the west, the tiny Gulf state of Qatar – the controversial site of the murderous construction of air-conditioned stadia for the 2022 World Cup – has provided bases for many of the warplanes involved in the Iraq and Afghan wars. Its Al Udeid Air Base also houses a huge 'Airspace Control' centre for the US military's Central Command (the strategic command focusing on the pivotal Middle East region).[10] The Al Udeid control centre had been responsible for organizing the unreal juxtaposition of our tourist flight above the war zone surrounding Baghdad.

Tellingly, Qatar's 'Airspace Control' centre was relabelled the 'Combined Air and Space Operations Center' – CAOC, pronounced 'KAY-ock' – in 2008. Such a shift reflects a strategic effort across the US military to deepen their control and use of extra-atmospheric space. Indeed, the Iraq War was deliberately used as an exercise in pushing such a shift.

The huge CAOC complex seeks minute control of the airspace and inner space above the twenty countries in the Centcom area in and around the Middle East, stretching from Sudan to Kazakhstan and from Pakistan to Egypt. The centre was thus the pivotal hub through which the wars in Iraq and Afghanistan were organized. CAOC is a crucial command centre for the prosecution of lethal drones strikes by the US military throughout the Middle East and the main complex organizing the fourteen-nation coalition air war against Islamic State in Iraq and the Levant (ISIS) since 2014.

Although bombing missions over Iraq and Afghanistan are now relatively rare, the extraordinary rise of ISIS in Syria and northern Iraq, as well as continued instability in Pakistan and Afghanistan, means that the vertical scrutiny of these regions is, if anything, intensifying: 'The center gathers more than 800 hours of surveillance video over the war zone every day'.[11]

Such is the UAE's strategic importance that plans are in place for an invisible 'dome' of strategic space above and around the city to be protected by one of the world's most sophisticated missile defence

---

10   Qatar is also the forward base for Centcom (the main headquarters is at Tampa, Florida).

11   Thom Shanker, 'Hagel Lifts Veil on Major Military Center in Qatar', *New York Times*, 11 December 2013.

systems – the Terminal High Altitude Area Defense (THAAD) system – as a deterrent to missile attack from Iran, just across the Gulf. These air defence missiles are designed to destroy attacking missiles in the upper atmosphere and even beyond the atmosphere's limits.

And so, after a mere twenty-six hours in Dubai, we moved on to our post-stopover flight to Mumbai to carry on a long-standing research project. This time our Emirates plane was equipped with the latest version of in-flight entertainment systems where video cameras on the underside and tail of the aircraft allow passengers a perfect view down on all they fly over. Travellers can now peruse the details of the topographies far below – their very own Google Earth.

For us, such a view was apposite, as our flight took off over the alter-ego to Dubai's vertical megalomania – a vast archipelago of artificial islands horizontally engineered up from the seabed, again with near-slave labour, to look good from Google Earth. For a final element of the 'Dubai model' has been the widescale manufacture of lucrative waterfront land through the literal sucking up of sensitive seabed ecosystems in a process mistakenly labelled 'reclamation'. With waterfront land generating real-estate premiums, this economic model involves the almost complete neglect of Dubai's horizontal desert hinterland in favour of the vast horizontal manufacture of artificial islands shaped with their appearance in mind to arrays of satellites, which in turn transmit the images to laptops, TVs and smartphones.

As we took off, our camera looked down on Dubai World's half-built archipelago of diminishing dune-islands. The rumour circulating at the time was that Rod Stewart had bought the 'United Kingdom' island (a rumour which sadly emerged as untrue; the actual owner, Safi Qurashi, was in jail for seven years for using false cheques).

As the dune-islands receded we readied ourselves, now even more dazed than we had been on landing, to confront a very different world of vertical politics: Mumbai. Another vertically stratified urban world awaited. This was full, as we shall see later in this book, of more elite towers rising to the skies (some marketed for the way they herald status as well as provide cooler air); of twenty-seven-storey single-family skyscrapers; and of growing networks of flyovers and walkways on stilts which raise up the city for the rich and mobile who can thus bypass the teeming streets below.

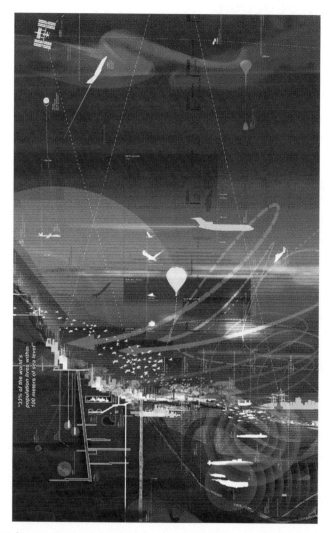

City of Volume: Harvard landscape architect Pierre Bélanger's cross-section showing verticalising cities tightly enmeshed in a world of drones, helicopters, aircraft and satellites above and subterranean infrastructures, mines and submarines below. He writes, 'This schematic cross-section view of the world opens a lens on the planet as an urban projection, pattern and process of overlapping change across different layers and level of space.' See Pierre Bélanger, 'Altitudes of Urbanization', *Tunnelling and Underground Space Technology* (2016).

Introduction: Going Vertical

vertical / ˈvɜːtɪk(ə)l

A adjective. **1** Of, pertaining to, situated at, or passing through the vertex or zenith; occupying a position in the sky directly overhead or above a given place or point.

2 Placed, extending, moving, or operating at right angles to a horizontal plane; perpendicular; upright.

Oxford English Dictionary

What does it mean to be above or below in today's rapidly urbanizing world? As humans excavate deep into the earth, build ever higher into the skies, and saturate airspaces and inner orbits with a myriad of vehicles, sensors and platforms, how might we understand the remarkable verticalities of our world?

Until recently, addressing such a question has been hampered by the dominance of remarkably *flat* perspectives about human societies in key academic debates about cities and urban life. In geography, especially, territory, sovereignty and human experience have long been flattened by a paradoxical reliance on flat maps – and, more recently, aerial and satellite images – projected or imaged from the disembodied bird's or God's eye view from high above. One powerful example here comes from the traditional geographic idea that geopolitics – the politics of state geography – is essentially the study of jostling nation states cartographically laid out on maps and globes. 'Geopolitics is a flat discourse', architectural scholar Eyal Weizman wrote in 2002 as part of a pioneering project on the political aspects of the vertical dimension. 'It largely ignores the vertical dimension and tends to look across rather than to cut through the landscape. This was the cartographic imagination inherited from the military and political spatialities of the modern state.'[1]

Such a flat tradition, indeed, was critical to the formulation and generalisation of modern nation states and the elaboration of the geographical and geopolitical sciences which surrounded and shaped that task. The key geographical idea dominating the world from the mid nineteenth to the mid twentieth centuries, after all, was that – following several centuries of colonial exploration, mapping and expansion by the dominant powers to fill in and claim the unknown territories of the earth – the horizontal and global extent of the earth's surface was both fully explored and fully claimed. Legally, no place could be left out of the world's system of solidifying sovereign states (a process completed after World War II with the colonial independence movements). The task of geography and geopolitics was to describe and understand how the territorial units of states jostled for power and territory within such a largely horizontal world view.

Such geographic traditions were in turn tightly bound up with deeper histories of Western culture in the critical period of colonial expansion between the fifteenth and nineteenth centuries. Broadly speaking, Western geographic thinking during this period was dominated by a largely horizontal and scenographic conception of geographic space – that is, with the study, exploration and control of the earth's surface. Ideas about geography thus became increasingly concerned with ideas of horizontal exploration and navigation beyond an immediate and stable horizon rendered through both cartography and linear perspective.[2]

These ideas were closely bound up with surface-level imperial 'discovery', exploration and competition to build Eurocentric empires. In the process new notions of property, law and territory were produced and enforced in colonial peripheries, absorbing colonial populations

---

1 Quote from Eyal Weizman, 'Introduction to the Politics of Verticality', *Open Democracy*, 2002, p. 3.

2 As film-maker Hito Steyerl puts it, 'The use of the horizon to calculate position gave seafarers a sense of orientation, thus also enabling colonialism and the spread of a capitalist global market, but also became an important tool for the construction of the optical paradigms that came to define modernity, the most important paradigm being that of so-called linear perspective.' Hito Steyerl, 'In Free Fall: A Thought Experiment on Vertical Perspective', *e-flux*, April 2011, p. 3.

into wage labour, servitude and colonial trading geographies. As this European discovery and exploration was completed, visually the modern world came to be pictured in globe, atlas or map form as the familiar series of curved surfaces or coloured flat surfaces. These equated the coloured territories of states and empires as proxies for their power and importance (a dominant technique in popular geography today).[3]

Beyond the occasional indication of geographic relief through use of contours or other cartographic techniques, or visual hints of the location of underground mineral deposits and fuel resources, *vertical* and *sectional* views that depict political claims of aerial or orbital worlds between the earth's surface and the rest of the cosmos have been very rare. Rarer still have been sectional or volumetric views of the critical subsurface and subterranean claims made by states to the key resources necessary to sustain their industrializing societies (soil, water, fossil fuels and a myriad of mined or quarried materials).

The powerful legacies of such 'flat' geographic thinking mean that, all too often, borders are still abstracted, unhelpfully, as little more than two-dimensional lines on a map. Such a perspective neglects the three-dimensional politics of the worlds above, below and around borders. It also makes it impossible to understand the increasingly common situation where airspace and subterranean resources are controlled by sovereign powers different to those with notional sovereignty over the surface. Flat imaginations of borders struggle even more to contend with occasions when *horizontal* structures effectively act as political and geopolitical borders – as when horizontal flyovers act to separate Jewish and Palestinian communities in contemporary Palestine, for example.

Outside the more fully three-dimensional debates in architecture, archaeology, climatology, geology or even philosophy,[4] 'flat' geographic traditions still too often represent cities, regions, nations and empires as planar areas of geography or sovereignty on the earth's

---

3   For a definitive history of thinking about the earth as a globe, see Denis Cosgrove, *Apollo's Eye: A Cartographic Genealogy of the Earth in the Western Imagination*, Baltimore: Johns Hopkins, 2001.

4   As we will see throughout this book, French philosopher Paul Virilio and German philosopher Peter Sloterdijk have done much work on questions of verticality and volume over the past few decades.

surface. The human and social life of cities is still often abstracted flatly through the diagrams and maps of traditional urban geography in ways which radically flatten imaginations of the politics of urban life. Such perspectives make it hard to take seriously the geographies and geopolitics of what lies above and what lies below the earth's surface. They make it difficult to fully appreciate sovereign space and territory as three-dimensional volumes that extend from the terrestrial surface both above and below. 'Just as the world does not just exist as a surface', British geographer Stuart Elden writes, 'nor should our theorisations of it.'[5]

Architect Léopold Lambert meanwhile contends that a fully three-dimensional view radically challenges the power of the traditional flat map. The paradigm of two-dimensional cartography, he contends, 'cannot be enough anymore to describe lands (sky, underground, space, other planets etc.) whose sovereignty had never [been] discussed in another way than theoretically in the past.' The contemporary period, he continues, 'opens a new paradigm in which the legal action of a State on a territory will be defined through the complexity of space and its multiple layers.'[6]

As the world's surface becomes more and more congested and contested and urbanisation girds more of our planet, so political and social struggle takes on an increasingly three-dimensional character, reaching both up from and down below ground level. This creates a world dominated increasingly, as French urbanist Henri Lefebvre suggested, by the growing 'independence of volumes with respect to the original land'.[7]

In practice, this means that human societies are increasingly dense and stacked societies, in which uses of space are built upwards and downwards with ever-greater intensity within geographical volumes. Thus, housing in many cities is dominated by stacked apartments reaching into the sky. Favela dwellers build houses up perilous mountain slopes directly atop the roofs of those below. Cruise ships,

5 Stuart Elden, 'Secure the Volume: Vertical Geopolitics and the Depth of Power', *Political Geography* 34, 2013, p. 35.

6 Léopold Lambert, introduction to *Funambulist Papers 20*, available at thefunambulist.net.

7 Henri Lefebvre, *The Production of Space*, trans. D. Nicholson-Smith, Oxford: Blackwell, 1984, p. 337.

ferries, container ships, trains, car parking, passenger aircraft, buses and even farms, warehouses and factories are being re-engineered to stack people, activities and commodities on top of each other, often in ever-increasing heights, scales and densities.[8] In Hong Kong the shortage of land is so acute that sports fields, container ports, markets, horse stables, IKEA-like big-box retailers and even cemeteries are now routinely stacked within bigger structures which are then linked together and integrated to the wider city through huge arrays of elevators, walkways, escalators and raised highways.

Complex subterranean spaces below major cities, meanwhile, are themselves three-dimensional labyrinths which stack and intertwine infrastructures and built spaces as deeply as many cites rise into the sky (again linked to the surface and beyond by remarkable complexes of essentially vertical infrastructures). Beyond the built spaces of cities, air and orbital spaces, in turn, are saturated by fleets of enigmatic vehicles and sensors that are stacked from ground to orbital levels (and beyond).

Although intensified stacking is far from new – ancient Roman apartment buildings could be seven storeys high – the world's major cities are thus increasingly organised as multilevel volumes both above and below ground level. And the integration of the world's rural peripheries tightly into urban means of production, exchange and extraction means that more invisible three-dimensional architectures and geographies are growing in those places as well. In such areas, intensifying excavations deep into subterranean spaces for fuel and resources are themselves organised through vast structures analogous to the skyscrapers that rise into the urban skies, but on even more gigantic vertical scales.[9] The world's deepest mines are over four times deeper than the world's highest skyscrapers are tall.

All such processes mean that struggles over the right to the city, to living space, to resources, to security, to privacy, to mobility, to food and water, to justice – and even, given the loitering power of

---

8   The latest cruise ships, stacked mobile cities in their own right, carry up to 8,000 passengers on sixteen decks; they are now too big to evacuate completely in a crisis.

9   Arguments in favour of stacking must be engaged with critically, however. Mid-height neighbourhoods can often accommodate more people than clusters of much-vaunted skyscrapers.

killer drones and bombers across large parts of the earth, to the right to live rather than die – are increasingly shaped across vertical as well as horizontal geographies of power. Making these central to our understandings of the contemporary world is pivotal because, as geographer Gavin Bridge argues, 'adding height and depth to the horizontal plane magnifies the possibilities of relative location, affording additional means of control.'[10]

Flat perspectives seen from the 'God's eye' view of the cartographer or satellite imager inevitably fail to support understanding of such three-dimensional geographies. This problem is especially acute when we try to understand contemporary cities. Though vast libraries and many disciplines in the social sciences are devoted to exploring the structuring of the horizontal aspects of cities stretched across the earth's surface, the attention to the vertical structuring of cities and urban life remains patchy and limited. This is especially so within Anglophone geography and urban studies traditions.[11] Take just one example: the *Blackwell Companion to the City*, an influential overview of critical urban studies published in 2002. This state-of-the-art compendium of urban social science in the Anglophone world fails to mention the word 'vertical' even once in its 784 otherwise excellent pages.[12]

Key urban geography texts, meanwhile, rarely mention the extraordinary extension of cities above and below ground beyond passing asides. One influential recent textbook admits early on that features like skyscrapers and undergrounds are features usually

---

10 Gavin Bridge, 'Territory, Now in 3D!' *Political Geography* 34, 2013, p. 55.

11 During a three-year geography degree in the UK in the mid 1980s, I recall perhaps two or three occasions not dominated by the vertical scrutiny of the earth's surface rendered as a flat plane.

12 Indeed, Anglophone urban studies and urban, political and economic geography have traditionally not even used the term 'vertical' to refer to the politics of above and below in urban or geographic life. Instead, the word has been used to describe how organizations, firms, social classes, cities and state bodies are related 'vertically' within hierarchies or supply chains at various scales – 'local', 'urban', 'regional', 'national' and 'international' – as imagined across a flat geographic surface. See, for example, Mark Casson, *Multinationals and World Trade: Vertical Integration and the Division of Labour in World Industries,* London: Routledge, 2012; Cindy Fan, 'The Vertical and Horizontal Expansions of China's City System', *Urban Geography*, 20:6, 1999, pp. 493–515.

found only in cities but says nothing more about such vertical geographies thereafter.[13] Vital current debates about uneven development, the 'reassertion' of space in social theory, the 'network' or 'digital' society, so-called 'planetary urbanisation', or the global spread of urban infrastructures and lifestyles way beyond traditional cities still tend to adopt the resolutely flat perspectives that derive from their reliance on traditional top-down cartography and horizontal geography.[14]

Only very rarely is it considered that uneven development and the remaking of geographical scales can happen across the vertical as well as horizontal dimension; that the spaces above and below the earth's surface are also being urbanised; or that these broad volumes are interconnected through a myriad of social and material relations that shape the politics of cities and urban life just as powerfully as do processes and relations organised to sustain the flat and horizontal ground levels of cities.[15] As far as this author is aware, only one book in English has thus far set out to systematically explore the many levels of cities, from the roofs of towers down through to street and subterranean levels.[16]

In this context, Swiss urban and political geographer Francisco Klauser, drawing on the work of German philosopher Peter Sloterdijk,[17] urges his colleagues to fully embrace 'spherical' and hence volumetric and verticalised imaginations of urban space and so to move beyond

---

13 See Doreen Massey, John Allen and Steve Pile, eds, *City Worlds*, London: Routledge, 1999, p. 4.

14 See, for example, Neil Brenner, 'Theses on Urbanization', *Public Culture* 25:1, 2013, pp. 85–114; Nikos Katsikis, 'On the Geographical Organization of World Urbanization', *MONU 20*, April 2014, pp. 4–11, available at http://urbantheorylab.net.

15 It should be noted that such perspectives are now starting to link mining and extraction to the growth of global cities – though still through a largely flat perspective. See Neil J. Brenner, ed., *Implosions/Explosions: Towards a Study of Planetary Urbanization*, Berlin: JOVIS, 2014.

16 See Ally Ireson and Nick Barley, eds. *City Levels*, Basel: Birkhauser, 2000.

17 See Peter Sloterdijk, *Bubbles: Spheres Volume I: Microspherology*, trans. Hoban W. Cambridge, Los Angeles: Semiotext(e); Peter Sloterdijk, *Globes: Spheres Volume II: Macrospherology*, Los Angeles: Semiotext(e), 2014; Peter Sloterdijk, *In the World Interior of Capital: Towards a Philosophical Theory of Globalization*, Cambridge: Polity, 2013.

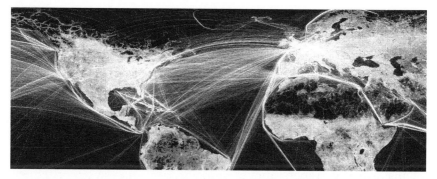

An example of the latest 'flat' mapping illustration of the planet's urbanisation from Harvard University's Urban Theory Lab. The global map showcases the multiple modes in which the planet is utilised, through a compilation of geographical data on land use intensification (agriculture, forestry, grazing); population density; density and distribution of artificial constructed surfaces; and major transportation networks (road, rail, marine, aviation). While extremely useful in mapping global flows of shipping and ground transportation, as well as the extending urbanisation of the planet across territory, such traditions inevitably struggle to deal with changes above and below the earth's surface because of their 'flat' treatment of the world.

contemporary approaches based 'almost exclusively based on two-dimensional planar metaphors'.[18]

In the urban design and urbanism traditions, meanwhile, despite many calls from urban scholars and policy makers to embrace, design and plan for density, what urban design scholars Barrie Shelton and his colleagues call '"flat earth"' viewpoints of urbanism' also remain remarkably dominant.[19] Despite a proliferating literature on the architecture of individual tall buildings, such perspectives remain wedded to the traditional idea of the urban ground, with its at-grade street networks and public encounters on sidewalks and in traditional public spaces.

Urban and architectural historians, always less dominated by such

18   Francisco Klauser, 'Splintering Spheres of Security: Peter Sloterdijk and the Contemporary Fortress City', *Environment and Planning D: Society and Space*, 28:2, April 2010, p. 326.

19   Barrie Shelton, Justyna Karakiewicz and Thomas Kvan, *The Making of Hong Kong: From Vertical to Volumetric*, London: Routledge, 2013, p. 20. On the problems of mapping population and social geographies in verticalising cities, see Nicholas Perdue, 'The Vertical Space Problem: Rethinking Population Visualizations in Contemporary Cities', *Cartographic Perspectives* 74, 2013.

flat discourses, planar metaphors and flat cartographic traditions than urban geographers, have already done much to start to explore the ways in which vertical urban life has been imagined, normalised, built or contested over the history of cities.[20] Within these traditions what Dutch architect Ole Bauman has called the 'metaphysics of verticalism' extends from classical structures through the city-cosmos geometries inherent in medieval city planning to modernist mass social housing towers and the contemporary global proliferation of massive skyscrapers and urban megastructures.[21] Unfortunately for the purposes of this book, however, rather than addressing the broader geographies, sociologies and politics of verticalising cities, such debates tend to focus rather on the aesthetics of vertical buildings as individual objects.[22]

'Flat' traditions in geography and urbanism clearly need to be overturned.[23] As we shall see in the chapters that follow, in many cities the urban 'ground' itself, rather than being the product of natural geological processes, is increasing manufactured and raised up as humans shape the very geology of cities in ever more powerful ways. In many verticalising cities, indeed, it is less and less clear what 'ground' level might actually be. Such disorientation emerges as people live their lives within complex three-dimensional volumes laced together by all manner of infrastructures and architectures located above, within and below the traditional terrestrial surface. As Shelton and his colleagues stress, this means that the 'principles of connection and connectivity that have been established for the ground plane must be revisited,

20 See, for example, Judith Dupré, *Skyscrapers: A History of the World's Most Extraordinary Buildings*, New York: Black Dog & Leventhal, 2013; Francesco Passanti, 'The Skyscrapers of the Ville Contemporaine', *Assemblage* 4, pp. 52–65; Gail Fenske, *The Skyscraper and the City: The Woolworth Building and the Making of Modern New York*, Chicago: University of Chicago Press, 2008.

21 Ole Bauman, 'In the Age of Horizontalization', in Ally Ireson and Nick Barley, eds, *City Levels*, Basel: Birkhäuser, 2000, p. 4.

22 See, for example, Ada Louise Huxtable, *The Tall Building Artistically Reconsidered*, University of California Press: Berkley, 1992; Thomas Van Leeuwen, *The Skyward Trend of Thought: The Metaphysics of the American Skyscraper*, Bambridge, MA: MIT Press, 1988; Scott Johnson, *Tall Building: Imagining the Skyscraper*, New York: Balcony, 2008.

23 See Andrew Harris, 'Vertical Urbanisms: Opening Up Geographies of the Three-Dimensional City', *Progress in Human Geography*, December 2016.

adapted and applied to cities which function effectively with *multiple grounds*.'[24]

When the often-disorientating effects of multiple digital screens, proliferating views from above, and the extended geographies of mobility, communication and globalisation are added to such vertical processes, many philosophers now talk of a wider collapse in the notion of a stable and grounded horizon altogether. Such ideas derive heavily from the pioneering work of philosopher Fredric Jameson. In 1991 he talked of human subjects, caught up in what he called 'postmodern hyperspace' – a fusion of bewildering vertical architecture, vast cities, globalised capitalism and electronic culture. This, he said, eclipsed the capabilities of individuals to situate and locate themselves in ways that allowed them to 'cognitively' map the world around them, both vertically and horizontally.[25]

'Many contemporary philosophers have pointed out that the present moment is distinguished by a prevailing condition of groundlessness', German film-maker Hito Steyerl adds. In the contemporary absence of any stable horizon, she argues that vertical perspectives help us to understand the ways in which such rapid and disorientating change brings with it the sense, as she puts it, of 'falling' in an urbanised, hyper-mobile and hyper-mediated world where 'there is no ground'. In such a context, 'traditional modes of seeing and feeling are shattered. Any sense of balance is disrupted. Perspectives are twisted and multiplied. New types of visuality arise.'[26]

Thus, stable linear perspective is of decreasing importance, in parallel with the reduced importance of the horizontal horizon. Stable views from a single point are replaced by multiple digital screens and increasingly immersive physical and electronic spaces

---

24   Shelton et al., *Making of Hong Kong,* p. 20. Author's emphasis.

25   A 'cognitive map' is a mental representation that humans hold of the world around them that helps them to navigate and make sense of the wider environment. See Fredric Jameson, *Postmodernism; or, The Cultural Logic of Late Capitalism*, Durham, NC: Duke University Press, 1991, p. 44; Kevin Lynch, *The Image of the City*, Cambridge, MA: MIT press, 1960. See also David Harvey, *The Condition of Postmodernity*, Oxford: Blackwell, 1989; and Edward Soja, *Postmodern Geographies: The Reassertion of Space in Critical Social Theory,* London: Verso, 1989.

26   Steyerl, 'In Free Fall'.

which offer a myriad of perspectives simultaneously – including those from satellites, aircraft and drones high above.[27] (In many places, of course, such technologies are also used to try and police, surveil, control and destroy the terrestrial surface and those on or below it.) Mobile subjects now increasingly inhabit and depend on complex volumes of infrastructure and built space strung out across the world and connected together through intense circulations and mobilities.

The resulting feeling of disorientation and 'falling', Steyerl speculates, radically challenges concepts of time and space, of subjects and objects and of human experience of the world. 'The lines of the horizon shatter, twirl around, and superimpose' in a 'multiplication and de-linearisation of horizons and perspectives.'[28] Thus, Google Maps, Google Earth, online surveillance panoramas and 3D virtual reality, simulation and cinema systems heavily emphasise the ground. But this ground is an unstable and radically contingent 'virtual' ground organised through a radically mobile and machinic gaze. Surveillance and simulation technology linked to screens creates a world of endless screen-based distraction where views from any perspective can be called up at any time. Such technological complexes, moreover, are increasingly automated to operate by remote control. In the process, power relations between the watchers on high and the watched below become ever more critical. Subversion of and resistance to militarised, vertical vision and targeting necessarily work to operate across increasingly vertical planes.[29]

As we will see in great detail in this book, such challenges of *de*-territorialisation parallel and combine with similar challenges to the sedimentation of class relations into *re*-territorialised vertical cities and vertical mobility systems. Always fragile, such emerging geographies of power and (attempted) control are vulnerable to the radical contradictions of an increasingly brutal and primitive mode of capitalism. This is based on the often violent exploitation of majorities by tiny cabals of the super-rich inhabiting vertical archipelagos of

---

27   See Nanna Verhoeff, *Mobile Screens: The Visual Regime of Navigation*, Amsterdam: Amsterdam University Press, 2012.

28   Steyerl, 'In Free Fall'.

29   See, for example, Eyal Weizman, *Hollow Land: Israel's Architecture of Occupation*, London: Verso, 2012.

protected spaces, using the mobility and communications grids that connect them together.

To Hito Steyerl, the perspective of 'free fall' is powerful because it makes us conscious that the planet is convulsing with radical-ised class war 'from above', as tiny elites grow unimaginably wealthy while seceding from the societies on which they depend. 'If the new views from above recreate societies as free-falling urban abysses and splintered terrains of occupation [which are] surveilled aerially and policed biopolitically', she emphasises, 'they may also – as linear per-spective did – carry the seeds of their own demise within them.'[30]

A key staring point for *Vertical* is that the continued flattening effects of both geographic and urbanistic traditions work to seriously under-mine the emergence of a fully three-dimensional understanding of these crucial transformations among disciplines – urban studies and geography – that should be at the core of such projects.

The continued, though diminishing, preoccupation with the surface as seen from some God's- or bird's-eye view has radically undermined critical treatments of the spaces and domains both above and below it. Issues of the height and depth of buildings, borders, airspaces, orbits, subterranean resource grabs, vertical mobilities, underground structures – and even the startlingly upright bodies of vertical, able-bodied humans – have all been remarkably neglected because of the persistent 'flatness' of geographical debates. (Urban inequality, for one, is almost always imagined to be constituted hori-zontally rather than vertically.)

Such 'flat' traditions neglect the real power of vertical and sec-tional thinking to provide much-needed insights into the politics and geographies of our world. In early 2016, Harvard landscape architect Pierre Bélanger published a piece called 'Altitudes of Urbanization', the most evocative demonstration of the power of such thinking yet. His startling graphical section (see the frontispiece to this chapter) portrayed the rising towers of terrestrial urbanism enmeshed within dense worlds of urban circulation and infrastructure both above and below both the ground level and an ocean surface which is rapidly rising because of global warming. Stretching up, fleets of helicopters

---

30   Steyerl, 'In Free Fall'.

and drones and myriads of orbital satellites and space craft peppered the skies; reaching down into the earth and oceans were labyrinths of tunnels, subways, mines and submarine craft.

'From 10,000 meters below the sea, to 35,000 kilometres in orbit above the surface of the earth', Bélanger stressed, 'the infrastructure that supports urban life has reached unimaginable extents below ground, in the water, and across outer space.' More than a mere pictorial novelty, however, Bélanger emphasises the radical analytical power of such a view. 'Seeing and seen in section', he continues,

> processes that are often isolated in plans, or divided in conventional categories from above, can be better understood and revealed … from the side, as being associative and integrative – often overlapping, intertwined and entangled. Opening a lens on the complex urbanization of the underground and of the atmosphere, this association of the quantitative with the qualitative made possible by seeing sideways offers three important observations on the once and future hinterlands of the underground, the ocean and the atmosphere.[31]

Given the power of such vertical and sectional views, why not a geography of lifts as well as urban highways and subways and of airspaces, drones and satellites as well as the terrestrial surface? Or a sociology of skyscrapers, sewers, bunkers, elite housing towers, domes of polluted and lethal air, raised walkways and personal helicopter commutes as well as 'flat' treatments of ground-level public space – and its inhabitants? Or a discussion of the cultural worlds of urban life which takes seriously the highly verticalised imaginaries and politics of religion, film, video games, science fiction and photography? Above all, is it possible for us to shift our perspectives sufficiently to see boundaries and relations between layers and levels within volumes of geographic space to be as important as those that horizontally demarcate traditional 'flat' notions of boundaries territory?

Vertical explores these themes – and more. The book has an ambitious agenda: to inscribe the politics of our three-dimensional world

---

31   Pierre Bélanger, 'Altitudes of Urbanization,' *Tunnelling and Underground Space Technology*, January 2016.

into critical debates about urban life, cities and geography. Building on an extensive range of recent work in geography,[32] where such a process has been under way for some time, as well as many other disciplines,[33] this book is a critical and international exploration of why and how verticality matters in the contemporary world.

In a sense, then, *Vertical* is an attempt to bring critical geographic debates more fully into line with the proliferating verticalities of our world, a highly mobile and uneven world of often disorientating vertical views, mobilities and structures which can only be understood in volumetric rather than two-dimensional, planar ways. The perspective of the book is thus deliberately critical, highly international and unusually interdisciplinary. In this most spectacular of fields, it is also as visual as it can be within the constraints of monochrome images within the form of an affordable book.

By necessity, *Vertical* draws on debates in history as well as engineering; in architecture as well as sociology and anthropology; in international relations as well as film and cultural studies; and in philosophy as well as geology and archaeology. As a way of focusing the debate on the key material structures of our increasingly vertical societies, *Vertical*'s fifteen chapters each explore the contested political and social relations which surround one key structure, site or cultural world. Geographically speaking, these tend to be vertically highly stratified.

Thus we enter each chapter through the initially above-ground worlds of satellites, drones, helicopters, bombers, flyovers, skyscrapers, raised walkways and urban airscapes as well as the human

---

32   See, for example, Gavin Bridge, 'Territory, Now in 3D!'; Elden, 'Secure the Volume', pp. 35–51; and Stephen Graham and Lucy Hewitt, 'Getting off the Ground: On the Politics of Urban Verticality', *Progress in Human Geography*, 37:1, 2013, pp. 72–92.

33   A full list here would include anthropology, archaeology, architecture, art, climatology, communications studies, cultural studies, economics, engineering, environmental studies, film studies, geology, history, housing studies, international politics/relations, landscape architecture, law, linguistics, literary and critical theory, philosophy, planning, physical geography, psychology, social theory, sociology, theology, urban design and urban studies. Some of these disciplines – architecture, archaeology and geology, for example – have of necessity developed much more three-dimensional views of the politics of geographic and urban space than has Anglophone human geography.

manufacture of the ground itself and initially subterranean burrow-ings of bunkers, basements, sewers, tunnels and mines.

As they work to address the political and social contestations sur-rounding key sites, structures or cultural worlds, *Vertical*'s chapters necessarily engage with some of the key historical dynamics through which their foci became sedimented into our world. Each synthesises into its narrative a wide range of critical debates on important exam-ples of social and political struggles drawn from an unusually wide and international range of cases.

As the influential British geographer Doreen Massey famously argued in 1994, the key point here is that places are not areas defined by boundaries on a map (or, in our case, a vertical section or three-dimensional volume). Rather, they are 'articulated moments in net-works of social relations and understandings'. Crucially, in these globalizing times, she continued, 'a large proportion of those rela-tions, experiences and understandings are constructed on a far larger scale that what we happen to define for that moment as the place itself, whether that be a street, or a region or even a continent.'[34] A key starting point for this book is that such points apply just as pow-erfully to relations organised vertically and volumetrically as they do to those connecting the world across the earth's surface. (In fact, of course, both operate simultaneously within broader volumes of geographic space.)

In confronting the vertical and volumetric geographies of our world it is vital at the outset to confront the ways in which vertical metaphors saturate – indeed, *constitute* – language about power, wealth, status and happiness. Indeed, their widespread and unthinking use works powerfully to stipulate and demarcate political and social power in ways that powerfully overlap with the human experience of material and geographical verticalities. Vertical and other spatial metaphors literally work to constitute and reconstitute social power: they both derive directly from the physical and phenomenological experience of social life and actively influence how people perceive and shape the social and political world.

---

34   Doreen Massey, *Space, Place and Gender,* Cambridge: Polity Press, 1994, p. 154.

It thus matters hugely that human life for able-bodied humans involves a perpetual struggle to maintain vertical stance to maintain the senses of the heavy human head against incessant gravity. It matters, too, that death, illness and defeat are always symbolised in humans by a lower bodily stature and, eventually, by succumbing into the very ground itself.

'The reason we say that we feel "up" when we are happy and "down" when we are unhappy or "depressed"', literary scholar Paul Haacke writes, is thus 'that our corporeal experience as vertically erect creatures has led us as a species to associate standing upright with awareness or vitality, and lying down with rest or death.'[35] Rather than being mere poetic or figurative devices of speech, then, vertical metaphors are deeply embedded in the way humans conceptualise and shape their lives and their worlds. As 'orientation metaphors' they are closely tied to their perceptual basis in the heads of upright humans and tend to be used instinctively and unthinkingly 'to provide a means of reasoning about and structuring entire, mostly abstract, domains in terms of other, more concrete, domains.'[36] That is why we describe social status or wealth as 'high' or 'low' rather than 'great' and 'small'.[37]

The latest developments in cognitive linguistics have explored how important vertical 'orientation' metaphors are in descriptions of social power.[38] This work has major implications for this book because it suggests that, far from being arbitrary examples of the evolution of language, vertical metaphors are directly related to the upright stance of the human body, continuous exposure to gravity, and the rich bodily experience of living within and through bodies that are particularly vertical and upright, and where the vast bulk of the human sensory apparatus is normally centred at the very highest level set within the raised-up head.

---

35   Paul Haacke, 'The Vertical Turn: Topographies of Metropolitan Modernism', PhD thesis, University of California, Berkeley, 2011, p. 9.

36   Daniël Lakens, Gün Semin and Francesco Foroni, 'Why Your Highness Needs the People: Comparing the Absolute and Relative Representation of Power in Vertical Space', *Social Psychology* 42:3, 2011, pp. 205–13; Michael Treichler, *Metaphor and Space: The Cognitive Approach to Spatially Structured Concepts*, Berlin: GRIN Verlag, 2004, p. 2.

37   Kern, 'Culture of Time and Space', p. 242.

38   See Lakoff and Johnson, ibid.

The argument here is that the vertical scale is used universally as a metaphor to describe hierarchies of power and worth in society because such 'image schemata' – the term cognitive linguists use to describe such metaphorical world views – offer the only effective way that humans can grasp and describe such abstract social forms. Gravity is important because effort and resources are continually required to move, stand or build upwards against it.

Consequently, weakness, poor status or vulnerability is associated for those who are physically low or who succumb to its power. Linguistically, 'lowness' suggests deceit, weakness, vulgarity or immorality.[39] Those exercising power from above also can exploit the power of gravity in their efforts – a pivotal point in the history of war and violence which still has crucial importance in a world of strategic bombing, drone warfare and satellite surveillance. 'The vertical dimension has gravity on its side.'[40] Many old fables and stories detail such ideas well: for generations, every British child instinctively learned to sing 'I'm the king of the castle and you're the dirty rascal!' when physically raised above their peers.

Vertical metaphors of social power – along with the two other, less important, metaphorical schema, left–right and front–back – thus gain their power from the way they are used ubiquitously in ways that are unintentional and unconscious. This binary opposition between above and below has moved seamlessly and stealthily from cosmology and metaphysics into the language of political rhetoric, geography and the social sciences.[41]

In English, for example, as well as the more obvious use of 'upper', 'lower' and 'under' to describe social class, the words 'status', 'stature', 'statute', 'estate' and 'institute' all derive from the verb 'to stand' (which also describe acts of assertiveness and bravery, as in 'to stand up' for something or 'to make a stand'). One can also be an 'upright' citizen. Words beginning 'super', meanwhile, demarcate achievement, status, power and order – 'superior', 'supervise', 'superman' – meanwhile,

---

39   Stephen Kern, *The Culture of Time and Space, 1880–1918,* Cambridge, MA: Harvard University Press. 1983, p. 242.

40   Kevin Murray, 'Verticalism and Its Underbelly', blog, 26 February 2009, available at http://ideaofsouth.net.

41   Haacke, *Vertical Turn*, p. 56.

all derive from the Latin 'super' (or 'above'). Dominant leaders in positions of authority are called the 'head'. And so on …

Conversely, words beginning with 'sub' (from the Latin for 'under') – 'subordinate', 'subaltern', 'subsume', 'subhuman' – all imply powerlessness, weak status, or experiences of violence and domination. Words commencing with 'infra', meanwhile – derived from the Latin for 'lower' or 'lower down' – include 'inferior' and 'infernal', and were originally related to the 'lower' cosmographic regions of hell.

Crucially for this book's discussions of vertical architecture, such linguistic histories overlap, reaffirm and valorise physical architectural traditions implying that status and power correlate with physical height above the ground.[42] Altars, athletes' podiums, penthouse offices and apartments, the 'high' tables at elite university dining rooms and mega skyscrapers connect seamlessly to the histories of medieval castles and cathedrals.

Even more profound links exist between the origins of the word 'story' (and hence 'history') – the idea of a narrative over time – and the architectural word 'storey' – meaning the stacked floor of a vertical building. (One possible explanation of the link is that medieval buildings often carried visual narratives across their facades to community to largely illiterate populations.) 'The very concept of history itself may be interpreted as implying multiple layers or stories of existence rather than a single, flat plane', humanities theorist Paul Haacke points out. 'Both English and Romance languages derive the term from the Latin *historia*, which contains the spatial metaphor of *storia*, meaning a succession of stages or series of layers, as in the architectural stories of a building.'[43]

More broadly, advertising universally invokes vague and simple parallels between vertical terminology, iconographies of vertical landscape and social and economic power and class. Because vertical metaphors are so ubiquitous and taken for granted, for example the apparently bizarre and illogical linkage of high snowy mountains with an advert for an executive MBA makes eminent sense. With so

---

42   For a brilliant discussion of this tradition in medieval Europe, see Keith Lilley, *City and Cosmos: The Medieval World in Urban Form,* London: Reaktion Books, 2009.

43   Haacke, *Vertical Turn*, p. 178.

many spaces and infrastructures geared towards the elite and power-ful in the contemporary world, it is no wonder that the production and use of vertical metaphors, floating free from any original mean-ings, overlap closely with the experiences of vertical spatial secession among powerful groups. (Note the verticality of all the terms used to describe them: the 'upper' class, the 'überwealthy', the super-rich and so on.)

Globally, vertical schemes for assigning value and worth have even been powerfully translated into horizontal cartography. Eurocentric colonial dominance was powerfully inscribed in the world maps pro-duced to celebrate and naturalise it. Thus, the global south or being 'down under' were (and are) often read as being geographically, eco-nomically or morally inferior simply because they fall in the lower parts of the dominant visual schemes used to depict the world's geog-raphy. (Such derogatory thinking stemmed from periods when a flat earth – the centre of the universe – was literally seen to lie below the firmament of heaven and above the fires of hell.)

For millennia, Eurocentric philosophers, theologians and geogra-phers routinely transposed their vertical religious and mythological schema on a binary world they separated between the civilised North and the inferior and morally questionable southern hemisphere. 'One pole is ever high above us', the Roman poet Virgil said in 29 BC, 'while the other, beneath our feet, is seen of black Styx and the shades infernal.'[44]

'This quarter of the earth, which is inhabited by all the people with whom we can have any contact, verges towards the north pole', the Roman philosopher Macrobius wrote in 420 AD. 'And the spheri-cal shape of the earth causes the south pole to be plunged into the depths.'[45] Such notions are still hidden deep within everyday language: to 'go South' is to fail or encounter a crisis. Those contesting such subtle but powerful prejudice, in turn, produce maps that upturn the usual north–south/up–down conventions by putting the south at the top within so-called 'upside down' maps.

---

44 The Styx was the river in Greek mythology that formed the boundary of the underworld. See Virgil, *Georgics*, Oxford: Oxford University Press, 1990, p. 194.

45 Quoted in Murray, 'The Idea of South'.

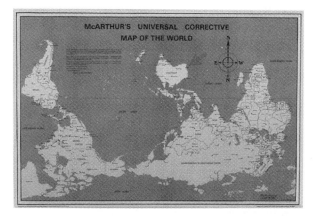

An 'upside down' world map based on Stuart McArthur's original 'Universal Corrective Map of the World'

The most famous of these maps was created by Stuart McArthur of Melbourne, who first drew it in 1970 for a primary school geography class. His teacher demanded that he re-do the map the 'correct' way up. After travelling to North America on a school exchange, he became sick of being the butt of jokes about being from a place on the 'bottom' of the Earth.[46]

Remarkably, McArthur produced his map, McArthur's Universal Corrective Map of the World, in 1979 aged only nineteen. It is now iconic, especially in the Antipodes. His map, he exclaimed, meant that Australia never again had to suffer 'the perpetual onslaught of "down under" jokes – implications from Northern nations that the height of a country's prestige is determined by its equivalent spatial location on a conventional map of the world.'[47]

Because they are so rarely exposed or challenged, the contemporary effects of the widespread and unthinking use of vertical of societal metaphors are especially insidious. This is because, as Stuart McArthur playfully demonstrated with his 'upside down' world map, they work to naturalise and hence obfuscate the reproduction of unjust and elitist societies. In other words, they work to detract attention from the remaking of societies through processes of neoliberalisation

46   Mike Parker, *Map Addict: A Tale of Obsession, Fudge and the Ordnance Survey*, London: Collins, 2010.

47   Jospeh Giovanninni, 'This Side up Please!' *New York Times*, 18 May 1986.

in ways that reallocate resources overwhelming to tiny numbers of super-rich transnational elites – at the expense of everybody else.

'These metaphors are so deeply embedded in the human conceptual system', writes cognitive scientist Michael Treichler, 'that they normally are not noticed as being metaphorical at all.'[48] They are, in other words, 'dead' metaphors where any intentional figurative purpose has long been abandoned and the terms have come to be used literally without metaphoric intention.[49] Who would now immediately consider phrases such as 'to look down on', or the 'upper and lower classes', to be geographic metaphors which pejoratively equate both physical and metaphoric 'lowness' to be proxies for reduced power, status or wealth?

In fact, so primitively woven into human cognition are such metaphors that they are mobilised instinctively and unthinkingly prior to the more conscious conceptual reasoning of the human brain. In the terms of linguistics, vertical metaphors are therefore both 'pre-conceptual' and 'pre-logical'. They therefore work to shape political and social thought before any deliberate logical reasoning comes into play.[50]

Vertical metaphors are also widely invoked in leftist strategies to build more egalitarian and less elitist societies. Challenging conservative and elitist ideologies which naturalise deepening 'vertical' hierarchies, social movements from the 1994 efforts of the Zapatistas in Mexico, the post-collapse mobilisations in Argentina in 2001 and the 2011 Occupy protests commonly invoke concepts of political and social horizontalism. Such ideas reject the violent verticalisation inherent in neoliberalisation and the rampant commodification of all means of life. They insist, instead, on 'horizontal', collaborative and autonomous social organisation of services, care, education, land development, production and infrastructure through locally organised democratic organisations.[51]

---

48   Treichler, *Metaphor and Space*, p. 9.

49   Graham Livesey, *Passages: Explorations of the Contemporary City*, Calgary: University of Calgary Press, 2004, p. 50.

50   Franson Manjali, 'On the Spatial Basis of Conceptual Metaphors', paper given at the International Conference on Narrative and Metaphor across the Disciplines, University of Auckland, July 1996, available at revue-texto.net/Inedits/Manjali_Metaphor.html.

51   See Marina Sitrin, ed., *Horizontalism: Voices of Popular Power in*

In Spanish, such movements are captured by the concept of *horizontalidad* ('horizontalism'). The political writer Marina Sitrin defines this as 'a social relationship that implies, as it sounds, a flat plane upon which to communicate. *Horizontalidad* requires the use of direct democracy and implies non-hierarchy and anti-authoritarian creation rather than reaction.' It is a break, she notes, from vertical 'ways of organizing and relating, but a break that is also an opening.'

This review of vertical language suggests two major tasks for this book's wider exploration of the vertical geographies of the contemporary world. The first is simple: to denaturalise and expose the taken-for-granted and often invisible ways in which deep vertical metaphors make up the very language that humans use to describe, experience and analyse all the cases, environments and cultural worlds explored throughout this book. The second is to problematise the way that this happens. The essays that follow, therefore, concentrate heavily on how value-laden and ancient vertical metaphors work to legitimise extreme inequality by subtly glorifying and naturalizing the wealth and power contemporary social, political and military elites – and the vertical geographies that reproduce and maintain it.

The dense and wide-ranging narrative of *Vertical* will, I hope, help readers to shake off any of the lingering shackles of the inherited flatness of world-views reliant on traditional geography and cartography – and to understand the limitations of these traditions. Once this is achieved, the book has been written to allow readers to 'see the world anew' by developing their own critical, vertical and indeed fully volumetric view of the politics of cities, urban life and geography in today's world. The motivating idea of the book is that it is only through such fully three-dimensional and critical perspectives that the political, social and urban struggles of our rapidly urbanizing world can possibly be understood.

Strap yourself in, then, for a wild and startling ride through the three-dimensional geographies of our world.

Argentina, New York: AK Press, 2006; and Marina Sitrin, *Everyday Revolutions: Horizontalism and Autonomy in Argentina*, London: Zed Books, 2012.

Part One: Above

Social scientists need to raise their eyes from the ground

Martin Parker

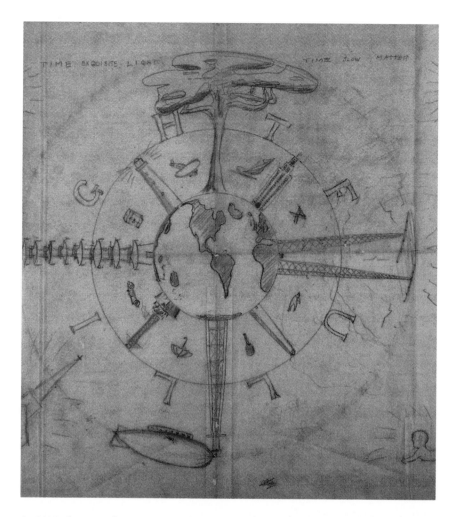

A 1928 drawing by visionary designer, architect and polymath Buckminster Fuller, emphasizing the global, spiritual, practical and vertical challenges facing engineering, architecture and human life inherent within his idea of 'Spaceship Earth'. (Fuller, *Operating Manual for Spaceship Earth*, 1968).

1.

Satellite: Enigmatic Presence

We live in a satellite enabled age. The satellites flying above us are not abstract agents of science but part of the critical life support system we all depend on, every day.
> – The UK Government's Satellites Application Catapult

There comes a point, as one ascends into the sky from the earth's surface – and the largely upright human experience of living on it – when the conventions that surround the human experience of the vertical dimension must inevitably break down.

At the margins of the earth's atmosphere and on the threshold of the vast realms of space we enter a world of orbits. At this point we start to encounter the crucial but neglected manufactured environment of satellites and space junk. 'Verticality pushed to its extreme becomes orbital', multimedia artist Dario Solman reflects. At such a point 'the difference between vertical and horizontal ceases to exist'. Such a development brings with it profound and unsettling philosophical challenges for a species that evolved to live upright on terra firma. 'Every time verticality and horizontality blend together and discourses lose internal gravity', Solman argues, 'there is a need for the arts.'[1]

The earth's fast-expanding array of around 950 active satellites – over 400 of which are owned by the United States – are central to the organization, experience – and also the destruction – of contemporary life on the earth's surface. And yet it remains difficult to visualise and understand their enigmatic presence.[2] Mysterious and cordoned-off ground stations dot the earth's terrain, their futuristic

---

1 Dario Solman, 'Air Attack', *Airfiles*, blog, 2001, available at filmlog.org.
2 See Doug Millard, *Satellite: Innovation in Orbit*, London: Reaktion, 2016.

radomes and relay facilities directed upwards to the satellites above. Small antennae lift upwards from a myriad of apartment blocks to silently receive invisible broadcasts from transnational television stations. Crowds might even occasionally witness the spectacle of a satellite launch atop a rocket.

Once aloft, however, satellites become distant, enigmatic and, quite literally, 'unearthly'.[3] At best, careful observers of the night's sky might catch the steady march of mysterious dots across the heavens as they momentarily reflect the sun's light. Such a small range of direct experience fails to equip us with the skills to disentangle the politics of this huge aerial assemblage of circling and (geo)stationary satellites.

It doesn't help that the literature on satellites in the social sciences is startlingly small. Communications scholars Lisa Parks and James Schwoch suggest that this is because scholars, too, struggle to engage with satellites because they lie so firmly beyond the visceral worlds of everyday experience and visibility. 'Since they are seemingly so out of reach (both physically and financially)', they point out, 'we scarcely imagine them as part of everyday life' at all. [4]

As we saw in the introduction, the continued tendency of many scholars of the politics of geography to maintain a resolutely horizontal view compounds our difficulties in taking seriously crucial the roles of orbital geographies in shaping life (and death) on the ground. Only very recently have critical geographers started to look upwards to the devices circling our Earth in their first tentative steps towards a political geography of inner and outer space.

Such a project emphasises how the regimes of power organised through satellites and other space systems are interwoven with production of violence, inequality and injustice on the terrestrial surface.[5] But it also attends to the importance of how space is imagined and represented as a national frontier; a birthright of states; a sphere of heroic exploration; a fictional realm; or as a vulnerable

---

3   Jim Oberg, cited in Trevor Paglen, *The Last Pictures*, New York: Creative Time Books, 2012, p. 2.

4   Lisa Parks, 'Orbital Performers and Satellite Translators: Media Art in the Age of Ionospheric Exchange', *Quarterly Review of Film and Video* 24, 2007, pp. 207–8.

5   An important book in this debate is Daniel Sage, *How Outer Space Made America*, Farnham, UK: Ashgate, 2014.

domain above from which malign others might stealthily threaten societies below at any moment.

The invisibility of the earth's satellites and their apparent removal from the worlds of earthly politics has made it very easy to place their organization and governance far from democratic or public scrutiny. Such a situation creates a paradox. On the one hand, widening domains of terrestrial life are now mediated by far-above arrays of satellites in ways so fundamental and basic that they have quickly become banal and taken for granted – when they are noticed or considered at all.

Global communications, navigation, science, trade and cartography have, in particular, been totally revolutionised by satellites in the last few decades. Military GPS systems, used to drop lethal ordnance on any point on Earth, have been opened up to civilian uses. They now organise the global measurement of time as well as the navigation of children to school, yachts to harbours, cars into supermarkets, farmers around fields, runners and cyclists along paths and roads and hikers up to mountaintops. Widened access to powerful imaging satellites, similarly, has allowed high-resolution images to transform urban planning, agriculture, forestry, environmental management and efforts to NGOs to track human rights abuses.[6]

Digital photography from many of the prosthetic eyes above the Earth, meanwhile, offers resolutions that Cold War military strategists could only dream of – delivered via the satellite and optic fibre channels of the Internet to anyone with a laptop or smartphone. A cornucopia of distant TV stations are also now accessible through the most basic aerial or broadband TV or Internet connection. Virtually all efforts at social and political mobilization now rely on GPS and satellite mapping and imaging to organise and get their message across.

Satellites, in other words, now constitute a key part of the public realms of our planet. The way they girdle our globe matters fundamentally and profoundly. And yet satellites are regulated and managed by a scattered array of esoteric governance agencies. They

---

6 On the latter, see Science and Human Rights Program, American Association for the Advancement of Science, 'Geospatial Technologies and Human Rights', 2015, available at aaas.org.

are developed and engineered by an equally hidden range of state and corporate research and development centres. When the obsessive secrecy of national security states is added to this mix, it becomes extremely hard to pin down even basic information about the ownership, nature, roles and capabilities of these crucial machines orbiting the Earth.

Such a situation has even led media theorist Geert Lovinck to suggest that it is necessary to think of the figure of the satellite in contemporary culture in psychoanalytical terms – as an unconscious apparatus that lurks away from and behind the more obvious or 'conscious' circuits of culture.[7] 'Publics around the world have both been excluded from and/or remained silent within important discussions about [the] ongoing development and use [of satellites]', Parks and Schwoch stress. 'Since the uses of satellites have historically been so heavily militarised and corporatised, we need critical and artistic strategies that imagine and suggest ways of struggling over their meanings and uses.'[8]

'Ultimate High Ground'

> Space superiority is not our birthright, but it is our destiny … Space superiority is our day-to-day mission. Space supremacy is our vision for the future.
>
> – General Lance W. Lord, commander of the
US Air Force Space Command, 2005

Even a preliminary study of the world of satellites must conclude that they have contributed powerfully to the extreme globalization of the contemporary age. Nowhere is this more apparent than in the murky and clandestine worlds of military and security surveillance satellites. Not surprisingly, the idea of colonizing inner space with the best possible satellite sensors has long made military theorists drool. Their pronouncements revivify long-standing military assumptions that to

---

7   Geert Lovink, interview with Lisa Parks, 'Out There: Exploring Satellite Awareness', *Institute of Network Cultures*, 1 November 2005, available at networkcultures.org.

8   Parks, 'Orbital Performers'.

be above is to be dominant and in control in the campaign to subjugate enemies.

The extraordinary powers of globe-spanning military and security satellites are only occasionally hinted at by whistleblowers or leaks. By communicating details about the earth's surface to secretive ground stations – its geography, communications, inhabitants and attributes – and by allowing weapons like drones to be controlled anywhere on Earth from a single spot, military and security satellites produce what geographer Denis Cosgrove called 'an altered spatiality of globalization'.[9]

Peter Sloterdijk stresses the way the increasing dominance of the view of the earth from satellites since the 1960s has revolutionised human imagination about the earth through a form of what he calls 'inverted astronomy':

> The view from a satellite makes possible a Copernican revolution in outlook. For all earlier human beings, gazing up to the heavens was akin to a naive preliminary stage of a philosophical thinking beyond this world and a spontaneous elevation towards contemplation of infinity. Ever since the early sixties, an inverted astronomy has … come into being, looking down from space onto the earth rather than from the ground up into the skies.[10]

This sense of global, total and seemingly omniscient vision from above allows military satellite operators in particular to render everything on the earth's surface as an object and as a target, organised through near-instantaneous data transmission linking sensors to weapons systems.[11]

Crucially, such 'virtual' visions of the world, wrapped up in their military techno-speak acronyms and euphemisms, are stripped of their biases, selectivity, subjectivity and limits. The way in which they

---

9 Denis Cosgrove, *Apollo's Eye: A Cartographic Genealogy of the Earth in the Western Imagination*, Baltimore: Johns Hopkins University Press, 2001, p. 236.

10 Peter Sloterdijk, 1990, cited in Wolfgang Sachs, *Planet Dialectics: Explorations in Environment and Development,* London: Zed Books, 1999, p. 111.

11 Philosopher Rey Chow calls this 'the age of the world target'. See Chow, *The Age of the World Target: Self-Referentiality in War, Theory, and Comparative Work*, Durham, NC: Duke University Press, 2006.

are used to actively and subjectively manufacture – rather than impassively 'sense' – the targets to be surveilled, and, if necessary, destroyed, is consequently denied. A further problem, of course, is that satellite imaging efforts also completely ignore the rights, views and needs of those on the receiving end of the technology on the earth's surface, far below satellite orbits – the people who are most affected by the domineering technology above. As with the closely allied worlds of the drone, military helicopter or bomber to be discussed in subsequent chapters, this imperial trick works powerfully. It manufactures the world below as nothing but an infinite field of targets to be sensed and destroyed, remotely, on a whim, as deemed appropriate by operators in distant bunkers. 'All the various aspects of satellite imagery systems … work together', writes communications scholar Chad Harris. They do this, he says, to create and maintain 'an imperial subjectivity or "gaze" that connects the visual with practices of global control.'[12]

To deny how constructed and subjective satellite visioning is, militaries and security agencies represent it as an entirely objective and omniscient means for a distant observer to represent the observed. This God-like view of satellite imagery is often invoked by states as evidence of unparalleled veracity and authenticity when they are alleged to depict weapons of mass destruction facilities, human rights abuses or nefarious military activities.

It does not help that many critical theorists mistakenly suggest that contemporary spy satellites effectively have no technological limitations or that a hundred Hollywood action movies – erroneously depicting spy satellites as being capable of witnessing anything – do the same. Critics often depict satellite surveillance as being omnipotent and omniscient – a world of complete dystopian control with no limits to the transparency of the view and no possibilities for resistance or contestation.[13] In suggesting, for example, that 'the orbital weapons [and satellites] currently in play possess the traditional attributes of the divine: omnivoyance and omnipresence', French theorist

---

12   Chad Harris, 'The Omniscient Eye: Satellite Imagery, "Battlespace Awareness", and the Structures of the Imperial Gaze', *Surveillance and Society* 4:1/2, 2002, p. 119.

13   See Paul Kingsbury and John Paul Jones, 'Walter Benjamin's Dionysian Adventures on Google Earth', *Geoforum* 40:4, 2009, pp. 502–13.

Paul Virilio radically underplays the limits, biases and subjectivities that shape the targeting of the terrestrial surface by satellites.[14]

Instead of invoking satellites as an absolute form of imperial vision, it is necessary, rather, to see satellite imaging as a highly biased form of visualizing or even simulating the earth's surface rather than some objective or apolitical transmission of its 'truth'.[15] It is also, as we shall see, necessary to stress the potential that satellites have for those challenging military-industrial complexes, environmental and human rights abuses and all manner of political and state repression.

Where maps are now widely understood to be subject to bias and error, satellite images are still widely assumed to present a simple, direct and truthful correlation of the earth. This occurs even when there is a long history of such images being so imperfect and uncertain – and as so manipulated, mislabelled and just plain wrong – that it necessary to be sceptical of such claims.[16] US military theorists offer an excellent case study of how attempted domination of satellite sensing is being combined with long-standing metaphors about the strategic power of being above one's enemies. In 2003 the US RAND think-tank declared that space power and its attendant satellites offered the 'ultimate high ground' in struggles for military superiority.[17]

14   Paul Virilio, *Desert Screen: War at the Speed of Light*, New York: Continuum, 2005 [1991], p. 53.

15   See John Pickles, ed., *Ground Truth: The Social Implications of Geographic Information Systems*, New York: Guilford Press, 1995.

16   The satellite images of the imagined 'WMD' facilities presented by the US government to justify the 2003 invasion of Iraq are a sobering example here. See David Shim, 'Seeing from Above: The Geopolitics of Satellite Vision and North Korea', *GIGA Institute of Asian Studies*, August 2012, available at http://giga.hamburg/de/.

17   Benjamin S. Lambeth, *Mastering the Ultimate High Ground: Next Steps in the Military Uses of Space*, Santa Monica, CA: RAND Corp., 1999. This 'high ground' of terrestrial space is split into three zones. Low Earth orbits (LEOs), between 150 and 2,000 km up, are dominated by fast-moving reconnaissance and communications satellites and inhabited craft for living astronauts. Here orbit the latest reconnaissance satellites – such as the US GeoEye-1, which can spot objects on Earth that are only 30 to 40 cm in size. Higher up, between 800 and 36,000 km above the earth's surface, are a range of communications, GPS and navigation craft in medium Earth orbit (MEOs). (GPS satellites orbit at around 20,200 km.) Finally, geostationary satellites – used for weather forecasting, satellite TV, satellite

The US military's vision for dominating space is characterised by dreams of being able to see anything on the earth's surface at any time, regardless of enemies' efforts to occlude their targets.[18] This ambition is linked with an obsession with the ability to use GPS satellites to organise the dropping of lethal ordnance on those self-same spots. Satellite dominance is seen as a critical prerequisite to the dominance of the airspace, landspace and maritime space below.

Finally, satellites are considered by US military theorists to be a crucial means of reducing the vulnerability of the home nation. This is done by using satellites to target incoming missiles – and, possibly in the future, by launching specialised weapons from one's own satellites against the satellite fleets of enemies.

'Black' Satellites: The Other Night Sky

How might critical scholars and activists penetrate the 'black' world of secret military satellites? Two linked strategies emerge here. On the one hand, a secretive group of satellites activists have done much recent work to expose the daily trajectories or geostationary orbits of the fleets of military spy satellites as they operate high above. Working with this community, artist and geographer Trevor Paglen, who helped to expose the CIA's system of extraordinary rendition in 2006, has spent many cold nights peering through sophisticated tracked telescopes in California's Sierra Nevada and other sites around the world. With his colleagues, he has been able to track, photograph, catalogue and calculate the orbits of 140 or so of the classified 'black' US satellites known to orbit the earth at any one time.[19]

Paglen and his colleagues have been able to do this because of a paradox: although 'black' satellites are so secret they aren't even

---

radio, most other types of global communications and military and security eavesdropping – orbit the equator at exactly 35,786 kilometres, a distance which allows them to remain permanently over their 'footprint' on one particular part of the earth.

18   As we will see in chapter 15, subterranean burrowing has long been the best strategy against satellite surveillance.

19   See Paglen, *Last Pictures*, chapter 1, and the satellite tracking community's two main websites: heavens-above.com and satobs.org/seesat/seesatindex.html.

supposed to exist, their large size means that, if you are able to calculate the places/times where they become clearly visible because they reflect sunlight, tracking orbital spy satellites is relatively simple. (Geostationary orbits, or GSOs, at exactly 35,787 km up, plus or minus a kilometre or two, are much harder to spot.)

Pulling scraps of data from satellite enthusiasts, publicly available military budgets and federal regulators' flight plan information, Paglen and his colleagues have done much to piece together what he calls the 'The Other Night Sky' – the clandestine world of US radar, radio, infrared and visual light–based military satellites. They even glean useful clues to the location and latitude of the launched satellites of the US National Reconnaissance Office (NRO) by decoding the military cloth badges that *are* made public about each launch.

Paglen's sketchy time-delay images offer a fleeting glimpse of a world that supposedly does not even exist, a world that, paradoxically, can be witnessed by anyone on the earth's surface simply by looking up on a clear night and catching the sun's reflections on the satellite body. 'The other night sky', Paglen writes:

> is a landscape of fleeting reflections: of giants, glimpses, traces and flares. Of unacknowledged moons and 'black' space craft moving through the pre-dawn and early evening darkness, where the rising and setting sun lights up the stainless steel bodies, and they blink in and out of sight as they glide though the backdrop of a darkened sky hundred of miles below. In most cases, the reflection is all we get.[20]

Fittingly for this book, Paglen's work, like the whistle-blowing leaks of Chelsea Manning and Edward Snowden, is an example of what has been called sous-surveillance – literally 'under surveillance' or 'surveillance from below'. In challenging the cloak of invisibility and secrecy that obscures top-down surveillance by national security states, Paglen and the satellite-tracking community fleetingly expose one crucial material embodiment of the increasingly secretive and authoritarian nature of security politics.[21]

---

20   Trevor Paglen, 'AFP 731; or, The Other Night Sky: An Allegory', in Lisa Parks and James Schwoch, eds, *Down to Earth: Satellite Technologies, Industries, and Cultures*, New Brunswick, NJ: Rutgers University Press, 2012, p. 244.

21   Lisa Lynch, '"As I Photograph the Night Sky, the Other Night Sky

Predictably, further exposures come from the strategic competitors of the United States. Between 2005 and 2010, for example, Russia managed to obtain detailed images of the NRO's enormous 'Lacrosse' radar reconnaissance satellites by using highly advanced ground-based telescopes in Siberia. These rare images, which can be contrasted with pictures of the satellites on the ground, were released for propaganda purposes.

Such tactics inevitably emerge, of course, as a reciprocal world of 'watching the watchers'. After completing his photographs, Paglen reflected that that his project was 'not a passive exercise: as I photograph the night sky, the other night sky photographs back'.[22]

There is also evidence that the Pentagon has responded to the satellite tracking community by reorienting some of their most secretive of satellites – those of the multibillion-dollar 'Misty' programme – so that they don't reflect sun down to the areas of the world where the main trackers live. 'We would prefer that these things not end up on the Internet', an NRO spokesperson noted dryly in 2006.[23]

Ground Stations: 'Fragments of America'

A complementary approach is to explore and map the ground-level infrastructure necessary to allow military spy satellites to function. Steve Rowell, an artist affiliated with the Center for Land Use Interpretation (CLUI) in Los Angeles, has completed one of the most thorough studies in this field. His analysis of the distribution of US satellite stations, both unmanned and manned, across the world is especially significant because such installations are not normally counted in conventional analyses of US military bases. As Rowell puts it, 'Every satellite in orbit requires a tremendous amount of infrastructure on the ground'.[24] He estimates that the United States alone has around 6,000 ground-based installations around the world.

Photographs Back": Surveillance, Transparency, and the Frenzy of Disclosure', n.d., available at academia.edu.

22   Cited by Lynch, '"As I Photograph the Night Sky"'.

23   Quoted in Patrick Raden Keefe, 'I Spy', *Wired*, 2 January 2006, available at wired.com.

24   Steve Rowell, *Ultimate High Ground*, 2008, available at steverowell.com.

'These sites', he writes, 'whether radar-detection posts, satellite-tracking bases, telecommunications-intercept centers, space ports, unmanned transmitter arrays, or overcrowded field offices, are fragments of America.'

Although they are fixed at the ground level, Rowell emphasises the changing roles of ground and earth stations in the shifting geopolitical strategies of the United States and other powers. Fenced-off, patrolled and enigmatic, their radomes and aerials can but hint at the roles of such facilities within a vast and largely unknowable and infinitely larger datascape of instant, encrypted, imaging, sensing, targeting and communications.

US satellite stations combine stations inherited from the British after World War II, a wide range of bases set up during the Cold War, and a newer set of installations that evidence that dramatic growth of the military-intelligence industry in the wake of the 'war on terror'. Steve Rowell's mapping of these facilities gives an indication of their reach and density across the earth.

Usefully, Rowell's work connects the abstract cartographies of the satellite-base surveillance with face-to-face confrontations with the eerie and secretive installations on the ground that sustain it. As part of his research, Rowell paid particular attention to the largest and most important of the National Security Agency's global satellite surveillance stations: the notionally British Royal Air Force base at Menwith Hill in North Yorkshire, England.

Steve Rowell's chance meeting with a Ministry of Defence police vehicle outside the Menwith Hill NSA Base

The 560-acre Menwith Hill site – known to the NSA and NRO as 'Field Station 83' – is one of three key US satellite bases at the heart of the globe-spanning communications surveillance system known as PRISM, a system powerfully exposed by the NSA whistle-blower Edward Snowden in 2011.[25] Like a dystopian film set, the base's architecture of over thirty Kevlar radomes sits rather incongruously within the pastoral landscapes of North Yorkshire's valleys. Its razor-wired peripheries are circled by US military guards, and its 2,300 employees are drawn from all of the three key players in the US satellite-surveillance complex.[26]

Menwith Hill's recently expanded and modernised fields of radomes house extraordinarily powerful systems for scooping up all electromagnetic wireless and satellite phone calls and data and video transmissions over large geographical areas. Its latest 'Taurus' or 'Collect-It-all' ground station antennae represent a step-change in the NSA's ability to monitor global satellite traffic.[27] Linked also with the NSA's systems for tapping terrestrial communications over ordinary radio transmissions, and secret optic fibre connections that can handle the equivalent at least 100,000 telephone calls simultaneously, bases like Menwith Hill to covertly collection, with agreement from IT service providers, of large swathes of the traffic of the whole Internet. This includes the monitoring of all traffic over the Microsoft, Google, Yahoo, Facebook, Paltalk, YouTube, Skype, AOL and Apple networks, data from which is transmitted back to the NSA's huge new 'data fusion' complex in Utah.

Using supercomputers and classified decryption software, Menwith Hill and its allied bases provide automatic analysis and classification of a huge range of intercepted data in order to track a wide assortment of identified 'targets'. These range from alleged insurgent leaders or

---

25   The others are in Australasia and Hawaii.

26   These are the National Security Agency (NSA), which runs the site; the National Reconnaissance Office (NRO), which operates surveillance and military satellites; and the National Geospatial Intelligence Agency (NGIA), which is responsible for geographic intelligence of many kinds. Staff from US military-contract corporations and the UK's GCHQ are also present at the base.

27   Desmond Ball, Duncan Campbell, Bill Robinson and Richard Tanter, *Expanded Communications Satellite Surveillance and Intelligence Activities Utilising Multi-beam Antenna Systems,* Berkeley: Nautilus Institute, 2015.

terrorist 'cells' in the Middle East to European politicians and businesses, as well as entirely legal and legitimate civilian protest groups and social movements within the UK, Europe and North America.

Menwith Hill's systems are also pivotal in globe-spanning systems organised to support the detection of ballistic missiles and the prosecution of lethal drone strikes. Indeed, Menwith Hill is a crucial hub in a massive US effort to be able to launch lethal power at any spot on the earth's surface at very short delay. Such 'time-critical targeting' is deemed to be crucial in a world where nonstate terrorist and insurgent threats are hard to distinguish from the background of the 'civilian' societies within which they hide. The aim of such global targeting is to build a fully integrated network, combining satellite imagery with interception of all types of electronic communications, in a way that provides the real-time intelligence necessary to identify targets and to carry out attacks anywhere in the world without the need for conventional armies.[28] Menwith Hill has thus played a pivotal role in the continuous prosecution of routine violence across vast geographic areas that have characterised US global covert wars over the past sixteen years or so.

Weaponising Space

> Let's hope the words 'commence the orbital bombardment' don't enter our vernacular in the near future.
>
> – Christian Sager, 'Death Metal from Space'

Since Sputnik was first launched in 1957, the orbits of satellites have given geopolitics a radically vertical fourth dimension.[29] Indeed, the last half-century has made the orbital domains of inner space a profoundly contested zone dominated by increasing processes of militarisation and weaponisation, despite notional international agreements such as the 1967 Outer Space Treaty prohibiting the process.

28   Yorkshire CND, 'Menwith Hill and the National Security State', 26 June 2013, available at yorkshirecnd.org.uk.

29   Lucio Caracciolo 'Assault on the Sky' *Heartland*, May 2004, available at temi.repubblica.it/.

As well as secretive launches of ever more sophisticated and powerful spy satellites and an extending range of ground stations, evidence of the deployment of armed satellites is emerging. Back in 2003, for example, the US military undertook research on the lethal effects of an orbiting satellite simply letting go of long, inert tungsten rods, targeted using simple gravitational force to any spot on earth in short order. Intended for destroying the deeply buried bunkers of adversary states, the six-metre-long rods – nicknamed the 'rod from God' – would impact the earth at ten times the speed of sound, unleashing energy on impact equivalent to that of a small nuclear explosion.[30]

To bolster the militarisation of space, a new field of 'astro-geopolitics' has emerged, largely in the United States. This is fuelled heavily by the use by metaphors linking the domination of inner orbits with the reach of empires across the horizontal planes of oceans in both pre-industrial eras and the competitive scramble between European empires in the eighteenth and nineteenth centuries. To the Heritage Foundation, a think-tank on the Republican right and a key player in deploying such metaphors, 'space is the high seas of tomorrow'.[31]

A range of hawkish astro-geopolitical theorists, meanwhile, now herald the domination of space as the key to controlling the earth below. Their thesis is a classic tautology: as a wider range of nations emerge to launch their own military space programmes, space will be weaponised; therefore space must be weaponised most powerfully and quickly by the United States in a pre-emptive effort to maintain its power. 'He who controls the lower orbits controls the near Space around Earth,' writes one influential theorist, Everett Dolman of the School of Advanced Air Power Studies at Maxwell Air Base in Alabama, and 'he who dominates the Earth determines the future of mankind'.[32]

---

30   See chapter 15. 'Rods from God' are referenced in both the 2003 *US Air Force Transformation Flight Plan*, available at au.af.mil, and the 2002 RAND report on *Space Weapons, Earth Wars,* available at rand.org.

31   B. T. Johnson, 'The New Space Race: Challenges for US National Security and Free Enterprise', Heritage Foundation Backgrounder no. 1316, 25 August 1999, available at heritage.org.

32   Everett Dolman, *Astropolitik: Classical Geopolitics in the Space Age,* New York: Frank Cass Publishers, 2002, p. 8.

Given the reliance of contemporary societies and economies on satellite-based communications, navigation and information, such systems constitute an Achilles heel the destruction of which would bring extraordinary disruption and economic destabilisation.

Italian journalist Lucio Caracciolo sees the orbital skein of communications and navigation satellites as an 'indispensable strategic nerve system of the more developed economies',[33] one that is highly vulnerable to anti-satellite weapons fired from the ground, aircraft or, conceivably, other satellites. 'Satellite constellations set up in peace are the fixed coastal defenses of the modern age', the US Naval Institute argue. They are 'easy to target and plan against – and most likely first on an enemy's targeting priority list.'[34]

Worryingly, the centrality of satellites to contemporary imperial power is being used by military leaders to urge for the exploration of a wide range of lasers and 'kinetic' (that is, physical) weapons that can actually hit the earth's surface from satellite orbits. 'We will fight from Space and in Space', General Joseph Ashby, then commander-in-chief of the United States Space Command, said, contemplating the future of his organisation in 1996. 'One day we will hit earthbound targets – ships, aircraft, objects on the ground – from Space. We will hit targets in Space from Space.'[35]

Anti-satellite weapons launched from below in fact have a long history. In the early days of the Cold War, huge nuclear warheads attached to modified ballistic missiles compensated for their lack of accuracy.[36] In 1962, to test this strategy, the United States exploded a 1.4-megaton nuclear weapons known as Starfish at an altitude of 400 km above Johnston Island in the Pacific Ocean.[37] Over the last forty years, the United States, Russia and China have each deployed a suite of anti-satellite missiles launched from ships, aircraft or ground stations.

---

33   Caracciolo, 'Assault on the Sky'.

34   CDR. Salamander, '...But Can You Sling One under an F-18 about to Shoot Off a CVN?', *US Naval Institute Blog*, July 2015, available at blog.usni.org.

35   Jennifer Heronema, 'A.F. Space Chief Calls War in Space Inevitable', *Space News*, December 1996, p. 4.

36   Lt. Col. James Mackey, 'Recent US and Chinese Antisatellite Activities', *Air and Space Power Journal*, Fall 2009, available at au.af.mil.

37   Puneet Bhalla, *Weaponisation of Space*, New Delhi: Centre for Land Warfare Studies, 2014, available at claws.in.

These systems are now so accurate that they use conventional explosive warheads. Although testing of such systems is not as common as it was between 1970 and 1990, anti-satellite missiles have been used on several occasions to destroy satellites deemed either to be a risk to inhabitants on the earth, or an intelligence risk when the satellites fall back through Earth's atmosphere after their operational lives are over or following a malfunction.

Such intercept operations create huge debris fields which in turn become a major hazard to other satellite and space operations. In 2007, the first Chinese anti-satellite launch, which destroyed a Chinese meteorological satellite, created a debris field made up of between 20,000 to 40,000 fragments of one centimetre or greater in size.[38] In this one intercept, China caused a 20 per cent increase in the number of small objects in lower Earth orbit – each one travelling at around 8 miles a second – which need to be tracked in order to minimise the damage to, or avoid the destruction of, other satellites or space vehicles. (Twenty-two years earlier, a similar US anti-satellite launch created 250 pieces of trackable debris, one of which almost collided with the International Space Station in 1999.) In total, there are already 500,000 fragments of potentially damaging space debris in orbit around Earth. Such debris is a grave concern because its impacts on states' satellites and other orbiting vehicles could easily be misinterpreted as deliberate anti-satellite warfare by adversary states. In 2016 the Russian Academy of Sciences warned that debris impacting orbiting vehicles might even provoke quick escalation towards global conflict because 'the owner of the impacted and destroyed satellite can hardly quickly determine the real cause of the accident.'[39]

Other development efforts in anti-satellite warfare centre on the use of high-powered lasers located on the ground, on ships or in aircraft. Microwaves, particle beams or electromagnetic pulse devices have also been explored as ways to damage or disable both incoming ballistic missiles and orbiting satellites. Another strategy is to launch anti-satellite satellites. Satellite researchers think that the

---

38   Kelly Young, 'Anti-Satellite Test Generates Dangerous Space Debris', *New Scientist*, 20 January 2007.

39   Cited in Spacedaily, 'Will Space Debris Be Responsible for World War III?' 1 February 2016, at spacedaily.com/reports/.

highly secretive MiTex fleet of tiny 250 kg US experimental geostationary satellites are already capable of stealthily tracking, inspecting, intercepting and even knocking out or disrupting the geostationary craft of adversary nations. One such interception has already been observed by South African satellite observer Greg Roberts.[40]

These weapons, as far as publicly known, have yet to be deployed into space itself, although President Reagan's ambitious 'Star Wars' Strategic Defense Initiative in the 1980s and 1990s involved wide-scale research and development of armed satellites as well as ground-based anti-missiles and anti-satellite systems. Indeed, the proliferation of ground-based anti-satellite weapons has rekindled the fear that weapons systems will soon be deployed into orbit around the earth.

Many US military theorists consider such deployments to be inevitable and suggest that the United States needs pre-emptively to lead such a move to maintain the nation's long domination of the 'ultimate high ground'.[41] It is clear, at least, that the United States is now developing a secret, reusable 'space-bomber' (the Boeing X37), and a range of satellites designed to destroy other satellites while in orbit have also been mooted.

Looking beyond the reliance of the military and the security services of satellites, the prospect of the use of anti-satellite weapons in conflicts is a daunting one. Such weapons contravene all of the key principles of international humanitarian law. In increasingly high-tech and automated societies, where more and more infrastructure and services rely continuously on GPS and satellite mapping and imaging in order to function, the use of such weapons would cause widespread, immediate and potentially even fatal disruptions. Destruction of a nation's satellites, warns Theresa Hitchens, director of the UN Institute for Disarmament Research (UNIDIR), would leave 'an entire country without effective communication systems, with very little access to the internet and phones, for a certain period of time'. It would also disrupt financial systems, telemedicine, ATMs and so-called 'just in time' logistics and delivery systems, as well the water supply, power grids and search and rescue operations.[42]

---

40   Paglen, 'What Greg Roberts Saw'.
41   Bhalla, 'Weaponisation of Space'.
42   'What if Space Was the Next Frontier for War?', *Time*, 3 October 2012. See

As societies automate rapidly, we can envisage further impacts. How murderous might a future highway system used by fleets of driver-less satellite-guided cars become if those satellites were suddenly disabled or their systems hacked? Anti-satellite attacks would also likely trigger waves of unstoppable tit-for-tat escalations between the main satellite powers. Many US war games simulating such attacks quickly escalate to nuclear exchanges.

Arms control lawyers are therefore now arguing that the proliferation and possible use of anti-satellite weapons is so significant that it needs to be subject to a range of treaties, proscriptions, regulations and inspections similar to those which have long attempted to regulate nuclear, biological and chemical weapons.

'Given the nearly unstoppable advance of modern military technology', international lawyer Robert David Onley writes, 'if space weapons are not banned, countries will be forced to build satellites equipped with counter-measures that destroy incoming anti-satellite missiles – and as a consequence, effectively guarantee the permanent weaponization of space.' At such a point, he suggests, 'there exists only a small leap in logic between the prospects of satellites armed with missiles for self-defence, to satellites (or space-bombers/orbiters) armed with missiles and bombs for offensive purposes.'[43]

World-Zoom: Google Earth

> Today the aerial view – the image *of* everywhere – seems to *be* everywhere.
>
> – Dorrian and Pousin, *Seeing from Above*

Perhaps the most profound effect of the contemporary proliferation of satellites centres on the way their extraordinary powers of seeing from above are now harnessed to computers and smart phones. Google Earth is obviously especially pivotal here. As a system of systems

also Stephen Graham, ed., *Disrupted Cities: When Infrastructure Fails*, New York: Routledge, 2009.

43   Robert David Onley, 'Death from Above: The Weaponization of Space and the Threat to International Humanitarian Law', *Journal of Air Law and Commerce* 78, 2013, p. 739.

linked to a computer or mobile smartphone, it offers almost infinite possibilities of zooming into and out of views of Earth's surface at local, regional and global scales.[44] Google Earth does this by 'mashing up' global satellite imagery, geopositioning coordinates, digital cartography, geolocated data, three-dimensional computerised maps, architectural drawings, street-level digital imagery and other social media, data and software. These are configured together as an 'always on', interactive and boundless datascape – a flexible and multiscaled portal of largely vertical images which now mediate life in profoundly new and important ways.

The apparently infinite 'scale-jumping' possibilities of Google Earth force us to revisit and update a long-standing debate about the politics of the aerial, 'God's-eye', or top-down view.[45] As we saw in the introduction, many cultural theorists argue that the new ubiquity of the digital view from above is an important part of contemporary shifts way from a world dominated by a stable and single sense of ground and horizon organised through linear perspective. Instead, contemporary societies are saturated by a multitude of 'always on' digital and screen-based perspectives; extending armies of prosthetic eyes laid across entire volumes of geographic space; intense and real-time globalisation; and, for many, unprecedented human mobility. Satellites and satellite vision are absolutely pivotal to this new sense of vertical 'free fall' that attends this new age.[46]

Google Earth is central to these transformations. It is the prime means through which vertical and oblique views of our world view have rapidly become radically accessible, zoomable and pannable in a myriad of ways. Many researchers suggest that mass public access to Google Earth fundamentally challenges long-standing assumptions that the view from above necessarily involves dispassionate, technocratic or privileged visual power.[47] In presenting a 'virtual globe' that can be navigated on screen and repeatedly zoomed, Google Earth

44   Ursula Heise, *Sense of Place and Sense of Planet: The Environmental Imagination of the Global,* Oxford: Oxford University Press, 2008, p. 11.

45   See Chris Tong, 'Ecology without Scale: Unthinking the World Zoom,' *Animation* 9:2, 2014, pp. 200–1.

46   See Hito Steyerl, 'In Free Fall: A Thought Experiment on Vertical Perspective', *E-Flux Journal* 4, 2011, available at e-flux.com/journal.

47   Mark Dorrian, 'On Google Earth', *New Geographies* 4, 2011, pp. 164–70.

thus presents a powerful imagination of the planet: one that is simultaneously global, corporate and saturated with commercial data and corporate location-based advertising. It is thus 'closely related to the production and movements of contemporary urbanization.'[48]

The active shaping of this 'virtual globe' by the viewer is crucial, however. In contrast to media like aerial or satellite photographs, users of Google Earth are no longer simply passive viewers witnessing the world as a zoom shot. Instead, participants can actively customise their own experience of Google Earth by building their own interfaces and adding their own data and imagery.[49] Indeed, the frame-by-frame animation of the Google Earth interface works to provide viewers and users with a virtual globe which they can manipulate to provide their own personal cinematic rendition of the planet that they can then view and manipulate in decidedly God-like ways. Media scholar Leon Gurevitch calls this the 'divine manufacturer of the very [Google Earth] environments [viewers] wish to travel through.'[50]

The addition of street-level visuals through Google Street View grounds this virtual world with imagery of current and historical street scenes. Now 'cloud' level and 'street' level worlds work seamlessly together, shimmering visual surfaces that occlude as much as they reveal to the inspecting subject. The system's interface 'provides the ability to come and go freely within a completely controlled universe', media scholar Daniel Laforest emphasises, 'while maintaining the sense of distance as a constant promise, a source of leisure, or even as an unexpected pleasure.'[51]

Despite its flexibility, the cultural and political biases of Google Earth are not hard to spot. Until recently, the system defaulted to a view that placed the US at the centre of the screen. The interface offers little evidence of the source or accuracy of the global surveillance that sustains Google Earth. The way Google Earth itself collects reams of data that is passed on to commercial information markets

---

48 Daniel Laforest, 'The Satellite, the Screen, and the City: On Google Earth and the Life Narrative', *International Journal of Cultural Studies*, July 2014.

49 Tong, 'Ecology without Scale'.

50 Leon Gurevitch, 'Google Warming: Google Earth as Eco-machinima', *Convergence* 20, 2014, p. 97.

51 See Daniel Laforest, 'The Satellite, the Screen, and the City: On Google Earth and the Life Narrative', *International Journal of Cultural Studies*, 2015, p. 6.

or security and surveillance services like the NSA is also carefully obscured.

Many areas are also censored or offered at deliberately low resolution. Under US law, for example, Google must represent certain parts of Israel/Palestine at low resolution. States have also been found to doctor Google Earth images. Hawkish security commentators stress the usefulness of Google Earth to those planning terrorist attacks and are now urging that such censorship be extended. 'Terrorists don't need to reconnoitre their target', Russian security official Lt. Gen. Leonid Sazhin said in 2005. 'Now an American company is working for them.'[52]

The social and cultural biases of Goggle Earth can also be stark. In post-Katrina New Orleans, for example, efforts to use Google Earth to allow communities affected by the crisis to share information and support across the various neighbourhoods of the city inevitably ended up being geared overwhelmingly towards more affluent and whiter neighbourhoods because of wider geographies of the so-called 'digital divide' in the city.[53]

Certain information, moreover, is dramatically prioritised within the system – information for users of corporate services, automobile drivers and so on. Google Earth's dominant, de facto data sets are heavily dominated by a cluster of key transnational corporations. To sustain their competitive advantages in tourism, travel, leisure services, oil consumption and food provision, these companies overlay the satellite surfaces with geolocation data geared towards exploiting their dominate position on this new screen interface. Other information – say about human rights abuses or the installations of national security states – is obviously obscured or inaccessible, sometimes through the crudest of censorship. Extreme biases in access, meanwhile, mean that user-generated content of Google Earth strongly reflects wider social and ethnic inequalities in society.

Beyond these disparities lies a burgeoning politics of urban legibility and camouflage, as state, commercial and nonstate actors work

---

52   Cited in Roger Stahl, 'Becoming Bombs: 3D Animated Satellite Imagery and the Weaponization of the Civic Eye', *MediaTropes* 2:2, 2010, p. 66.

53   Michael Crutcher and Matthew Zook, 'Placemarks and Waterlines: Racialized Cyberscapes in Post-Katrina Google Earth', *Geoforum* 40:4, 2009, pp. 523–34.

to appropriate the new vertical views to conflicting ends. As financial collapse hit the Greek state in 2009, for example, the government tried to locate wealthy Athenians guilty of tax avoidance by using Google Earth to find their swimming pools. The immediate response was to drape tarpaulins over the tell-tale azure rectangles.

Meanwhile, many social and political movements have mobilised Google Earth and satellite imagery in their efforts to expose war crimes and state violence in places as diverse as Darfur, Zimbabwe, the Balkans, Syria, Burma and Sri Lanka.[54] Satellite images have been very helpful in securing convictions of war criminals in the International Criminal Court at The Hague.[55]

Activists in Palestine, meanwhile, have actively used the system to generate maps that depict widening Israeli control there in an effort to undermine the cartography produced by the Israeli state to legitimise or minimise its degree of colonial control.[56] The system has also been a boon to those aiming to expose, hack and contest the scale and power of national security states, military forces and corporate power.[57] Perhaps the most famous example in this regard was the discovery in China in 2006 of a military training area that mimicked precisely the exact terrain of a part of the Indian–Chinese border that has been in dispute since 1962.

In Bahrain, Google Earth's ability to trace aggressive efforts to vertically build up 'reclaimed' land to fuel elite real estate speculation had a huge impact in 2011.[58] The mass uprising of the Shiite majority against the dictatorial Sunni elite – brutally suppressed by local security forces with the help of Saudi paramilitaries – was ignited partly by circulation of Google Earth images depicting the scale of corrupt land

54   See Lisa Parks, 'Digging into Google Earth: An Analysis of "Crisis in Darfur"', *Geoforum* 40:4, 2009. pp. 535–45; Andrew Herscher 'From Target to Witness: Architecture, Satellite Surveillance, Human Rights', in Bechir Kenzari, ed., *Architecture and Violence,* Barcelona: Actar, 2010, pp. 127–48.

55   James Walter, 'Archimedean Witness: The Application of Remote Sensing as an Aid to Human Rights Prosecutions', PhD thesis, Los Angeles, UCLA.

56   Linda Quiquivix, 'Art of War, Art of Resistance: Palestinian Counter-Cartography on Google Earth', *Annals of the Association of American Geographers* 104:3, 2014, pp. 444–59.

57   Chris Perkins and Martin Dodge, 'Satellite Imagery and the Spectacle of Secret Spaces', *Geoforum* 40:4, 2009, pp. 546–60.

58   This case is described in more detail in chapter 12.

'reclamation' by those very elites to radically remodel and further privatise the tiny nation's coastline.

More broadly, the vertical gaze of Google Earth helped the poor Shiite majority in Bahrain to realise that the nation's tiny Sunni elite owns and controls 95 per cent of country's land and has, along with wealthy tourists, exclusive private access to 97 per cent of its beaches. The geographies of exploitation and repression became startlingly clear in full-colour, high-resolution imagery. 'When Google Earth was introduced', Middle East specialist Eugene Rogan relates, 'Bahrainis for the first time could see the walled palaces and rich homes that normally were hidden from view. Bahrainis got a bird's-eye view of how rich people there lived.' Although the Bahraini state blocked Google Earth in response, activists outside the country responded by circulating the same images in PDF format.[59]

Although Google Earth clearly has enormous potential as an aid to activism and critique, it is easy to forget that such new, GPS-enabled activism relies fundamentally on 'dual-use' devices that can function only because of military rocket launches. Such efforts are also based on the deployment of a series of twenty-four geosynchronous satellites used continually to drop murderous ordnance of a wide range of countries. And they are inevitably mediated through imperial networks of militarised ground stations and data centres, relying fundamentally on a network of atomic clocks run by the US Air Force.

In this context, media theorist Roger Stahl emphasises the military origins of the whole aesthetic of Google Earth. It 'began its life as the very picture of war', he stresses. During the 2003 Gulf War, he relates,

> a certain 3D aesthetic appeared in the form of virtual flybys, as part of more complex computer animations, in studio surveys of bomb damage, in speculations on the whereabouts of Saddam Hussein, and a range of other uses. It is not an exaggeration to say that this aesthetic took center stage in the high-tech spectacle of US television coverage.[60]

Such a perspective forces a deep appreciation of the ways in which, despite its widening civilian use, Google Earth remains a highly

59   Michael; Byrne, 'Google Earth and the Bahraini Uprising', *Motherboard*, 17 February 2011, available at motherboard.vice.com/.

60   Stahl, 'Becoming Bombs', p. 67.

militarised domain embedded fundamentally within a broader military-technology-geotechnology-security complex. This means that the system is a key means through which citizens now consume state military violence, a process which adds to the mythology of 'clean' war and 'precision weapons' that contemporary US militaries are eager to circulate. 'Rather than say that the 3D satellite image has been "demilitarized" as it has entered civilian life', Stahl emphasises, 'it may be more accurate to say that the transference has draped the planet with a militarized image of itself.'

The militarised nature of GPS systems – a crucial basis for Google Earth – also requires emphasis. Media activist Brian Holmes, for one, questions the powers of GPS-based art and activism in a world where the broader technological structures of power are dominated powerfully by what he calls a 'hyper-rationalist grid of Imperial infrastructure'. When you use a GPS-locating device such as Google Earth, he argues, 'you respond to the call. You are interpellated into Imperial ideology.'[61]

Finally, the vertical gaze of satellite imagery that is now so remarkably accessible offers important new perspectives on how the horizontal geographies of our planet's surface are changing. For it is only from such distant heights that we can begin to make sense of the extraordinary territorial formations currently being created by the rampant growth and sprawl of the world's urban areas. 'To truly exist', Rice University architect Professor Lars Lerup writes, 'every city needs its perspective. Its point of view. Its eyes.'[62] And yet the dominant experience at the edges of many sprawling urban areas – beyond the clusters of rapidly rising skyscrapers and elite housing towers – is one of apparently endless horizontality. In such landscapes obtaining a sense of the wider city becomes all but impossible.

Google Earth allows such landscapes to be understood. Only the zoomable and extending top-down gaze of the satellite can really stretch to encompass what Lerup calls the 'striated, spread-out geographies' of contemporary urbanised regions and 'megalopolitan'

---

61   Brian Holmes, 'Drifting through the Grid: Psychogeography and Imperial Infrastructure', May 2003, available at springerin.at.

62   Lars Lerup, 'Vastlands Visited', in Alan Berger, ed., *Drosscape: Wasting Land in Urban America*, New York: Princeton Architectural Press, 2006, p. 242.

corridors. Writing about Alan Berger's remarkable maps of the geographies of sprawl and wasted land in urban America, Lerup points out that 'from a satellite, this neglected in-between [of drosscape or "pure unadulterated waste"] is the real grammar of the horizontal city, requiring a new mathematics whose nature, strength and intelligence lies embedded in its apparent incoherence.'[63]

With the satellite view of the city now a normal way of representing urban areas for mass consumption, navigation, planning and, increasingly, marketing, it is perhaps the way in which cityscapes are increasingly engineered to be brandscapes visible from space that is the most immediate example of Google Earth's impacts on the ground. Here, Mark Dorrian points out that 'the terrestrial surface itself becomes manipulated as a media surface, not just virtually on the Google Earth interface, but literally.'[64] This democratization of verticality has important effects: In this new, mass market medium, corporations are now concerned with how their spaces and buildings look from satellites and aircraft.

On the one hand, there is growing evidence that city boosterists increasingly work to ensure that their branded, spectacularised urban 'products' work well when viewed through Google Earth. (The design of corporate advertising for aerial and satellite consumption is also increasingly common.) A consultant involved in the staging of the 2012 London Olympics, for example, remarked that 'it's a media event, so it will look great from the air.'[65] Sometimes city authorities, keen to show their new developments off vertically, are unhappy at the slow updating of the vertical imagery of their cities.[66]

Commentary is also already emerging of the relative aesthetic merits of the 'fly-through' experience above and through the increasingly 3D virtual renditions of major global cities. 'As a city to fly though or play with', geographer David Gilbert remarks, 'London works better than the homogeneity of Haussmann's Paris or the regular order and rectilinear street plans' of Manhattan. Gilbert argues that both Paris's long

---

63   Lerup, 'Vastlands Visited', p. 243.
64   Dorrian, 'On Google Earth', p. 169.
65   Ibid.
66   An example was Liverpool in 2006. See *BBC News*, 'Online Map "Misses" Regeneration', 26 November 2006, available at news.bbc.co.uk.

Poet Raúl Zurita's 3-kilometre poem in the Atacama desert

boulevards and Manhattan's endless avenues through canyons of high towers 'become less interesting than a cityscape of roads that change direction or end unexpectedly, of labyrinthine lanes and alleys that repay close investigation, and of rapid variety in the characteristics of districts and built forms.'[67]

On other occasions artists and activists are undertaking ambitious projects to use the very surface of the earth as a canvas for their efforts, to be consumed, via the Google Earth system, on the laptops and smartphones of a global audience. Most notable here is the project by the Chilean activist and poet Raúl Zurita, who suffered incarceration and torture at the hands of the Pinochet regime, to use earth-moving machinery to inscribe a four-word poem in a 3 km stretch of the bone-dry Atacama desert. The line – *ni pena ni miedo* ('no pain no fear') – is a deep reflection of Zurita's response to his experience of political tyranny.

Much more familiar, as we will discuss later in chapter 12, is the widespread engineering of manufactured earth to create distinctive megastructural urban brandscapes which are carefully designed with their representation through Google Earth in mind. Most notable here, as we have seen already, are the 'Palm' and 'World' developments in Dubai – gargantuan projects marketed as 'today's great development epic'.[68] Here civil engineering, land art and landscape architecture

67 David Gilbert, 'The Three Ages of Aerial Vision: London's Aerial Iconography from Wenceslaus Hollar to Google Earth', *London Journal* 35:3, 2010, p. 298.

68 See the world.ae/au_overview.html.

blur together to create vast manufactured islands designed as gigantic vehicles for real estate speculation whose prime marketing advantage is their unique appearance, via satellites, on the mobile Google Earth interfaces carried on a billion smartphones in a billion pockets and a billion laptops in a billion bags.

2.

Bomber: Death from Above

In 2005, the Estorick Collection, a small private gallery in London dedicated to twentieth-century Italian art, put on an exhibition titled 'Futurist Skies'.[1] Exploring the influential movement of 'aeropainting' (*aeropittura*), the show displayed a range of original art, set to canvas in Mussolini's Italy in the 1920s and 1930s. The canvasses offered lavish praise to the new possibilities that aircraft offered for perspective, art and culture.

Part of the wider Futurist movement, aeropainters celebrated – indeed, fetishised – aircraft and flying for the sense of the radical rupture they seemed to offer against a ground-level society deemed to be bound up with corruption and stasis. Like all good Futurists, the aeropainters offered a manifesto.[2] 'The changing perspectives of flight', it argued, 'constitute an absolutely new reality that has nothing in common with the reality traditionally constituted by a terrestrial perspective'.[3] Their efforts to help Italy's population become 'air-minded' were motivated by the goal of helping the country to emerge as a first-rate aerial military power.

Perhaps the most famous aeropittura painting is Tullio Crali's *Nose-diving on the City* (1939).[4] The painting, emblazoned across the gallery's publicity for the show and its publications, might seem at first

---

1   See Renato Miracco, *Futurist Skies: Italian Aeropainting*, Rome: Mazzotta, 2005.

2   Giacomo Balla, Benedetta, Fortunato Depero, Gerardo Dottori, Fillia, F.T. Marinetti, Enrico Prampolini, Mino Somenzi and Tato, 'Manifesto of Aeropainting' [1929], in Lawrence Rainey, Christine Poggi and Laura Wittman, eds, *Futurism: An Anthology*, New Haven, CN: Yale University Press, 2009.

3   Enrico Crispolti, 'Aeropainting', in Pontus Hulten, ed., *Futurism and Futurisms*, London: Thames and Hudson, 1986, p. 413.

4   Incuneandosi Nell'abitato (In Tuffo Sulla Città).

Tullio Crali's *Nose-diving on the City* (1939)

sight to offer little more than a Futurist celebration of the danger and speed of modern aerobatics, set against the bewildering canyons and modern towers of some giant, futuristic city modelled obviously on Manhattan.[5] The gallery's brochure, indeed, says little else, suggesting that the paintings being displayed were merely innocent celebrations of the romance of aeronautics. But like all aeropittura pieces, the painting was completed for a much darker purpose: the aesthetic celebration of the new power of the bomber to embody long-dreamt Fascist and Futurist fantasies of systematically destroying cities and societies from above.

Crali's work is an invitation to the supposedly spiritual and 'hygienic' act of 'cleansing' through total aerial warfare. When it was first shown, the painting was widely celebrated in Fascist and Futurist circles as marking Italy's imperial ambitions, symbolising the virility of Mussolini's regime and evoking the martial notion of 'the new Fascist man'.[6]

---

5   Jonathan Jones, 'Birds of Prey', *Guardian*, 5 January 2005.

6   Fernando Esposito, *Fascism, Aviation and Mythical Modernity*, London: Palgrave Macmillan, 2015, p. 327. 'We will glorify war', the manifesto for the Italian Futurists declared, 'the world's only hygiene.' Filippo Marinetti, 'The Founding and Manifesto of Futurism', in Robert Flint, ed., *Marinetti: Selected Writings*, London: Secker and Warburg, 1972 [1909], pp. 39–44.

Completed two years after the bombers of Germany's Condor Legion killed 1,654 out of Guernica's population of 7,000 in April 1937 (as well as committing atrocities in other Spanish cities), and just before the Stuka-led Blitzkrieg attacks on Poland, it takes a spectacular piece of self-deception see Crali's painting as anything but an act of Fascist praise to the act of aerial urban annihilation.[7]

'It was painted in 1939', journalist Jonathan Jones emphasises, criticising the show as an example of the 'moronic complacency of the art world.' Who, he wonders, 'in 1939, would have got this kind of view of a city, if not the pilot of a Stuka dive-bombing an east-European city? Is there really any doubt this painting praises the dynamism of blitzkrieg?'[8]

The complete silence of the gallery, in a show supported by the Italian state and its president, Silvio Berlusconi, is telling but all too predictable. For, as we shall see, throughout the history of the visual depiction of the aerial bomber, the gory details at ground level, when the bombs explode amid the soft, fleshy and all-too-vulnerable bodies of densely packed citizens, almost always remains hidden.

The Estorick's catalogue accompanying the show says nothing about what Stukas did to those in the way on Germany's Blitzkrieg offensives. It also neglects to address how aeropittura artists, linked closely to the first theorist of aerial bombing, Giulio Douhet (1869–1930), glorified the Italian air force's use of bombs and mustard gas in committing atrocities against civilians in colonial wars in Libya and Ethiopia between 1911 and 1936.

Once at war, the Fascist regimes in Germany and Italy, long accustomed to celebrations of aerial annihilation by bombers such as those

---

7   Indeed, many critics see the Aeropittura movement as the progenitor of today's glorification of bombing through 'shock and awe'. See Emily Braun, 'Shock and Awe: Futurist Aeropittura and the Theories of Giulo Douhet', in Vivien Greene, ed., *Italian Futurism 1909–1944: Reconstructing the Universe*, New York: Guggenheim, 2014, pp. 268–86.

8   Jones, 'Birds of Prey'. Christopher Adams, a British art historian who has worked at the Estorick gallery, has countered this view by suggesting that the 1940s Aeropittura artists were not a single coherent group of painters; that many had ambivalent attitudes to war; and that they had complex links to the three-decades-old Italian Fascist movement. See Christopher Adams, 'Historiographical Perspectives on 1940s Futurism', *Journal of Modern Italian Studies* 18:4, 2013, pp. 419–44.

offered by the aeropittura, committed many atrocities against civilians in cities as part of their campaigns. Beyond the bombing of Guernica and other Spanish towns in the civil war, German bombers destroyed the centres of Polish, Dutch and British cities between 1939 and 1942. Indiscriminate German terror bombing during the attack on Poland in 1939 and 1940 killed at least 100,000 civilians; the better known 'Blitz' on British cities in 1940 and 1941 killed at least 40,000 more.

Often such atrocities were treated by the protagonists as aesthetic events celebrating the ascendant power of Fascist violence over their cowering victims below. In 1934 Mussolini's own son, commenting on the 'good sport' of bombing Ethiopian villagers as part of Mussolini's violent push for a 'second Roman Empire' across North Africa, remarked how a direct hit meant that their bodies 'opened up like a flower'.[9]

The dominance in Germany and Italy of a military doctrine emphasising air support for the armies meant, however, that both air forces lacked truly heavy or 'strategic' bombers throughout World War II. This meant that they were unable to field air forces that could systematically lay waste to well-defended cities over sustained periods. The huge fleets of heavy bombers built up later in the war by the British and US air forces, by contrast, meant that they were able to systematically annihilate entire systems of German and Japanese cities between 1942 and 1945.[10] Despite sometimes devastating defences and the provision of civilian bunkers, the Allies killed between 1 million and 1.2 million urban civilians through their bombing. The unprecedented violence of these campaigns, certainly, meant that the traditional sites of urban refuge and safety – basements, shelters and cellars – themselves often became the sites of greatest carnage. 'One could not escape by retreating below ground', historian David Bell writes:

---

9   Cited in Hendrik Van Loon, *The Story of Mankind*, London: Digireads, 2004, p. 545.

10   In keeping with the theme of this book it must be remembered that such technological achievements were possible because of the Allies' unparalleled ability to drawn on vast reserves of subterranean resources, especially the oil, bauxite and iron necessary to create the fleets of aircraft as well as the huge masses of explosives dropped from them. See Mimi Sheller, *Aluminum Dreams: The Making of Light Modernity*, Cambridge, MA: MIT Press, 2014.

when the whole point of the bombing tactics was precisely to bring about the utter destruction of the edifices attacked – that is, to cause buildings, no matter what their architectural structure, to collapse upon themselves, completely leveled and returned to the flat barrenness of the surrounding plains, thereby rendering them literally and completely uninhabitable, whether above or below ground.[11]

The carnage meant that the vertical metaphors deployed by Hermann Goering, head of the Luftwaffe – who repeatedly stressed that his air force would keep a 'roof over Germany' – rang decidedly hollow as the incendiary bombs rained down and firestorms raged throughout German cities.

The destruction of these cities was very carefully engineered. The chemical composition of incendiaries was carefully tailored to the targeted cities using authentic copies of Japanese and German housing designed by architects originally from those nations. These structures, including furnishings, clothing and interiors, were built, burnt and rebuilt in the deserts of Nevada in comprehensive preparations for firestorm attacks on each system of cities.[12] Air power advocates had long looked at Japan's cities, in particular, as easily combustible. 'Japan offers an ideal target for air operations', Billy Mitchell, a US general who many regard as the father of the US Air Force, said in 1932. '[Its] towns, built largely from wood and paper, form the greatest aerial targets the world has ever seen … Incendiary projectiles would burn the cities to the ground in short order'.[13]

The experimental use of two different atom bombs on Nagasaki and Hiroshima in 1945 was thus only the final act of systematic ruination of two highly urbanised nations. Indeed, this violence was so systematic that historians Eric Markusen and David Kopf have even argued that it can be considered genocidal in the way it systematically sought to burn entire systems of cities; dehumanised its victims; used euphemisms to disguise the horror on the ground;

---

11   David F. Bell, 'Bunker Busting and Bunker Mentalities, or Is It Safe to Be Underground?', *South Atlantic Quarterly* 107: 2, 2007, p. 218.

12   See Mike Davis, *Dead Cities and Other Tales*, New York: New Press, 2002, chapter 3.

13   Cited in H. Bruce Franklin, *War Stars: The Superweapon and the American Imagination*, Minneapolis: University of Minnesota Press, 2008, p. 98.

and built up a complex world of technological and organizational routine.[14]

Grounds for Denial

> When the United States Air Force (USAF) revised their slogan in 2008 they chose the simple motto: 'Above All'. Full stop.
>
> – Adey, Whitehead and Williams, *From Above: War, Violence and Verticality*

The ways in which the victims of these the Axis and Allied bombing campaigns have been rendered visible (or not) within post-war history and collective memory have contrasted starkly. The fates of the victims of the German Blitz on British cities are known and have been reported in great detail. By contrast, many taboos still inhibit dispassionate analysis and discussion of the fate the civilians in the Allied aerial annihilations of German and Japanese cities (although, in both Germany and Japan, these are now slowly being overcome[15]).

In the US and the UK, in particular, the World War II 'air war' is still widely glorified in militaristic TV shows, books, toys, video games, air shows and films – what war theorist Chris Hables Gray calls the culture of 'bomber glorioso'.[16] Powerful taboos, and continued official and unofficial censorship, have meant that the perspectives here, like those in aeropittura paintings, have been overwhelmingly aerial: the view from the plane; the God's-eye view of before-and-after maps and aerial or satellite pictures; the almost sublime view of the flaming or exploding city below.

More recently, mainstream media culture has been awash with infrared video footage of 'smart bombs' destroying targets on the ground taken from the launching aircraft or even from the bomb itself.

---

14 Eric Markusen and David Kopf, *The Holocaust and Strategic Bombing: Genocide and Total War in the Twentieth Century*, New York: Westview Press, 1995.

15 See Winfried Sebald, *On the Natural History of Destruction*, London: Random House, 2004.

16 Chris Hables Gray, *Postmodern War: The New Politics of Conflict*, London: Routledge, 2003, p. 87.

Stacked bodies and vertical annihilation: German soldiers burning piles of dead German civilians in Dresden after the firestorm caused in the city by British and US 'area bombing' raids between 13 and 15 February 1945

As in aeropittura Futurism, images of what this ordnance does to the densely clustered human bodies at the point of impact is heavily – sometimes violently – censored. Instead, militarised and technical jargon and euphemism work to render abstract the act of bombing from above, technical and radically removed from the bloody realities on the ground.[17] Far away from this continuing cult of aerial war – and the 'shock and awe' bombing campaigns against Iraq in 2003 show deeply troubling similarities with Italian Futurism within the genealogy of bombing – the annihilated cities, and the maimed, ruptured or burned dead on the ground, barely exist at all in these narratives.[18]

When the fleshy remains of victims are represented, huge controversy still ensues. Although the unimaginable spectacle of the piled bodies of emaciated Holocaust victims in death camps in 1945 has rightly been brought fully and persistently into view, the piled-high bodies of victims of urban firestorms unleashed by Allied fire-

17   See Derek Gregory, 'Lines of Descent', *Open Democracy*, 8 November 2011, available at opendemocracy.net.

18   See Jessica Palmeiri, 'Shock and Awe: The Troubling Legacy of the Futurist Cult of War', paper presented at the event Shock and Awe: The Troubling Legacy of the Futurist Cult of War, Kaye Playhouse, Hunter College, New York, 2009.

bombing in Hamburg, Dresden and Tokyo remain marginal to collective memory and popular discourse about atrocity and war.

Such obfuscations also mark the tragedies of the two atomic bombings in Japan in 1945. Since those attacks, the most commonly available images of the bombings have been the familiar mushroom clouds seen from the bombers. In the immediate aftermath, to minimize international criticism of the bombings, a plethora of trivializing aerial photos and maps were released which glorified the power of the atom bombs and justified their use. An aggressive campaign of censorship and confiscation between 1945 and 1951 dramatically limited the circulation of colour and black-and-white ground-level images and newsreel footage taken on the streets of Hiroshima and Nagasaki which showed the terrible human and urban realities of 'ground zero'.[19]

All evidence of the medical effects of radiation was confiscated as well.[20] Censorship of the effects of the second, plutonium-based bomb used on Nagasaki – dropped partly as an experiment to study its effects relative to the other type of bomb dropped on Hiroshima three days earlier – was particularly strict.[21]

As a result, the aerial images of the mushroom clouds taken from the bombers dominate collective and media memories of the two bombings. Beyond this, images of the flat, lifeless and unbodied plain of the annihilated cities also endure. Later, in Cold War memorialization, such obfuscations aided the remaking of the sites of the two bombings into universal, disembodied and metahistorical symbols of peace.[22]

The actual bomber aircraft that dropped the atomic bombs, meanwhile, have been refurbished, glorified and proudly put on display.

19   Jiyoon Lee, 'A Veiled Truth: The US Censorship of the Atomic Bomb', *Duke East Asia Nexus* 3:1, 2011, available at dukenex.us.

20   Janet Farrell Brodie, 'Radiation Secrecy and Censorship after Hiroshima and Nagasaki', *Journal of Social History* 48:4, 2015, pp. 842–64.

21   It did not help, of course, that many people were literally vapourised by the blasts; tracing their absence was possible only by looking for the shadows they cast behind them. The danger here, though, is that such shadows deny the burns and radiation poisoning of tends of thousands of victims whose bodies – alive or dead – very much endured the blasts.

22   See Ryan Bishop and Gregory Clancey, 'The City as Target', in Stephen Graham, ed., *Cities, War, and Terrorism: Towards an Urban Geopolitics*, London: Wiley & Sons, 2004, pp. 58–62.

In 1995, the newly restored *Enola Gay*, the aircraft that dropped the first atomic bomb on Hiroshima in 1945, was put on display at the Smithsonian Institution's National Air and Space Museum in Washington, D.C. Initially, the display placed artefacts from the ground which hinted as the suffering of the civilian victims – such as a partially melted child's lunch box – alongside the bomber. Huge controversy ensued. A wide range of right-wing, veterans' and patriotic groups, arguing that the display failed to emphasise the efforts of US military personnel as heroic benefactors in supposedly using the bombs to terminate the war against a fanatical and criminal Japanese regime, lobbied to have the initial exhibition closed down. They succeeded.

Six months later a revised exhibition was opened. In it the merest hints of the ground-level impacts of the atomic bomb, and the one dropped three days later on Nagasaki, were entirely absent. No mention was made of the 200,000 civilian victims who died in the attacks – or of the many thousands more who suffered devastating effects of radiation poisoning for generations to come. Artefacts from the ground that even hinted at the suffering of the victims had been removed from the display.

'The exhibit, having excised almost all artefacts and voices from "Ground Zero" in Hiroshima and Nagasaki, arguably erased the shocking destruction of these atomic bombings', Virginia Tech political scientist Tim Luke wrote. Paradoxically, he argued, 'displaying the *Enola Gay*, a real weapon of mass destruction, seems only to have hidden Hiroshima deeper in the past century, growing dimmer each day.'[23]

To Luke and other critics, the revised, 'uncontroversial', display was only one of many efforts to deny ground-level annihilation and long-term health crises as a means to bolster the nationalist mythology of the unproblematic heroism of US military personnel in pursuing glorious national objectives – whether in the World War II, the Cold War or contemporary bombing campaigns.[24] The defence of the

23 Timothy Luke, 'Displaying the "Enola Gay": Hiding Hiroshima', *Arena Journal* 22, 2004, pp. 73–81.

24 The latter have been justified, paradoxically, by huge efforts to memorialise and sanctify victims of nonstate bombing using civilian airliners at a newer 'ground zero' at the World Trade Center.

omissions by Tom Crouch, then curator of the Smithsonian Air and Space Museum, was both telling and startlingly honest. 'Do you want an exhibit to make veterans feel good?' he asked. 'Or do you want an exhibition that will lead our visitors to think about the consequences of the atomic bombing of Japan? Frankly, I don't think we can do both.'[25]

The vast infrastructure of cultural militaria adds further to this celebration of the Western aerial bomber from or in the air. Aircraft museums, air shows, digital simulations, video games, propagandist war films, children's toys, gun-ho *Discovery Channel* documentaries, and 'profiles' of weapons in newspapers all combine to fetishise both contemporary and historic (or even what are now called 'heritage') bombers.

At the same time, the aircraft and the wider weapons systems within which they operate are abstracted completely from the reality of what they do, or did, to the fragile masses of civilian bodies in cities far below on the receiving end of their rain of military ordinance. Civilian victims of more recent US bombings in Korea, Vietnam, Laos, Panama, Kabul, Baghdad, Tripoli and elsewhere have meanwhile been rendered equally invisible by the continuing power of Western propaganda and self-censorship.

With irony of the darkest kind, the 'information operations' campaigns that are so important in contemporary war have sometimes involved US forces bombing independent television stations that show the civilian carnage that inevitably results on the ground, even when so-called precision strikes are actually 'on target' – the inevitable reality behind the repulsive euphemisms of 'collateral damage' in urban bombing.

In April 2003, for example, a journalist was killed when the offices of Al Jazeera, the Qatari-based news channel, were bombed by a US warplane following its widespread transmission of ground-level views of the bodies of civilian men, women and children killed by the wider bombing campaigns of the Second Gulf War.[26] A notorious leaked

25 Quoted in Robert Newman, *Enola Gay and the Court of History*, New York: Peter Lang, 2004, p. 109.

26 Lisa Parks, 'Insecure Airwaves: US bombings of Al Jazeera', *Communication and Critical/Cultural Studies* 4:2, 2007, pp. 226–31.

memo communication from a meeting in April 2004 between George W. Bush and Tony Blair shows that they even discussed bombing the main headquarters of Al Jazeera in Qatar for the same reason.[27]

The most powerful denial of the ground view, however, is reserved for the bomber pilots themselves. Their world of machines, sensors, screens, two-dimensional maps and defensive countermeasures – and in World War II, of terrifying risk and mass death themselves at the hands of flak and fighters – tends to be totally removed from the detail of what their actions are actually doing to human bodies on the ground. Such distancing – and the complex apparatus of euphemisms, dehumanising propaganda and abstract organizational and technological routinisation – makes it easy for politicians and military leaders to justify and legitimate bombing campaigns against densely populated cities that will, inevitably, maim, disable and kill large numbers of civilian men, women and children – however 'precise' the targeting.

The testimony of RAF bomber crews recalling the Dresden raid in 1945 – which killed over 40,000 civilians in a few hours – underlines their sense of distance from the realities on the city streets far below their aircraft. 'Normally, everything was very remote, even when there were colossal fires burning down below', one pilot remembered. 'In general you saw a light on the ground, which was the fires', another recalled. Mainly, though

> you saw a glowing light in the smoke. Then searchlights above and ack-ack [anti-aircraft shells] around you. There was always a weird feeling of unreality in Bomber Command. You were living in, say, Cambridgeshire or Norfolk; you were thinking of friends, pubs, girls, even intellectual pursuits. Then you launched for 8 hours into a different world at 20,000 ft. over Germany.[28]

---

27 Wadah Kanfer, 'They Bombed Al Jazeera's Reporters: Now the US Is After Our Integrity', *Guardian*, 10 December 2010.

28 Both quotes from Alexander McKee, *Dresden 1945: The Devil's Tinderbox*, London: Souvenir Press, 1982, p. 234. Cited in Derek Gregory 'War and Peace', *Transactions of the Institute of British Geographers* 35:2, 2010, pp. 154–86.

Historian Howard Zinn, prompted by Elin O'Hara Slavick's extraordinary artworks mapping the diverse sites and cities across the world bombed by the US Air Force over the last century,[29] comments on how darkly ironic it is that her abstract and 'God's-eye' maps – so apparently similar to the aerial surveys and photographs that sustained bombing campaigns – should powerfully evoke the visceral and bloody horror at ground level. 'As I look at her drawings', Zinn – himself a bomber pilot in World War II – wrote,

> I become painfully aware of how ignorant I was, when I dropped those bombs on France and on cities in Germany, Hungary, Czechoslovakia, and of the effects of those bombs on human beings. Not because she shows us bloody corpses, amputated limbs, skin shredded by napalm. She does not do that. But her drawings, in ways that I cannot comprehend, compel me to envision such scenes.[30]

Occasionally, however, the horrible realities on the ground below have managed to puncture the technological capsule of the bomber thousands of metres above the flames. When strategic bombers operated at lower altitudes, macabre hints of the terrible realities of the urban firestorms that they unleashed did occasionally rise to the planes above to traumatise the bomber crews themselves. Arriving back at their island bases in the Pacific in 1944 and 1945, after turning Japanese cities into huge firestorms that burned up to 900,000 civilians to death within a few months, the very bomb bays of US B-29 bombers sometimes held and carried the nauseating stench of thousands of burning bodies. 'When the crews returned to their bases', military historian Wilbur Morrison writes, 'they handed in their reports with hands that shook, with shock and horror still reflected in their eyes from what they had witnessed just hours before'.[31]

---

29   See Elin O'Hara Slavick and Carol Mavor, *Bomb after Bomb: A Violent Cartography*, New York: Charta, 2007.

30   Howard Zinn, foreword to Slavick et al., *Bomb after Bomb*, p. 9.

31   Wilbur Morrison, *Point of No Return: The Story of the Twentieth Air Force*, New York: Times Books, 1979.

Aerial Living, Aerial War

> The airplane indicts the city.
>
> – Le Corbusier, *Aircraft*, 1935

Other neglected links surround the relationships between aerial bombing to destroy cities and the planning and architecture necessary to reconstruct them. Although few architecture courses mention it, arch-modernist architect Le Corbusier, like the Italian Futurists, celebrated both the modernism of the aircraft-machine and its vertical destructive power. 'What a gift to be able to sow death with bombs upon sleeping towns', he wrote in his 1935 book *Aircraft*.[32]

Le Corbusier's response to the 'sinister apotheosis' of death and destruction heralded by aerial bombing was the production of plans for the total demolition of the old cities of dense, ground-level streets and their systematic replacement by modern utopias that were specifically designed to be 'capable of emerging victorious from the air war'.[33] Le Corbusier's obsession with loosely spaced high-rise towers set in parkland, most famously elaborated in his *Ville Radieuse* or 'Radiant City' concept city of 1933,[34] were not just a celebration of the well-known combination of light, air, sunlight and the modern house as a 'machine for living in'.[35] The towers were also a reaction to a widespread obsession in 1920s and 1930s Europe with the need to completely re-plan cities to present the most resilient targets to the massed ranks of bombers then being fielded or planned by the major powers. Reflecting his notion that urban planning was analogous to waging war, Le Corbusier's towers were spaced widely partly to make them difficult targets for bombers. They were also designed to lift residents above expected gas attacks and were to be fitted with bomb-resistant roofs.

'The threat of attack from the air demands urban changes', the modernist architectural theorist Sigfried Gideon wrote in 1941, as the devastating impacts of strategic bombing on cities were quickly being manifested in horrible detail:

---

32 Le Corbusier, *Aircraft*, Barcelona: Abada Editores, 2003 [1935], pp. 8–9.
33 Ibid., pp. 60–1.
34 Le Corbusier, *La Ville Radieuse,* Paris: Vincent, Freal & Cie, 1964 [1924].
35 See chapter 8.

Great cities sprawling open to the sky, their congested areas at the mercy of bombs hurtling down out of space, are invitations to destruction. They are practically indefensible as now constituted, and it is now becoming clear that the best means of defending them is by the construction, on the one hand, of great vertical concentrations which offer a minimum surface to the bomber and, on the other hand, by the laying out of extensive, free, open spaces.[36]

Post 9/11 – an event which seemed to underline the extreme *vulnerability* of skyscrapers – it seems painfully ironic that the dreams of that arch celebrator of skyscrapers was, in fact, partly intending to reduce the city's exposure to aerial annihilation.[37]

As the scale and scope of devastation became clear in the wake of the so-far unequalled bombing campaigns of World War II, preservationists achieved some limited success in rebuilding parts of some cities along the old lines. Many ruined buildings – churches especially – were preserved as war memorials. The British art historian Kenneth Clark even argued that 'bomb damage itself is picturesque'.[38]

However, many devout modernists – keen to radically rebuild cities as vertically stratified megastructures of raised walkways, huge towers and massive highways – actually saw the unimaginable devastation from above as an unparalleled opportunity. As part of the 'brave new word' of post-war reconstruction, modernist planners and architects seemed in many cases to be almost grateful that the deadly work of the bombers had laid waste to urban landscapes of traditional, closely built streets and buildings. What better way to achieve their longed-for tabula rasa?

One pamphlet, published by UK architect John Mansbridge, seems a particularly tactless example of such arguments from a contemporary stand point. Mansbridge expressed gratitude to the devastation wreaked by that modernist icon, the aeroplane. Not only had it 'given us a new vision', he argued, but it had also offered Britain 'a new chance by blasting away the centres of cities'. Thus, the leaflet continued,

---

36   Siegfried Gideon, *Space, Time and Architecture*, Cambridge, MA: Harvard University Press, 1941, p. 543.

37   See chapter 8.

38   Cited in Christopher Woodward, *In Ruins*, London: Chatto and Windus, 2002, p. 212.

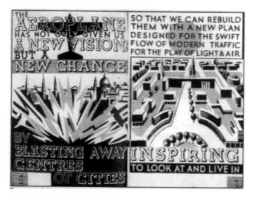

Illustrations from John Mansbridge's 1943 British pamphlet *Here Comes Tomorrow* celebrating both the modernism of aircraft and the 'new chance' that bombing offered British cities to rebuild along modernist lines

modernist reconstruction could now be delivered to sustain 'the swift flow of modern traffic; for the play of light and air'.[39]

The aerial annihilation of total war – an unprecedented act of planned urban devastation in its own right – thus served as a massive accelerator of comprehensive urban planning, architecture and urbanism along vertically stratified, modernist lines. The tabula rasa that every devoted modernist craved suddenly became the norm rather than the exception, particularly in the city centres of postwar Europe and Japan.

As a result, in a very real sense, 'the ghosts of the architects of urban bombing – Douhet, Mitchell, Trenchard, Lindemann – and the praxis of airmen like Harris and LeMay, still stalk the streets of our cities'.[40] Perhaps urban planning and history teaching should focus on these luminaries of twentieth-century bombing theory as much as their more usual cast of iconic architects and planners.

---

39   Nick Tiratsoo, Junichi Hasegawa, Tony Mason, and Takao Matsumura, *Urban Reconstruction in Britain and Japan, 1945–1955: Dreams, Plans, Realities*, Luton, UK: University of Luton Press, 2002.

40   Kenneth Hewitt, 'Place Annihilation: Area Bombing and the Fate of Urban Places', *Annals of the Association of American Geographers* 73:2, 1983, p. 278. The first four were key visionaries in the development of strategic bombing in the early and mid twentieth century in, respectively, Italy, the US, and Britain (both Sir Hugh Trenchard and Frederick Lindemann). 'Bomber' Harris was central to RAF strategic bombing in World War II. Curtis Le May organised the fire- and nuclear bombing of Japan's cities in the same way, and commanded US nuclear bombing forces in the early Cold War.

3.

Drone: Robot Imperium

April 2014. From ground level the grassy field looks to be covered with the kind of plastic sheeting commonly used to shelter intensively farmed fruit and vegetables. But this is no agricultural device: it is an image on the Earth. It is only when the sheet is seen from an aerial view that the image becomes startlingly clear.

Staring up from this anonymous field in the drone-killing heartland of Khyber Pukhtunkhwa within the Federally Administered Tribal Areas in Pakistan (known as FATA), the gigantic image, placed there by a group of French, American and Pakistani political artists, is that of a local girl. According to Pakistan's Foundation for Fundamental Rights, the nameless child lost both her parents and her brother, Syed, as 'collateral damage' to a Hellfire missile fired by a US armed drone on 21 August 2009.

'Viewing the body through a grainy-green video image' that drone 'pilots' use when launching their weapons, *#NotABugSplat* artists emphasise, 'gives the sense of an insect being crushed.'[1] As with developments in bombers, satellites and armed helicopters, such a view reminds us of the ever-tightening connection between the act of killing through a weapons system and the use of visual technologies to find a target.

As the time between sensing and shooting has been reduced by new communications and sensing technologies, so has the military obsession to 'compress the kill chain'. The dream here is to move to a world where weapons and imaging systems are so totally integrated

---

1 Insideoutproject.org, 'Not a Bug Splat: Undisclosed Location, Khyber Pakhtunkhwa Region, Pakistan', April 2014, available at insideoutproject.net. The name derives from a type of target calculation software first used in 2002, which US drone pilots routinely label using the dehumanising euphemism 'bug splat'.

The '*#NotABugSplat*' project viewed from the air. It is the work of French, American and Pakistani political artists. Khyber Pukhtunkhwa, northern Pakistan, April 2014.

that the acts of seeing and killing become effectively one and the same.[2]

Drones linger over and annihilate people from above. Sociologists who have studied viewer comments to YouTube footage from drones of the targeting and killing of 'insurgents' note a widespread tendency. In keeping with deep traditions in Western culture and language, commentators see their top-down view as one of inherent superiority over the subjugated, less important, and racialised people – or even dehumanised non-people – far beneath the gaze.[3] Most of the 1,600 or so comments from viewers addressed in the study inscribed their views – that is, the view of the murderous weapon itself – with a sense of moral and all-seeing superiority. 'I want, to see for myself that they are dead and dying', one comment read. 'Just for my own satisfaction'.[4]

---

2   See Derek Gregory, 'The Everywhere War', *Geographical Journal* 177:3, 2011, pp. 238–50.

3   The very term 'superiority' derives from the Latin prefix 'super' meaning 'high' or 'above'; conversely, the term 'subjugated' derives from the Latin prefix 'sub' meaning below.

4   Henrik Fürst, and Karin Hagren Idevall, '"Drone Porn" and Violence: Comments on YouTube to a Drone Attack', unpublished paper presented at the 10th Conference of the European Sociological Association, 7–10 September 2011, p. 12; cited in Mark Dorrian, 'Drone Semiosis: Weaponry and Witnessing', *Cabinet Magazine*, Summer 2014, p. 52.

The drone's-eye view plays well on YouTube, as well as in a whole host of militarised video games. This only adds to the ways in which drone killing operates through complex webs of electronic technology. Together, these work to blur the line separating weapons systems and entertainment systems. Perhaps for this reason, the US Air Force is directly targeting the recruitment of gamers – especially those with experience of home aircraft and drone simulators – as drone pilots. The actual controls used by drone pilots to undertake the killing now sometimes directly mimic the familiar Sony PlayStation controls that recruits have been using since early childhood.[5]

In 2005, Noah Shachtman of *Wired* magazine discussed the experience of a new Predator pilot named Joe Clark. Private Clark has, in a sense, 'been prepping for the job since he was a kid. He plays videogames', Shachtman stressed. 'A lot of videogames. Back in the barracks he spends downtime with an Xbox and a PlayStation … When he first slid behind the controls of a Shadow UAV [Unmanned Aerial Vehicle], the point-and-click operation turned out to work much the same way.'[6] Once drone operators begin to launch lethal strikes, however, their need to linger over the carnage unleashed by their weapons quickly disabuses them of any lingering notion that they might be participating in some 'PlayStation war'.

In such a context, the uncanny power of *#NotABugSplat* derives from the way it upscales and upturns that most human of all images – the face – in a way that fundamentally upsets the logic of distant, vertical and mechanistic vision. It questions the surveillance and dehumanisation that the rise of routine drone-based killing relies on.

More important still is the way the girl's eyes 'look back' vertically towards the distant sensors that support the drone attacks.[7] On

---

5   Charlie Fripp, 'Do Gamers Make for Perfect Drone Pilots?' *IT News South Africa*, 10 October 2013, available at itnewsafrica.com.

6   Noah Shachtman, 'Attack of the Drones', *Wired* 3:6, 2005. Tightening such connections further still, some of the latest video games themselves re-create the world of the drone 'pilot'. For example, in the 'unmanned' game released by the Molleindustria company in 2012, a player 'control[s] … unmanned attack aircraft by day, and by night goes home to a suburban life.' The game is marketed under the strapline: 'When the war is fought on screen, where is the real damage experienced? See gamesforchange.org/play/unmanned/.

7   Dorrian, 'Drone Semiosis', p. 55.

seeing the girl's image on the field, it's tempting for a brief moment to wonder whether its appearance enforces a more symmetrical gaze between targeter and targeted as the image of the girl's eyes meets the digital sensor. Did the image momentarily undermine the normal operation of drones, which, as media scholar Tim Blackman has put it, 'are designed to stay in the dark and bring enemies into the light where they can be destroyed'.[8]

Mike Pearl wonders about the impact of the image on an actual drone pilot located in a virtual reality 'cave' in Creech Air Force Base, located in the northern suburbs of Las Vegas:

> When you're looking down from a Predator drone's point of view seeing a child's face would be a startling change from the usual Google Earth view I think we all assume they're looking at. The pilot seated at the remote terminal would, I suppose … be so stirred with empathy that he or she would be forced to stand up and quit the drone programme once and for all. If that's overly optimistic, maybe the pilot is just meant to be too distracted to properly target the toddler he or she was planning to shoot, or at least compelled to try extra, extra hard not to shoot toddlers this time.[9]

It is doubtful whether such a chain of events actually occurred, however: once the image was photographed, and those images had gone viral globally, local villagers used the valuable sheeting as building materials.

Vertical Orientalism

The #NotABugSplat project exposes the myths that the military and the political supporters of drone wars endlessly repeat. Drone killing, these arguments stress, involves 'precision' attacks and 'targeted killings'. They operate through all-seeing sensing and targeting systems.

---

8   Tim Blackmore, *War X: Human Extensions in Battlespace*, Toronto: University of Toronto Press, 2011, p. 137.

9   Mike Pearl, 'This Giant Art Piece in Pakistan Won't Be Making Drone Pilots Feel Empathy', *Vice*, 7 April 2014, available at vice.com.

And they lead to negligible, and justifiable, civilian deaths – 'collateral damage'.

In one of many such examples, White House spokesman Jay Carney in January 2012 urged reporters that one of the hallmarks of US counterterrorism efforts 'has been our ability to be exceptionally precise, exceptionally surgical and exceptionally targeted in the implementation of our counterterrorism operations.'[10] Lt. Col. James Dawkins of the US Air Force underlines that armed drones are 'a very appealing option for the politicians faced with use-of-force decisions due to reduced forward basing requirements and the possibility of zero friendly … casualties.'[11]

In drone attacks a risk remains, of course, that the machine may be lost during operations. But even if this happens, the UAV crews will remain utterly untroubled and unscathed, embedded as they are in bunkers on bases thousands of miles away. Above all, 'there will be no widow-making, no embarrassing prisoners of war.'[12] This complete invulnerability is radically new and profoundly important: never before has war offered up such a completely asymmetric vision of the cosseted and far-distant targeter, equipped with all manner of electronic eyes and godlike weaponry, being completely invisible to, and immune from, those upon whom he or she unleashes their violence. 'For whoever uses an armed drone', French philosopher Grégoire Chamayou notes, 'it becomes, *a priori,* impossible to die as one kills.'[13]

The US use of killer drones is widely celebrated by large sections of the civilian population as a strategy that puts machines at risk in order to save US military personnel. Indeed, Republican congressman Brian Bilbray has even argued that the Predator drone should be seen as an American 'folk hero'. 'If you could register the Predator for

10   'Press Briefing by Press Secretary Jay Carney', 31 January 2012, available at whitehouse.gov.

11   James Dawkins, *Unmanned Combat Aerial Vehicles: Examining the Political, Moral, and Social Implications*, Air University, Maxwell-Gunter Air Force Base, Montgomery, Alabama, 2005.

12   Tim Blackmore, 'Dead Slow: Unmanned Aerial Vehicles Loitering in Battlespace', *Bulletin of Science, Technology and Society* 25, 2005, p. 199.

13   Grégoire Chamayou, *A Theory of the Drone*, New York: New Press, 2014, p. 13.

President', he suggests, 'both parties would be trying to endorse it.'[14] Recently, parts of the US military have even urged that medals should be awarded to successful drone pilots.

In challenging the myths and euphemisms of drone killing, *#NotABugSplat* exposes the gaze of the killer drone from above as little more than a racist gaze used in imperial killing. The image emphasises, above all, how the racist mechanisms through which imperial power constructs humans to be of differential value between a notional 'us' in the 'homeland' and a threatening and racialised enemy – a 'them' – have been switched through drone killing from a largely horizontal to a vertical frame (although one organised though satellites, communications systems and military technologies that are horizontally organised across continental scales).[15]

One example is Israel's switch from a permanent military occupation of Gaza to a policy of dominating the area from above through drone surveillance and strikes. Although it is difficult to disentangle Israeli drone strikes from assaults by artillery, helicopters and warplanes, the Gazan human rights group al-Mezan calculates that drone strikes killed at least 760 Gazans between 2006 and 2012.[16] During its 2012 'Pillar of Defence' bombardment of Gaza, 36 of the 162 Palestinians killed died through drone strikes, and a further 100 were seriously injured. Of those 36 killed, two-thirds were civilians.[17]

In analysing such violence, architectural researcher Eyal Weizman invokes Edward Said's influential critique of the tradition of Western 'Orientalism' – the construction of an imaginary, primitive and exotic Other in the Middle East and Asia to justify violent Western colonialism and militarised control.[18] Weizman argues, however, that Israel's approach to Gaza now involves a vertical – rather than a traditionally

---

14   Brian Bennett, 'Homeland Security Adding 3 Drone Aircraft Despite Lack of Pilots', *Los Angeles Times*, 27 October 2011.

15   See Keith Feldman, 'Empire's Verticality: The Af/Pak Frontier, Visual Culture, and Racialization from Above', *Comparative American Studies* 9:4, December 2011, p. 330.

16   Cited in Jonathon Cook, 'Gaza: Life and Death under Israel's Drones', *Al Jazeera*, 28 November 2013, available at aljazeera.com.

17   See also Anne Wright, 'Israeli Drone Strikes in Gaza in November 2012 Attack: Two-Thirds Killed Were Civilians', *Op.Ed. News*, 2 June 2013, available at opednews.com.

18   Edward Said, *Orientalism*, New York: Pantheon, 1978.

horizontal – form of Orientalism. 'The geography of occupation', he writes, has 'completed a ninety-degree turn: the imaginary 'orient' – the exotic object of colonization – was no longer beyond the horizon, but now under the vertical tyranny of western airborne civilization that remotely managed its most sophisticated and advanced technological platforms, sensors and munitions in the spaces above.'[19]

Since the first attack by a US drone in Yemen in 2002, drones have become the mainstay of both US military air power and of covert strikes by the CIA. Between 2002 and 2010, the US inventory of drones increased forty-fold, from 167 to around 7,000.[20] They now constitute more than 40 per cent of the US military's entire fleet of aircraft.[21]

Following the routine use of drones in Afghanistan, Pakistan, Yemen and Iraq, the US now launches armed drone strikes in Libya and Somalia under Obama's policy of extending drone operations. The US also runs routine drone surveillance operations in a wide range of other African and Middle Eastern countries. With extraordinarily broad and vague rules of targeting and engagement, the 'war on terror's' drone wars have in effect turned large parts of the world into a free-fire zone.[22]

However, Pakistan, Iraq and Afghanistan overwhelmingly dominate US drone killings. The CIA's covert drone operations against the northern regions of its notional ally of Pakistan – in breach of every tenet of international law – have been especially controversial. The Bureau for Investigative Journalism in London has produced robust estimates of the civilian toll of dead and injured over the various periods of these operations. They estimate that drones had killed between 524 and 1,169 civilians in Pakistan, Yemen and Somalia, up to 18 March 2015; that they had killed between 186 and 226 children; and that they had seriously injured between 1,319 and 2,068 people in

19 Eyal Weizman, *Hollow Land: Israel's Architecture of Occupation*, London: Verso, 2007, p. 237.

20 Mark Neocleous, *War Power, Police Power,* Edinburgh: Edinburgh University Press, 2014, p. 153.

21 Rob Blackhurst, 'The Air Force Men Who Fly Drones in Afghanistan by Remote Control', *Daily Telegraph,* 24 September 2012.

22 See Derek Gregory, 'Drones and the World as Free-Fire Zone', *Geographical Imaginations* (blog), 23 June 2013, available at geographicalimaginations.com.

that time. The same study calculates that CIA drone strikes in Pakistan killed between 2,445 and 3,945 people. Between 421and 960 of them were civilians, with between 172 and 207 children were among that number.[23] Between 1,142 and 1,720 civilians were also seriously injured, with many left permanently disabled and impoverished.

On the back of the massive expansion in the deployment and use of lethal military drones, drone manufacturers have grown enormously in size, profitability and lobbying power. General Atomics Aeronautical Systems, a branch of General Dynamics that manufacturers the most widely used Predator and Reaper drones, is a particularly powerful case. From an annual turnover of only $110 million in 2001, rapid growth of the drone programme pushed this figure to $1.8 billion by 2012.[24]

Drones, moreover, are rapidly becoming more sophisticated and capable. As they do so, weapons manufacturers label them using monikers drawn from ancient mythology, names chosen deliberately to add to the sense that they are murderous and all-seeing cyborg-like monsters loitering far above. Beyond the now-familiar Predator and Reaper, for example, DARPA, the US military research agency, is building a drone with ninety-two cameras called Argus after the mythic all-seeing servant in Greek mythology with a hundred eyes.

The Sierra Nevada Corporation, meanwhile, make a system called Gorgon Stare, named after the female figure in Greek mythology with hair of live snakes who turned those who looked on her to stone. Aimed at surveilling whole cities to build up patterns of supposedly 'normal' life against which the 'abnormal activities' of 'targets' might be identified, the company claims that the system can completely survey a 4 km radius. The system even has its own motto: *oculus semper vigilans* ('an always watchful eye').[25]

Understanding the impacts of living in Pakistan, Afghanistan or elsewhere, under a permanent system drone surveillance – as well as the possibility of being killed or maimed at any moment – is not easy.

---

23   See Bureau of Investigative Journalists, 'Get the Data: Drone Wars', 2015, available at thebureauinvestigates.com.

24   James Risen, *Pay Any Price: Greed, Power and Endless War*, New York: Houghton Mifflin Harcourt, 2015, p. 54.

25   Dorian, 'Drone Semiosis', p. 48.

Few journalists or human rights groups venture to the places where drone strikes occur; even fewer manage to interview locals and relatives of victims. Instead, the perspectives, including those on sites like YouTube, remain almost entirely aerial.

The dark paradox here is that drone killings are sustained, like modern bombing, military helicopters and satellite surveillance, by a deeply technophiliac and militarised myth of total vertical vision and an obsession with seeing all. This perspective is combined, however, with an almost complete absence of knowledge about, and media coverage of, those on the ground unlucky enough to get in the way of the Hellfire missiles fired down upon them from the sky.[26] In northern Pakistan the mysterious machines flying far above have entered local folklore: the term 'I will drone you' has even entered day-to-day conversation as a morbid joke.[27]

Research efforts are also starting to reveal the impacts of drone strikes on the people and communities below. Like the artists behind #NotABugSplat, Stanford University's Living Under Drones project has recently challenged the dominant narratives surrounding drone strikes. The Stanford group document in detail the deep psychological trauma of whole communities living with the persistent threat of instant and unknowable death and destruction from usually invisible vehicles far above. Beyond the deaths and injuries they cause, the Stanford team argue, 'US drone strike policies cause considerable and under-accounted-for harm to the daily lives of ordinary civilians'. Drones, they continue,

---

26　This invisibility makes forensic analysis of the impacts of drone strikes by critical architects and lawyers especially important. Such experts are helping the UN Human Rights Council to investigate drone killings of civilians as human rights abuses and potentially as war crimes. Eyal Weizman's group at Goldsmiths College, London, has been especially important here. 'In order to hold … governments [that undertake drone killings of civilians] to account', Weizman argues, 'we need to demonstrate the devastating reality of such attacks on civilians directly hit and on entire communities living under drones.' Goldsmiths News, n.d., 'Research into Devastating Drone Strikes Hampered by Government Secrecy, United Nations Told', available at gold.ac.uk. See also Forensic Architecture, ed., Forensis: The Architecture of Public Truth, Berlin: Sternberg Press, 2014.

27　Lila Lee, 'Drone Warfare: War in the Age of Digital Reproduction', master's thesis, Lund University, Lund, Sweden, 2012.

hover twenty-four hours a day over communities in northwest Pakistan, striking homes, vehicles, and public spaces without warning. Their presence terrorizes men, women, and children, giving rise to anxiety and psychological trauma among civilian communities. Those living under drones have to face the constant worry that a deadly strike may be fired at any moment, and the knowledge that they are powerless to protect themselves.[28]

Psychologists in Gaza, meanwhile, talk of a whole generation of Gazan children suffering deep psychological trauma because of the continual exposure to the buzzing sounds of drones high above, machines that can spit lethal violence upon them and their families at any moment. 'When you hear the drones, you feel naked and vulnerable', Hamdi Shaqura, deputy director of the Palestinian Centre for Human Rights in Gaza City asserts. 'The buzz is the sound of death. There is no escape, nowhere is private.'[29]

Stanford's Living Under Drones researchers, meanwhile, have shown that civilians in Pakistan and Afghanistan are reluctant to help those hit by the first strikes because rescuers themselves have often been killed by follow-on drone strikes. Injured relatives in the rubble of the first strike have been known to tell their relatives not to help rescue them because of the frequency of these so-called 'double-tap' strikes. People also avoid gathering in groups in visible places. Many children are permanently kept indoors and often no longer go to school. Other children struggle with permanent disabilities caused by drone strikes; many amputees have to use poor-quality prosthetic limbs. One example is Sadaullah Wazir, a teenager and former student from the village of Machi Khel in Mir Ali, North Waziristan. He lost both of his legs and one of his eyes in a September 2009 drone strike on his grandfather's home. 'Before the drone strikes started, my life was very good', he relates to the Stanford team,

I used to go to school and I used to be quite busy with that, but after the drone strikes, I stopped going to school now … Two missiles [were] fired at our *hujra* [home] and three people died. My cousin and I were

28   Living Under Drones Project, *Living Under Drones,* Stanford University, Stanford, CA, 2012, p. vii, available at chrgj.org.
29   Cited in Cook, 'Gaza: Life and Death'.

injured. We didn't hear the missile at all and then it was there … Now I have to stay inside … Sometimes I have really bad headaches … [and] if I walk too much [on my prosthetic legs], my legs hurt a lot. [Drones have] drastically affected life [in our area].[30]

Myths of Total Vision

Rather than being the result of all-seeing sensors that can identify armed insurgents and execute them with precision, the realities of drone warfare reveal a dangerous absence of knowledge about the people targeted far below.

As well as discussing their rules of engagement, drone pilots happily talk about the powerful and seductive aesthetics of their job – as well as the boredom. One anonymous pilot famously talked in Omer Fast's film *5,000 Feet Is the Best* about that altitude being the most enjoyable one at which to patrol. 'I love it when we're sitting at 5,000 feet', he related,

> You have more description, plus, at 5,000 feet I mean, I can tell you what kind of shoes you're wearing from a mile away! I can tell you what kind of clothes a person is wearing, if they have a beard, their hair color and everything else … We have the IR, infra-red, which we can switch to automatically, and that will pick up any heat signatures or cold signatures … If someone sits down, let's say, on a cold surface … and then gets up … it kind of looks like a white blossom, just shining up into heaven. It's quite beautiful.[31]

Speaking of the targeting sequence through which drone operators launch their deadly Hellfire missiles, the pilot also emphasises both his sense of omniscient, vertical power and the aesthetic beauty of the process:

---

30 Living Under Drones Project, *Victim Stories*, Stanford University, Stanford, CA, 2013, available at livingunderdrones.org.

31 Omer Fast's film *5,000 Feet Is the Best*, cited in Matt Delmont, 'Drone Encounters: Noor Behram, Omer Fast, and Visual Critiques of Drone Warfare', *American Quarterly* 65:1, 2013, pp. 193–202.

We call [the drone] in, and we're given all the clearances that are necessary [to fire], all the approvals and everything else, and then we do
something called the Light of God … the Marines like to call it the Light
of God. It's a laser targeting marker. We just send out a beam of laser
and when the troops [on the ground] put on their night vision goggles
they just see this light that looks like it's coming from heaven. Right on
the spot [where the missile will hit] coming out of nowhere, from the
sky. It's quite beautiful.[32]

Canadian anthropologist Gastón Gordillo points out that large-
scale civilian deaths are an inevitable result of a US policy of deploying
lethal drones when backed up by myths that drone operators benefit
from God-like omniscience. These, he points out, stem from widespread attitudes in the military about the way drones and other digital
technologies bring with them 'total information awareness' through
'persistent surveillance'.[33]

Despite the high-resolution digital CCTV cameras, heat sensors,
motion-detecting systems and other sensors, however, Gordillo
stresses that the sheer mass of imagery and data often means that
drone controllers are completely overloaded with too much data to
process or interpret while they are making decisions to fire. In 2009
alone, US drones collected the equivalent of twenty-four years' worth
of video footage; DARPA's Argus system, mentioned already, can
generate eight years' worth of continuous video from a single day's
operations. [34]

In addition, the sheer immensity of the huge foreign geographies
that drone pilots target means that the pilots are often culturally
ignorant of those they target and kill. Crucially, they have no way
of reliably distinguishing actual armed insurgents from the rest of
the surrounding population. Because of this, they work hard to fill
completely unreliable visual clues – people holding objects or 'loitering' suspiciously, say – with the imagined and violent intent
necessary for them to launch their missiles under standard rules of
engagement.

---

32   Ibid.
33   Gordillo, 'Opaque Zones of Empire'.
34   Dorrian, 'Drone Semiosis'.

As with records of the conversations of attack helicopter pilots discussed in the next chapter, transcripts of the conversations of drone pilots repeatedly show their desperation to use Orientalist cliché. This imperialist apparatus of knowledge can turn any aspects of normal, civilian life into clear evidence that they are watching 'insurgents' or 'terrorists' who can be fired upon at will. The language of drone operators effectively enrols all adult men in the vicinity of drone strikes as 'combatants' by labelling them 'military age males'. Even the US military has admitted that such a terminology encourages drone strikes against civilians because it 'implies that the individuals are armed forces and therefore legitimate targets.'[35] As a result, the US does not count dead adult men as 'civilians' unless there is clear posthumous intelligence proving that they were.

Constant effort is also made to assimilate other Afghans, Pakistanis or Iraqis on the screens into the set of legitimate targets. Obvious evidence that images of innocent children or civilians are filling their screens is often wilfully ignored or – worse still – interpreted as further evidence of malevolence because of assumptions that they have been deliberately placed there by 'terrorists' or 'insurgents' to thwart drone pilots' ability to kill. As ever, intense training works to dehumanise the 'enemy' people below while glorifying and celebrating the killing process. 'Ever step on ants and never give it another thought?' Michael Hass, an ex-US drone operator said in November 2015:

> That's what you are made to think of the targets – as just black blobs on a screen. You start to do these psychological gymnastics to make it easier to do what you have to do – they deserved it, they chose their side. You had to kill part of your conscience to keep doing your job every day – and ignore those voices telling you this wasn't right.[36]

Grégoire Chamayou's analysis of one three-hour-long surveillance and attack operation on a convoy of three of SUVs that killed civilians in Afghanistan in February 2010 shows a notorious case. Throughout

---

35   Center for Army Lessons Learned, 'The Afghanistan Civilian Casualty Prevention Handbook', Fort Leavenworth, Kans., 2012, p. 5.

36   Pilkington, 'Life as a Drone Operator: "Ever Step on Ants and Never Give it Another Thought?"' *Guardian,* 18 November 2015.

the operation there is a sense of the drone controllers' desperation to destroy the people and their vehicles – whatever the evidence of their clearly civilian nature. The transcript is full of statements like 'that truck would make a beautiful target'; 'Oh, sweet target!'; 'The men appear to be moving tactically'; and 'They're going to do something nefarious.' The mission controller later spots an 'adolescent near the rear of the SUV'. 'Well', the operator responds, 'teenagers can fight! … twelve or 13 years old with a weapon is [sic] just as dangerous!' (Children are often called 'fun-size terrorists' by drone operators.[37])

'Screener said at least one child near SUV', the coordinator says on another occasion 'Bullshit! Where?' replies the sensor operator. 'I don't think they have kids out at this hour … Why are they so quick to call fucking kids but not to call a fucking rifle?'[38]

Based on an alleged 'weapon' sighting, the decision is then made to fire Hellfire missiles from nearby armed helicopters called to the scene; the first and third vehicles in the convoy are destroyed. The Predator pilots immediately fly in to assess the carnage. Viewing a scene of dead and maimed men, women and children, the safety observer remarks 'No way to tell, man.' The camera operator agrees: 'No way to tell from here.'

US military officials admitted that on this occasion the missiles killed sixteen civilian men and severely injured a woman and three children. However, Afghan elders from the victims' home villages said in later interviews that the attacks had killed twenty-three, including two boys, Daoud, three, and Murtaza, four. As is common in such cases, the US military compensated families of the dead with the equivalent of $4,800 for the relatives of each person killed. Each survivor was given $2,900.[39]

Stressing the regular inevitability of such killings, Gastón Gordillo continues his crucial analysis. 'The gaze guiding the drones', he writes, 'follows a binary logic that seeks to distinguish "normal" from "abnormal activity" from amid an extremely heterogeneous and complex spatial universe.' In such a context, he stresses that the enormous

---

37 Ibid.

38 Chamayou, *Theory of the Drone,* pp. 1–11. This attack is also analysed in David Cloud, 'Anatomy of an Afghan War Tragedy', *Los Angeles Times*, 10 April 2011.

39 Cloud, 'Anatomy of an Afghan War Tragedy'.

pressure on drone pilots to interpret what they see as 'insurgent activity', combined with the fact that drone operators have no reliable way of distinguishing civilians from 'insurgents', means that the killing of large numbers of civilians is in no way an 'accident' or an 'error'. In all such cases, rather, 'operators and image analysts navigating [received imagery] "saw" mundane objects as "rifles", people praying as a sign that they were "Taliban", or children as potentially hostile "adolescents".'[40]

The acts of watching the grainy video feed from the drone, and of launching a missile on humans below, create a sense of extraordinary power among drone operators. One admits that he sometimes felt 'like a God hurling thunderbolts from afar'. [41] Another relates that 'you see a lot of detail … we feel it, maybe not to the same degree [as] if we were actually there, but it affects us … When you let a missile go', he continues, 'you know that's real life, there's no reset button.'[42] There are even some reports of drone pilots struggling with post-traumatic stress disorder after they have killed civilians, especially children. Unlike bomber pilots, moreover, drone operators linger long after the explosives strike and see their effects on human bodies in stark detail.

Drones to the Homeland

As domestic policing agencies begin to deploy drone technologies in urban areas with greater regularity, we will see a shift in the ways that these spaces, and the populations that inhabit them, are constructed, surveilled, and governed.

– M. Hyane, 'The Ghetto Bird, the Drone, and Policing from Above', 2014

---

40   Gordillo, 'Opaque Zones of Empire'.
41   Matt Martin and Charles Sasser, *Predator: The Remote Control Air War over Iraq and Afghanistan*, Minneapolis: Zenith Press, 2010, p. 3, cited in Derek Gregory, 'From a View to a Kill: Drones and Late Modern War', *Theory, Culture & Society* 28:7/8, 2011, p. 198.
42   Lara Logan, 'Drones: America's New Air Force', *60 Minutes*, CBS News, 14 August 2009; and David Zucchino, 'Drone Pilots Have a Front-Row Seat on War from Half a World Away', *Los Angeles Times,* 21 February 2010.

As Western military budgets shrivel, a concerted drive is being made by a complex constellation of lobby groups, arms manufacturers and industry associations to construct drones developed initially for war and vertical killing as a panacea for all manner of security and police operations in civilian airspace within domestic 'homelands'.[43]

Many barriers confront such efforts, however. Their murderous use in Asia and the Middle East means that drones, to say the least, have something on an image problem. Civilian airspace regulators are also concerned about the potential for drones to cause widespread fatalities through ground crashes or collisions with civilian aircraft. Civil liberties and anti-surveillance lobbyists, meanwhile, are working hard to expose the ways in which domestic drone programmes are closely connected to deepening cultures of surveillance and police militarisation.

Drone manufacturers, as might be expected, are adamant that their products have been unfairly maligned and that they can be extremely useful for a wide range of civilian applications. Included here are humanitarian and disaster response, mail delivery, crop monitoring, weather forecasting, TV news reporting, search and rescue operations and policing.

'As with any emerging technology', the US-based Aerospace Industries Association (AIA) argue, 'public opinion regarding these systems often begins in the imagination, and may harden into myth through misconception, popular culture and an inability to imagine the non-military benefits of a platform that has traditionally been used for national defense.'[44] The figure of the drone has even been projected as a much-maligned victim of public misunderstanding based on the widespread myths that drone killings along the war on terror's frontier and war zones are already entirely autonomous. 'It's

---

43 Such a shift is a classic example of what Michel Foucault called a 'boomerang effect': the deployment of security, surveillance and military technologies in the domestic, civil world once they have been honed and normalised within the war zones of colonial and frontier operations. See Michel Foucault, *'Society Must be Defended': Lectures at the Collège de France, 1975–1976*, London: Allen Lane, 2003, p. 103.

44 Aerospace Industries Association, *Unmanned Aircraft Systems: Perceptions & Potential*, Washington, DC, 2013, p. 3, available at aia-aerospace.org.

tough being a "drone"', the AIA continue, 'especially when the public doesn't even recognize you for what you are: an unmanned aerial vehicle under human control through a sophisticated ground-based control system.'[45]

Despite such barriers, civilian markets for drones are burgeoning. Israeli-made Hermes drones, and more recently General Atomics' Predators, have been routinely deployed along the US–Mexico border since 2003. Indeed, many conservative and nationalist US lobbyists have worked to encourage the 'return' of military drones from the war zone to the homeland; the latter were deployed as 'a result of widespread enthusiasm for the surge in Predator operations in Iraq and Afghanistan.'[46] Linked to military-standard surveillance systems built by US and Israeli arms companies along the ground border, drone patrols have been used to 'identify and intercept potential terrorists and illegal cross-border activity.'[47]

It is crucial to stress that the current shift towards the domestic deployment of drones is a key result of the growing militarisation of security within Western nations that has occurred as a key element of the 'war on terror' – and especially the widening adoption of the concept of 'homeland security'. The concept originated with the lockdown of Israel in the 1990s; it was honed in the US after the terrorist attacks there in 2001; and it is now being diffused throughout Europe and elsewhere. Homeland security concepts project all aspects of civilian life as domains of permanent existential threat requiring militarised responses based on extending the powers of networked surveillance and targeting.[48]

In the process, everything beyond the worlds of full weapon-on-weapon warfare becomes a 'low-intensity operation' or 'military operations other than war' (or 'MOOTW' to its friends) within an all-encompassing and never-ending 'battlespace'. Such shifts radically blur already vague distinctions between policing, intelligence and

---

45 Ibid., p. 14.

46 Tom Barry, 'Drones over the Homeland: How Politics, Money and Lack of Oversight Have Sparked Drone Proliferation, and What We Can Do', Center for International Policy, Washington DC, April 2013, p. 6.

47 Ibid., p. 3.

48 See Ben Hayes, 'Homeland Security Comes to Europe', *Statewatch*, 2006, available at statewatch.org.

military deployment and between local, national and international policy. They also blur the legal and doctrinal separation between the domestic and foreign spheres.

Reinforced by such concepts, security operations everywhere increasingly merge into a mobilisation based on permanent deployment of high-tech military sensors such as drones aimed at pre-emptively highlighting threats and 'targets' from the background civilian population or city. Crucially, such ideas are fuelled by the same fantasies of total vision against vague and existential threats deep within the normal circuits of civilian life.

Such shifts mean that domestic domains that were dominated previously by a rhetoric of policing against criminal activities among citizens are gradually reconstituted as paramilitarised 'wars' against lurking existential threats. In a powerful example, the US Department of Homeland Security now routinely refers to the US–Mexico border in the same language that the US military uses to describe its war zones: a limitless 'battlespace' encompassing a world where civilian life camouflages 'targets' and where drones and other high-tech surveillance systems are the key to 'persistent situational awareness' achieved through 'network-centric' operations.[49]

Such scenarios are further supported by the latest theories of so-called 'fourth-generation warfare'. These regularly posit immigrations as invasions, immigrants as threats to the cultural and political integrity of nations and all flows of 'illegal' immigrants as Trojan Horse–like harbingers of drug trafficking or terrorism. 'In Fourth Generation war', US military theorist William Lind wrote in one demonstration of this view, 'invasion by immigration can be at least as dangerous as invasion by a state army.'[50]

Already, there is evidence that the identities of Border Security agents in the US are changing in keeping with this wider shift: many now talk about their role as one of paramilitary force deployment rather than law enforcement. The Department of Homeland Security, meanwhile, are already exploring ways of arming Predator B drones

---

49   See Jim Hightower, 'The Border Industrial Complex', *Other Words*, 7 August 2013, available at otherwords.org.

50   William Lind, 'Understanding Fourth Generation War', *Military Review*, September/October 2004, pp. 12–16, available at au.af.mil.

with what DHS calls 'non-lethal weapons designed to immobilize' targets.[51]

Fuelled by xenophobic and bellicose political rhetoric, the latest US legislation on border security – the Secure Our Borders First Act (introduced in January 2015) – added an additional $10 billion for further drone acquisition and deployment.[52] The act calls for the Department of Homeland Security to use new technologies such as drones to 'seal' what is deemed to be an unacceptably leaky frontier. The language is highly militarised: the challenge is to work towards 100 per cent 'defence in depth' through radically improved 'situational awareness'. This, the argument goes, is necessary so that nine out of ten migrants can be intercepted within a 100-mile strip of territory just inside the US–Mexico border.[53]

Despite evidence that drones have been an extremely expensive and highly ineffective means of securing the border,[54] myths of total vision and absolute panopticism permeate the politics of drone deployment. Already, the Department of Homeland Security's Predator drones capture video of the border zones that they monitor which is analysed to automatically identify changes in the terrain below.

Beyond this is a sense of dramatic albeit highly profitable over-kill. Expensive militarised systems of vertical patrolling and sensing are deployed when on-the-ground staffing might be a much more capable and cost-effective approach. 'Surely it is enormously waste-ful and a perversion of homeland security priorities', wonders Tom Barry of the Center for International Policy, 'to have Predator drones patrolling the skies on the hunt for immigrants and marijuana?'[55]

What James Risen of the *New York Times* has termed the 'homeland-industrial security' complex,[56] of course, is only too happy to amplify the militarisation of discourses about the insecurity of

---

51   Phillip Bump, 'The Border Patrol Wants to Arm Drones', *The Wire* 2:13, 2 July 2013, available at thewire.com.

52   Sarah Launius, 'The Border Security Complex', paper at the conference 'From Abortion Rights to Social Justice', Hampshire College, Amherst, MA, 12 April 2014, available at academia.edu.

53   Ibid.

54   Barry, 'Drones over the Homeland'.

55   Ibid.

56   Risen, *Pay Any Price*.

civilian life and feed the myths of total vision in the hope that their weapon systems can reach widespread civilian deployment. This is especially so since drone markets are predicted to triple in value between 2015 and 2025, totalling $93 billion over that period.[57] Global drone manufactures also work hard to lobby US and European governments to get them to undermine barriers to the widespread civilian deployment of drones.

In the US, a sixty-strong lobby group of immigration hardliners and conservative 'hawks' has established the Congressional Caucus on Unmanned Systems (CCUS). The purported aim of the group is to 'educate members of Congress and the public on the strategic, tactical, and scientific value of unmanned systems, actively support further development and acquisition of more systems, and to more effectively engage the civilian aviation community on unmanned system use and safety.'[58] In addition, the main industry lobby group in the US, the Association for Unmanned Vehicle Systems International, spent at least $22 million on lobbying in 2011 alone.[59]

The power of the lobbying of drone companies is especially startling to anyone who uses Washington's futuristic metro system. The walls of the stations are a veritable *Jane's Defence Weekly* plastered with huge ads for high-tech drones and other weapons. In flagrant attempts to curry favour with key decision makers, stations have been reconstructed as an extraordinary symbol of the militarisation of US culture and politics.[60] The usual myths of precision targeting and perfect vision are again the mainstay here: drone technology is projected as a flexible panacea for all security and military challenges at home and abroad.

Recently, adverts for the latest versions of Northrop's autonomous strategic strike drones have even appeared in the subway cars themselves – between the line maps and safety instructions. Bizarrely, as

---

57 Beth Stevenson, 'UAV Market Set to Triple in Value in Next Decade', *Flight Global*, 18 August 2015, available at flightglobal.com.

58 Barry, 'Drones over the Homeland', p. 21.

59 See First Street Research Group, *Drones in US Air Space: The Next Lobby Frontier*, Washington, DC, 1 May 2012, available at firststreetresearch.wordpress. com.

60 Stephanie Westbrook, 'Occupied Washington, DC', *Common Dreams*, 10 April 2010, available at commondreams.org.

they travel deep underground, passengers are repeatedly reminded as they move towards the subway car's doors of the sentient and God-like power of murderous machinery flying high in the skies on their behalf over far-flung 'enemy' territories.

Other lobbying efforts in the US and Europe are working to normalise drone use within civilian police forces. In the US the Departments of Justice and Homeland Security have established grants, training programmes and 'centers of excellence' to support the introduction of drones in policing. Early drone policing activities, to bolster the surveillance capabilities of narcotics squads and SWAT teams, have already been established in Montgomery County, Maryland; Arlington, Texas; and in Miami.[61]

In Europe, meanwhile, a powerful concert of EU policy makers and defence manufacturers is similarly bent on selling drones as a panacea for domestic security problems.[62] Statewatch calculates that the EU has spent fully €500 million, without democratic oversight or public scrutiny, to support such a shift since the late 1990s.[63] Once again, drone manufacturers are pressing hard for civilian expenditure to naturalise drone use within a wide spectrum of civilian applications. A key motivation in Europe is industrial policy: to bolster the growth of European drone makers in a market dominated by US and Israeli companies. Another reason is Europe's burgeoning migration crisis, as millions of African and Middle Eastern migrants and refugees risk all making sea and land crossings to flee poverty and war.

In October 2010, Dani Stroli of Israel Aerospace Industries made a presentation to one of the EU's drone policy consortia (of which he was a member at the time). The challenge, he said, was to discover ways to 'make people perceive [drone] technology as a natural part of future society'; to 'create positive interest in [drones]'; and to 'create a multidisciplinary promotional campaign'.[64] The UK lobby group for the drone industry have suggested that adverts for drones should depict their work in humanitarian emergencies. They also suggest

61   Barry, 'Drones over the Homeland', p. 14.
62   Ben Hayes, Chris Jones and Eric Toepfer, *Eurodrones Inc.*, Statewatch, 2014, p. 7, available at statewatch.org.
63   Ibid., p. 7.
64   Ibid., p. 25.

that civilian drones should be painted in bright colours to distinguish them from their murderous cousins in war zones.[65]

The problems with the deployment of drones within domestic space are the same that attend all radical extensions of systems of digital surveillance and tracking at a distance within contemporary cultures of policing – especially those based on re-purposed military systems. A permanent and radical extension of vertical surveillance of entire societies through live-feed cameras, communications surveillance, infrared monitoring and video analysis will be the inevitable result.[66]

Drone technologies, moreover, would inevitably be deployed based on existing techniques of racial, ethnic and geographical profiling, possibly even through the use of automated software looking for 'abnormal' or 'threat' signatures, or even targeted individuals, on the ground below. The sorts of drone-based dragnetting of the electronic signatures of the populations of whole cities that are the focus of programmes that feature in the Argus and Gorgon Stare projects would likely emerge as the cornerstone of domestic drone policing. The use of sensors to see through walls and roofs can also be expected.

Combined with the existence of large databases of individual facial images, communications records and so on, automated manhunts are easily envisaged. Although face recognition is in its infancy, and is only as good as the facial images in the databases used, its capabilities are improving rapidly. Working face-recognition drones, trawling images from all manner of high-resolution social media and image and other biometric and information databases, would, at a stroke, radically undermine remaining notions of public anonymity on city streets.

Again, military drone systems provide a worrying precedent. Tim Faltemier of the Progeny Systems Corporation talked in 2011 about a project his company is developing for US Army drones using 3D models of people's faces to track them biometrically from above: 'If this works out, we'll have the ability to track people persistently across wide areas … A guy can go under a bridge or inside a house.

---

65   Ibid.
66   See the Bill of Rights Defense Committee, 'Drone Talking Points', 2013, available at constitutioncampaign.org.

But when he comes out, we'll know it was the same guy that went in.'[67] In such 'noncooperative' tracking of people by their biometric signatures, the upturned face of the human beneath the drone, rather than a means of challenging the eye of the drone, as in the #NotABugSplat project, becomes instead the very signature that allows the drone to secure its domination.

It is very likely that new drone-based policing methods would be particularly concentrated, of course, on intensifying vertical scrutiny of those places or populations deemed, a priori, to be the source of threats, agitation, criminality and 'otherness'. In the US, as with the deployment of police helicopters after widespread rioting in US cities in the late 1960s, it seems highly likely that police drone squadrons within increasingly polarised cities will overwhelmingly be used to police black and Latino neighbourhoods while working to secure downtowns and affluent white suburbs.[68] Focusing on political movements in the vein of the Occupy protests, which aim to interrupt the logistical flows of city life, will be an important focus.

As in the deployment of lethal drones abroad, moreover, the use of police drones, inevitably, will rely on the internal prejudices of policing cultures in stipulating what or who is an enemy in a world where it is only such prejudices that can help to simplify the radical complexity and opaqueness of the world viewed below. Once established, regular drone patrols would inevitably be the source of mission creep as more and better sensors and weapons become available to be added to existing, highly expensive, platforms.

In the US, the Bill of Rights Defense Committee has already stressed that the domestic deployment of armed drones, building on the Department of Homeland Security's efforts to arm its border drones, is a very real possibility. 'Drones are easily affixed with lethal and "less-lethal" weapons', they point out. 'And assurances that they will not be armed domestically lack credibility.'[69] The committee cite an example in Houston where police have deployed a drone armed with a 12-gauge shotgun and a grenade launcher. The local sheriff is,

---

67   Noah Shactman, 'Army Tracking Plan: Never Forget a Face', *Wired*, 11 September 2011, available at wired.com. The project is called the 'Long Range, Noncooperative, Biometric Tagging, Tracking and Location' system.

68   Hyane, 'Ghetto Bird'.

69   See Bill of Rights Defense Committee, 'Drone Talking Points'.

moreover, 'open to the idea of adding non-lethal weapons like tear gas, rubber bullets or Taser-style rounds to the drone.'[70]

The prospect of armed drones in domestic policing, motivated in the US by highly racialised and militarised policing tactics, inspires particularly grave concerns. They also bring the prospect of an especially powerful Foucaudian boomerang: the use of high-tech drones piloted from a distant place to deploy violence against racialised Others far below both at home and abroad. The 'disregard for constitutional restraints on killing and transparency' in US drone operations abroad, the Bill of Rights Defense Committee emphasise, 'leaves little reason to believe that the Department of Justice would ensure that local law enforcement's use of drones abided by constitutional and legal standards.'[71]

Contesting the Dronesphere

How, then, to contest the dronesphere? A widespread and powerful range of loosely coordinated social movements, legal and human rights movements, demonstrations and activism campaigns are working hard at many scales to challenge the progressive normalisation of drones at home and abroad.

The *#NotABugSplat* project is only one particularly visual campaign among many. Resistance to drone-based killing is manifest in continuous demonstrations by veterans and other protestors at Creech and other drone air bases; widespread demonstrations against all aspects of the drone-related military machine; forensic analysis of drone strikes to try to hold to account those perpetrating human rights abuses or war crimes; and a wide spectrum of legal, communications and journalistic critiques and challenges.[72]

An anonymous group of activists have also produced a 'Drone Survival Guide' – a guide to 'twenty-first century birdwatching' as they call it, outlining types of drones, as viewed from below, as well

---

70   See 'Groups Concerned over Arming of Domestic Drones', CBS LOCAL – DC, 23 May 2012, available at washington.cbslocal.com.

71   Bill of Rights Defense Committee, 'Drone Talking Points', p. 3.

72   See, for example, the International Committee for Robot Arms Control, available at ICRAC, icrac.net.

Essam Attia's satirical anti-drone poster, which he distributed on the streets of New York in December 2012

as ways to challenge their power. 'Our ancestors could spot natural predators from afar by their silhouettes', it reads. 'Are we equally aware of the predators in the present-day?'

Central here is the challenge of rendering visible the secretive and geographically peripheral process of drone-based killing. In 2013, for example, US artist Josh Begley tried to get Apple to accept his Drones+ smartphone app, which would notify users each time a US drone strike was reported. (Apple refused because, they said, too many people would find the app 'objectionable'.)[73]

More theoretically, architect Asher Kohn has even explored the types of physical urban structures that might be installed above urban roof tops to prevent a city being subjugated from above by drone patrols or strikes.[74]

Anti-drone campaign groups are working hard to problematise the ways in which unarmed and armed drones are crossing over from the colonial frontier to the domestic metropolis. In 2012, in a famous case, the New York–based artist Essam Attia was arrested for pasting 100 satirical posters around the city attacking the prospect of drone-based policing in the city. Triggered by the decision of the New York Police Department to authorise drone use, Attia's simple aim, he said, was to 'create a conversation' about the politics of drone-based policing.[75]

Elsewhere, activists themselves are exploring the adoption of drone-based systems to extend their own powers of surveillance

73   Derek Gregory, 'Drone Geographies', *Radical Philosophy* 183, 2014, pp. 7–19.

74   Sarah Goodyear, 'Imagining a Drone-Proof City', *CityLab*, 6 February 2013.

75   Joshua Kopsteain, 'Street Artist behind Satirical NYPD "Drone" Posters Arrested', *The Verge*, 2 December 2012, available at theverge.com.

'from the grassroots' against state and corporate power (what has been termed 'sous-surveillance'). This is part of a broader shift in urban activism towards recognising the need to address the volumes of city spaces rather than merely occupying the flat terrain of urban streets. 'Where does [Occupy] go from here?' Californian activist Teo Ballvé reflected in 2011, following a range of efforts – including aerial banners, helium balloons, floating tents and the like – to move their protests into three dimensions. 'How about up?'[76]

With drone hobbyism growing rapidly, and basic drones with video cameras now accessible from any toyshop for extremely low prices, prospects for democratising the drone are emerging. Might drones be repositioned away from the monopolistic control of the world's high-tech militaries and police authorities towards routines of citizen activism, research and critique?

In an initial example, Occupy protestors in New York in December 2011 repurposed a simple drone bought from a toystore as an 'Occucopter'. An attempt to distribute the vertical gaze beyond the security forces or corporate media to the activists and demonstrators themselves, and their channels of communication, the Occucopter represents one example of the ways in which the democratisation of military technologies can be used to challenge the militarisation of civil society.[77]

In practice, the Occucopter helped activists become aware when groups of demonstrators were being illegally incarcerated, when they were being geographically confined by 'kettling' tactics or when journalists were illegally barred from accessing sites of demonstrations. Recorded footage from the drone was also useful in countering the efforts of the police or corporate media to brand activists and demonstrators as a mere gang of 'violent anarchists'. (Further successful drone use by protestors and critical researchers has occurred in Estonia, Russia, Poland and in Washington, DC).

More than this, though, drones might offer excellent opportunities for human rights groups to expose brutality, violence and atrocities.

76   Teo Ballvé, 'Occupy Volume, Occupy Verticality', *Territorial Masquerades,* 1 December 2011, available at territorialmasquerades.net.
77   Noel Sharkey and Sarah Knuckey, 'Occupy Wall Street's "Occucopter" – Who's Watching Whom?' *Guardian,* 21 December 2011.

They might also help develop powerful communications strategies to build support and legitimacy. 'No more do citizens need to wait for news choppers to get aerial footage of a major event', *Wired* editor and personal drone-builder Chris Anderson emphasises. 'With drones, they can shoot their own overhead video.'[78]

Capturing the violence of political regimes against nonviolent protestors, in particular, can be a huge boon in efforts to bolster campaigns while quickly undermining the legitimacy of those in power. Technology researcher Patrick Meier even wonders whether drones could be used more strategically to paint entire skies with key activist slogans or to follow key public officials during protests.[79]

The first challenge for such campaigns, however, is to prevent the a priori criminalisation of activist drones at the outset. Just as citizen drone use is proliferating, national security states are trying to assert their hegemony of the skies. As journalists, activists and researchers have extended their use of the technology to gain previously impossible footage and imagery of proscribed and securitised spaces, so civilian use of such technologies is increasingly being criminalised as a 'security threat'. In 2015, three Al Jazeera journalists were arrested on suspicion of using drones without a license in Paris, and a photojournalist using a drone near Gatwick airport was arrested and held even though he had such a license.

Many states are introducing much tighter legislation criminalising the use of hobbyist drones based on the same vague and ill-specified 'security' concerns so often used to justify homeland deployment of drones in the first pace. With particular irony, scare stories are often used in such arguments about the possibility of terrorists using drones with weapons attached.[80] In February 2005, four weeks before a hobbyist drone controller was arrested for accidentally flying his machine above the White House while drunk,[81] a wide range of US state

---

78   Cited in Patrick Meier, 'The Use of Drones for Nonviolent Civil Resistance', *Irevolutions*, 18 February 2012, available at irevolution.net.

79   Meier, 'The Use of Drones for Nonviolent Civil Resistance'.

80   Kevin Poulsen, 'Why the US Government Is Terrified of Hobbyist Drones', *Wired*, 2 May 2012, available at wired.com.

81   The Chinese manufacturer of the drone promptly distributed a software update equipped with a virtual 'geo-fence' organised through GPS which disabled

security departments had held a summit exploring the dangers posed by the possible weaponisation of hobby drones. Videos of fighters in the Syrian civil war using drones equipped with automatic weapons were shown. An exhibition was organised of hobby drones with various weapons attached. The emphasis was that the enormous expenditure fortifying government facilities against surface-level terrorist attacks might be simply traversed by those using the third, vertical, dimension.

More prosaically, police forces in Japan unveiled an anti-hobbyist drone in December 2015. It is equipped with a net to pluck drones seen as troublesome out of the Tokyo skies. Such cat-and-mouse, drone-versus-drone conflicts are rapidly intensifying in the airspaces above cities.

---

all of its drones from flying within 15.5 miles of the White House. (It already programmes its drones to avoid most airports.)

4.

Helicopter: Direct Arrival

Ever since they were imagined, helicopters have inspired dreams of frictionless, three-dimensional mobility for the masses. Virtually every depiction of future cities by film-makers, cartoonists, science fiction authors and architects since the 1920s has been predicated heavily on the possibilities of a fully tri-dimensional urbanism liberating a population from the ground either through personal helicopter travel or the generalisation of a more exotic vertical take-off and landing vehicle.

Fritz Lang's dystopian city in his 1927 film *Metropolis* – set in 2026 – was laced together by swarms of aerial vehicles. Broadacre City, Frank Lloyd Wright's influential suburban utopia of 1932, was animated by an enormous fleet of aerial helicopter-like flying pods. And countless cartoon worlds, dystopian movies and sci-fi visions have centred on personalised vehicles that can, at a moment's notice, leap into the skies.

Surely, many protagonists have asked, the limits of gravity, of the street, of worsening congestion, and of the city multitude trapped together on the urban surface require the ultimate form of transcendence: a personal flying vehicle that can sustain door-to-door mobility within a completely three-dimensional urban environment?[1]

Dreams of helicopter urbanism have sustained more than the presses of pulp science fiction and comic book publishers. Serious experiments, commercial flights and widespread investment occurred between the 1940s and 1960s to try to make mass urban helicopter travel a reality. In the 1940s the American Historical Association produced a pamphlet linking the promise of the helicopter with post-war possibilities of modernist renewal and suburban mobility in the

---

1 For a contemporary exploration of such possibilities, see MDRVD, *Skycar City: A Pre-Emptive History*, Barcelona: Actar, 2007.

United States. Titled *Will There Be a Plane in Every Garage?* the pamphlet explored the promise of this novel machine:

> If your home is in a suburban or rural district, the helicopter can take you to and from work daily in comfort and with speed. You won't get tied up in a traffic jam or have to stop for red lights or wait for a ferryboat. You will not need an elaborate landing field. Any level plot of ground 50 feet in diameter will suffice. This plot need not be adjacent to your helicopter garage. It can be several blocks away, for it is thought that helicopters will be built so that they can be driven along streets for short distances.[2]

Though they have been almost completely forgotten, these efforts to bring widespread helicopter use into post-war cities in Europe and North America were considerable. Commercial passenger-carrying helicopters were designed and built for scheduled services. Inter-city services were inaugurated (for example, between Liverpool and Cardiff in 1961 in the UK). And urban planners worked hard to integrate heliports and their complex three-dimensional demands into their plans for the comprehensive redevelopment of city centres.

'I believe that we are on the threshold of a helicopter age in Britain for internal passenger transport', one British MP predicted in a parliamentary debate on heliports in 1953. 'The point that I wish to emphasise is that only by the erection of elevated stations in the centre of our principal cities can we gain the maximum benefit from all the time-saving potentialities of these brilliant little machines.'[3]

London alone witnessed fifteen serious proposals for city-centre helipads to accommodate the expected proliferation of commercial and personal helicopter use.[4] As well as the heliport that was actually

---

2   Cited in Saulo Cwerner, 'Vertical Flight and Urban Mobilities: The Promise and Reality of Helicopter Travel', *Mobilities* 1:2, 2006, p. 196.

3   Mr Gerald Nabarro, MP for Kidderminster, House of Commons debate on 'Helicopter station, London', 2 February 1953 [Hansard, HC Deb 02 February 1953 vol. 510 cc1615-26], cited in Martin Dodge and Richard Brook, 'Helicopter Dreaming: The Unrealised Plans for City Centre Heliports in the Post-War Period', Department of Geography, University of Manchester, 2013, available at personalpages.manchester.ac.uk.

4   Martin Dodge, 'Vertical Urbanism and the Forgotten Plans for Heliports',

Early 1950s vision for a huge raised 'helidome' on top of London's Hungerford Bridge and Charing Cross rail station. Anticipating complex webs of intercity helicopter services that never materialised, the helidome would have been equipped with a large flight deck (centre), an arrivals area (left), departures area (right), passenger lounges and elevators integrating it with the rail station below.

constructed on the Thames at Battersea, plans emerged to retrofit all the major rail stations as well as some of the City's markets and bridges with rooftop heli-decks. The multistorey car parks that were built to stack cities' proliferating cars when stationary were, in some cases, topped off by (ultimately unrealised) plans for municipal heliports.

The widespread assumption was that such facilities would quickly become as banal and ubiquitous as municipal bus stations. Visions for helipads seemed to fit perfectly into a wider world of three-dimensional urban planning in the UK, elsewhere in Europe and in North America, a world that also led to the widespread construction of vertically segregated walkway systems, modernist high-rise housing and both elevated and sunken freeways.

The most famous operational heliport was constructed in 1965 by Pan American Airways atop its gleaming new modernist tower on Park Avenue in Midtown Manhattan. Fully exploiting the nexus of futuristic imagery linking modernist skyscrapers, express elevators,

Department of Geography, University of Manchester, 2013, available at personalpages.manchester.ac.uk.

international air travel and helicopter urbanism, the roof of the tower was equipped with a particularly elaborate heliport. This was serviced by double-rotor Boeing helicopters that whisked business-class passengers direct to the stairways of the company's waiting intercontinental airliners at New York airports.

Elite passengers excitedly embraced the possibility of bypassing the notorious congestion that afflicted the city's surface and subsurface means of reaching its airports. Journey times to LaGuardia were slashed to four minutes; those to Newark to six minutes; and those to Idlewild (soon to be renamed John F. Kennedy) to seven minutes.

The whole journey offered a new, futuristic experience of vertical urbanism and apparently frictionless, three-dimensional mobility. 'Once ticketed, passengers would walk but a few steps to an express elevator for a thirty-second ride to the fifty-seventh floor of the building', architectural historian Meredith Clausen writes. They would then 'take an escalator to a heliport lounge one flight up and a short elevator ride to the boarding lounge next to the control tower and roof pad. The speed, travel and convenience – it was all pretty futuristic stuff.'[5] Journalists, too, fell under the spell of a new three-dimensional urban spectacle. The trip 'was like nothing else' gushed a *New York Times* reporter; the take-off in particular offering 'breathtaking views of Manhattan 800 feet below.'[6]

Regular helicopter service drew major public resentment, however. The enormous noise generated by the large and relatively primitive machines operating so close to densely inhabited space resulted in many complaints. Others were appalled at the extreme elitism and obvious public dangers of the service. 'It is a promotional idea, pure and simple', one disgruntled New Yorker wrote in a letter to the *New York Times*. Worse still, he felt that the idea had been 'foisted upon our city at huge risk to public safety.'[7] Such predictions proved prescient. On 16 May 1977, following the recommencement of services after a lull, a helicopter with broken landing gear skewed sideways on the helipad as it landed. Its rotor blade snapped off, scything to death

---

5   Meredith Clausen, *The Pan Am Building and the Shattering of the Modernist Dream*, Cambridge: Mass.: MIT Press, 2005, p. 314

6   Cited in Clausen, *Pan Am Building*, pp. 311–14.

7   Ibid., p. 311.

four of the waiting passengers. Part of it then plunged off the heliport to kill a fifth person on the teeming street sixty storeys below.

The fatal accident, as well as wider concerns about noise pollution and simple economics, fatally undermined the drive to make municipal heliports as common as municipal bus stations. It also dealt a bitter blow to longstanding 'dream[s] of "direct arrival" for the masses by air into the heart of city centres (a dream as old as the Empire State Building in the same city, whose long rooftop mast was also conceived as a mooring point for airships).'[8] Across the planning offices of the West, helipads were thus quietly deleted from plans for the roofs of concrete multistorey parking garages. Prosaic lines of parked cars took the place earmarked for ranks of futuristic helicopters.

Kinetic Elites Take to the Skies

Such controversies failed to kill off helicopter urbanism completely, however. Instead, urban helicopter mobility and 'direct arrival' were progressively reinvented as privileges of hyper-individualised super-elites within sprawling megacities. Indeed, elite helicopter travel has emerged to be perhaps the ultimate symbol of the secession of the tiny numbers of überwealthy from the constraints, limits and struggles that surround urban life on the earth's surface. Through it, the 'upper' classes assert monopolistic access to the third dimension: the 'Z-access' of verticality, a domain denied to all but the select few. For the kinetic elite, unparalleled riches allow them to project their everyday routines into aerial space, radically re-engineering their urban geographies in the process.

What geographers call 'time-space compression' – the use of new technologies to pull disparate sites into a functional routine through speed – thus takes place across the volume of air above the city, region and nation, rather than on the surface of the earth, the subsurface (through subway trains), or the higher atmosphere (through air travel). While elites radically speed their journeys through the air, the mass of the megacity population below can only look up while their own movement often slows to a snail's pace because of worsening congestion.

---

8   Dodge, 'Vertical Urbanism'.

The Brazilian commercial capital of São Paulo, a city where 1,880 individuals have net assets of $30 million or more,[9] is by far the most dramatic case of these three-dimensional geographies of elite succession. Helicopter use is so widespread among São Paulo's elites that in 2004 the city was the first in the world to develop an air-traffic control system designed solely for the movement of personal helicopters.[10]

The city of 20 million people now has over 420 helipads – 50 per cent more than the whole of the UK – and 470 registered helicopters (the biggest urban fleet in the world). São Paulo's helicopter business is growing at over 20 per cent per year. Even so, assuming that the city's helicopters accommodate on average three passengers, this aerial transportation system can shuttle around only three-quarters of one hundredth of one per cent of São Paulo's population at a time.

Sociologist Saulo Cwerner notes that a municipal planner in São Paulo argued recently that 'elevated helipads are fast taking the role that swimming pools had a decade or so ago: every building, including residential ones, wants to have one!'[11] Indeed, helipad use is so normalised amongst São Paulo's super-elite that architectural firms specialise in designing helipads with appropriate upscale looks to add status to corporate headquarters buildings. 'Today we define the sculptural rooftop helipad as a good architectural result', Carlos Freire, an engineer with a company that has dominated this market, pointed out in 2005.[12]

In one of the world's most unequal societies, Cwerner argues that the personal helicopter, despite its $1,300 per hour cost, provides a 'fresh and, in many respects, ideal form of social distinction for a privileged social class increasingly obsessed by barriers and separation.'[13] Lacing together corporate office towers, fortified residential enclaves, elite shopping malls, five-star hotels, exurban country clubs, beach resorts and airports across a sprawling 1,500 km² megacity, personal

---

9 'São Paulo's Millionaires Use Helicopters to Avoid Traffic Jams', *South China Morning Post*, 26 April 2013.

10 Saulo Cwerner, 'Vertical Flight and Urban Mobilities: The Promise and Reality of Helicopter Travel', *Mobilities* 1:2, 2006, p. 199.

11 Ibid., p. 203.

12 Ibid., p. 208.

13 Ibid., p. 203.

A São Paulan business executive commuting to his central city office tower from the home helipad on his gated country estate

helicopter and helipad use has become the ultimate status symbol for super-rich Paulistas. It is the perfect response to their concerns about the city's extraordinary traffic jams – officially, the world's worst, according to *Time* magazine, with an average, and worsening, traffic speed of 14 km per hour – and worrying rates of kidnapping and car-jacking.[14] Hopping between secure spaces at 200 kilometres an hour, the helicopter offers a radical reinvention of urban life for the elite, providing a succession of vertical 'direct arrivals' onto what has been called in the different context of Los Angeles a 'geometric terrain of helipads'.[15]

In São Paulo, elite helicopter urbanism works to sustain and integrate a broader process of vertical succession for the super-elite, who

14   Andrew Downie, 'The World's Worst Traffic Jams', *Time*, 21 April 2008.

15   The unique building regulations in LA mean that all buildings taller than seventy-five feet built after 1974 must have flat-top helipads for rescue and fire-fighting purposes. This requirement has had dramatic effects on the city's skyline. 'There are no Postmodern pyramid-topped buildings, no neo-Gothic or Modern spires, topped by an antenna mast', Center for Land Use Interpretation, 'Elevated Descent: The Landingscape of Helipads', *Lay of the Land*, Spring 2010, available at http://clui.org/newsletter/.

gravitate upwards in their living, working and leisure environments towards a plethora of roof-top helipads. São Paulo's elites thus now ascend over, and cease to rely on, the city's chronically saturated ground-level streetscapes, taking minutes to complete journeys that previously took hours. (The journey time to the city's main airport is five minutes compared to the hour to hour and a half that is usual by car.)

As with the use of flyovers, air travel, skyscrapers, cable cars, elevators and Google Earth, helicopter-based urban lifestyles in turn work to produce powerful new aesthetic sensibilities of megacity life. Along with the proliferation of TV news helicopters and paramilitary police helicopters, elites now consume the city as an aestheticised landscape from above. The notorious 130-mile traffic jams in rush hour; the struggles by the city's 7 million vehicles to access an ageing and increasingly jammed road system; the snail-like progress of the city's totally inadequate public transport system; the city's deadly ground-level smog – all are rendered as little but a backdrop. From the helicopter cabin, the city becomes 'a seemingly endless sea of concrete dotted with swimming pools, helipads, shantytowns and abandoned warehouses.'[16]

'I cannot even remember what a traffic jam is', Amilcare Dallevo, Junior, the president of the RedeTV station, admits.[17] In five minutes, Dallevo can get from his home in the superwealthy enclave in Alphaville to his office in the city's downtown – a distance of 23 kilometres. 'If I didn't take a helicopter, I would not be able to get to all of my appointments.'

The ascension of the elites in São Paulo has not gone uncontested, however. Since 2009, rising public protests over the interminable noise pollution caused by helicopters have led city authorities to rein in the proliferating infrastructures of helicopter travel and to limit their times of use. Thirty per cent of helipads have been closed because of environmental restrictions regulating their distances from schools, universities and hospitals.

---

16   Tom Phillips, 'High above São Paulo's Choked Streets, the Rich Cruise a New Highway', *Guardian*, 20 June 2008.

17   Verena Brähler and Solveig Flörke, 'São Paulo: The World's Biggest Helicopter Fleet', *LAB: Latin American Bureau*, 1 September 2011.

Predictably, in a series of legal battles dubbed 'helicopter wars' by the *Folha de S. Paulo* newspaper,[18] coalitions of elite groups, banks, hotels and real estate owners are contesting these bans in the courts. Carlos Alberto Artoni, the former president of the Brazilian Association of Helicopter Pilots (ABRAPHE), argues forcefully that unfettered helicopter-mania among the wealthy is good for the city, a sign of modernity and progress.

Dismissing allegations that the noise pollution causes lost sleep and psychological disturbance to millions, he snapped back a riposte: 'Those who want to hear birds sing should live outside São Paulo. Here you have to get used to modernity.'[19] These struggles, which have their parallel in Los Angeles and elsewhere, have been complicated by revelations of the degree to which São Paulo's political elites themselves frequent the city's skies. For example, a magazine revealed recently that the six-mile commute of Sergio Cabral, the governor of Rio de Janeiro state, involved a three-minute helicopter ride at an annual cost to the Brazilian taxpayer of $1.7 million.

It was also revealed that Cabral routinely ferried his nanny, family and even dog around the city and beyond on routine trips and excursions to his country home.[20] 'People are protesting over public transportation', Eduardo Militão, a lobbyist for political transparency, argues. 'And then you discover the authorities are taking joy rides [in helicopters] with public money'.[21]

Frisking the Streets

Beyond São Paulo and another limited selection of 'global' cities, elite sky-taxis buzzing between elevated helipads are still uncommon. Much more common are the world's burgeoning fleet of ambulance and rescue and, of course, police helicopters. Symbolising the increasing deployment of military-standard surveillance and targeting

18   Claire Rigby, 'Watch the Skies: São Paulo's Helicopter Wars', *From Brazil*, 13 September 2012, available at frombrazil.blogfolha.uol.com.br.

19   Ibid.

20   Lourdes Garcia-Navarro, 'Highflying VIPs Face Backlash over Air Travel', *NPR.Org*, 19 July 2013, available at npr.org.

21   Cited in Garcia-Navarro, ibid.

technologies in civilian policing, the latter vehicles are increasingly marketed by military–industrial and security corporations as magical solutions to urban disorder.

Adverts in arms brochures and military and policing magazines routinely depict the helicopter, electromagnetic sensors ready, loitering above troublesome urban neighbourhoods ready to penetrate the labyrinthine landscapes of cities to bring criminals to heel. 'The most sought-after provision that will open up the megacity to state scrutiny', British geographer Pete Adey stresses, 'is the police helicopter'.[22]

Some ads for military and police helicopters hint at what French philosopher Michel Foucault called the 'boomerang effect' – the propensity for imperialist societies and empires to bring the military technologies honed within frontier counter-insurgency wars to the domestic worlds of social control and urban policing. In the research for my 2010 book *Cities Under Siege* – an extensive investigation of the links between the burgeoning world of 'homeland security' and the wars in Iraq, Afghanistan and Israel/Palestine – I came across the best visual depiction of a contemporary 'boomerang effect' imaginable. The advert was for the infrared sensors that both military and police helicopters use to track – and sometimes destroy – warm human bodies in cities.[23]

Depicting a two-sided, hybrid helicopter – a military side with rockets, and a police one with aerial cameras – the message reads, 'Every Night, All Night – No. 1 Multi-Sensor Thermal Imaging – From Baghdad to Baton Rouge – We've Got Your Back!' (Baton Rouge is the largely African-American city that is capital of the US state of Louisiana.)

The suggestion here is that the task for army and police across an urbanising world is pretty much identical: rise above the city with a God-like transcendence, subject it to permanent lock-down and surveillance from above and from afar using helicopters (as well as

---

22   Peter Adey, 'Vertical Security in the Megacity: Legibility, Mobility and Aerial Politics', *Theory, Culture and Society* 27:6, 2010, pp. 51–67.

23   It is these infrared sensors that provide the ghostly white images of human bodies starkly exposed against the cooler blackness of the wider city beyond that are so familiar from the replaying of this footage on TV, YouTube and Hollywood action movies.

Foucault's boomerang: An advert from sensor manufacturer Forward-Looking Infra Red (FLIR) extolling the crossover between paramilitary and military helicopters

drones and satellites); and use military sensors to target, assail – or, if necessary, eliminate – those urban subjects below deemed to be enemies or those whose behaviours are deemed 'abnormal'.

The deliberate imitation of military-style helicopter operations in civilian policing started in Los Angeles in 1965. It emerged as a crucial part of that city's police forces' effort to replace beat policing on the ground with technological capital sustaining systematic aerial surveillance. Helicopter operations quickly became the 'cornerstone of a policing strategy for the entire city'.[24] In the pre-GPS era, LA's rooftops were daubed with large numbers to facilitate helicopter navigation around the sprawling metropolis.

In the late 1980s, the Los Angeles Police Department's helicopters started to mimic military attack helicopters by using infrared sensors, massive 'night-sun' illumination systems and heavily armed SWAT (Special Weapons and Tactics) teams to be dropped down at any moment onto the streets. Since then, such systems have been generalised across the police forces of the world's major cities. The military helicopter industry has grown rapidly. Meanwhile, the crossovers between urban policing and the burgeoning worlds of 'homeland security' have meant a bonanza time for hybrid aircraft colonising the blurring worlds between domestic policing, pacification and all-out warfare. In the United States, a recent market report noted that, while US military 'operations in urban environments will be more frequent, thus increasing demands for rotorcraft', the 'Department of Homeland Security is expected to acquire hundreds of helicopters to support its expanded efforts at US borders.'[25]

The allure of helicopter-based policing is such that police forces in Global South megacities such as Lagos and Mumbai have announced their ambitions to imitate the Hollywood-style police operations of the LAPD that have been featured – along with their footage of the city below – in a thousand films, police drama shows and reality TV series.

Some helicopter TV events, such as the real-time chase of O. J. Simpson in LA in 1994, have in turn become pivotal moments in

24   Mike Davis, *City of Quartz*, pp. 251–2.
25   Daniel Goure, *Military Helicopter Industrial Base*, Washington DC: Lexington Institute, 2005.

the cultural history of aerial security. A whole genre of 'scary police chases' captured by the digital cameras of TV and police helicopters – as well as those in cars and roadside systems – is a major part of the reality TV and pulp documentary industry.

Such systems and deployments fit perfectly into a world where the enemy is deemed to be 'within' the domestic megacity; mobilisation is permanent within boundless 'wars' against drugs, terrorism, insurgency or political disruption; and the labyrinthine worlds of urbanised terrain sprawls toward, and beyond, the horizon. 'Domestic' helicopter deployments to the 'badlands' of the homeland thus become less and less distinguishable from full-on counterinsurgency operations against occupied colonies.

A case in point of such 'military policing'[26] is the helicopter-based counter-insurgency war against Brazil's urban favelas. In these aerial incursions by the notorious paramilitary forces – who killed 983 people in Rio in 2004 alone[27] – into favelas, paramilitaries smash open 'tin rooftops, break down doors and windows, ransack houses and bully their occupants, [fire] weapons indiscriminately, close down stores and schools, and carry out mass arrests for "vagrancy" (apprehending *favelados* who do not bear identity cards on them as required by the law).'[28]

Such urban helicopter operations rest on attempts by aerial police to assert a moral geography based on the tacit judgments of personnel and organisations: which people, and which neighbourhoods, are 'bad' and require forceful, masculinised, control; and which ones are 'good' and require protection.[29] The city thus ceases to be a lived social world of communities, places and people with attachments. Instead, it 'reduces … space to a zone of tactics.'[30]

In the rundown parts of LA subject to the most intensive helicopter operations, journalist Andrian Kreye reports that police helicopters

---

26   The term comes from Lea Andyouno, *What Is to Be Done about Law and Order*, Harmondsworth, UK: Penguin, 1984.

27   Adey, 'Vertical Security', p. 61.

28   Ibid.

29   Steve Herbert, '"Hard Charger" or "Station Queen"? Policing and the Masculinist State', *Gender, Place and Culture: A Journal of Feminist Geography* 8:1, 2001, p. 60.

30   Ibid.

now regularly 'drop down from the night sky above the urban terrain, light up whole blocks with their search lights, frisk the streets with their infra-red sensors and high-powered cameras, corral fleeing suspects like cattle through the city streets until the ground troops can nail them down and put on the handcuffs.'[31]

Increasingly, however, as in the wider military shift towards the automatic identification of targets, efforts are being made to imbue computer software itself with the capability to automatically identify people or vehicles deemed to be 'targets' from within the stream of digital imagery. In 2002, for example, the Bavarian police became one of the first to use 'automated target recognition' software linked to its helicopter's infrared sensors. These scan 'for predefined objects such as persons or vehicles, these being indicated upon recognition by appropriate optical symbols on a display unit or by acoustic signals.'[32]

Backed by highly pejorative language about the 'good' and 'bad' parts of cities among many helicopter police,[33] the temptation here is to render the human subjects in the 'bad' parts of town as racialised and criminalised targets necessitating a permanent culture of aerial tracking and interdiction via helicopter – and, increasingly, drone – systems. All too easily, these deployments slip into a world where the city below is 'populated only by [police] officers and suspects.'[34]

Such warlike deployments and imaginaries are often inscribed with starkly racialised and anti-urban politics. They fit into a wider culture within urban security forces and sympathetic right-wing commentators which often work to render poorer cities, and poorer parts of cities, as intrinsically feral, inhuman and racially defined places beyond the bounds of normal law – intrinsically sinful and demonic environments always on the brink of chaos requiring heavy-handed, military-style intervention.[35]

---

31 Andrian Kreye, 'Above the Neon Prairie: On Patrol with the LAPD's Helicopter Squad', *andriankreye.com*, 2009, available at andriankreye.com/LAPDE.html.

32 'EADS-Developed AUTOPOL Helps Police Helicopters to Spot People and Vehicles', 1 May 2002 available at http://northamerica.airbus-group.com/.

33 Herbert, 'Hard Charger'.

34 Kreye, 'Above the Neon Prairie'.

35 See Steve Macek, *Urban Nightmares: The Media, the Right, and the Moral Panic over the City,* Minneapolis: University of Minnesota Press, 2006.

Foucault's boomerangs also operate in the linguistic register to justify and normalise the deployment of militarised helicopter operations against domestic cities. After Hurricane Katrina hit New Orleans, one US Army magazine referred to the need to 'take back' the city from 'insurgents'. Two years later, right-wing commentator Nicole Gelinas argued in the Manhattan Institute's *City Journal* that post-Katrina New Orleans was little less than a 'Baghdad on the Bayou'. She argued that the city required a similar militarised response to bring order and investment amid its supposed pathologies of crime and violence.[36]

The aerial surveillance of the helicopter's infrared or target sensor provides a highly militarised way of treating the city – and its people – below the scanning, computerised eye. Increasingly, the infrared register of warm bodies against the cooler dark cityscape effectively *becomes* the city as the increasingly high-tech helicopter cockpit works to progressively exclude the operator's or pilot's direct sensory engagement with the areas below.[37]

Police helicopter cockpits thus start to mimic the cockpits of military attack helicopters. The obsession becomes one of penetrating the veil of an urban environment deemed to be devious and deceptive as a means of exposing targeted bodies. The reliance on a suite of digital sensors is used to perceive the world on the ground. This creates a virtual image of target registers while at the same time allowing personnel very limited direct use of their own bodily senses.[38]

The infrared night-time gaze of the police helicopter receives a rapturous reception among police, the military-industrial complex and sympathetic media alike. A case in point was the discovery of Dzhokhar Tsarnaev, on the run after the bombing of the Boston Marathon on 13 April 2013. Hiding beneath a boat as the entire city of Boston sheltered at home within an unprecedented martial-law lock-down,[39] he

---

36   See Nicole Gelinas, 'Baghdad on the Bayou', *City Journal*, Spring 2007, pp. 42–53, available at city-journal.org.

37   Ryan Bishop and John Phillips, *Modernist Avant-Garde Aesthetics and Contemporary Military Technology: Technicities of Perception,* Edinburgh: Edinburgh University Press, 2010, chapter 2.

38   Ibid., p. 25.

39   See Henry Giroux, 'Lockdown, USA: Lessons from the Boston Marathon Manhunt', *Truthout.Org*, 6 May 2013, available at truth-out.org.

was unaware that his heat signature made him entirely visible to the helicopter sensors.

'When I heard it was Massachusetts State Police, I knew it was our camera,' said Andy Teich, president of FLIR Commercial Systems (the company that makes infrared sensors). When he made it back to the company's Oregon headquarters the employees, sensing the huge growth in contracts the company could garner within booming homeland security and surveillance markets, cheered. 'This imager is a mid-way thermal imager,' Teich continued. 'Meaning that it looks in a certain area of the infrared spectrum in the 3-5 micron range. Why that was significant in this case is that in that particular spectrum, many plastics become transparent.'[40]

Rotorwars

For all their awesome firepower and totalizing gaze, paramilitary and military helicopters are far from omnipotent. Efforts to use them to achieve vertical omniscience and omnipotence have been contradictory, incomplete and contested.

As with the deployment of lethal drones, fantasies that high-tech sensors genuinely unveil the complex worlds below, distinguishing accurately and automatically between friends and enemies, are deluded and dangerous. Indeed, these systems deliver the real-time video and then starkly expose the inability of the operators to make sense of it. This is a reality with murderous consequences, for three reasons.

First, as anthropologist Gastón Gordillo suggests, as with armed drones, these systems merely expose the inability of pilots and operators to deal with what he calls the 'textured density of the terrain' below the unblinking gaze of the electronic eye.[41] Into this disorientating vacuum of understanding steps a potent cocktail of militaristic and neocolonial hubris, masculine omnipotence fantasies, racist imagination and an increasingly detached, video game–like experience.

40   Paul Peluso, 'Thermal Imaging Plays Major Role in Bombing Manhunt', *SecurityInfoWatch.com*, 23 April 2013.
41   Gastón Gordillo, 'Opaque Zones of Empire', *Space and Politics*, 25 June 2013, available at spaceandpolitics.blogspot.co.uk.

'If I had to sum up current thinking on precision missiles and saturation weaponry', Former US Under-Secretary of Defense W. J. Perry, boasted in the late 1980s, 'I'd put it like this: once you can see the target, you can destroy it.'[42] For attack helicopter crews, such a logic works to render the killing process a video game–like experience. During his deployment as the weapons officer in one of the UK's Apache attack helicopters in 2013, Prince Harry said his job was a 'joy'. This, he continued, was 'because I'm one of those people who loves playing PlayStation and Xbox, so with my thumbs I like to think I'm probably quite useful'. Zabiullah Mujahid, a Taliban spokesman, responded by saying, 'I don't believe that he participated in the fighting. Maybe he has seen the Mujahideen in a movie, but that's it.'[43]

Second, this situation is even more lethal because today's military ideologies completely fetishise the linking of sensing and killing with ever-faster speed. In armed helicopters, as in police helicopters, this involves integrating the feed from sensors directly into the helmet goggles of the pilots used to target and fire weaponry.

Such integration means that the pilot merely has to look at the 'target' to ensure that the weapons are sighted on it – ready for the kill. Cultural theorists Ryan Bishop and John Phillips emphasise that such a progressive blurring of seeing and killing centres on the 'desire to make target perception and target striking virtually the same act'.[44]

Finally, the lethal rotorcraft is the source of a deeply aestheticised and sexualised adulation by those who make it and use it. Although far from new – as the famous 'Ride of the Valkyries' scene in Francis Ford Coppola's 1979 film *Apocalypse Now* will demonstrate – these seductive aesthetics work to further the normalisation of lethal helicopters while obscuring the dead civilians left lying on the ground in their wake.

One recent advert for the Bell Super Cobra attack helicopter, for example, claims a sublime beauty, as well as a lethal power and omniscient gaze, for the machine's frontal view. The image in the advert

---

42   Cited in Paul Virilio, *War and Cinema: The Logistics of Perception*, London: Verso, 2009, p. 4.

43   Jon Boone, 'Taliban Retaliate after Prince Harry Compares Fighting to a Video Game', *Guardian*, 22 January 2013.

44   Bishop and Phillips, *Modernist Avant-Garde Aesthetics*, p. 52.

is labelled 'goodbye', and the strapline reads: 'We made it beautiful. Because it's the last thing some people will ever see.'[45] The helicopter, Bishop and Phillips write, thus 'itself addresses its victims, who indeed may feel for a moment – who would know? – the sadness of its might or the richness of its anger.'[46]

These three factors have worked with lethal inevitability in recent helicopter-based counterinsurgency operations in Iraq and Afghanistan. The obsession with speedy targeting, combined with the imprecise perception and gun-ho militarism of operators, have had lethal consequences for a large number of civilians. And, as with drone attacks, startlingly, the digital footage of the killings – along with recordings of pilots' real-time commentaries – can be replayed repeatedly on YouTube and other video sharing websites.

There are many examples here of such 'YouTube wars'. Some show the brutality in daytime, when the human figures are recognisable. Night-time operations offer the ghostly rendition of killing by infrared. Many are obviously war crimes preserved to be replayed, ad infinitum, via the Internet. As media theorist Kari Andén-Papadopoulos stresses, now that footage from the actual sensors of weapons systems is available for global consumption, 'the representation of war, becomes one with the waging of war itself.'[47]

Often the excited commentary of the operators and pilots displays both humorous and sexual pleasure in the killing. Again, a highly aestheticised and sexualised process reveals itself – an experience which overlaps disturbingly with video game culture. Conflict researchers Chris Cole and colleagues call this the 'PlayStation mentality'.[48]

'See that car, I lit that fucker up! He got 30 rounds in that bitch!' gloats one US Apache weapons operator after two cars drive into the helicopter's line of cannon fire and their passengers scatter to be gunned down in turn. 'Oooh, my bitch is fucking done, dude!'

---

45 This discussion, and the advert, draw from Bishop and Phillips, *Modernist Avant-Garde Aesthetics*, p. 52.

46 Ibid.

47 Kari Andén-Papadopoulos, 'US Soldiers Imaging the Iraq War on YouTube', *Popular Communication* 7:1, 2009, pp. 17–27.

48 Chris Cole, Mary Dobbing and Amy Hailwood, *Convenient Killing: Armed Drones and the 'PlayStation' Mentality*, Fellowship of Reconciliation, 2010, available at dronewarsuk.files.wordpress.com.

Advert for a US Bell Super Cobra attack helicopter.

screams another. 'Dude, *look* at it! We fucked those people all to shit down there!'[49]

Although there are many examples, the 2010 release via WikiLeaks of the so-called 'Collateral Murder' video – captured in 2007 – exposes these logics with the most brutal clarity. This captured the digital video sensed by the helicopter, and beamed direct to the pilot and gunner's helmet-sights, of an US Apache helicopter as it gunned down two Reuters journalists and ten colleagues in Baghdad.

'Look at those dead bastards', one pilot says, after the first shells explode and the bodies lie dismembered on the ground.

'*Nice!*' the other enthuses.

The pilots then urge one of the wounded men to pick up a 'weapon' – actually his TV camera – so that they can fire again and finish the job. 'All you gotta do is pick up a weapon', a pilot says.[50] Minutes later, as a van driver attempts to come to the aid of the first victims, he is attacked, too: several more people die and two children within the vehicle are injured. When they become visible one of the crew members remarks: 'Well, it's their fault for bringing their kids into a battle.'

And yet, despite their awesome firepower and surveillance capabilities, (para)military helicopters remain inherently fragile. When weapons are brought against them, helicopters – especially those

49   Cited in Andén-Papadopoulos, 'US Soldiers Imaging the Iraq War'.
50   Elisabeth Bumiller, 'Video Shows US Killing of Reuters Employees', *New York Times,* 5 April 2010. See collateralmurder.com.

not designed as attack helicopters – remain spectacularly vulnerable. 'The helicopter is an unlikely war tool', media theorist Tim Blackmore writes. 'Delicately structured with an almost papery aluminium skin [...], the aircraft body veined by exposed fuel lines and connector rods', the helicopter is 'chaos reified, an object at war with itself.'[51]

As the notorious 'Black Hawk Down' events in Mogadishu in 1993 – and the many downings of military helicopters in Iraq and Afghanistan – demonstrate, helicopters can be easily shot down with rudimentary weapons. Highly armed drug gangs have even been known to shoot down paramilitary helicopters during their incursions into favelas. (The Rio police are now acquiring fully armoured attack helicopters in response.) 'Those who use the helicopter understand its true delicacy', continues Blackmore. Despite the occasional addition of armour, 'the helicopter is not, after all, a flying tank; inside, the human body is vulnerable to all kinds of damage.'[52]

(Para)military helicopter operations, meanwhile, also struggle to 'hold' the territory below. 'Because their presence is so fleeting, the police can only cling on to territory for a time.'[53] During the Vietnam War and in Brazil's favelas, permanent incursions by ground forces have been necessary to permanently reshape the political geographies of conflict. Some also worry that, like drone and submarine use, it's only a matter of time before nonstate insurgencies and drug gangs gain their own helicopters.

A final problem is the chronic unreliability of these unwieldy rotor-craft. Without wings, engine failure in helicopters is an exercise in the immediate and unexpected power of gravity. As with the police helicopter suffering from double engine failure that killed ten people as it crashed into a Glasgow bar in December 2013, the machine plummets to the earth like a stone. The distance to the ground is usually too limited for pilots to take evasive action to avoid an almost infinite range of obstacles and barriers to crash into.

It should be no surprise, then, that in the decades since the Pan Am crash in New York 1977, fatal crashes have remained a serious

---

51   Tim Blackmore, 'Rotor Hearts: The Helicopter as Postmodern War's Pacemaker', *Public Culture*, 15:1, 2003, p. 98, available at publicculture.org.

52   Blackmore, 'Rotor Hearts', p. 98.

53   Adey, 'Vertical Security in the Megacity'.

problem in all helicopter operations, even when helicopters are mobilised for the virtuous roles of rescue and life saving. In 2008 – an admittedly exceptional year – twelve air ambulances crashed in the US alone, killing twenty-nine crew and patients.[54] Civilian helicopters crash, on average, forty-three times more often than winged aircraft per 100,000 hours of flying time.[55]

54   Stephen Pope, 'Air Ambulance Safety: A Closer Look', *FlyingMag.Com*, 26 July 2013, available at flyingmag.com.

55   At 7.5 per 100,000 hours versus 0.175 per 100,000 flying hours. See HelicopterLawyers.Com, 'What Causes Helicopter Accidents?', n.d., available at helicopterlawyers.com.

5.

Favela: Tenuous City

At least one in every sixth human – over a billion people in all – lives in a self-built shanty, favela or informal settlement (often pejoratively labelled a 'slum'). In sub-Saharan Africa, this proportion rises to 62 per cent (200 million people in all); in Southern Asia it is 35 per cent (another 190 million); in East Asia, 28 per cent (a further 200 million); and in Latin America and the Caribbean there are a further 125 million slum dwellers (24 per cent of the population).[1] Over 25 million people move into informal settlements every year.

Informal settlements are individual and collective claims to space in the city necessarily mobilised by the poor and marginalised. By definition, such people tend to claim vulnerable or tenuous urban locations yet to be colonised through formal urban construction. They thus trade a small claim of space and some security of tenure against often extreme vulnerability to various risks and hazards. Very often, especially in mountainous cities, this means a rush up the most precipitous – and potentially lethal – slopes. These might be the slopes of mountains and ravines, of waste and chemical dumps, or of volcanoes, geological faults, infrastructural cuttings, coastal ravines, mining spoil heaps, landfill sites or river and canal banks.[2]

Across many cities in Africa, Asia and Latin America, especially, informal cities have long colonised the most treacherous and vertiginous slopes – spaces deemed too dangerous or unstable

---

1   Data are from United Nations, *Millennium Goals Report*, New York: United Nations, 2013.

2   Indeed, the very origins of the word 'favela' in Brazilian Portuguese expose the deep connections between such housing and extremely precipitous slopes. The first such community in Rio, built in the Morro da Providência district of the city in the 1880s, was named by the settlers after a thorny hill-loving plant in Northeast Brazil.

for mainstream real estate development or requiring protection to preserve water supplies, forests or natural habitats. In many contemporary US and European cities, affluence can increase with elevation as the wealthy colonise hilltops for better views and air quality, but historically hills have often been colonised by the urban poor because of the extreme difficulties in using prevailing means of transport – walking and horses – to access the wider city from such sites.[3]

The incremental accretion of dense, self-constructed settlements up vertiginous slopes, in the absence of formal planning, engineering or building controls, is an extremely perilous business. Floods and landslides are deadly problems accentuated both by the impervious nature of concrete and the increasingly violent rainstorms, flash floods and storm surges caused by global climate change and rises in sea levels.

With informal cities struggling to house growing populations, self-built structures often themselves rise skywards, increasing their vulnerability to collapse through flooding, seismic shocks, landslides or just the uneven battle between gravity and poor building quality. In Quito, Ecuador, for example, dwellings often use the roof slabs of lower buildings as the foundation for new construction. In Rio, meanwhile, MIT Professor Janice Perlman notes what she calls a 'volcanic upward thrust of vertical expansion' as the city's burgeoning favelas have become much more dense over the last few decades. This has happened, she stresses, in the context of a 'total freedom from zoning regulations or construction codes.'[4] (As shanty communities become 'regularised', such codes are introduced.)

Vertical Favelas, Urbanised Hazards

In our world so-called 'natural' hazards are anything but natural.[5] Rather, they are hazards that are shaped and exaggerated by

---

3 See William Meyer, 'The Poor on the Hilltops? The Vertical Fringe of a Late Nineteenth-Century American City', *Annals of the Association of American Geographers* 95:4, 2005, pp. 773–88.

4 Janice Perlman, *Favela: Four Decades of Living on the Edge in Rio de Janeiro*, Oxford: Oxford University Press, 2010, p. 28.

5 See Gregory Squires and Chester Hartman, eds, *There Is No Such Thing as a Natural Disaster: Race, Class, and Hurricane Katrina*, New York: Taylor & Francis, 2006.

Catastrophic floods and landsides on Rio's slopes, January 2011

anthropogenic changes in climate, oceans, landscapes and biospheres which, in turn, impact on manufactured, urban environments, and the engineered infrastructures that sustain and protect them.

Invariably, such manufactured environments – as demonstrated when Hurricane Katrina flooded central New Orleans in 2005 – are constructed in ways that systematically expose the urban poor to the most perilous risks. The combination of intensifying storms, landslides and flood risks caused by climate change and slums clinging to perilous slopes is a powerful example of such a political ecology of highly politicised vulnerability. 'Shanties are most likely to be located in marginal or hazardous geographical areas such as flood plains, within 10m of sea level or on unstable terrains and hillsides prone to landslides.'[6]

In Bogotá, for example, the intensification of vertical slums on perilous mountainsides now means that 60 per cent of the city's

---

6   Abbas Norozi and Sebastian Messer, 'Feral City: A Dystopia', Built and Natural Environment Research Paper, *Architecture* 5:1, 2012, p. 14.

population – over 4 million people – live on steep slopes subject to landslides.[7] Mike Davis notes that many of Brazil's most famous favelas, especially in Rio, are pushed up to the most perilous granite mountaintops long denuded of protective vegetation.[8]

Rio, in fact, condenses multiple politics of risk and verticality since different parts of the population live very different vertiginous lives cheek by jowl. Simulations of major future flooding and storm events conclude that the vulnerable poorer communities of Rio live in favelas near waterways and on perilous slopes, while the relatively wealthy tend to live in modern, high-rise apartment towers away from the riskiest terrain.[9] To complicate this pattern further, as we shall see, some mountainside shanty communities are now being gentrified, bringing the middle-class into areas where they previously feared to tread.

Such trends reach their apogee in Caracas, Venezuela – the global capital of the vertical favela in more ways than one. Here, fully two-thirds of the city's 5.2 million people live in favelas on denuded, unstable and seismically active hillsides on the fringes of the city. Lethal floods and landslides are common in such verticalised shanty settlements. In the most dramatic, in mid December 1999, a year's worth of rain fell over several days in and around Caracas, killing more than 32,000 people and leaving 140,000 homeless. More prosaic and highly lethal favela collapses are almost routine: 200 people died in landslides in Rio's favelas in February 1988. And in Niteroi in Rio in 2010, more than 200 people died when a slum built on the slope of a garbage heap collapsed after a storm.

In the absence of major public engineering works to mitigate the risks of vertical slum living on perilous slopes, the challenge is to fund and sustain pro-poor adaptations and upgrades in building quality, infrastructure, flood protection, and urban design – as well as other key improvements such as potable water supplies, transportation,

---

7   Ebru Gencer, *The Interplay between Urban Development, Vulnerability, and Risk Management*, Berlin: Springer, 2013.

8   Mike Davis, 'Slum Ecology', *Orion Magazine*, March 2006, available at orionmagazine.org.

9   Alex De Sherbinin, Andrew Schiller and Alex Pulsipher, 'The Vulnerability of Global Cities to Climate Hazards', *Environment and Urbanization* 19:1, 2007, pp. 39–64.

education, health services, public security, waste disposal and proper sewerage.

The challenge, though, as we shall see, is to organise such so-called 'upgrade' programmes in ways that avoid the very real risks that shanty settlements will simply become exclusionary sites of gentrification. Such processes tend to force out the very people who first made the tenuous claim on the right to the city, as real estate speculators move in to commodify the spectacular views and newly improved accessibility and infrastructure.

Vertical Appropriation

In Caracas a further verticality of improvised living has occurred in the downtown area, demonstrating other links between vertical high-rise structures and informal occupation. In the central finance district the seventh highest building in Latin America – the forty-five-storey Torre de David, formerly the Centro Financiero Confinanzas – emerged between 2007 and 2014 as an unexpected icon of the global economic crisis and the creative dynamics of informal city life. An icon of the financialisation and structural adjustment stemming from Venezuela's oil boom in the 1980s, the building was left unfinished after the death of its developer.

In 2007 the tower was colonised by 750 families, amounting to a more or less stable community of around 3,000 people.[10] It was widely labelled as the ultimate 'vertical slum', or, less pejoratively, an 'informal vertical community'.[11] The modernist glass-faced side of the tower was no longer a domineering glass cliff: missing panels and satellite dishes hinted at the remarkable improvisations under way within. Spaces inside were reconstructed as landscapes of roughly built brick houses. Rather than the intended corporate offices, hotel, swimming pool, luxury apartments and helipad, instead hair salons, a football pitch, a basketball court, churches, day-care centres, shops, workshops, barbers and even a few bodegas dotted the vertical structure.

10   In the 1980s, a parallel occupation, this time of drug gangs, pimps and prostitutes, occurred in the fifty-five storey Ponte tower in Johannesburg before it was returned to its original use as luxury apartments after 2001.

11   Alfredo Brillembourg, *Torre David*, Berlin: Lars Müller, 2012.

The appropriation of the tower seems like a second episode of J. G. Ballard's famous dystopian sci-fi novel *High Rise*, architect Sepideh Karami suggests. This time, however, the colonisation of the semi-ruined tower 'is a model of survival in a brutally segregated city' – an idea 'of how collective life can emerge out of a desire to access relatively safe and proper housing' in Caracas.[12]

Sadly, Torre David's residents were eventually evicted in July 2014 and relocated to remote margins of Caracas. The tower is now being gentrified as an elite housing tower. While they existed, however, the community governance systems of the Torre David's colonisers worked more or less effectively. Collective regulation of security was largely successful. An organic urban community blurred the rigid and hierarchical architectural partitions of the modernist tower, creating a complex vertical social geography which, though ridden with conflicts, was also equipped with some of the means of reconciling them.

As well as improvised power, water and sewerage systems, pathways were burrowed through walls to facilitate movement. In the absence of functioning elevators, a vertical transport service was provided by young men who drove motorbikes up the first ten floors of parking garages. 'We might say that the language used on the inside is much more complex than we first thought and not because it is spectacular, but because it is organic', wrote artists Ángela Bonadies and Juan José Olavarría, who worked on Torre David:

> Everyone wants to live in the best possible conditions. When you are inside, you're not in the tower, you are in shared corridors, on the stairs or in a person or a family's home. The tower disappears when you are on the inside and it becomes a compendium of atomized languages that live together within the overall layout.[13]

Given the global financial crisis's legacy of modern ruins around the world and the severe housing shortages faced by virtually all cities, architect Alfredo Brillembourg and colleagues wondered, before the

---

12   Sepideh Karami, 'De/ascending: Torre David, the Second Episode of Ballard's High-Rise', *Lo-Res* 1, 2015, p. 82.

13   Ángela Bonadies and Juan José Olavarría, 'La Torre de David', *El Nacional*, 14 April 2012.

evictions, whether Torre David, far from being a toxic and criminal threat to the body politic – as argued by Venezuela's elites – might actually be a model of urban improvisation that should be copied around the world.[14]

With states doing so little to address the desperate need for social housing, Torre David, and other examples like it, demonstrate the power of collective appropriation of the vertical and elitist spaces that have long been erected to symbolise the 'globalness' of cities. Amid the banking and corporate head offices of central Caracas, Torre David demonstrated the importance of the improvised takeover of vertical spaces just as powerfully as the precarious favelas on the hillsides a few kilometres away on the city's periphery.

'Favela Chic' and Vertical 'Pacification'

The most fascinating emerging example of the tensions and contradictions between the upgrading of vertically stacked favelas in Latin America in recent years has been the translation of the cable car, that icon of ski and mountain tourism, into an everyday form of urban mobility for vertically structured favelas. Metro cables have already been installed to link verticalised favelas to wider cities in Medellín, Colombia; Caracas, Venezuela; and the Alemão favelas in Rio. They are one element within the wider current trend for selective, design-based interventions to improve favelas – what urban planner Adriana Navarro-Sertich has called 'urban acupuncture'. This she defines as 'making design a central component in the approach and aiming to minimise displacement while improving conditions in the area.'[15]

Favela cable car systems are justified by state policy makers as a radical means to overcome the extreme inaccessibility and peripheral positioning of vertical favelas, lacing the areas into the wider city. The new cable cars tie in well with city leaders' propensity to fund dramatic and highly visible infrastructure and are central to a radical aesthetic turn which works to undermine the deep stigma faced by favelas. Their very rarity, moreover, makes it easy to fetishise cable

---

14   Brillembourg, *Torre David*.
15   Adriana Navarro-Sertich, 'Favela Chic: A Photo Essay', *Berkeley Planning Journal* 24, 2011.

The new cable car system over Rio's Alemão favela

car projects, casting them as symbolic and messianic solutions to the needs of very poor communities (when such places often remain without mains water, piped sewerage or decent health and education services).[16]

The aestheticisation of favelas often has troubling overtones. It often heralds a form of 'favela chic' which helps to open up newly 'pacified' favelas to the gaze, and acquisitive speculation, of the outside world. Too often, it is linked to a wider process of aggressive, militarised 'pacification' which, while reducing drug and gang crime, works to signal the formal 'civilising' of often demonised favelas.

In the process, favelas – or at least those in strategic and desirable locations adjacent to richer, tourist zones of the city – are opened up as prime real estate markets and to a whole suite of new 'legal' market laws. Often this shift signals spirals of eviction, gentrification, the imposition of dramatic increases in rents and service charges, and the

---

16   It should be noted that many favela communities are actually also positive about the need for favela cable systems to have positive symbolic as well as material impacts on their communities. For a review of the case in Cazucá, Colombia, for example, see Rivadulla Álvarez, María José and Diana Bocarejo, 'Beautifying the Slum: Cable Car Fetishism in Cazucá, Colombia', *International Journal of Urban and Regional Research* 38:6, 2014, pp. 2025–41.

in-migration of professionals increasingly priced out of the adjacent 'formal' city.

Such risks have been especially prominent in the favelas adjacent to the tourist city within Rio's build-up to host both the 2014 World Cup and the 2016 Olympics. It is these favelas that have been the main focus of the thirty-three special pacification policing units set up so far in Rio.

Drawn by the stunning aerial views, low costs and its now booming restaurant scene, the favela of Babilonia, with views over the Copacabana beach and the ocean, has been dramatically transformed by speculative capital. 'It's a hot property market', noted Nelio Pereira da Silva, a local real estate agent, in 2013, a year before the World Cup. Speculators from Germany, the US, France and Italy were heavily involved. Houses that in 2006 went for $25,000 in 2013 were selling for $75,000.[17]

As part of Brazil's tourism boom, Brazilian scholar Alvaro Jarrin meanwhile predicted that 'favelas that have the nicest views of the city, particularly those located in close proximity to wealthy neighborhoods, will likely see family homes being replaced by hostels, as tourism in the favelas becomes a popular option for those who seek a more "authentic" Brazilian experience.'[18]

Elsewhere in Rio, urban tourism companies now sell 'urban adventure' tours where tourists travel above the favelas by cable car gazing voyeuristically at the labyrinthine landscapes below. Alcebíades Fonseca of Rio's Engineers' Club has noted that, far from being a main form of transport for favela residents, some cable systems, such as the one in Alemão, are mostly used by tourists. The *Guardian*'s feature on Rio's booming favela tourism business in the run-up to the World Cup and the Olympics warns that, though the favelas will leave Western tourists 'wide-eyed', they 'should be aware that these are tours of places where very poor people live – which some might find difficult'.[19]

17   Lourdes Garcia-Navarro, 'Once Unsafe, Rio's Shantytowns See Rapid Gentrification', National Public Radio, 6 June 2013, available at npr.org.

18   Alvaro Jarrin, 'The "Pacification" of Rio's Favelas', *Ethnolust*, 22 December 2011, available at ethnolust.wordpress.com.

19   Dom Phillips, 'Favela Tourism in Rio de Janeiro', *Guardian*, 4 November 2013.

Protestors complain about the housing demolitions to build the systems, the appropriateness of such expensive investments in places with such poor-quality sanitation, power, waste, health and education services, and, above all, the systems' intended users. The lurking suspicion is that a key motivation for the cable car system is to bring global prestige to elite politicians. 'If only the money would have been spent just fitting drains and sewerage into the old favela'. Leona Deckelbaum, an activist challenging in one cable-car development in Manguinhos, said, in 2014. 'But then, sewers do not look good at world urbanisation conferences – not like cable cars!'[20]

A further criticism is that the new cable car systems are primarily oriented towards commodifying the startling views that they create for wealthy residents and tourists while at the same time stealthily developing a new, premium-level infrastructure for the rebranded and re-engineered 'global' city of Rio. 'If you really want to experience the life and energy of our people', Daiene Mendes, a resident of the Alemão favela says of the streams of tourists who gawk on her community from the cable car, 'you have to walk through the community, not just stare down from above.'[21] (Far from being a simple, top-down process, many favela communities are responding to their new aerial audience with a proliferation of roof-top art projects.)

'Cable car for whom?' is the protestors' main slogan.[22] Anthropologist Lana Schissel notes that the new cable car system for the Porto Maravilha, as well as leading to the demolition of 800 homes 'will facilitate movement to places of interest like the Cruzeiro [a multisport club for affluent groups] at the top of the community with a specular 360° view of Rio.' Other proposed lines, she notes, will connect to the cruise terminal, Museum of Tomorrow, and the Samba City, an upmarket entertainment venue.[23]

---

20   Quoted in Simon Jenkins, 'Vision of the Future or Criminal Eyesore: What Should Rio Do With Its Favelas?', *Guardian*, 30 April 2014.

21   Daiene Mendes, 'Rio Olympics: View from the Favelas – "Hopes of Pacification Are Shattered"', *Guardian*, 14 December 2015.

22   See Malte Steinbrink, 'Festifavelisation: Mega-events, Slums and Strategic City-Staging – The Example of Rio de Janeiro', *Die Erde* 144:2, 2013, pp. 129–45.

23   Lana Schissel, *Rio 2016: Mega-Event Urban Planning Politics and Anti-Olympics Protest*, Saarbrücken, Germany: Lambert Academic Publishing, 2013.

Discussing his recent trip on a gleaming new Austrian-made Doppelmayr cable car – this time freshly installed on the line up to Rio's Sugarloaf Mountain, ready for the imminent influx of World Cup and Olympics tourists – Canadian professor Thomas Heise notes the classic process of a depoliticised 'Othering' though the distant, vertical gaze. 'Laid out before the eye, the shantytowns – 950 in Rio alone', he writes, provide the 'glamorous city's darker doppelgänger that Doppelmayr makes visible from above, as one rides on the back of a mechanical Christ the Redeemer gracefully sailing on an airstream out to the ocean.'[24]

What is striking is that this verticalised voyeurism forms a close parallel to the widespread use of military helicopters by the often violent and unregulated SWAT teams whose task is to 'pacify' Rio's favelas in the run-up to forthcoming sporting mega-events. Here the favela becomes a war zone within domestic territory as the notorious *policia militaria* use helicopters to drop into selected favelas periodically in violent pacification raids to carry out widespread arrests for 'vagrancy'.[25]

The difference now is that, rather than retreating after the operations, paramilitary 'Pacifying Police Units' (UPPs) remain permanently in the favelas. The policy enforces a permanent pacification symbolised by the snake-like extension of the cable cars into areas where police previously did not venture, as well as the demolition of favelas to make way for sports facilities and tourist infrastructure. The largest UPP police stations are notably positioned on the tops of the hills next to important cable car stations.

Such permanent presence has undoubtedly heralded a partial retreat by drug cartels and gangs. But it has also often led to violent abuses of power normally associated with full-scale military counter-insurgency operations: raids, arrests, curfews, ID checks, harassment, summary evictions and disappearances.

---

24   Thomas Heise, 'From Slumdogs to Millionaires: How Poverty Tourism Is Changing What It Means to Be Poor', *Berfrois*, 19 August 2013, available at berfrois.com. See also Matthew Gandy's critique of Rem Koolhaas's helicopter-based research of Lagos in Gandy, 'Learning from Lagos', *New Left Review* 2:33, May/June 2005, p. 42.

25   Loïc Wacquant, 'The Militarization of Urban Marginality: Lessons from the Brazilian Metropolis', *International Political Sociology* 2, 2008, p. 66.

In a city where around 10,000 citizens have been killed or 'disappeared' by the various forms of police and state militaries in recent years,[26] many favela residents, though welcoming the benefits of the retreat of the drug gangs, complain that by its nature 'pacification' has merely implanted one murderous force into the everyday environment – the often highly corrupt police – in place of another. 'We were used to having 40 heavily armed criminals standing at the entrance of Rocinha', local activist José Martins said. 'But now the clandestine weapons have been switched to official ones'.[27] To complicate this picture further, in many cases, corruption means that the line separating the state police and the drug gangs is a very thin one.

Favela Futures? Megastructural Fantasies

The instinct to suggest the wholesale re-engineering of entire favela complexes through vertically structured mega-design projects – ostensibly as a solution to problems of density and population growth – also operates in the imaginative realm. Here, influenced perhaps by the spectacular improvisations of Torre David in Caracas, the favela skyscraper has become a common feature of the imaginative rendering of future urbanism, especially by architects. The French architect Léopold Lambert, for example, has speculated that the densification of favelas within ever-growing cities will inevitably lead to the emergence of informally constructed vertical favelas. Pointedly, the ways in which such structures might be realistically and safely engineered, financed, built, operated or inhabited is not discussed. How on earth would vertical transportation work in such structures?

Meanwhile, New York architects Reese Campbell and Demetrios Comodromos imagine rebuilding Cairo with a series of vertical 'favela skyscrapers', linked by skybridges, as the solution to the challenges of increasing density in a city deemed to lack a history of tall living structures.[28] In this case, the towers are ostensibly designed both to

26   Lourdes Garcia-Navarro and Melissa Block, 'A Cable Car Ride Gives Insight into Rio's "Pacified" Favelas', National Public Radio, 18 September 2013.

27   Rio activist José Martins, quoted in Paula Dalbert, 'Brazil Activists Question Favela Policing', Al Jazeera, 10 August 2013.

28   Reese Campbell and Demetrios Comodromos, 'Urban Morphology + The

Reese Campbell and Demetrios Comodromos's designs for informal Cairo skyscrapers

mimic the horizontal social life of medieval neighbourhoods in the city and to reproduce some of the flexibility that is so central to shanty architecture.

Once again, though, the fetish for mere form takes precedent in such imaginings over any concept of how such structures might be realistically built and safely maintained by resident populations whose very reason for building adaptable shanty cities is an absence of power and capital.

Social Vernacular: A Speculative Skyscraper for Islamic Medieval Cairo', *Journal of Architectural Education* 63:1, October 2009, pp. 6–13.

6.

Elevator/Lift: Going Up

Looming high above the Japanese city of Fuchu, a dense suburb twenty kilometres to the west of central Tokyo, a 213-metre-high building dominates the low suburban skyline. Seemingly too thin to be of any commercial use, the G1 Tower sits, surrounded by a glade of trees, rather incongruously at the heart of a huge research campus owned by the giant Hitachi Corporation. Opened in 2010, the tower does not whisk affluent urbanites above the smog, noise and traffic. Nor is it some material embodiment of hubris and ego in the material 'race' upward that is so evident in the global spread of super-tall skyscrapers. It is, rather, a vertical test track: the world's highest elevator research tower, a living testament to the central role of Japanese engineers in, as anthropologist Ryan Sayre so pithily puts it, 'technologically reworking the innards of "up".[1]

Key to developing the high-capacity and high-speed elevators now demanded by the world's vertically sprawling cities, the tower – the world's tallest lift research structure – is a series of lift shafts unadorned with surrounding residential or commercial space. The G1 Tower is thus a perfect monument to the skyward reach of the world's cities and, more particularly, to the crucial but often ignored roles of new vertical transportation technologies in facilitating this reach. Hitachi are using the $61 million tower to design and develop a new generation of elevators that will be like the bullet train of the urban skies: super-fast, high-capacity and high-tech elevators that will exceed one kilometre a minute in speed.

Hitachi, like other big elevator manufacturers, are using the tower to design a whole new array of high-tech elevator technologies.

---

1 Ryan Sayre, 'The Colonization of the "Up": Building up and to the Light in Postwar Japan', *Architectonic Tokyo*, 2011, available at architectonictokyo.com.

The world's tallest elevator research and testing facility: Hitachi's 213-metre G1 Tower in Fuchu, Tokyo

There are new designs, power sources and materials technologies to construct lighter, smaller lift shafts and elevator cars. There are double-decker lift cars (in effect, elevators stacked one on top of the other). There are 'destination dispatch' elevators that assess the preferred destinations of potential riders in advance of their entering the elevator and use algorithms to assign them to specific cars to reduce overall movement. There are even pressurisation systems that automatically compensate riders' ears for the changes of air pressure during ascent and descent.

The first of these is especially important as 'super-tall' skyscrapers of over 100 storeys proliferate across the world because elevator shafts consume a higher proportion of overall space as the floor-plate of buildings shrinks in size as they reach greater heights (from 7 per cent to 20 per cent as towers rise from 70 to 100 storeys, for example).[2] The weight of steel ropes and lifting systems, meanwhile, has so far limited vertical ascents to around 500 metres in one go. Elevators are thus now thus 'the bottleneck of the super high-rise building', as

---

2   See Jeannot Simmen, 'Elevation: A Cultural History of the Elevator', in Wolfgang Christ, ed., *Access for All: Approaches to the Built Environment*, Basel: Birkhauser, 2009, pp. 15–30.

Johannes de Jong, of the KONE elevator company, pointed out to *Business Week* in 2013.[3]

Echoing the long but often overlooked co-evolution of skyscraper and mine elevators or 'cages', KONE's 350-metre research elevators, built to research the same challenges as Hitachi's tower, are placed in a disused limestone mine in the Helsinki suburb of Lohja. Capturing this coevolution perfectly, the deep subterranean shaft is called the 'High Rise Laboratory'. KONE executives are especially hopeful that their new carbon-fibre rope technology – which they claim is the 'holy grail' in skyscraper engineering – will allow elevators to safely ascend 1,000 metres in one go (double the current limit). This would allow the widespread construction of skyscrapers way beyond the current target height of 1 km. In the longer term, engineers are planning electro-magnetically powered elevators that will operate along tracks like vertical MagLev (magnetic levitation) trains. Such systems, being pioneered by ThyssenKrupp AG, will also allow elevators to move sideways as well as vertically.

'Today most engineers will tell you', futurist Len Rosen, writes, 'that the limit of vertical height in buildings has more to do with the steel cable in elevator shafts than any other factor.'[4] *Construction Week* magazine calculate that the steel ropes for a 400 m elevator weigh 41,116 pounds; carbon-fibre ropes for the same system weigh only 2,500 lbs.[5]

Despite such remarkable developments, startlingly, beyond a few technical articles in the trade press, 'vertical transportation' industry structures like the G1 Tower and the elevators they help shape remain almost invisible within social science debates about cities and urbanism.[6] Similarly, beyond its appearance within certain genres of film, or during periods when elevators were carefully designed as ornamental spaces in their own right, elevator urbanism has received little

---

3   Quoted in Tim Catts, 'Otis Elevator Vies for the Ultratall Skyscraper Market', *Business Week*, 31 January 2013, available at businessweek.com.

4   Len Rosen, 'Materials Science Update: New Discovery May Lead to Mile-High Buildings', *21st Century Science*, 21 June 2013, available at 21stcentech.com.

5   Nick Ames, 'KONE Wins Elevator Pitch for World's Tallest Tower', *Construction Week Online*, 5 June 2014, available at constructionweekonline.com.

6   See George Strakosch and Robert Caporale, *The Vertical Transportation Handbook*, London: Wiley, 2010.

of the wider poetic celebration of the mobilities underpinning urban life that have centred on airplanes, automobiles, subways or railroads. 'While anthems have been written to jet travel, locomotives, and the lure of the open road, the poetry of vertical transportation is scant.'[7] Entire libraries can be filled with volumes exploring the cultures, politics and geographies of the largely horizontal mobilities and transportation infrastructures that are intrinsic to urban modernity – highways, railways, subways, buses, cars, cycling and so on. By contrast, the geographies and politics of vertical transportation within and between the buildings of vertically organised cityscapes have been largely ignored by social scientists and humanities scholars.

Not surprisingly, this neglect is being overcome first in the densest and most verticalised cities, starting with Hong Kong. 'To think of Hong Kong's "public transport" only in terms of conventional vehicles', urban designers Barrie Shelton and colleagues argue, 'is too limiting and should rightly be extended to include '"public movement infrastructure services" like lifts and elevators, escalators, moving walkways and so on.'[8]

Despite such calls, the social science and urban literatures on lifts, elevators and vertical people movers remains both minuscule and esoteric.[9] It is paradoxical, indeed, that the world's geographers and urbanists gather in their thousands every year in a major corporate skyscraper hotel in a US city for the main American geography conference. During this meeting they perform complex vertical movements using elevators to move between multiple sessions discussing 'mobilities', 'time-space compression', 'logistical urbanism', 'transport geography' and so on. Completely absent from these discussions, however, is their total reliance on the ubiquitous and crucial power of the elevator.

Indeed, geographers face particular difficulties coming to terms with a mode of transport that moves entirely on the vertical axis. One

---

7 Nick Paumgarten, 'Up and Then Down: The Lives of Elevators', *New Yorker*, 21 April 2008.

8 Barrie Shelton, Justyna Karakiewicz and Thomas Kvan. *The Making of Hong Kong: From Vertical to Volumetric*, London: Routledge, 2013, p. 6.

9 See Alisa Goetz, ed., *Up, Down, Across: Elevators, Escalators, and Moving Sidewalks*, Washington, DC: National Building Museum, 2003.

of the discipline's main frameworks for mapping how people move in both time and geographic space, a perspective called 'time geography', is completely unable even to represent such movement. In the 3D maps used in time geography, a vertical line actually means a person is standing still or at rest.[10]

Elevator Histories

The elevator has a history of at least 2,000 years: Rome's Colosseum had a system of twelve winch-powered elevators operated by slaves to lift wild animals and gladiators straight into the bloody action of the arena. Without a means of drawing power greater than that available from human or animal muscle, however, such systems were inevitably highly limited in their speed and reach. It was Elisha Otis's invention of a safe, automatically braking elevator in Yonkers, New York, in the 1850s that created a technology enabling the vertical movement of people as well as goods that has been central to the rapid colonisation of vertical space through urban growth.

Otis's innovation opened up the vertical frontier to architectural construction like no innovation in human history. Through facilitating rapid movement against the pull of gravity to ever more lofty heights, the elevator made it possible to rebuild cities along the startlingly vertical lines that had long obsessed writers, artists, futurists, film-makers, novelists and architects. The elevator – a 'veritable machine for making cities'[11] – as Ryan Sayre puts it, thus allowed 'up as a habitable territory ... to be made. Sometimes forcefully but always without precedent.'[12]

When combined with electric or hydraulic power and cable drum innovations adopted from the mining industry, safely braked or 'safety' elevators released cities from the millennia-old constraints created by the need for the human ascent of stairs. The overcoming of

10   See Alan Pred and Gunnar Törnqvist (eds), *Space and Time in Geography*, Lund: Lund University,1981.

11   Alanna Thain, 'Insecurity Cameras: Cinematic Elevators, Infidelity and the Crime of Time', *Intermédialités: Histoire et Théorie des Arts, des Lettres et des Techniques* 14, 2009, p. 51.

12   Sayre, 'Colonization of the "Up"'.

gravity for the movement upward of human inhabitants was able to match the overcoming of gravity through innovations in skyscraper construction and operation. Since its invention, the elevator, as Rem Koolhaas puts it, 'has been the great emancipator of all horizontal surfaces above the ground floor'.[13] By 1916, the Woolworth Building in Manhattan – the world's highest skyscraper at the time – boasted twenty-nine elevators that ascended at 3.5 metres per second to an altitude of 207 metres.[14]

Faster, bigger and more reliable elevators have been fundamental to the skyward shift in architecture and engineering ever since. In an overlooked process of acceleration or 'time–space compression' every bit as dramatic as that on roads, railways or airways, Hitachi's research elevators in the G1 Tower are now running at speeds 300 times faster than those in New York a hundred years ago.

The availability of elevators has been pivotal in changing the social geographies of stacked housing. As we shall see later in this chapter, living at higher levels without elevators is an exhausting logistical nightmare. In the stacked housing of pre-elevator societies, consequently, the top stories were often extremely unattractive and reserved for those who could afford little else. An absence of power, water and sanitation infrastructures compounded this vertical geography. In Victorian and Edwardian London, for example, as well as inhabiting airless basements, 'the poor lived in the attic, farthest from the street-level toilets and water supply; the rich occupied flats on ground and first floors, with higher ceilings, larger windows and fewer stairs to climb.'[15]

During the late nineteenth and early twentieth centuries, elevators also played less obvious roles in the iconic growth upwards of the skyscrapers of corporate America, especially in Chicago and New York. Social historian of technology Ithiel de Sola Pool stressed that the history of the skyscraper has, in fact, been inseparable from the history of both the elevator – which allowed the ingress and egress of

---

13   Rem Koolhaas, *Delirious New York: A Retroactive Manifesto for Manhattan*, New York: Monacelli Press, 1978, p. 82.

14   Simmen, 'Elevation: A Cultural History'.

15   Richard Dennis '"Babylonian Flats" in Victorian and Edwardian London', *London Journal* 33, 2008, p. 228.

required office workers – and of equally new, horizontally stretched networks of electronic communication (the telegraph and then telephones) – that allowed those people to attempt to exercise control at a distance over dispersed sites once there.[16] Without telephones to allow the central power of the modern metropolis to concentrate and pile high into the sky, so many lift shafts would have been necessary to carry the multitudes of messenger boys to the destination of the message – factories, warehouses, shipping centres and the like – that there would have been far too little office space left for the buildings to be commercially viable.

Elevator travel has long been a central component of cultural notions of urban modernity. This relationship is complex, however. In one sense, the experience of being crammed in a box with strangers moving rapidly upward, pulled by a suite of hidden motors and cables, can induce powerful, almost primeval anxieties. Indeed, psychologists recognise fear of elevators as a serious and widespread phobia. Such anxieties are rapidly compounded with unexpected delay and malfunctions – hence the introduction of 'elevator music' in 1928 to help compensate for the removal of elevator operators. The shift away from staffed elevators to automated ones added to the sense of desocialised vulnerability and was paralleled by a shift from ornate to utilitarian styles of design of elevator interiors.[17]

Elevators are, however, by far the safest form of powered transport: only sixty-one people lost their lives within them in the US while at work between 1992 and 2001.[18] However, the becalmed normality and hushed voices of habitual vertical ascent merge into the purest horror with the prospect of being trapped completely, the (extraordinarily rare) breakage of a cable or – rarer still – the collapse of the overall building.

---

16   Ithiel de Sola Pool, *The Social Impact of the Telephone,* Cambridge, MA: MIT Press, 1977.

17   Peter A. Hall, 'Designing Non-space: The Evolution of the Elevator Interior', in Goetz, ed., *Up, Down, Across,* pp. 59–78.

18   Sally Wilk, 'Elevator Safety: What to Do if Someone Is Trapped', *Elevator World,* September 2006, pp. 129–32.

Vertical (Post)Modernities

> This small room, so commonplace and so compressed … this elevator
> contains them all: space, time, cause, motion, magnitude, class.
> – Robert Coover, 'The Elevator', from *Pricksongs and Descants*

Elevator ascent is essentially modern. It has even been likened to a rather banal form of vertical teleportation via the ultimate socio-technical 'black box', in which a person merely walks into a room at one heights and out of it at another. 'I enter a small room,' philosopher Mark Kingwall observes. 'The doors close; when they open again, I am somewhere else. The taken-for-granted elevator is perhaps the closest thing we have to the *Star Trek* transporter device, and it is so ordinary we hardly even think to think about it.' 'Unlike ship, air or rail travel', Berlin curator Jeannot Simmen continues, elevator travel 'does not entail journeying from place to place and offers nothing to see. Instead of passage over time, the relevant parameter is the time wasted while ascending.'[19]

Human enclosure within elevators is a particularly fascinating exercise in urban anthropology. 'Passengers seem to know instinc-tively how to arrange themselves in an elevator', writes the *New Yorker*'s Nick Paumgarten. 'Two strangers will gravitate to the back corners, a third will stand by the door, at an isosceles remove, until a fourth comes in, at which point passengers three and four will spread toward the front corners, making room, in the center, for a fifth, and so on, like the dots on a die.'[20]

Experiences of elevator travel, an exercise in delegating agency first to a human operator and then to unknowable electromechan-ical or digital systems, is also over-coded with a rich history of fictional, filmic, poetic and science-fictional imagination. From the mysterious and secret seven-and-a-half floor in the 1999 film *Being John Malkovich*, to a whole chapter of urban folklore, or a myriad of unfortunate and filmic deaths and catastrophes, the elevator stalks the interface between the banal and the fearful or unknown within the vertical and technological cultures of the contemporary – and the projected – metropolis.

---

19   Simmen, 'Elevation: A Cultural History', p. 28.
20   Paumgarten, 'Up and Then Down'.

Elevators are 'public yet private, enclosing yet permeable, separate from but integral to the architectural spaces that surround them', American historian Susan Garfinkel writes, and 'invite us to expect the unexpected in certain predictable ways.'[21] She shows how elevators have been used in film to symbolise, variously, the 'corporate ladder'; aspirations of social or economic advancement or sexual liaison (or sexual predation); the democratisation of public space; anxieties of technological collapse or lurking monsters; the monotony of corporate life; and fears of urban anomie.

In Depression-era American cinema 'physical proximity and the elevator's rapid upward thrust are meant to augur the heterosexual liaisons that follow.'[22] Sometimes, as in Woody Allen's 1997 film *Deconstructing Harry*, elevators are even used to symbolise anxieties about the how vertical connections might operate as thresholds to the vertical religious cosmographies of heaven or hell.[23]

Importantly, the relatively standardised and enclosed experience of the modern elevator is increasingly shifting, at least in high-end office buildings or the celebrated and spectacular vertical structures visited by tourists. Since transparent rocketship-style elevators were first installed along the interior atrium of architect John Portman's influential Hyatt Regency hotel in Atlanta in 1967, exterior, glass or 'panorama' elevators on the insides or outsides of buildings have become increasingly common.

Such a shift resonated powerfully with long-standing tropes of science fiction and space-age futurism. In 1914, Italian Futurist Antonio Sant'Elia's vertical city ideas centred in particular on the idea that 'elevators should no longer hide way like solitary worms in the bottom of stairwells' but should, instead, 'swarm up the facades like serpents of glass and iron.'[24] The notion of putting the elevator

---

21   Susan Garfinkel, 'Elevator Stories: Vertical Imagination and the Spaces of Possibility', in Goetz, ed., *Up, Down, Across*, pp. 173–95,

22   Merrill Schleier, *Skyscraper Cinema: Architecture and Gender in American Film,* Minneapolis: University of Minnesota Press, 2009, p. 68.

23   On the depiction of elevators in film, see Alanna Thain, 'Insecurity Cameras'.

24   Cited in Umbro Apollonio and Leonardo Mariani, *Antonio Sant'Elia: Documenti, Note Storiche e Critiche a Cura di Leonardo Mariani,* vol. 18, Milan: Il Balcone, 1958, p. 200.

on the façade, or of removing it from the building altogether, was further developed by H. G. Wells 1936 in his film *Things to Come* and in Charlie's journey skyward in Roald Dahl's *Charlie and the Great Glass Elevator* (1972). In both, the vertical journey itself is increasingly exposed, untethered and celebrated. Within some early façade elevators – most obviously at Seattle's Space Needle, built in 1972 – the vertical journey also became packaged to directly resemble the Apollo astronauts' vertical elevator ride up an Apollo gantry to be strapped into a Saturn V rocket for a moon launch.

As with other celebrated postmodern architectural projects by John Portman – LA's Bonaventure Hotel (1976) and Detroit's Renaissance Center (1977) – his transparent 'gondola' elevators ascending and descending along the interior of the vast atrium of the Hyatt Regency hotel in Atlanta, opened in 1967, were crucial in creating the sense of the complex as a self-contained mini-city. The oscillating elevators provided the sense of movement, animating an interior world of space of consumption and spectacle as urbanism turned away from the world beyond the curtilage.[25] 'The elevator really established the dynamics of the whole space', Portman recalled. His aim, in the design, he relates, was to 'pull the elevators out of the wall [to make] them like moving seats in a theatre.'[26] In turn, the kitschy transparent pods quickly became icons of Atlanta's rapid growth in the 1970s and symbols of a much broader geographic rebalancing of US urban growth towards the South.

After the opening of Portman's hotel, architecture critic Phil Patton recalls that 'visitors from the rural hinterlands around Atlanta made special trips to the city to see the elevators. The multiple cars, rising as others fell, were tapered at the ends like candies in twist wrappers and lit like miniature riverboats ... The elevator ride was worth the whole trip: a rocket launch take off, then the passage through the building's roof to the Polaris rotating restaurant.'[27]

---

25   See Fredric Jameson's extraordinarily influential discussion of the façade elevators in Portman's Los Angeles's Bonaventura Hotel in his *Postmodernism: or, The Cultural Logic of Late Capitalism*, Durham, NC: Duke University Press, 1991. p. 578.

26   Cited in Phil Patton, 'Hovering Vision', in Goetz, ed., *Up, Down, Across*, pp. 110–11.

27   Ibid., p. 106.

No longer hidden inside the building's core, the spectacular transparent gondola elevators animate the atrium of John Portman's Hyatt Regency hotel (1967)

Notably high or fast vertical journeys within iconic towers, meanwhile, are increasingly fetishised as part of wider fantasy landscapes of urban tourism and consumption. The elevator ride increasingly becomes a commodified destination and spectacle in and of itself. Elevators in glitzy new towers on Australia's Gold Coast, for example, now have video screens on the ceilings depicting the image of the receding lift shaft above – along with indicators of speed and location – so that occupants can be more exposed to the nature of the journey.

Sky Shinkansen

The spread of vertical cities and skyscrapers, not surprisingly, is closely linked to a global boom in the industries of vertical transportation. In 2012 there were roughly 11 million elevators and escalators in service across the world; 700,000 a year were being sold; and the global market was expected to grow at 6 per cent per year and be worth $90 billion a year by 2016, up from $56 billion in 2008.[28]

Not surprisingly, Asia, and especially China, totally dominates this growing market: half of all investment was in China in 2010.[29] And yet the market has some surprises. For example, the country with the highest numbers of elevators per capita, perhaps surprisingly, is Spain – a legacy of the systematic rebuilding of Spanish cities into apartment complexes during the Franco era.

Rapid advances in lift/elevator technology are as fundamental to the global proliferation of super-tall skyscrapers as are innovations in materials science and civil engineering. In Japan, new elevator technology has been central to relatively recent moves beyond long-standing earthquake-limited height controls (30-metre limits were in place until 1968). These have spawned a series of multi-use 'city within city' vertical complexes. In some ways, these resemble scaled-up and vertically stretched versions of John Portman's 1970s and 1980s North American designs.

The Roppongi Hills towers in Tokyo are key examples here. These 'vascular shafts' encompassing super-thin malls, elite condominiums, multi-storey parking garages, corporate HQs and expensive hotels and restaurants are serviced by some of the world's fastest elevators.[30] Such systems are marketed publicly as icons of national modernity every bit as symbolic of the use of faster infrastructures to overcome geographical barriers as the more familiar Shinkansen bullet train networks that lace together the country's cities horizontally. 'With four of the world's five fastest elevators today produced by Japanese companies', writes Ryan Sayre, 'Japan has actively promoted velocity as a worthy rival to altitude in the colonization of "up".'[31]

Indeed, super-fast elevators are now being lauded by the world's business press as proxy indicators of what's really going on in the fast-changing economic geographies of globalisation, urban growth

28   Matt Bodimeade, 'Global Elevator Market Led by Otis Elevator Company', *Companies and Markets*, 2012, available at companiesandmarkets.com.

29   Koncept Analytics, *Global Escalator and Elevator Market Report: 2010*, London: Koncept Analytics, August 2010.

30   Sayre 'Colonization of the "Up"'.

31   Ibid.

and real estate speculation. 'If you want to know where the world's hottest economies are', *Forbes* business magazine gushes, 'skip the GDP reports, employment statistics and consumer spending trends. All you need to do is answer one question: Where are the fastest elevators?'[32]

The world's fastest elevators, installed by Toshiba in the Taipei Financial Center in Taiwan, currently peak at a vertical speed of 60 km per hour and are pressurised to avoid ear damage among riders. In April 2013, Hitachi excitedly announced that they were taking over this vertical speed record with the construction of even faster elevators – developed in the G1 Tower – for a new 530-metre tower in Guangzhou, China. These will climb 95 floors in a mere 43 seconds, a maximum speed of 72 km per hour.

Much higher super-tall towers, served by unprecedented vertical transportation systems, have long featured in modernist architectural imaginaries. In 1956, for example, Frank Lloyd Wright designed a mile-high tower, a 528-storey city-tower for Chicago. This was replete with sixty-six nuclear-powered, quintuple-decker elevators traveling at 60 miles an hour. Ever since, much architectural fantasy has centred on constructing ever-higher and more grandiose vertical visions.

Way beyond even the gigantic scale of projected architecture, the dream of a functioning elevator linking the earth's surface to a geostationary satellite – or even the moon – has long gripped science fiction writers. The International Academy of Astronautics even argued in 2014 that a 100,000 km 'space elevator' will be feasible by 2035 by applying emerging research into super-strength carbon nanotube materials. A means of radically reducing the costs of launching satellites, such a project – built as a 'tether' to winch loads vertically into space – would also, they argue, be a crucial step to much more intensive extra-planetary exploration and colonisation.[33]

---

32   Tom Van Riper and Robert Malone, 'The World's Fastest Elevators', *Forbes*, October 2007, available at forbes.com.

33   Peter Swan, David Raitt, Cathy Swan and Robert Penny, *Space Elevators: An Assessment of the Technological Feasibility and the Way Forward*, London: Virginia Editions, 2013.

Street People, Air People

> There were the Street People and there were the Air People. Air people
> levitated like fakirs ... access to the elevator was proof that your life had
> the buoyancy that was needed to stay afloat in a city where the ground
> was seen as the realm of failure and menace.
>
> – Jonathan Raban, *Hunting Mister Heartbreak*

As such vertical megaprojects are imagined, marketed and constructed – whether as putative responses to sustainability challenges, demographic and urban growth, the changing possibilities of speculation and construction technology, or sheer megalomania – so the uneven social geographies surrounding vertical mobility are likely to become more and more stark.

Social inequalities in access to vertical transportation are very poorly researched. Clearly, though, elevator layouts are already starting to mimic increasingly the sorts of 'splintered' geographies which combine premium transport systems geared to the wealthy with deteriorating systems left for the poor, which have long characterised the evolution of much horizontal transport infrastructure.[34]

Ascension of the super-tall towers of the 1930s, limited by the elevator technology of the time, involved several time-consuming changes between elevators that were vertically staggered in sequence within the structure. These elevators were able to stop at every floor. The time consuming experience of these repeated journeys in the Empire State Building, Mark Kingwall writes, served to remind the upward traveller of their 'constant and continued suspension'. There is nothing, he continues, 'like having to change elevators three times to show that cable does not stretch indefinitely far.'[35]

The design of stronger cables, though, allowed single-leap elevators to reach the tops of tall towers. Such new technologies facilitated the engineering of 'unbundled' and 'splintered' elevator experiences: radically diversified elevator speeds and leaps, organised to allow elite, premium or long-distance travellers to experience faster ascent and

---

34 See Stephen Graham and Simon Marvin, *Splintering Urbanism*, London: Routledge, 2001.

35 Kingwell, *Nearest Thing to Heaven*, p. 192.

descent, 'bypassing' less valued users who were removed into more prosaic and slower elevators.

Since the architects of New York's World Trade Center introduced the idea of the 'sky lobby' in 1973 – a lobby half-way up super-tall towers where 'express' and 'local' elevators can exchange traffic – super-high towers, mimicking the pattern of subway trains on the New York subway, have increasingly been built with fast, long-distance or 'shuttle' elevators and 'local', slower ones which stop on every floor. Such approaches are starting to allow designers and architects to carefully customise different elevator speeds and experiences to different classes of residents or visitors.

In effect, such transformations work to diversify and differentiate experiences of vertical mobility. They replace single, public passage points up and down with a spectrum of vertical elevators organised using the latest card- and radio chip-based access-control technologies familiar in many hotels. Compounding widening fears about the vertical secession of elites in the world's cities, express and VIP elevators can bring elite users occupying the prestigious penthouse spaces of towers radically 'closer' to the ground while conveniently bypassing the mass crowds confined to the shuttles that stop at every floor below.

Already, a variety of lifts provide highly varied ways to ascend the world's tallest building, the Burj Khalifa in Dubai. Those lucky enough to access the VIP lift to the luxury restaurants and viewing platforms on the 123rd floor ride upwards in a luxurious lift car in around a minute beneath a sign that reads 'the stars come out to play' (hence extolling both the status of the selected passengers and the rate of their velocity upwards). Meanwhile, super-luxury hotel towers like the Waldorf Astoria in Ras al-Khaimah, also in the UAE, are keen to extend the personal and protected geographies that their clients demand: they now advertise that their penthouse suites are newly equipped with entirely private VIP lifts.

Many corporate office towers are also being equipped with VIP lifts. These whisk CEOs and top executives straight to their offices at the apex of buildings without having to stop at intervening floors or rub shoulders with the company's workforce from the 'lower' tiers of corporate hierarchies.

A range of emerging elite residential towers take the idea of

Parking spaces linked to 'sky garage' car elevators in the Hamilton Scotts housing tower in Singapore. The Ferrari on the right is being eased into its in-apartment parking space next to the adjacent Porsche after being lifted up to the apartment by the automobile elevator system.

individualised elevator travel much further still. They offer dedicated elevators for residents' extremely expensive automobiles as well. In a startling example of the suburbanisation of Manhattan, for example the recently completed condo complex for the super-wealthy at 200 Eleventh Avenue in Chelsea offers New York's first 'en-suite sky garage' facility. This is a system of elevators that lift residents and their vehicles from street level to a personal garage adjacent to their $20 million apartment. Built for the cars of the super-rich, the elevators can take vehicles weighing up to 8,000 lbs. The 'sky garage' system at the Hamilton Scotts tower in Singapore, meanwhile, offers separate elevators for drivers and vehicles. Here the system automatically shepherds the upscale car to a glass-encased aerial garage so that it can be fetishistically admired from the apartments' living space.

Trapped: Vertical Transport Crises

> Good high-rises rely on good elevators.
> – Kat Cizek, 'Poverty Is Vertical – and the Elevators Are Terrible'

Beyond the glitz of the VIP and auto elevators serving elite residential towers, the vertical movement sustained by elevators remains highly contested. On the one hand, the complete dependence of occupants in towers on elevators means that they can become the ultimate 'ransom strip' – a means to extort higher and higher service charges from dependent tenants. Many residential tenants renting out some of the 1,000 apartments in the Burj Khalifa, for example, have recently found themselves electronically locked out of some of the luxurious spas, gyms and other facilities that they had assumed their £40,000 annual rent allowed them to access.

Such communal services have been withdrawn because the tenants' landlords have been failing to pay the building's owners the high maintenance and service charges stipulated in their contracts. In 2013, typically, these costs amounted to around £155,000 for owners of a £1 million apartment, increases well beyond rates of inflation. In 2012 they rose 27 per cent. When property owners can't or won't pay these fees, building owners resort to locking tenants out of key communal facilities or posting 'name-and-shame' lists of nonpaying tenants next to elevator doors.[36]

On the other hand, and more prosaically, unreliable, vandalised and poorly maintained elevators have long been an Achilles heel of modernist dreams of mass social housing in vertical towers, especially in North American and European cities. Given that 'the elevator is an utterly essential technology for high-rise housing,'[37] problems of elevator breakdown or unreliability create immediate crises for residents, especially those who find staircases impassable. Without functioning elevators, these Corbusian blocks, rather than emancipating 'machines for living' or modern spaces projected into the light and air of vertical space, quickly reduce to dystopian places of extreme isolation and enforced withdrawal, especially for those with children or the less mobile.

Recognising this, better managers of mass vertical housing systems, such as the Singaporean Government's Housing Development Board, maintain an emergency twenty-four-hour response team to allay

---

36 Jim Armitage, 'Trouble at the £1bn Burj Khalifa Tower: Spiralling Service Costs See Landlords Falling Behind on Their Bills', *Independent*, 13 February 2014.

37 Jane M. Jacobs and Stephen Cairns, 'Ecologies of Dwelling: Maintaining High-Rise Housing in Singapore', in Gary Bridge and Sophie Watson, eds., *The New Blackwell Companion to the City*, Oxford: Blackwell, 2011, pp. 79–95.

residents' concerns about vertical isolation caused by elevator failure. In many social or low-income housing towers, however, the costs and difficulties of maintaining elevators present a perennial problem. Often, vertical transport crises caused by decrepit, obsolescent or unreliable elevators lead to problems of social isolation in cities just as powerfully as the more visible and familiar crises of horizontal mobility through failed or disrupted rail, subway, auto or air travel systems.[38]

Thus far, most debates about vertical living in Canadian cities have centred on the spectacular proliferation of private condo towers there. However, many on low incomes are often marooned in the sky by the failure to maintain continuous elevator services in the cities' stock of increasingly decrepit high-rise rented towers that are populated by low-income communities. The United Way organisation, which lobbies on behalf of Toronto's poor, warns that Canada's biggest city, for one, is becoming a city of 'vertical poverty' where the physical renewal of these towers' elevators – as well as the rest of the buildings – is necessary to prevent a major infrastructural crisis which systematically isolates the city's most vulnerable populations high in the sky. Growing up in a decrepit tower in an inner city in Toronto, Jamal, a participant in the study, recalls that 'the elevator would skip floors, jumping and jolting, moving up and down. I used to wonder if we would survive if the elevator dropped from the 13th floor to B2.' He was so terrified when his family visited that he 'had disturbing thoughts that they wouldn't come out.' Even now, after moving out of the tower, he remains scared of elevators.[39]

In France, meanwhile, the vertical abandonment of immigrant communities living in high-rise *banlieues* – places where elevator services have become ever more perilous – has become a symbol of the troubled politics of assimilation in the post-colonial Republic since the 2005 riots. Clichy-sous-Bois, the largely French-African neighbourhood on Paris's north-eastern periphery where the 2005 riots started, has become a particular symbol of processes of

---

38   See Stephen Graham, ed., *Disrupted Cities: When Infrastructure Fails*, New York: Routledge, 2009.

39   Quoted in Cizek, 'Poverty Is Vertical'.

vertical as well as social and horizontal abandonment. Since the riots, as the physical spaces of high-rises have deteriorated, elevator maintenance has collapsed (especially in private rented blocks). Many families have found themselves isolated in the sky for long periods.

In 2013, Margareth, a Congolese immigrant living near the top of a high tower, was interviewed by the French *Les Inrocks* magazine.[40] The elevators in Margareth's block are now 'mere ornaments', the magazine reported. Repairs take several months, at best. When she was interviewed, it had been over a week since Margareth had been to ground level to shop. 'With the kids just the trip would take me almost an hour', she says. When she does shop, she minimises weight to make the ascent of the stairs easier. 'I have techniques. I take the [concentrated] syrup to avoid packs of juice.'[41]

A complex support and barter system among neighbours, along with an improvised pulley system to raise shopping bags to higher floors, is the only thing keeping the less mobile tenants from real hunger. In 2013, as tenants waited for elevator repairs, the local mayor intervened and organised a system of 'live elevators', volunteers to help residents ascend the stairs.

The reliance of modern elevators on electricity adds a further twist to the vulnerability of high-rise occupants. Although power outages never featured in the imaginings of the modernist architects who postulated life in vertical towers, the fragilities of contemporary power grids can also quickly turn vertical living into vertical isolation. This was powerfully demonstrated in October 2012 as Hurricane Sandy tore into New York City. As they faced abandonment in their new penthouse apartments, the downsides even for the wealthy of living at the tops of glittering new towers during power blackouts became starkly obvious. Residents were forced to discover the often hidden circuits of stairwells within buildings that they had not seen in years (if at all).

The 400,000 residents in public housing projects were even more badly hit, with over 430 elevators shut down in such blocks

---

40   David Doucet, and Cerise Sudry-le-Dû, 'Clichy-sous-Bois, Entre Abandoné et Solidarité', *Les Inrocks*, 28 January 2013, available at lesinrocks.com.

41   Quoted in Doucet and Sudry-le-Dû, 'Clichy-sous-Bois'.

due to power outages. The outages also stopped water and sewage pumping, forcing often vulnerable, disabled and frail residents and children to try to improvise carrying water – as well as food – up long stairways.

7.

Skyscraper: Vanity and Violence

The skyscraper is still the stuff of heroes. Superman and Superwoman can aspire to the executive floor, or even higher. The timid out-of-towner can suitably palpitate on entering the auspicious lobby. The only problem is, as a designer, how to make your tall box different from the rest.

– Peter Cook

November 2014. Twenty kilometres north of the ancient city of Jeddah, on the banks on the Red Sea, lies an unprepossessing building site. One of countless similar sites dotted across Saudi Arabia and the Gulf States, its cluster of cranes, geometric concoctions of steel girders and concrete, and busy groups of bonded South Asian workers are common sights across the region's fast-expanding cities.

On the margins of Jeddah, the building abuts hundreds of miles of dusty desert. Empty, hard-baked ground stretches away from the busy cranes and trucks to the sandy horizon. It's hard to imagine that there could ever be sufficient demand from businesses, residents, tourists or investors for a super-tall tower in such a location. Certainly, anyone schooled in the traditional geographic idea that it is intense competition for prestigious sites at the centres of large 'global' cities that drives skyscraper development would laugh at the prospect.[1]

And yet by 2018 the building under construction on this site will stretch vertically upwards for over a kilometre to become –for a time at least – the tallest skyscraper in the world. From the dusty desert floor a tapering tower of steel, concrete, glass and aluminium will ascend skywards for fully three-quarters of a mile. Such a realisation

---

1   See Donald McNeill, 'Skyscraper Geography', *Progress in Human Geography* 29:1 (2005), pp. 41–55.

Construction of the Kingdom Tower, Jeddah, February 2015

becomes even more remarkable when you realise that this tower has actually been downsised. A combination of the 2009 financial crisis and in-depth geological excavations meant that an earlier design – intended to reach a full vertical mile to mimic Frank Lloyd Wright's 1956 design for 'The Illinois', a proposed tower for Chicago – was reduced in scale.

Anchoring a major new city, like most Saudi megaprojects, the $1.2 billion tower is being directly driven forward by the Saudi royal family. Prince Alwaleed bin Talal, nephew of the recently deceased King Abdullah, is chairman of the company building the tower. At least in part, Alwaleed is clearly building 'his' tower – a gateway to the holy Islamic cities of Mecca and Medina – in a personal bid to out-do Sheikh Mohammed bin Rashid Al Maktoum's Burj Khalifa skyscraper in Dubai (currently the world's tallest).

Jeddah's Kingdom Tower symbolises perfectly how the geographies and politics of the world's tallest skyscrapers have been revolutionised over the last few decades. Once, the tallest of such towers clustered only at the centres of the world's most important corporate and finance capitals in the capitalist heartlands of the Global North. Vertical symbols of the dominance of major corporations and capitalist business elites, they fed off extreme competition for sites, super-high land values and struggles to materialise corporate prestige in stone, steel, aluminium and glass.

Through real estate industry links to both speculators and to extending subterranean mining operations across the world to provide construction materials, the mushrooming of towers in New York and Chicago between 1885 and the 1980s, in particular, created a new type of volumetric city where previously only the small area above the surface could be commodified and leased. Air, in other words, could itself be monetised and enclosed into rising towers, a process that architecture academic Eric Höweler has called a 'new speculative terrain of vertical extension'.[2]

Improved and safety-braked electric or hydraulic elevators and steel-frame construction technologies, brought in from the mining industry, were central to the emergence of skyscrapers as a building form. Just as important, though, was the new supermetal aluminium, which allowed the taller parts of the super-tall towers built from the 1930s onwards to be light enough to be borne safely by the structure and foundations below.[3] 'The modern skyscraper', the industry's Aluminium Association claim, 'would not have been possible without aluminium.'[4]

The rising clusters of downtown skyscrapers in cities such as Chicago and New York in turn acted as powerful signifiers on the symbolic plane. In cinema, skyscrapers were widely portrayed metaphorically as symbols of career advancement 'up' within deeply hierarchical corporate organisations. Indeed, corporate skyscrapers were carefully designed to physically materialise the 'vertical' hierarchical structure of the large corporation. 'The height of the building is a concrete metaphor of the company turnover', Italian journalist Marco d'Eramo emphasises. The luxury offices of CEOs look down from the highest floors in the heavens; the corporate minions slave away down near the ground; and career advancement can be measured by physical ascent up to be 'on top of the pile'.

'While its costs may be astronomically high', d'Eramo continues, 'the skyscraper performs well its symbolic duty; only those above you, or your "superiors", count, while your "inferiors" fade quietly into

---

2   Eric Höweler, *Skyscraper: Designs of the Recent Past and for the Near Future*, London: Thames & Hudson, 2003.

3   See Mimi Sheller, *Aluminum Dreams: The Making of Light Modernity*, Cambridge, MA: MIT Press, 2014.

4   See aluminum.org/modern-skyscraper.

insignificance. From the office window, your gaze may wander down, but your aspirations are upward (on the social ladder). Mirroring the bitter struggle to the top, the skyscrapers themselves often compete with each other in their bid for the sky.[5]

Crucially, corporate skyscraper headquarters also became a symbolic representation of the power, reach and identity of corporations themselves. Architects, developers and corporations searched hard for unique building forms and silhouettes which could be used to distinguish them from their competitors as cultural signifiers.[6] They sought larger and taller structures to symbolise the financial and economic power of the tenant. And they worked to project 'their' building as an icon of the established and continuing power of their corporation. 'This is a discourse of stature, status, stability, establishment and estate', urban theorist Kim Dovey explains. 'And [it] shares with these words the Greek root *sta*: "to stand".'[7]

In designing headquarters of large companies, architects sought the symbolic powers of height, splendour and a memorable silhouette as means of generating maximum commercial and cultural impact. (The assemblage of a range of identifiable skyscraper silhouettes, in turn, were quickly manufactured and celebrated as iconic skylines immediately identifying particular cities – a process ongoing today.[8])

The prolonged skyscraper 'race' between New York and Chicago dominated the building form for much of the twentieth century. Above all, the new towers were symbols of the aggressive, centripetal pull of capitalist urbanism, and of the growth of corporate headquarters organised to remotely control disparate and widely spread sites of manufacturing, marketing and distribution. As new building, materials and elevator technologies combined with the massive growth of the power and reach of corporations, insurance companies, airlines, retail operations, telecommunications companies, banks

---

5 Marco d'Eramo, *The Pig and the Skyscraper: Chicago: A History of Our Future*, London: Verso, 2003, p. 56.

6 See Thomas Van Leeuwen, Thomas, *The Skyward Trend of Thought: The Metaphysics of the American Skyscraper*, Cambridge, MA: MIT Press, 1988.

7 Kim Dovey, 'Tall Storeys: Corporate Towers and Symbolic Capital', *EDRA* 22, 1991, p. 286.

8 Christoph Lindner, 'New York Vertical: Reflections on the Modern Skyline', *American Studies*, 2006, pp. 31–52.

and conglomerates, rising skyscrapers embodied a period of intense 'Manhattanism' – the structuring of a few dominant central cities based on skylines made up of clusters of skyscrapers.[9]

'All Manhattan's tall buildings had been content to confront each other in a competitive verticality', French philosopher Jean Baudrillard wrote in 2002. 'And the product of this was an architectural panorama reflecting the capitalist system itself – a pyramidal jungle, whose famous image [of Manhattan] stretched out before you as you arrived from the sea.'[10]

Just as the skyscraper skyline emerged as the dominant symbol of the US central city,[11] so skyscrapers loomed large as images of modernity and futurity within fiction, cinema, comic books, art, architecture and urbanism.[12] 'The skyscraper is not only the building of the century', the *New York Times*'s legendary architecture critic Ada Louise Huxtable wrote in 1984. 'It is also the single work of architecture that can be studied as the embodiment and expression of much that makes the century what it is.' Skyscrapers, she continued, were key symbols of the power of consumer and corporate culture; they romanticised power and the intensity of the twentieth-century metropolis; they were literal embodiments of the promise of modernity, technology and 'progress'; and they were powerful icons of the most powerful nation on Earth. To Huxtable, 'The tall building probes our collective psyche as it probes the sky.'[13]

Crucially, it was the combination of the vertical skyscraper and horizontal street grid that came to symbolise US urbanism in the second

9   Rem Koolhaas, *Delirious New York: A Retroactive Manifesto for Manhattan*, New York: Monacelli Press, 1978, p. 291.

10   Jean Baudrillard, *Requiem for the Twin Towers: The Spirit of Terrorism*, trans. Chris Turner, London: Verso, 2002, pp. 42–4.

11   On the importance of skyscraper skylines to contemporary 'global' cities, see Nebosca Čamprag, 'Frankfurt and Rotterdam: Skylines as Embodiment of a Global City', *Council for Tall Buildings and Urban Habitat*, 2015, available at global.ctbuh.org.

12   See, for example, Merrill Schleier, *Skyscraper Cinema: Architecture and Gender in American Film*, Minneapolis: University of Minnesota Press, 2009; and James Saunders, *Celluloid Skyline: New York and the Movies*, New York, Alfred, 2001, pp. 4–6.

13   Ada Louise Huxtable, *The Tall Building Artistically Reconsidered*, New York: Pantheon, New York, 1984.

half of the twentieth century. Rem Koolhaas, in his extravagant 1978 paean to New York's skyscrapers *Delirious New York*, revelled in the ways 'the Grid's two-dimensional discipline also creates undreamt-of freedom for three-dimensional anarchy.' The street grid, he argued, 'defines a new balance between control and de-control in which the city can be at the same time ordered and fluid, a metropolis of rigid chaos.'[14]

To feminist critics, the skyscrapers of twentieth-century Chicago and Manhattan, symbols of a muscular and heroically masculinised notion of US modernity, also inevitably reeked of an extreme, phallic-centred patriarchy. 'The twentieth-century urban skyscraper', architectural commentator Leslie Kanes Weisman writes, 'a pinnacle of patriarchal symbology, is rooted in the masculine mystique of the big, the erect, the forceful – the full balloon of the inflated masculine ego.' Urban skyscrapers, she believed, 'compete for individual recognition and domination while impoverishing human identity and the quality of life.' To symbolise such masculinised competition, New York skyscraper architects even paraded at balls dressed in effigies of their own towers and were not slow to celebrate their structures in highly sexual terms.[15]

For example, Chicago architect Louis Sullivan, the first to exploit new steel-frame construction techniques in skyscraper design and often referred to as the 'father of the skyscraper', described a building by his colleague Henry Hobson Richardson – built using Sullivan's innovation of the girder box surrounded by non-load-bearing walls – as follows: 'Here is a man for you to look at,' Sullivan gushed,

> A virile force, an entire male. It stands in physical fact, a monument to trade, to the organized commercial spirit, to the power and progress of the age, to the strength and resource of individuality and force of character. Therefore I have called it, in a world of barren pettiness, a male, for it sings the song of procreant power, as others have squealed of miscegenation.[16]

14   Koolhaas, *Delirious New York*, p. 20.

15   Leslie Kanes Weisman, 'Prologue: 1 "Women's Environmental Rights: A Manifesto"', in Jane Rendell, Barbara Penner and Iain Borden, eds, *Gender, Space, Architecture: An Interdisciplinary Introduction*, London: Psychology Press, 2000, pp. 1–5.

16   Louis Sullivan, *Kindergarten Chats and Other Writings*, New York: Dover, 1947.

Manhattan's architects, dressed as their own skyscrapers, perform 'The Skyline of New York' at the city's Beaux Arts Ball in 1931. From left: A. Stewart Walker as the Fuller Building, Leonard Schultze as the new Waldorf-Astoria, Ely Jacques Kahn as the Squibb Building, William Van Alen as the Chrysler Building, Ralph Walker as One Wall Street, D. E. Ward as the Metropolitan Tower and Joseph H. Freedlander as the Museum of the City of New York.

And yet not all twentieth-century skyscrapers emerged as powerful icons of the imagination. On the one hand, architect Minoru Yamasaki's twin World Trade Center towers, opened near the tip of Manhattan in April 1973, were almost universally loathed. The towers, built by the Port Authority of New York and New Jersey as what it called a 'vertical port' to directly parallel the authority's horizontal infrastructure of ports and airports,[17] quickly emerged as overbearing symbols of the crass extremes of domineering and destructive capital. They particularly came to symbolise both the widespread destruction of street life by monolithic modernist structures and the growing economic monoculture of 'Fordist' corporations in New York in the 1970s, with their concentration of corporate headquarters specializing in finance, insurance and real estate.

---

17   Eric Darton, 'The Janus Face of Architectural Terrorism: Minoru Yamasaki, Mohammad Atta and the World Trade Center', *Open Democracy*, 8 November 2001, available at opendemocracy.net.

Urban critic Marshall Berman lambasted the towers as 'brutal and overbearing ... expressions of an urbanism that disdained the city and its people.'[18] He especially decried the destruction of large swathes of older streetscapes in Downtown Manhattan necessary to build them as a 'manifestation of terrorism ... a destructive act.' In an eerie parallel to the mechanism of the towers' demise nearly three decades later, other critics of the project also condemned the towers' construction as a brutal act of 'urbicidal' violence – that is, violence against the city.[19] Sixteen acres of dense streetscape, including 'Little Syria' – a thriving Middle Eastern neighbourhood – were erased to clear the ground for the construction of the Twin Towers.[20]

French philosopher Paul Virilio meanwhile saw the World Trade Center towers as the ultimate embodiment of the fetishising of radically vertical and orthogonal forms within Western urbanism, one that needed to be resisted at all costs. Virilio even invoked the biblical myth of the Tower of Babel by calling the development of the Twin Towers an example of the wider 'Babelization of the city'.[21]

By startling contrast, 1930s icons like the Empire State and Chrysler Buildings have often attracted extraordinary adulation and generated their own mythology.[22] 'Even at its inception', Toronto

---

18   Marshall Berman, 'When Bad Buildings Happen to Good People', in Michael Sorkin and Sharon Zukin, eds, *After the World Trade Center: Rethinking New York City*, New York: Routledge, 2002, pp. 1–12.

19   Ada Louis Huxtable, *Will They Ever Finish Bruckner Boulevard? A Primer on Urbicide*, New York: Macmillan, 1970.

20   See Terry Smith, *The Architecture of Aftermath*, Chicago: University of Chicago Press, 2006, chapter 5.

21   Paul Virilio and Sylvère Lotringer, *Crepuscular Dawn*, Mike Taormina, trans., New York: Semiotext(e), 2002. See Julian Reid, 'Architecture, Al-Qaeda, and the World Trade Center: Rethinking Relations between War, Modernity, and City Spaces after 9/11', *Space and Culture* 7:4, 2004, pp. 396–408. 'The Genesis narrative of the fall of the Tower of Babel', writes theologian Graeme Davison, 'links worldly pride to the rise and catastrophic fall of an imperial city ... The pride of these city-dwellers, so the story goes, leads to a great fall. God, noticing that they had got above themselves, decides to sow linguistic confusion among them, they leave off building their tower and are scattered to the ends of the earth.' Davison, 'The Fallen Towers: Pride, Envy and Judgement in the Modern City', *Bible and Critical Theory* 1:3, 2005, available at novaojs.newcastle.edu.au.

22   Daniel Libeskind, in pushing through his designs for the 'Freedom Tower' – later renamed 1 World Trade Center – on the site of the World Trade Center

philosophy professor Mark Kingwell writes of the Empire State Building, 'the building was a strange palace of dreams, a heaven-seeking tower made of solid metal and stone, and serving the needs of business. Standing so firm, technology's latest last word, it appears nevertheless to shimmer and shift before our eyes.' The site of countless movies, the Empire State Building is a site of intense cinematic memory. As part of the rising skyline of twentieth-century Manhattan, it has long acted, with other towers, as a key symbol to migrants across the world of the opportunities offered by America. And as a (now historic) symbol of the future, the tower has had huge global cultural and architectural impact. 'As with so many parts of New York', Kingwell suggests, 'even if this is your first visit, you know you've been here before.'[23]

Gigantic Logos: Nowhere into Somewhere

Skyscrapers for corporate headquarters and banks in the centres of 'global cities' have not disappeared completely, of course. However, the processes of globalised urbanisation over the last few decades have led, in cities like Jeddah, Riyadh, Baku and Dubai, to the growth of the super-tall skyscraper as urban or national brand. Such structures are being brought into being by super-rich national elites as attempts to quickly manufacture sites and cities that matter, and that have pulling power, within the contexts of intense globalisation of leisure, tourism, finance, business and real estate. 'Skyscraper megalomania … is never only about attracting foreign investments', anthropologist Aihwa Ong stresses, 'but fundamentally also about an intense political desire for world recognition.'[24]

---

towers, often talked of his new skyscraper as a way of restoring the 'spiritual peak' of New York. See Blair Kamin, *Terror and Wonder: Architecture in a Tumultuous Age,* Chicago: University of Chicago Press, 2010, p. 36.

23   Mark Kingwall, *The Nearest Thing to Heaven: The Empire State Building and American Dreams*, New Haven, CN: Yale University Press, 2006, pp. 14–28.

24   Aihwa Ong, 'Hyperbuilding: Spectacle, Speculation, and the Hyperspace of Sovereignty', in Ananya Roy and Aihwa Ong, eds, *Worlding Cities: Asian Experiments and the Art of Being Global,* London: John Wiley & Sons, 2011, p. 210. See also Leslie Sklair, *The Icon Project: Architecture, Cities, and Capitalist Globalization*, Oxford: Oxford University Press, 2016.

Real estate specialist William Murray puts it succinctly: 'Supertall buildings are gigantic logos – brand identifiers for the countries that built them. They create a skyline, a marker and a recognizable shape that help us to remember, relate to and form positive associations about a place.'[25]

Changes in the technologies used in financial and corporate services, meanwhile, have made large towers less appropriate as the headquarters of large corporations. Many such firms now occupy lower, boxier structures in downtowns or on the edges of big cities in order to accommodate the complexes supporting contemporary trading flows and financial services.

Both remaining and new corporate towers in the centres of New York and Chicago, meanwhile, are less and less marked as the symbols of large corporations. Indeed, in the aftermath of 9/11, such corporations have increasingly sought more anonymous real estate; their efforts to build symbolic capital now relate less and less to the building of physical structures. And many of the largest corporations associated with skyscrapers across the twentieth century have been swept away by economic changes.

'Visibility is no virtue in the late capitalist society', writes architectural theorist Kazys Varnelis, perhaps over-emphasising the demise of the skyscraper as corporate symbol:

> The first outrageously tall skyscraper of the twentieth century, the 792 [-foot] tall Woolworth building, completed in 1908, emptily symbolizes a chain of discount stores that closed in 1997, mainly due to competition from Wal-Mart which replaced the now-empty symbolic value of the towering corporate headquarters with the real economic utility of a computer database reputedly second in size only to that of the Pentagon.[26]

Some central office towers in London and New York have in turn been converted to now more profitable residential use; most new towers in

---

25   William Murray, 'Selling Tall: The Branding and Marketing of Tall Buildings', *Council for Tall Buildings and Urban Habitat,* 2012, available at global. ctbuh.org.

26   Kazys Varnelis, 'Revision of a Brief History of Horizontality', 13 October 2005, available at varnelis.net.

these cities are residential and are built to attract the superwealthy. Other skyscrapers blend commercial, residential and leisure uses.[27]

Beyond the cores of older global cities, skyscraper construction has a different logic. Driven less by escalating land values and corporate semiology, the new skyscrapers are instead material embodiments of contemporary dynamics for circulating the vast capitalist surpluses of oligarchs, oil sheikhs and global financial and super-rich elites. Since 1996, when the Petronas Towers opened in Kuala Lumpur, the tallest towers have been developed in the Middle East and Asia – the first time since the building of Europe's Norman and Gothic cathedrals that the world's tallest structures have not been in the West.[28]

Indeed, geographer Andrew Harris now identifies what he sees as a 'vertical fix' in the fast-moving political economies of capitalism.[29] By building highly vertical structures carefully orchestrated to emerge as the centre of huge cycles of hype, spectacle, branding and advertising, the new super-tall towers work to transform complex debt, investment and speculation into lucrative real estate assets more powerfully than do other less visible or less vertical structures. The new tower can thus emerge pretty much anywhere such surpluses become grounded within ambitious megaprojects backed by hubristic local elites. The argument, these days, is very much: 'If we build it, they will come.'

Most arguments that the new skyscraper towers are necessary to improve urban densities, reduce sprawl, increase 'sustainability' and so on are almost entirely specious. French urbanist Jean-Marie Huriot sees such discourses as little more than a smokescreen camouflaging the powerful symbolism of extreme vertical architecture. He emphasises the much higher build and operational costs of very tall compared to conventional buildings. Huriot also stresses that overall urban densities are often higher in densely built streets than in cities dotted with clusters of huge towers. The population density in Paris's 13th Arrondissement, for example – a Haussmann-style neighbourhood of classic six- or seven-storey apartment buildings

27   See James Barton and Steve Watts, 'Office vs. Residential: The Economics of Building Tall', *Council of Tall Buildings and Urban Habitat Journal*, 2013, available at global.ctbuh.org.

28   Deyan Sudjic, *The Edifice Complex: How the Rich and Powerful – and Their Architects – Shape the World*, New York: Penguin, 2006, p. 356.

29   Andrew Harris, 'Vertical Urbanisms'.

built in the nineteenth century – is significantly higher than that in Les Olympiades, a nearby district made up of more recent 100-metre towers.

Calling the new towers 'deplorable symbols', Huriot concludes that, beyond the camouflaging rhetoric, the main reason for their proliferation can be found simply in 'the intimately linked symbolisms of performance, prestige and power.' Interrogating the lust for height as a de facto objective of planning policy in many contemporary cities, Huriot questions the motives of the radical verticalisation of cities in the name of 'urbanity' or 'iconicity':

> One must build higher, ever higher. But with what aims for society? To sell, to speculate, to generate profit at the expense of truly urgent social issues? These towers are nothing but deplorable symbols … Decision-makers, get your feet back on the ground and desecrate these towers and all that they symbolise![30]

The fact that a growing proportion of the height of super-tall skyscrapers is actually so narrow that it is 'vanity height' – little wider than the lift shafts and utility conduits and therefore completely unlettable – adds further weight to Huriot's arguments. If the new towers were really a response to the need to house booming populations, increase urban density or improve sustainability, why design them so that large portions of the building are little more than unused and energy-hungry monuments to the hubris of developers or the super-rich?

In 2013, the *ArchDaily*'s James Taylor-Foster calculated the proportion of new skyscrapers made up of unusable vanity height around the world. In the UAE, the country with the largest proportion of vanity height, he found that, on average, fully 19 per cent of the height of UAE skyscrapers was completely unlettable and unoccupiable. Of the combined height of the ten tallest skyscrapers in the world in 2013, moreover, fully 27 per cent was entirely superfluous vanity height.[31] Fully eighty-five floors of Jeddah's Kingdom Tower are too narrow to

---

30   Jean-Marie Huriot, 'Towers of Power', *Metropolitiques*, 25 January 2012, available at metropolitiques.eu.

31   James Taylor-Foster, 'Vanity Height: How Much of a Skyscraper Is Usable Space?', *ArchDaily*, 6 September 2013, available at archdaily.com.

be lettable in any way whatsoever. Such statistics powerfully reaffirm architecture critic Deyan Sudjic's conclusion that 'there is of course something ludicrously childish about the irrational urge to build high, simply for the sake of being the world's highest.'[32]

It is clear that the new super-tall towers act at key anchors within the wider construction of what Mike Davis and Dan Monk have called 'Dreamworlds of neoliberalism'[33]: enclaves of largely unregulated capitalism organised around the production of speculative, fantasy landscapes for leisure, consumption, investment, finance and tourism. In a world of extending, identikit suburbs and transnational urban regions stretching to, and beyond, the horizon, the towers are engineered in ways that allow extreme verticality to signal (at least ambitions of) significance, power and centrality.

The competitive and much-hyped 'race' to build the tallest skyscraper only adds to the search for centrality, spectacle and symbolic capital in a struggle to evidence 'national arrival' on the world stage.[34] A typical projection of this 'race' is a vertical diagram of the 'mega-tall' towers constructed as of 2010 from the global lobby and industry group for ever-taller skyscrapers, the Council for Tall Buildings and Urban Habitats, based in New York. They calculate that, in July 2013, there were seventy-three 'super-tall' skyscrapers in the world over 400 metres high and two 'mega-talls' over 600 metres – a category that didn't even exist a few years ago. Research and design efforts are already under way, moreover, for the next generation of 'ultra-talls': towers higher than 1.6 kilometres.[35]

It is important not to neglect the political and geopolitical aspects of contemporary skyscraper development. Aihwa Ong emphasises the ways in which the building of spectacular vertical megaprojects can

32　Sujdic, *Edifice Complex*, p. 358.

33　Mike Davis and Daniel Bertrand Monk, eds, *Evil Paradises: Dreamworlds of Neoliberalism*, New York: New Press, 2011.

34　Currently, 'super-tall' skyscraper projects in Azerbaijan, China and Qatar are at various stages of development in the struggle to top the Burj Khalifa's current record of 830 metres. They may even surpass the height of Jeddah's 1 km Kingdom Tower. See Aihwa Ong, 'Hyperbuilding'.

35　See Andy Davids, 'The Next Generation of Ultra High-Rise Buildings', *Council for Tall Buildings and Urban Habitat*, 2012; David Malott et al., 'Next Tokyo 2045: A Mile-High Tower Rooted in Intersecting Ecologies', *Council for Tall Buildings and Urban Habitat*, 2015, both available at global.ctbuh.org.

be seen as part of an effort by Asian and Middle Eastern states and their associated elites to attract speculative capital while asserting a confident sovereignty in the face of extremely mobile flows of finance, people and imagery. The frenzied building of spectacular structures, Ong stresses, leverages real estate values while also raising hopes among many local stakeholders about urban and national futures. It helps build a world where competition between rival cities and states becomes indexed and fetishised through the relative size and scale of vertical urban forms and spectacles.[36]

Here, as with the skyscrapers of Chicago and New York in the early and mid twentieth century, mega-tall buildings gain their power through their inspiration of wonder, awe and terror: a technological sublime that makes it easy to connect them in some putative vertical 'race' with other similar structures around the world.[37] 'This is the sublime terror of the abyss and the peak', business theorist Martin Parker writes, 'of elevation and descent.'[38] Above all, the structures work to offer what Ong calls 'promissory values about the geopolitical significance of the city and the country' within the changing geo-economics and geopolitics of global capitalism. In other words, 'a huge tower makes nowhere suddenly into somewhere.'[39]

In such a context, the new super-tall towers tend to house little or no commercial space. Much more important are hotels, restaurants, leisure attractions, viewing platforms and extremely expensive super-luxury apartments from which owners and investors can look over their new domains.[40] In 2000, only five of the world's twenty

---

36   LSE urbanist Marijn Nieuwenhuis, when discussing the obsession with skyscraper building in contemporary China with a academic architect in Hong Kong, recounts the story of Chinese tourists visiting neighbouring Thailand. 'Visiting Chinese tourists disappointingly complain that the buildings there are not high enough, not modern enough' he was told. Marijn Nieuwenhuis, 'Experiencing China's Verticality and Exposing Abstractions in Altitude', *Field Research Method Lab* at LSE, 24 April 2014, blog entry, available at wp.me/p46hMd-5P.

37   See David Nye, *American Technological Sublime*, Cambridge, MA: MIT Press, 1996.

38   Martin Parker, 'Vertical Capitalism: Skyscrapers and Organization', *Culture and Organization* 21:3, 2015, p. 218.

39   Sudjic, *Edifice Complex*, p. 358.

40   Fully 160 of the Kingdom Tower's more than 200 floors will be used for

tallest skyscrapers were mixed use; by 2020, only five won't be.[41] Such a shift symbolises and reflects wider transformation of many cities from landscapes of production to centres of consumption and leisure.

Crucial to the success of the new towers is the way the buildings themselves become the focus for a myriad of symbols and promotion and marketing drives to represent the places from which they spring – and associated commercial and elite capital. 'The symbolic function of the iconic skyscraper in the contemporary metropolis is to define the presence of the city on a world stage', UCL's Michele Acuto emphasises. Acuto stresses how the towers emerge as dominating of aspiration and status locally; as symbols of the 'aspiration of local political, planning and real-estate elites on the world stage, and, as short-hands to signal and represent the locality in myriad of adverts, product placements and tourist and investment drives.

Also important to the rise of the new towers are the complex ways in which their ascent is lauded by a myriad of supine, superficial and boosterist media and architectural commentary. These endlessly reinforce discursive formulations simplistically equating vertical height with power, wealth, importance, quality or modernity.

'Our vision for Kingdom Tower is one that represents the new spirit of Saudi Arabia', Adrian Smith, one of the tower's Chicago-based architects and a key designer as part of the SOM practice of super-tall towers across the world, stated in 2011. Not surprisingly side-stepping the House of Saud's truly execrable record of human rights abuses and its global promotion of terrorist violence, Smith continues:

> This tower symbolizes the Kingdom as an important global business and cultural leader, and demonstrates the strength and creative vision of its people … With its slender, subtly asymmetrical massing, the tower evokes a bundle of leaves shooting up from the ground – a burst of new life that heralds more growth all around it. We're thrilled to be working with His Highness [Prince Alwaleed bin Talal] and Jeddah Economic Company to help define this path for the Kingdom.'[42]

apartments, hotels and viewing platforms; the tower's largest penthouse will have its own private exterior gardens over 2,000 feet up in the air.

41   Clay Risen, 'The Rise of the Supertalls', *Popular Science*, 15 February 2013.

42   Architecture and Design, 'World's Next Tallest Tower – Being Built by Bin Ladens', 5 August 2011, available at architectureanddesign.com.au.

As we note throughout this book, deep vertical linguistic traditions and metaphors are intrinsic to such boosterism. 'Saudi shoots for the stars', the UAE's national newspaper declared in its reportage on the Kingdom Tower.[43] *Design Middle East* magazine, meanwhile, excitedly analysed the 'lift off' of the tower's sixty-five super-fast elevators, five of which will be double-decked, made by the Finnish company KONE and tested in their test facility in a mineshaft near Helsinki.[44] The tower's new elevators, will, CNN gushed, allow 'high-rolling residents [to] be able to communicate directly with the lifts through their phones.'[45] Some will reach 'the world's highest liveable floor' in only fifty-two seconds (a speed of 35 km/hour). Others will race 660 metres uninterrupted to the observation deck – the world's highest single rise elevator.[46] Such a leap is possible only because of KONE's new carbon-fibre elevator cables.

To understand the contemporary fetish for 'iconic' tall towers and their super-fast elevators from a broader perspective, geographer Maria Kaika draws important links between the hypermobility of the world's corporate and super-rich elites and the often craven efforts to brand new skyscrapers as easily identifiable everyday objects. Here, London's new range of skyscrapers – nicknamed the 'Gherkin', the 'Shard', the 'Cheesegrater', the 'Walkie Talkie', and so on – offer especially powerful examples.

Kaika calls such structures, appropriately, 'autistic icons' or 'serial objects'. She links their proliferation to the hypermobility of global elites and the ways in which such groups no longer link their identities and financial fortunes to growth coalitions within one specific city (as did the likes of Guggenheim or Rockefeller in the twentieth century). Instead, those in control of processes of neoliberal globalisation now seek to operate within networks of key global cities while not being limited – or, indeed, responsible – to any one of them.

43   Lucy Barnard, 'Saudi Shoots for the Stars as 1km-tall Kingdom Tower Set to Rise', *The National*, 13 March 2013, available at thenational.ae.

44   Nick Ames, 'Jeddah's Kingdom Tower Lifts Off', 5 November 2015, at designmena.com/.

45   See cnn.com/2014/07/01/world/meast/kingdom-tower-how-will-the-elevators-work/.

46   Excluding that below ground in mines.

The most (in)famous of London's supposedly 'iconic' crop of new skyscrapers: the 'Cheesegrater' – left, behind; the 'Walkie Talkie' – left, front; the 'Gherkin' – middle; and the 'Shard' – right – viewed from South London

By developing strings of obviously identifiable toy-like skycrapers which quickly become crassly packaged as 'iconic', the 'transnational capitalist class' of occupiers,[47] developers, rentiers and investors benefit from the construction of extremely lucrative 'premium' products that saturate global media circuits. Local planners and politicians, Kaika notes, in turn support the increased development of super-tall structures as necessary so that they are not left behind in some putative 'race' between global cities. In global financial centres like London, the stress falls on the ways in which the new buildings will ostensibly become emblematic of the status of their cities as powerful and instantly recognizable global hubs. Again, the naïve equation of height with economic power, and the desperation, as real estate economist William Murray puts it, to 'stand out in a congested landscape', runs riot.[48]

Caught in the pincers between these forces and the growing privatism and elitism of many urban planning regimes in neoliberalising cities, the city's resident population, Kaika argues, is often left to deal with arrogant landscapes of power made up of strings of poorly

47 Leslie Sklair, *The Transnational Capitalist Class*, Oxford: Blackwell, 2001, pp. 5–6.
48 Murray, 'Selling Tall'.

designed, highly secured and unbreachable 'objects of desire' that are inaccessible to all but a wealthy elite.[49]

To compound matters still further, concerns about 'security' are now widely used to fortify the new skyscrapers and to remove them – with their interior gardens, expensive rooftop restaurants and penthouse terraces – ever further from the wider public and the rest of the city. Such a process only accentuates the extreme exclusivity that surrounds the new towers. In London, 'public spaces' around the base of the new towers are actually highly secured and privatised plazas patrolled by private security forces who prohibit even photography.

'Even if the next skyscraper to be erected in London's or New York's skyline does not relate to anything that Londoners or New Yorkers can identify with', Kaika emphasises, 'the city's public is nevertheless bombarded by many expert opinions on its significance, sublime design, and aesthetic value.' Once the tower is raised to the sky, all that remains for London's citizens, she continues, is to 'kneel down and admire it, hoping that the subsequent ritualisation of the building into the city's everyday life might justify this belief.'

Worse still, the hype surrounding new towers often works to override already squeezed traditions of democratic accountability in urban planning. Maria Kaika emphasises how the public enquiry over the 'Walkie Talkie' tower completed in late 2014 in central London – and memorably described by the *Guardian* as 'bloated, inelegant an thuggish'[50] – was dominated by promises that the structure would emerge as 'iconic'. Francis Golding from the developer Land Securities exemplified this attitude when he prophesised that the '"Walkie Talkie" [will] become as iconic a part of London's skyline as the Swiss Re "Gherkin".'[51]

---

49   Maria Kaika, 'Autistic Architecture: The Fall of the Icon and the Rise of the Serial Object of Architecture', *Environment and Planning D: Society and Space* 29, 2011, pp. 969–84.

50   Rowan Moore, 'Walkie Talkie Review – Bloated, Inelegant, Thuggish', *Observer*, 4 January, 2015.

51   P. Clift, 'Walkie Talkie Would Become Loved Symbol of London', *EGI News*, 8 March 2007. Instead, this execrable building has merely generated anger, bewilderment and satire. Indeed, in 2015, it was 'awarded' the 'Carbuncle Cup' award for the UK's worst new building of that year.

Renzo Piano's 'Shard' meanwhile was widely lionised within messianic discourses about the future of London before it was even constructed. 'Something … significant [is] simmering south of the Thames', gushed the *Independent*. 'Something that transcends iconic architectural statements, and is poised to deliver a key step-change in vertical city planning. We're talking size, and we're talking clumps. The Shard, designed by the brilliant Renzo Piano, may prove to be a building of the highest quality and drama …'[52]

London's emerging skyline, violently and rapidly reshaped by a growing number of apparently arbitrary shapes jutting into the sky, lends itself to parody. 'Oh, man, and just look at London's privatised skyline', urges journalist Ian Martin. 'It would be hilarious if it wasn't so cartoonishly tragic. This one looks like a Nespresso machine. And that one, a cigar, is it? Potato? Full nappy? The utter capitulation of London's planning system in the face of serious money is detectable right there in that infantile, random collection of improbable sex toys poking gormlessly into the privatised air.'[53]

Fallen Towers: Destructural Works

Gamers playing the hugely popular *Battlefield 4* urban warfare video game, meanwhile, are already desperate to incorporate the Burj Khalifa into the simulated cityscapes within which they continually do virtual battle. 'As someone who lives in Dubai and sees this tower everyday', one of them exhorts, 'I would love to see Dubai as a map in *Battlefield 4*. Destroying the Burj Khalifa would be an awesome sight!'[54]

The destruction of skyscrapers has, indeed, long been a preoccupation within popular and media culture. Manhattan's towers have been brought to the ground so many times and in so many ways that a book of several hundred pages has been necessary to encompass

52 Jay Merrick, 'Architecture: The Sky's the Limit', *Independent*, 11 February 2008, p. 12.

53 Ian Martin, 'The City That Privatised Itself to Death', *Guardian*, 24 February 2015.

54 *Battlefield 4* discussion forum, 'Wouldn't [a part of] Dubai be a GREAT map for BF4?' 2013, available at reddit.com.

its myriad of devastations within cartoons, films, novels and video games.[55] Just as the erection of New York's towers became the cliché of rampant modernity and futurity, so their rapid and violent demise has long been the signifier par excellence of rapid and apocalyptic Armageddon. A swathe of recent post-apocalyptic films have so shaped the collective culture of urbanism that a stock response to the all-too-real 9/11 catastrophe was that 'it was just like a scene in a movie!' The 9/11 attacks 'were organised as epic horror cinema with meticulous attention to the *mise-en-scène*', urban critic Mike Davis writes:

> The hijacked planes were aimed precisely at the vulnerable border between fantasy and reality ... Thousands of people who turned on their televisions on 9/11 were convinced that the cataclysm was just a broadcast, a hoax. They thought they were watching rushes from the latest Bruce Willis film.[56]

The perpetrators of the 9/11 attacks were of course interested in much more than the chain of apocalyptic media events that their violence would set off – and their resonances with Western popular culture. Their actions were a careful, premeditated strategy of attacking the connections between extreme vertical modernism, aerial mobility and the geo-economic power of the West – while also bringing a real-time spectacle of death and mayhem to the heart of metropolitan power. 'A great tower is ... vulnerable', theologian Lilli Nye stresses. 'By virtue of its height and its hubris, it is inevitably precarious; it's always exposed – to instability, to attack, to forces greater than itself, such as the downward pull of gravity.'[57]

Detailed research into the background of Mohamed Atta, the leader of the 9/11 attackers and the pilot of the plane to crash into the north tower of the World Trade Center, suggests that targeting the most vertical and extreme examples of modernist verticality – out of the full gamut of possibilities of metropolitan America – was no accident.

55   Max Page, *The City's End: Two Centuries of Fantasies, Fears, and Premonitions of New York's Destruction*, New Haven, CN: Yale University Press, 2008.

56   Mike Davis, *Dead Cities*, p. 5.

57   Lilli Nye, 'Axis Mundi: The Meaning of Towers – September 11, 2011', available at tparkerchurch.org.

Atta was a graduate in architecture from Cairo University and had a master's degree in urban planning from Hamburg-Harburg Technical University. Already radicalised, he completed a research dissertation in Hamburg in 1994 on the tumultuous architectural changes them emerging in the ancient city of Aleppo, Syria (a long-standing research focus of Dittmar Machule, dean of the department, and a city since massively damaged in the Syrian civil war).

Atta's thesis, *City Planning in the Syrian Town of Aleppo,* lambasts the local employment of Western planners in the modernisation of the city and decries the destruction of traditional neighbourhoods and ancient, labyrinthine souks with raised flyovers, fast-food outlets and ramparts of high-rise modernist housing blocks and hotels. Atta argued that high-rise modernizing buildings in Aleppo – and elsewhere – needed to be destroyed because they both desecrated the traditional Islamic townscape and symbolised the invasion of Western culture into Islamic heartlands.

To restore traditional Islamic culture, Atta earmarked all the accoutrements of Western modernism for demolition with his suggested planning scheme. They were be replaced once again by the dense, finely woven souks and neighbourhoods of what he called the 'Islamic-oriental city'. Such a process would, Atta stressed, also remove all non-Islamic kufrs and tourists. 'The traditional structures of the society in all areas should be re-erected', Atta wrote. Enclosed housing along traditional lines would be used to incarcerate women so as not to 'engender emancipatory thoughts of any kind', a development which he viewed as 'out of place in Islamic society.'[58] On receiving the highest mark for the oral defence of his thesis by his professors, Atta's radicalisation had progressed to the stage where he refused to shake the hand of one – because she was female.

Atta met some of his fellow hijackers through an Islamic student group that he founded in Hamburg. Further radicalised at Hamburg's al-Tauhid mosque, Atta deepened his loathing of Western skyscraper and modernist architecture both during trips to his fast-changing home city of Cairo and during professional work at the Hamburg architectural firm Plankontor. Arriving eventually at a Jihadi training

---

58   The term from the Quran for nonbelievers or infidels; see Daniel Brook, 'The Architect of 9/11', *Slate,* 10 September 2009.

camp in Afghanistan, Atta became committed to martyrdom through apocalyptic violence.[59]

Though selected by Osama Bin Laden to lead the 9/11 strikes, Atta did not personally choose the World Trade Center as the main targets for his attacks. This decision fell to Khalid Sheikh Mohammed, a mechanical engineer by background whose nephew Ramzi Yousef had attempted but failed to level the buildings with a truck bomb in 1993. Indeed, the two had long looked through illustrated books of US skyscrapers to identify suitable targets.[60]

The Twin Towers targets – attacked by repurposing Western systems of vertical and aerial mobility as aerial weapons – were certainly in keeping with Atta's broader views. Representing modern verticalised urbanism, they were obvious targets for Wahabbist ideologues mobilised against the globe-spanning economic and cultural power of Western modernity. A perceived affront to God Himself in their verticality, they were the culmination of a Manhattan skyline that itself symbolised, to the attackers, all the decadence and immorality of Western urban culture.

Constructed to force people to take notice of their height and bulk, their destruction would kick off the ultimate global media spectacle – in real time. 'The modern city', philosophers Avishai Margalit and Ian Buruma write in *Occidentalism*, 'representing all that shimmers just out of reach, all the glittering arrogance and harlotry of the West, has found its icon in the Manhattan skyline, reproduced in millions of posters, photographs, and images, plastered all over the world. You cannot escape it … It excites longing, envy, and sometimes blinding rage.'[61]

The attacks were clearly designed to represent divinely inspired retribution against the ways in which extreme vertical modernism symbolised the concentration of wealth and power within the geopolitical heartlands of the dominating Western metropolis. Given Atta's

---

59   See Jonathan Raban, 'Rebels with a Cause', *Guardian*, 4 March 2002.

60   As well as being highly symbolic prestige targets, skyscrapers were also relatively easy to see from the air amid the complex landscapes of cities. See Terry McDermott, *Perfect Soldiers: The 9/11 Hijackers: Who They Were, Why They Did It*, New York: Politico, 2005, p. 167.

61   Avishai Margalit and Ian Buruma, *Occidentalism: The West in the Eyes of Its Enemies*, London: Penguin, 2005, p. 4.

lack of formal religious training, US novelist Jarett Kobek, who has written a semi-fictionalised account of Atta's life, thus emphasises strongly that 'looking at 9/11 architecturally makes a lot more sense than looking at it through the lens of religion'.[62]

Osama Bin Laden, himself a trained civil engineer, applauded the atrocities in New York in September 2001, citing the vertical elevation of the targeted structures as an affront to his fundamentalist cosmographic conception of an all-powerful Islamic God controlling a ground-based humanity from the heavens. 'There is America, hit by God in one of its softest spots', he said in a speech on 7 October 2001:

> Its greatest buildings were destroyed, thank God for that. There is America, full of fear from its north to its south, from its west to its east. Thank God for that … To America, I say only a few words to it and its people. I swear by God, who has elevated the skies without pillars, neither America nor the people who live in it will dream of security before we live it in Palestine, and not before all the infidel armies leave the land of Muhammad, peace be upon him.[63]

We can only imagine what Osama Bin Laden would have made of the rapid skyward growth of the 1-kilometre-high 'pillar' of the Kingdom Tower on the edge of Jeddah, a city with a revered Islamic history in which he lived for long periods as a child and student. His comments, though, leave us with a startling paradox. For the huge construction company established by Osama bin Laden's father in 1931 – now one of the largest of global construction corporations – is both a key investor in and main contractor for the building of Jeddah's Kingdom Tower.[64]

There is also irrefutable evidence that various members of the Saudi royal family, along with a brigade of their Wahabbist clerics, were the

62   Noura Wedell, 'Jarett Kobek's Portrait of a Hijacker', *Bomb Magazine*, 8 March 2012, available at bombmagazine.org.

63   Osama bin Laden, untitled speech, Doha, Qatar: Al Jazeera TV, 7 October 2001.

64   See Verushti Mawami, 'Kingdom Tower by Bin Laden Group Will Be the World's Tallest Building', *Industry Leaders Magazine*, 5 August 2011, available at industryleadersmagazine.com.

principal financiers of al-Qaeda and the Taliban in the 1990s, in the run up to the 2001 attacks as part of their long-standing support for Islamist Jihad across the world. Between 1921 and 1991 it has been estimated that Saudi royals and religious elites spent between $100 billion and $200 billion exporting the Wahabist ideology that is at the root of the Islamist violence of the Taliban, al-Qaeda and ISIS. (Fifteen of the eighteen hijackers were also Saudi nationals.)[65]

At this juncture the profound and unsettling links between the creation and destruction of skyscrapers within the past two decades become clear, though darkly ironic. As ever, the politics of creation and destruction connect seamlessly. Social and architectural theorist Ben Bratton has drawn close parallels between the operation of al-Qaeda as a kind of 'transnational firm' or 'figurative corporation' bent on what he calls architectural 'destructural works' and Osama bin Laden's father's immense construction conglomerate.[66]

'It is not surprising', Bratton writes, 'that this New Economy transnational firm [al-Qaeda] would be led by the son of one of the most powerful public works engineers in all of Saudi Arabia, of the man who literally built that kingdom, and would subcontract urban planners, like Mohammed Atta, to carry out its plans.' Reflecting on such a situation, he continues, 'it's not just fitting skills to tasks, nor ironic coincidence, it is a spiritual politics of space.'[67]

And yet, as we saw with our earlier discussion of the construction of the World Trade Center, the profound parallels between skyscraper construction and skyscraper terrorism run deeper still. Unusually, Eric Darton, author of *Divided We Stand: A Biography of New York's World Trade Center*, directly compares the figures of the towers' prime destroyer – Mohamed Atta – and their creator – Japanese architect, Minoru Yamasaki – at a metaphysical level.

---

65   Yousef Butt, 'How Saudi Wahhabism Is the Fountainhead of Islamist Terrorism', *Huffington Post*, 20 January 2015; Anthony Summers and Robin Swan, 'The Kingdom and the Towers', *Vanity Fair*, August 2011; Ben Hubbard and Scott Shane, 'Pre-9/11 Ties Haunt Saudis as New Accusations Surface', *New York Times*, 4 February 2015.

66   The term 'destructural works' is Ben Bratton's. See his 'Figures of Destructuration: Terrorism, Architecture, Social Form', November 2009, available at bratton.info.

67   Ibid.

Darton identifies what he calls 'a kindred spirit linking the apparently polar realms of skyscraper terrorist and skyscraper builder.'[68] He argues that the enormous physical forces necessary to both create and destroy skyscrapers can succeed only though extreme and violent levels of abstraction – what he calls 'daydreams of domination'. The immense scale of the acts of creating and destroying monumental towers, Darton elaborates, work to radically distance their authors from the fine-grained, day-to-day human habitation of real people and real bodies on the ground in real urban places.

Both construction and violent erasure also entail the use of professional and calculative power or architects and engineers. On the one hand, this power is used to push up an immense and abstract set of modernist or neomodernist towers against the forces of gravity; on the other, to 'unbuild' them through calculating the structural properties of the target and the capabilities of the truck bomb or the velocity and power of the impacting aircraft.[69] 'We are creatures of the Earth and air', Darton concludes, 'capable of functioning with our heads in the clouds – so long as our feet remain on the ground.' He finishes, however, by drawing metaphysical connections between the arrogance of those who's hubris raises – or brings down – vast towers. 'Rising toward the stratosphere', Darton writes, 'we feel we have broken free of gravity. When that illusion possesses us, it is not long before our ascent finds its opposite number in the terror of the fall.'

---

68   Darton, 'Janus Face of Architectural Terrorism'.

69   It must be stressed here that there is no evidence that Atta and his colleagues had any way of predicting, let alone planning, the final collapse of the buildings once they had been struck by the two aircraft.

8.

Housing: Luxified Skies

Building Up to 'Save' the City?

In March 2011, Harvard economics professor Edward Glaeser wrote a manifesto for the building of vertical cities in the *Atlantic* magazine.[1] Arguably the world's most influential urban economist, Glaeser playfully invoked the Book of Genesis, citing the builders of the legendary Tower of Babel when they declared, 'Come, let us build us a city and a tower with its top in the heavens. And let us make a name for ourselves, lest we be scattered upon the face of the whole earth.'

To Glaeser, there is a simple solution to the contemporary impasse combining extraordinary rates of urbanisation, rapid population growth, a predilection for conserving large swathes of older, lower housing stock and crises in the supply of affordable urban housing. Such a situation, he argues, means that there is little choice but to build up, to build high and to build quickly. Asserting that gentrification and spiralling house prices in many cities are squeezing out lower income groups – an undeniable problem – Glaeser argued that 'growth, not height restrictions and a fixed building stock, keeps space affordable and ensures that poorer people and less profitable firms can stay and help a thriving city remain successful and diverse.'

In an argument that has a long and contested history, Glaeser urges that the sheer economics of building stacked, vertical housing on a large scale mean that doing so is the only way to deliver affordable housing to the masses in contemporary urban contexts. Without such a programme, he argues, many poor nations and cities will be unable

---

1   Edward Glaeser, 'How Skyscrapers Can Save the City', *Atlantic*, March 2011. See also his *Triumph of the City: How Our Greatest Invention Makes Us Richer, Smarter, Greener, Healthier and Happier*, New York: Penguin, 2012.

to emerge as middle-income nations and cities, since decent and accessible urban housing will always be confined to wealthy elites.

Glaeser emphasises the economies of scale that vertical housing provides. Once buildings rise above seven storeys or so, the extra fixed costs of buying or leasing the scarce plot of land and providing elevators and the other requirements for vertical living contribute much less in terms of marginal costs because they are spread among more units. This means that 'building up has its own economic logic, since those fixed costs can be spread over more apartments.'

He is especially scathing about the tendency for wealthy city dwellers who move into gentrified historic urban neighbourhoods to use their power to proscribe new, taller urban housing that might be both affordable to the non-wealthy and accessible to the highest levels of demand in city cores (rather than being marginalised to cheaper housing in the metropolitan periphery or beyond where transport difficulties and costs exclude them from services and jobs and create traffic crises). 'In 2000, people who lived in historic districts in Manhattan were on average almost 74 per cent wealthier than people who lived outside such areas', Glaeser writes. In addition, 'average people are barred from living in central Paris just as surely as if the city had put up a gate and said that no middle-income people can enter.'[2] With a bourgeois sensibility for preserving historic urban fabric in aspic prevailing in many Western city cores, the numbers of new housing units are utterly inadequate – adding to spiralling costs and reductions of supplies of social housing.

Glaeser's ideas on high-rise housing have been enormously influential in shaping urban planning and housing agendas in big cities across the world in the past decade or so. Partly in response to his and other similar arguments, cities with historically low height restrictions as diverse as London, Toronto, Vancouver, Johannesburg, Panama City and Melbourne – to name but a few – have embraced tall and super-tall residential towers as a de facto housing policy. The building of housing towers in central cities has chimed powerfully with a laudable orthodoxy that equates the vertical densification of city cores with increasing environmental sustainability and generating the much-vaunted phenomenon of 'smart growth' – urban and economic

---

2   Ibid.

development that is, relatively, environmentally benign. Importantly, ideas of vertical growth have also resonated with city leaders and development agencies keen to engineer glitzy, futuristic skylines as a means of building urban 'brands' that compete with other so-called world or global cities for investment, tourism, media exposure and the 'creative class' (mobile and well-educated high-tech elites).[3]

The problem with Glaeser's arguments, however, is that they invoke densification and verticalisation for cities as a simple economic imperative while completely ignoring the structural social and political forces shaping the production and consumption of urban housing in contemporary cities.[4] In economic terms, Glaeser focuses exclusively on alleged links between inelastic housing supply (caused by constrained building and low building heights) and housing affordability. At the same time, in line with the wider neoliberal rhetoric within which his arguments fit,[5] he argues that state regulation is merely a barrier to the building of housing in cities. The implication is that housing and planning regulations and subsidies – rent controls, social and collective housing provisions, height restrictions – need to be cut away in the interests of an entirely privatised housing regime unleashing the vertical growth processes that they supposedly constrain.

In many cities, the result of this confluence of ideas concerning densification, 'smart' growth, neoliberal vertical housing and 'global' city planning – despite Glaeser's rhetoric – has been profoundly regressive socially. In many ways, Glaeser's arguments are merely the latest in a long line of 'trickle-down' economics that have been handed out by a stream of neoliberal urban theorists over the past four decades. Such theorists continually proffer the capitalist utopia of unleashed and unregulated global capital operating to the alleged benefit of all.

---

3 See Richard Florida, 'The Rise of the Creative Class', *Washington Monthly* 34:5, 2002, pp. 15–25.

4 Jamie Peck, 'Edward Glaeser's City: A Triumph of Economism', unpublished paper, 2014.

5 Glaeser is affiliated with the neoconservative Manhattan Institute, which was a key intellectual player behind George W. Bush's two presidential tenancies. See Jamie Peck, 'Economic Rationality Meets Celebrity Urbanology: Exploring Edward Glaeser's City', *International Journal of Urban and Regional Research*, 2016 (forthcoming).

In the absence of nonmarket mechanisms to create and allocate mass urban housing as an affordable living space for those who need it, however, all that remains when city planners allow tall housing towers to rise above their streetscapes are global engines of unregulated financial speculation. Such financial mechanisms treat the new housing towers – and the land they rest on – purely as investment assets for the world's booming and dominant – but numerically small – class of super-rich (who often buy off-plan at distant marketing events in cash). The urban growth skyward often thus becomes merely a process of the marketisation of land and real estate organised more for the 'housing' of elite capital than for a city's people (let alone a city's poorer population). New condominiums for elites in cities like London, Vancouver, Toronto, San Francisco, Miami, Melbourne, Sydney and New York thus need to be understood primarily as what Paul Goldberger in *Vanity Fair* has called 'tradable commodities, perfect for the speculatively inclined'.[6]

Because the profit margins in building prime housing for increasingly wealthy elites far exceed those in serving the lower ends of housing markets, cities thus become saturated with extremely expensive housing towers. In volatile economic contexts where elite investment is fleeing more risky commodity and stock markets, for the relative safe haven of real estate in a select group of core global cities, the competitive scramble of investors works to radically increase housing prices.

Culturally, too, the new vertical shift in urban housing is being tellingly coded. The vertical ascent by the relatively small numbers of (often absent) owner occupiers in new elite housing towers is widely celebrated and marketed as the answer to all their narcissistic and anti-urban fantasies. The new towers are invariably marketed as luxury cocoons of über wealth and fortressed security that float serenely above the urban landscape, while offering large amounts of living space and astonishing private services and luxuries. The wider city is usually rendered as a mere aesthetic backdrop of startling (and expensive) views: a premium panorama to be consumed from on high, at a safe distance from the people who actually inhabit it far below.

---

6   Paul Goldberger, 'Too Rich, Too Thin, Too Tall', *Vanity Fair*, May 2014.

The shimmering promises that forests of new housing towers – often marketed and clumsily designed to be 'iconic' while being poorly integrated into the darkened and windswept streetscape below – will resolve the housing crises in the world's big cities is therefore chimeric in the absence of powerful social housing and planning policies.[7] Very often, indeed, the processes through which new housing towers are constructed amount to programmes of engineered gentrification, which forcibly evict or sweep away the remnants of earlier periods where housing was at least to some extent organised collectively based on criteria of social need.

Many urban critics are now widely lambasting the simplistic equation that building high necessarily results in cheaper housing, higher densities and greener urbanism. 'All the experts say that if we want a greener, healthier city then we have to roll back the regulations, get rid of the NIMBYs [Not In My Back Yard-ers] and let a thousand towers bloom', urban critic Lloyd Alter writes. 'But what are we getting when we throw away height limits and barriers to development, stop worrying about shadows and views, and let the developers loose? Also importantly, *who* are we getting?'[8]

Alter surveys the new housing towers being erected in London, New York and Toronto. He finds that the emerging housing is overwhelmingly dominated by large, multi-million-dollar, super-luxury condos within isolated high-end architectural towers designed by the likes of Frank Gehry and geared to global investors and the super-rich. 'Buildings are not isolated Frank Gehry sculptures', Alter retorts. 'They exist to house people and give them places to work. They are part of a culture and a society [they are] not monuments. They should serve a societal need, not just park money for the very rich.'[9]

We will come back to the details whereby current elites are taking over the urban skies through housing towers built for the super-rich in various cities later in this chapter. To understand the significance of this shift, though, we need to place it in its historical context. In

---

7   As well as blocking out light, new towers often create wind systems at ground level that can be uncomfortable and even dangerous to those on the street.

8   Lloyd Alter, 'It's Time to Dump the Tired Argument That Density and Height Are Green and Sustainable', *Treehugger*, 3 January 2014, available at treehugger.com.

9   Ibid.

particular, we need to understand how the current orthodoxy of building elite housing towers in Western cities has risen to dominance after half a century during which the provision of mass social housing – often in modernist towers – was derided and undermined by often simplistic arguments that worked to produce the myth that low-income vertical housing in city cores must necessarily be doomed to fail.

The Rise and Fall of Mass Social Housing

Between the 1930s and 1970s radically new and highly ambitious programmes of mass social housing in Western cities came to dominance. Essentially, such programmes, however misguided and problematic, focused on efforts to democratise aerial living in cities. As the possibilities of steel-framed construction, elevators and industrialised prefabrication fused with modernist urban ideas, elevated apartment blocks were widely lauded as a powerful force of social and economic modernisation in response to industrial poverty, rapid urbanisation and the mass strategic bombing of cities.

Central to this process was the idea of leaving the ground-level street, with its pollution, congestion, conflict and poverty, for raised-up and rationally planned three-dimensional urban worlds that were emancipatory because they were designed in toto. To their advocates, mass vertical housing blocks 'offered a social and political response to the chaos of cities rocked by an age of industrial poverty, population explosion, mass migration, and total war.'[10]

The rhetoric signified a step-change in mass industrial society, a planned and designed revolution through vertical, designed housing which mimicked the parallel rise of mass vertical housing in socialist and communist societies. The obsession was with the creation of a *tabula rasa* through massive demolition of what was there before so that a radically new society could be engineered.

'A breach has been made with the past', Walter Gropius declared in 1965. Leader of the hugely influential Bauhaus school of design

---

10   Samuel Zipp 'The Roots and Routes of Urban Renewal', *Journal of Urban History* 39:3, May 2013, p. 372.

in Weimar Germany and a pivotal figure in the spread of architectural modernism in the West after his emigration to Harvard in 1937, Gropius argued this break 'allows us to envisage a new aspect of architecture corresponding to the technical civilisation of the age we live in; the morphology of dead styles has been destroyed; and we are returning to honesty of thought and feeling.'[11]

To modernists, lifting the urban masses up into the light, sun and air of functionalist towers, above the surrounding parks that were supposed to accompany them, would bring social and morale improvement that the 'lower' life of the teeming streets of the slums, and their fetid basements and terrible sanitation, could never hope to achieve. In the interwar period, distributing huge towers across park-like environments was also thought to have an added advantage in moving urban populations away from expected gas attacks and making them a difficult target for strategic bombing.

Architectural modernism in the mid and late twentieth century was a crucial element of wider trends in European and American modernist art, literature, film and culture which linked verticality to ideas of power and freedom – ideas that were radically questioned as part of the shift to postmodernist forms of culture from the late 1960s onwards.[12] Modern architectural ideologies also linked notions of modernity, utopianism and industrialism intrinsically to the built forms of concrete. 'Being economical, flexible and indestructible', architects Fosco Lucarelli and Mariabruna Fabrizi write, 'concrete became a metaphor for "the future" and acquired enough respect to be emphatically exposed on the façades of large buildings.'[13]

A range of influential movements – of modernist architecture and 'scientific' planning; of mass industrialisation and consumption; and of the 'rational' reengineering of bureaucratised social welfare and planning – fused to create a widespread utopian ethos that vertical

---

11   Walter Gropius, *The New Architecture and the Bauhaus*, Cambridge, MA: MIT Press, 1965, p. 146.

12   Paul Christoph Haacke, 'The Vertical Turn: Topographies of Metropolitan Modernism', PhD thesis, University of California, Berkeley, 2011, available at escholarship.org/uc/item/1857736f.

13   Fosco Lucarelli and Mariabruna Fabrizi, 'The Trellick Tower: The Fall and Rise of a Modern Monument', *San Rocco Magazine* 5, Fall 2012.

mass housing offered a revolutionary break from the pitfalls of the nineteenth-century industrial city – and its streets.

Sigfried Giedeon, another key figure in the modernist architecture movement, urged the mass production of entirely new modern house types offering the 'greatest possible overcoming of gravity'.[14] In 1947, the most important figure of all, Le Corbusier – a figure now known to have had strong links to the French Fascist movement – urged what he called an 'upward spirit' in housing design. Recalling his obsession with building for an idealised, modular, upright and male human, for Le Corbusier, 'geometrical engineering and glass' were little less than 'tutelary deities enabling [man] to make with his proportion the cube with exact right angles which is his niche, his cell, his shell, his haven: man in the cube'. Through a range of utopian projects and proposals – most famously his utopian *Ville Contemporaine* of 3 million (1922) and his *Plan Voisin* (1925), a vast series of huge towers on a totally demolished tract of central Paris – he sought to completely replace terrestrial urbanism with what he called 'a vertical city'. This new city form would 'pile up the cells which have for so long been crushed on the ground, and set them high above the earth, bathed in light and air.'[15]

Housing was thus to be much more than shelter: rather than merely the inhabitation of private space, it was to emerge as the fully modern, collective and mechanised social and technical experience of an entire 'environmental matrix' organised and designed around the figure of the standardised (able-bodied male) human body.[16] Thus, freeways, parks, schools, leisure facilities, elevated walkways, raised megastructures and all the other accoutrements of modernist living needed to be planned for as well.

Planners and architects in turn ascended to the skies to adopt aerial views and offered comprehensive designs of the entire complex, organised to create geometric patterns that looked aesthetically powerful from above (as in Brasilia and Chandigarh). It seemed only

---

14   Sigfried Giedeon, *Building in France, Building in Iron, Building in Ferroconcrete,* Santa Monica, CA: Getty Center for the History of Art and the Humanities, 1995 [1928].

15   Le Corbusier, *The City of Tomorrow and Its Planning*, New York: Dover, 1987 [1927], p. 280.

16   This term comes from the US Citizens Housing Council, 1940. Cited in Zipp, 'Roots and Routes', p. 274.

fitting that the view of the autocratic designer looking down from his (and it was invariably 'his') bird's-eye view using maps and aerial photographs emerged as the blueprint for the re-engineering of human life in its totality.

The power of this ideological confluence was torrential. If corrective mobilisation was necessary to forcibly re-engineer entire cities and their populations to reach this goal – while also clearing poorer groups from central cities so the economic value of 'higher' land uses could be achieved – so be it. The modernist challenge, after all, was the remaking of people as well as physical environments. Le Corbusier's 'machines for living' were to be standardised and mass-produced machinic environments welded intimately to the new age of capitalist mass production and circulation. J. J. P. Oud, the municipal architect for Rotterdam, even called his worker's houses 'dwelling Fords' to signal the deep linkage between the vertical apartment as a machine and the assembly-line automobile.[17]

Vertical Pathologies? Critique and Erasure

> We had to believe that problems in public housing were inevitable because there is something naturally wrong with poor people living together.
>
> – Maya Dukmasova, 'Tricknology'

Since the widespread construction of mass social housing towers in Western cities between the 1950s and 1970s, the highly complex situations surrounding their successes and failures have often been reduced to simplistic clichés. These have been essential to construct a prevailing mythology that all mass social housing programmes in the West have been abject failures and that social housing built vertically for lower-income residents must necessarily be problematic.

Critics – many residents included – lambasted the violent erasure of old neighbourhoods, the often poor design and building standards of those projects that were built, inadequate levels of services and maintenance, and the psychological and social alienation that

---

17   Cited in Zipp, 'Roots and Routes', p. 376.

sometimes came with inhabiting 'streets in the sky'. Many lamented that the obsession with the modernist aesthetics of the new towers had not been matched by detailed sociological thinking about how they would benefit the lives of those who inhabited them.

In the fierce debates about the design and management of vertical mass housing that developed in France, the UK, the US and elsewhere from the late 1960s, vertical mass housing began to be read off as an (often racialised) proxy for pathologically rooted 'urban problems': crime, poverty, gang violence, ghettoisation and drug misuse. Jane Jacobs, the most influential critic of all, complained of the 'great blight of dullness' in the cheap and poorly designed US public housing projects.[18] Dutch planner John Habraken, meanwhile, criticised modernist planners and architects for being 'bewitch[ed] by partially understood technical possibilities' which resulted in a soul-destroying '"automatism" and uniformity in housing design.'[19]

Certainly, the forcible and arrogant rehousing and removal of populations into warrens of cell-like apartments within badly sited, poorly designed and under-landscaped housing towers was often socially disastrous. The Liverpool poet Ken Rogers reflects on the comprehensive redevelopment of terrace housing in that city:

> The Council sent us far away
> They called it our Slum Clearance Day
> They built us flats ten storeys high
> With 'streets' that floated in the sky
> They said we wouldn't have it hard
> But High Rise flats don't have a yard
> And how are mams supposed to dream
> Without a sandstone step to clean?
> Why bother with an open door
> When Mary's on another floor?[20]

---

18   Jane Jacobs, *The Death and Life of Great American Cities*, New York: Random House, 1961, p. 46.

19   Cited in Jacobs, Cairns and Strebel, 'A Tall Storey', p. 614.

20   The poem, by Ken Rogers, comes from his tribute to people who were rehoused and often moved as part of the slum clearances in Liverpool in the 1960s. See Ken Rogers, *Lost Tribe: The People's Memories: 2.* Liverpool: Trinity Mirror North West and North Wales, 2012, p. 7.

The backlash, when it came, rejected all high-rise housing ideas in its obsession with giving residents a territorial, ground-level space that they could survey and control. Drawing on architect and planner Oscar Newman's argument that humans, as territorial beings, necessarily require a 'defensible space' they can control, an important example here was Alice Coleman's 1985 UK book *Utopia in Trial.*[21] Coleman saw a simple, direct and universal link between high-rise apartment living and the prevalence of raised walkways and processes of social alienation and the growth of crime. Coleman even offered data which, she argued, suggested that simple correlations existed between a whole host of data indicating the existence of 'urban problems' in the high-rise projects that she studied with distance from the ground.

Such ideas have a continued salience on the political right. Despite his wider advocacy of building upwards to create urban housing, Glaeser suggests that vertical housing for those in poverty is necessarily problematic: 'The combination of height and social disorder can be very, very bad. New York and Chicago built many of those projects, and they proved very unsuccessful. They concentrated large amounts of poor people on very small amounts of land, which made it difficult to create law and order.'[22]

The problem of such arguments is that they tend to generalise the experiences of a few highly problematic cases across all vertically constructed affordable social housing, everywhere. 'By the 1990s', urban writer Maya Dukmasova points puts, 'the dismal reputation of public housing high-rises had grown to such monstrous proportions that it overshadowed the reality on the ground ... But the idea of pervasive and irrevocable dysfunction in the system was the first necessary component of an agenda to eradicate public housing.'[23]

Simplistic clichés about public and social housing have, as a result, produced one of the crucial 'manufactured realities' widely used to justify neoliberal policies for the systematic disassembling of public

---

21   Oscar Newman, *Defensible Space,* New York: Macmillan, 1972; Alice Coleman, *Utopia on Trial: Vision and Reality in Planned Housing,* London: Shipman, 1985.

22   Douglas Gorney, 'City Limits: A Conversation with Edward Glaeser', *Atlantic,* 8 February 2011.

23   Dukmasova, 'Tricknology', p. 25.

housing systems and their distribution into private hands. 'To man-ufacture the neoliberal reality', Dukmasova continues, 'it is necessary to establish a baseline of truths, such as "public housing is doomed to fail." Sometimes history and reality speak to the contrary!'[24] Indeed, myths about the inevitable failure of vertical public housing have been so widely generalised that they are endlessly repeated as accepted facts in many Western societies.

This process has been crucial in the widespread destruction and privatisation of public housing programmes. Often, the myths have been used to justify the wholesale dismantling of all public and social housing provision, or their systematic neglect and impoverishment. Dukmasova recounts, for example, how the alleged failures of vertical public housing were used by authorities in Atlanta to destroy many successful, popular and well-designed tower schemes in that city, such as the Techwood and Clark Howell projects. In what were seen as bold neoliberal experiments at the time, tenants were dispersed to the four winds while sites were allocated to private house builders as part of Atlanta's 'clean-up' to host the 1996 Olympics.

In many places, the backlash against mass vertical housing – and the grand stories of their 'failure' – have succeeded so powerfully that their systematic erasure and demolition is proceeding apace. The demolition of St Louis's Pruitt-Igoe complex, on 3 March 1972, has even been widely cited as an iconic moment signalling the social tran-sition from modernism to postmodernism. 'Happily, it is possible to date the death of Modern Architecture to a precise moment in time …' wrote Charles Jencks, in a famous statement in 1977. 'Modern Architecture died in St. Louis, Missouri on July 15, 1972 at 3:32 pm (or thereabouts) when the infamous Pruitt-Igoe scheme, or rather several of its slab blocks, were given the final coup de grâce by dynamite.'[25]

Built in the 1950s, the Pruitt-Igoe project became in the 1960s and 1970s a symbol of the racialised decay of inner urban cores and white flight as the middle classes rushed to the suburbs. Redlining, dein-dustrialisation and the growing emergence of racialised ghettos in

---

24   Ibid., pp. 25, 26.
25   Charles Jencks, *The Paradigm in Architecture*, cited in Charles Jencks and Karl Kropf, *Theories and Manifestoes of Contemporary Architecture*, New York: Academy Press, 1997, p. 9.

Pruitt-Igoe and similar projects allowed mainstream media to demonise such places and their inhabitants. Pruitt-Igoe thus emerged as a symbol of urban decay, collapse and hopelessness. Its spectacular erasure was widely used as shorthand for a period in the US where 'those who lived in cities no longer cared for them, and those who lived elsewhere feared and detested them.'[26] The fact that communal housing was widely deemed to chime with socialist thinking didn't help.

The demolition of Pruitt-Igoe's thirty-three cheaply built slab towers powerfully symbolises the shift towards the systematic erasure of mass vertical housing in many Western nations. The site is now a 'messy plot of trees with an electrical substation,'[27] and the project still haunts debates about the links between modernity, urbanity, public architecture and vertical housing. Featured in films (most notably, perhaps, in Godfrey Reggio and Philip Glass's 1982 *Koyaanisqatsi*), documentaries and sociological treatises, the after-image of Pruitt-Igoe's collapsing towers has had a complex and influential cultural life all its own. 'Through all its phases of ruination', geographer Garrett Dash Nelson points out, 'Pruitt-Igoe has been a kind of document, first in bricks and blueprints, then in graffiti lines and trash heaps, and finally in films and essays, of the different ways of imagining, executing, and then remembering Modernist ideals.'[28]

Appropriately enough for an event deemed to mark the commencement of postmodernism, Pruitt-Igoe's iconic demolition has been followed by the growth of a whole cultural industry focused on demolishing tall housing blocks as urban spectacle. Floodlit, choreographed and thoroughly hyped, such demolitions have been enrolled into the entrepreneurial packaging of cities for tourism and consumption. They present the violent destruction of place – and the erasure of collective and architectural memory – as a live media event to be consumed globally, in real time, by millions.

Tactless at the very least, such events raise major controversies. When authorities in Glasgow announced the 'live' demolition of five

---

26   Garrett Dash-Nelson, 'Pruitt-Igoe: Facts and Memories of an American Ruin', unpublished paper, 2009, p. 4, available at http://people.matinic.us/.

27   Ibid., p. 1.

28   Ibid., p. 2.

(Above) Glasgow's Red Road Estate after construction; (below) demolition of some of Glasgow's modernist housing blocks on Red Road, June 2012

of the city's tallest Red Road housing blocks as part of the opening ceremony for the Commonwealth Games in 2014, for example, the reactions were particularly fierce.[29] 'We are going to wow the world', Gordon Matheson, leader of Glasgow City Council, proudly announced:

> with the demolition of the Red Road flats set to play a starring role. Red Road has an iconic place in Glasgow's history, having been home to thousands of families and dominating the city's skyline for decades.

---

29 The planned media spectacle of the demolitions followed a long series of previous destructions that were merely reported by the usual TV and news outlets; 25 per cent of Glasgow's high-rise blocks were demolished between 2005 and 2015.

Their demolition will all but mark the end of high-rise living in the area and is symbolic of the changing face of Glasgow, not least in terms of our preparations for the Games.[30]

However, people who had lived in the flats over the previous half-century were disgusted with the idea. Many Glaswegians were 'immobilized in disbelief' at the announcement;[31] a mass petition to cancel the decision quickly followed.

'Certainly it's not an appropriate celebratory spectacle', Carolyn Leckie, a former member of parliament for Scotland, responded. 'What on earth were the people who decided this thinking of?' she wondered. 'You couldn't make it up! They say it's celebrating Glasgow's renewal. Can you imagine if Danny Boyle's celebration of the NHS at the [2012 London] Olympics opening ceremony involved blowing up an NHS hospital?'[32] Following a sustained campaign to stop the games organisers cancelled the televised demolition because of 'safety and security' concerns.

In the context of contemporary housing crises, mythical assumptions that any high-rise housing for lower-income residents must necessarily be a bad idea are profoundly unhelpful. In their preoccupation with reading off social 'impacts' from abstract design ideas, critics of vertically stacked social housing have tended to neglect a wide range of important factors that have often contributed heavily to the failures of vertical social housing projects. Here we must confront the often tawdry machinations of land markets, the profiteering of industrial housing firms and the excessive zeal of messianic architects and planners. Poor housing management policies, racialised policing and catastrophic drugs policies must also be considered. We should also address the often shoddy and cheapskate design of the resulting tower blocks, the failure to deliver promised infrastructure, services or jobs, poor communication between architects and housing offices and the power of demonising stigma. Above all, we must recognise the systematic deindustrialisation of and disinvestment in many of

---

30   Severin Carrell, 'Glasgow 2014: Red Road Flats to Be Blown Up During Opening Ceremony', *Guardian,* 3 April 2014.

31   Tracey McVeigh, 'Backlash at Plans to Demolish Red Road Flats Live on Television', *Observer,* 6 April 2014.

32   Ibid.

the surrounding local economies imagined to sustain the towers and the severe problems of mass unemployment that followed.

Perhaps more important, though, is the need to stress that many examples of high-rise social housing throughout Europe and North America – including modernist high-rise housing – have been extremely successful.[33] In hundreds of cases, socially oriented and publicly built and managed vertical housing remains tremendously popular. 'From the nearly universally negative coverage of public housing', write housing scholars David Madden and Peter Marcuse about the United States, 'you'd never know that far more people are trying to get into it than leave it. Nearly all of the nation's more than 3,000 public housing authorities have waiting lists. New York City's public housing has a 1 per cent vacancy rate and more than 270,000 families waiting for a spot.'[34]

As the British architecture critic Owen Hatherley remarked in 2008, the better modernist social housing projects from the 1930s to the 1970s are 'well worth rescuing from the dustbin of history and the blandishments of heritage.' Such projects, he argued, 'continue to be *useful*: a potential index of ideas, successful or failed, tired, untried or broken on the wheel of the market or the state. Even in their ruinous condition, they can still offer a sense of possibility which decades of being told that 'There is No Alternative' has almost beaten out of us.'[35]

Successes in vertical social housing have occurred when design, maintenance and management have been of a high quality; where residents have been able to maintain their economic fortunes amid dramatic processes of urban restructuring; and where residents have had continued inputs into the design and management of their homes. The careful integration of socially rented housing and avoidance of ethnic ghettoisation have also often also been crucial. In nations where mass high-rise housing has been organised for whole popula-tions – as in Singapore and Hong Kong – high levels of maintenance, rent regulation and the provision of mass transit, decent public and

33   Williams Goldhagen, 'On Architecture: Living High', *New Republic*, 7 June 2012.

34   David Madden, 'Five Myths about Public Housing', *Washington Post*, 11 September 2015.

35   Owen Hatherley, *Militant Modernism,* London: John Hunt Publishing, 2009, p. 13 (emphasis in original).

commercial services and quality landscaping have helped to make tower living relatively popular, even for families.

We must be wary, then, of writing residential towers into simplistic 'grand stories' while ignoring their complex and varied histories and politics. Such a point is especially important in confronting the current boom of super-elite housing towers and in asserting again the imperative that current housing crises are such that vertical social housing must rise again (though in ways that learn the lessons from past failures).

'The residential high rise has been, in a variety of guises, drawn up into a range of indisputably grand stories', writes geographer Jane M. Jacobs. Such stories have involved 'utopian visions for living, stellar architectural careers like that of Le Corbusier, bureaucratic machineries of mass housing provision, national projects of modernisation, the claims of critical social sciences, spectacular instances of failure, as well as popular and academic imaginaries about globalisation.'[36] Jacobs, who has done some superb work on the lived realities of high-rise housing with various colleagues, makes the important argument that the small details of mass housing provision, and their variations, tend to evaporate from such grand narratives.

In Singapore, for example, excellent planning, design, maintenance and infrastructure standards have been complemented by tight regulation of a range of imaginative financial mechanisms to deliver excellent and relatively affordable mass housing to the mass of the population. The fact that 80 per cent of Singapore's population of 5.5 million live in public housing has been pivotal to the success of this land-starved island state.[37]

Here policy and research need to attend, minimally, to the politics of maintenance and neglect; the varied political economies of finance, land, building and speculation; the highly diverse experiences and cultures of tower living; the complex politics of design, technology and maintenance; and the ways in which different societies represent –

---

36   Jane M. Jacobs, 'A Geography of Big Things', online paper archived by the Institute of Geography, School of Geosciences, University of Edinburgh, 2005, available at era.lib.ed.ac.uk.

37   Elena Generalova and Victor Generalova, 'Designing High-Rise Housing: The Singapore Experience', *Council for Tall Buildings and Urban Habitat,* 2014, at global.ctbuh.org.

and sometimes demonise – social housing towers and those who inhabit them.[38] It is also important to stress that the communities who inhabit modernist high-rises can shape and transform them in important ways that often belie the apparently monolithic architecture of such structures.[39]

Elite Takeovers of the Urban Skies

It is clear that the circulation of images of the spectacular demise of housing projects like Pruitt-Igoe or Red Road increasingly ceases to connect to any reasoned discussion of the complexities surrounding vertical social housing. Instead, in bolstering grand stories about social high-rises, they stand as incitations to never build vertical socially oriented housing in the West again. Like Alice Coleman's essentialising critiques, they stifle creative debate about how well-designed, well-managed and affordable housing in Western cities in the future might take other forms than low-level apartment blocks or the ground-hugging neo-traditional houses with their Newmanian defensible space, so beloved of New Urbanists. Meanwhile, bolstered by trickle-down ideas like those Ed Glaeser, in parallel with the evisceration and privatisation of the inheritance of social housing, city cores are being systematically re-engineered through speculative real estate and financial bubbles as the spaces for neoliberal elites.

With mass social housing projects largely undermined by processes of neoliberalisation within many contemporary cities, vertical housing – as with so many aspects of the politics of verticality – has transmuted in a generation into a secession of the elites into super-expensive condo towers. Indeed, the widespread construction of vertical, gated towers for the merely wealthy and the super-rich in

---

38   For a brilliant discussion of these factors in the rise and fall of the Aylesbury 'sink' estate in southeast London, see Ben Campkin, *Remaking London: Decline and Regeneration in Urban Culture*, London: IB Tauris, 2013. chapter 4.

39   Migrant Bangladeshi communities in Toronto, for example, have dramatically reshaped some of the city's modernist towers. See Sutama Ghosh, 'Everyday Lives in Vertical Neighbourhoods: Exploring Bangladeshi Residential Spaces in Toronto's Inner Suburbs', *International Journal of Urban and Regional Research* 38:6, 2014, pp. 2008–24.

many cities now rivals their more familiar horizontal shift to gated suburban, exurban or resort enclaves.

While not completely ignored, the politics surrounding this process remain under-explored. As already discussed, this is partly because the growth of glitzy housing towers for the wealthy in city cores is often being camouflaged by suggestions that such towers are part of a needed movement to 'densification' and increased urban 'sustainability'. The elite take-over of the urban skies is also neglected because overwhelmingly horizontal frames are used – especially in the Anglophone world – to discuss and imagine urban inequality. Thus far, arguments about the clustering of elites into fortressed enclaves have tended to be, as anthropologists Kevin Lewis O'Neill and Benjamin Fogarty-Valenzuela put it, 'supremely horizontal observations'[40] linked with studies of gated communities and fortified enclaves in the suburbs and exurbs scattered to the peripheries of cities.[41]

A growing range of urban writers and activists are, however, starting to address the ascension of the fortressed elites. Anti-gentrification social movements in cities as diverse as San Francisco, Istanbul, Tokyo, London, Hong Kong, Manila, Delhi, Mumbai, Vancouver. Melbourne and Toronto – where over 85 per cent of all central housing construction is now in the form of condominiums – now actively suggest that the central landscapes of these cities are being transformed through processes of 'vertical sprawl' erecting large numbers of 'vertical gated communities'.[42]

The Vancouver critique is especially important because of the way in which the city authorities there have concentrated housing investment into a large number of central glass-covered condo towers as

40   Kevin O'Neill and Benjamin Fogarty-Valenzuela, 'Verticality', *Journal of the Royal Anthropological Institute*, 19:2, 2013, p. 379.

41   See Teresa Caldeira, *City of Walls: Crime, Segregation and Citizenship in São Paulo*, Berkeley: University of California Press, 2000; Edward Blakeley and Mary Gail Snyder, eds, *Fortress America: Gated Communities in the United States*, Washington, DC: Brookings Institution Press, 1997; Setha Low, *Behind the Gates*, New York: Routledge, 2003.

42   See SFConnection, 'The "Vertical Gated Communities" of San Francisco', 2007, available at http://thesfconnectionwordpress.com; Alex Waterhouse-Hayward, Vancouver's Vertical Gated Communities', 2010, available at blog .alexwaterhousehayward.com.

part of their influential 'smart growth' programme. Vancouver's authorities have 'consciously willed [the city] into becoming a model of contemporary city-making.'[43] Such 'Vancouverism' is based heavily on the construction of luxury condo towers through the central area, located sometimes on sites where low-rise, lower-income and social housing stood previously.[44] As in many other cities, the experience of Vancouver's vertical housing growth powerfully demonstrates that 'densification processes that lack social measures for securing tenure for long-time residents lead to the displacement of poorer people, and to increased socio-spatial disparities.'[45]

As geographers Jamie Peck, Elliot Siemiatycki and Elvin Wyly argue, the Vancouver model has been sold as a 'winning combination of density, livability and sustainability – all rendered seductively real in the forest of glass-walled condominium towers that has colonised the downtown core since the late 1980s.'[46] Beneath the boosterist gloss, however, and despite laudable efforts of planners to protect key sightlines and integrate towers into the streetscapes below, they diagnose an effective suburbanisation of Vancouver's downtown. This has occurred, they argue, as the gentrifying speculation of condo towers, fuelled by the flow of money from wealthy Asian investors, has remade the central city as an increasingly homogenous, exclusionary and – because many condos are bought as assets that are rarely used – sometimes even *uninhabited* space.

Vancouver's formulaic repetition of architecturally cloned, squeaky-clean and socially homogenous towers can be seen, indeed, as an implantation of suburban logics into a previously much more diverse and unpredictable – that is to say, urban – landscape. 'If the condos of Vancouverism were once seen as edgy and innovative, by virtue of their challenge to North America's picket-fence hegemony', Peck and his colleagues write, 'their subsequent

43   Lance Berelowitz, *Dream City: Vancouver and the Global Imagination*, Vancouver: Douglas & McIntyre, 2010, p. 1.

44   See Jamie Peck, Elliot Siemiatycki and Elvin Wyly, 'Vancouver's Suburban Involution', *City* 18:4/5, 2014, pp. 386–415.

45   Marit Rosol, 'Social Mixing through Densification? The Struggle over the Little Mountain Public Housing Complex in Vancouver', *Die Erde: Journal of the Geographical Society of Berlin* 146:2/3, 2015, p. 151.

46   Peck et al., 'Vancouver's Suburban Involution', p. 387.

commodification, materially and culturally, is reducing them to vehicles for capital gains accumulation and marketing clichés.' Startlingly standardised, with their hardwood floors, high-end appliances and granite worktops, the condos in Vancouver have become 'highly fungible [that is, interchangeable] and slickly marketed investment commodities'.[47]

Designed to consume the most spectacular views of Vancouver's alluring combination of ocean and mountain vistas, and offering a gamut of luxury facilities and services within street-facing podium structures – tanning salons, private cinemas, pools, bars and shops – Vancouver's condo towers have been widely lauded by planners across the world as means of improving urban 'sustainability' and 'localism' and sustaining 'smart growth'. Such structures, the argument goes, increase the density of core populations within walkable neighbourhoods. At the same time, they are praised for reducing shifts of the wealthy to auto-dependent suburbs, bolstering municipal coffers and paying, through real estate taxes, for wider infrastructure improvements and public services that the whole city can use.

Such arguments are often questionable. Central-city condos for the wealthy tend to be built with lavish parking garages. Social and lower-cost housing also tends to be notable by its absence within such blocks. In a study of condo developments in Toronto, architecture researcher Michael Panacci found that the top of the building podiums, replete with lighted lagoons and luxury bars, often tends to be more active than the real street below, which is often now fringed by the highly securitised buildings and their car-garage entrances.[48]

The result is often a simulated urbanity – but one that is elitist, controlled, sterile and removed from the wider public city. 'As these jointly owned spaces increase in complexity and use, they begin to form a new interior urban realm,'[49] Panacci continues. 'If Jane Jacobs'

---

47   Ibid., pp. 404–5.

48   Leslie Kern, in a detailed analysis of condo culture in central Toronto, found that women condo residents were especially appreciative of the presence of strong security measures, especially when condo complexes are built on the 'urban frontier' of gentrification, adjacent to 'dodgy' parts of town. See Leslie Kern, *Sex and the Revitalised City*, Vancouver: University of British Columbia Press, 2010.

49   Michael Panacci, 'Vertical Urbanity: Urban Dwelling in an Age of

view of urbanity centred on the street and neighbourhood block in the 60's, it is becoming abundantly clear that to the current generation, urbanity must now surely include the condo corridor, elevator, its amenity spaces and the lobby.'[50]

Panacci's research also shows that neighbourly interaction between the residents of new condo towers is often minimal. Such mixing is now made especially difficult by the design of exit-only stairwells and securitised elevators that allow residents access only to their 'home' floors. Instead, the 'repetitive residences become hermetic pods, supported by luxurious facilities and in-house amenities. It's an easy matter to emphasise suitability when the rest of the city is pushed to the perimeter, visually and mentally.'[51] This distancing is in fact emphasised in the marketing and naming of new towers. Gleaming structures are depicted in brochures and ads as completely isolated structures surrounded by wooded parks that don't exist; one tower in central Toronto is even labelled a block of 'flying condominiums' invoking the raising up of living space as a shift away from the terrestrial city altogether.[52]

Vancouver's condo boom is even more problematic because of the relative weakness of the city's economy and labour market. Indeed, the city's main industries in the last three decades have centred on the very real-estate complex involved in the physical remaking – and marketing – of the Vancouverist myth as a means to draw in further investment from far-off places. 'Someone recently said, "No one knows what drives Vancouver"', a former Vancouver city councillor related recently. 'Well, what drives Vancouver is that people make wealth in unpleasant places and they come here and spend their wealth in a pleasant place – that's it!'[53]

Far from reducing the cost of housing for people who already live in the city – a central tenet of Ed Glaeser's argument – the powerful and globe-spanning speculative forces unleashed by this process

---

Programmatic Promiscuity', masters thesis, University of Waterloo, 2012, available at uwspace.uwaterloo.ca.

50   Ibid.

51   M. McMains, 'New Urban Lifestyle: Fracture/Segmentation?', n.d., unpublished paper.

52   Kern, *Sex and the Revitalised City*, p. 32.

53   Peck et al., 'Vancouver's Suburban Involution', p. 412.

have merely hiked up housing prices ever more beyond levels that can be sustained by locals drawing wages from the relatively weak local economy. Vancouver has by far the highest housing costs of any Canadian city. And yet some of the new condo districts in the downtown are eerily quiet because they are in effect resort spaces bought up by wealthy elites in Asia and elsewhere in North America, to be used during the odd skiing or summer vacation. Far from being a model of sustainability, affordability, and liveabiliy, then, Vancouver, as local architect Bing Thom puts it, has been remodelled into 'a tourist resort and a place to park money'.[54]

New York: 'Inequality Is Literally Blocking Out the Sun'[55]

In a very different case, the recent rise of a forest of slender, super-tall residential towers into the airy heights above midtown Manhattan presents more powerful evidence that building high does not necessarily enhance environmental sustainability or increase the supply of affordable housing. Designed by star architects like Frank Gehry, Richard Meier, Jacques Herzog, Jean Nouvel, or Robert Stern, these super-tall structures, which reach between 800 and 1,800 feet, now dominate skyscraper construction in New York. The construction of these towers represents the latest phenomenon in a thirty-year process of hyper-gentrification whereby the global super-rich – Malaysian financiers, Indian building moguls, Mexican power brokers, Russian ministers (some of dubious provenance) and the like – have used untraceable shell companies to aggressively assert increasing control in Manhattan.[56] In 2016 the US state is so concerned about the role that Manhattan's elite real estate is playing in the laundering of 'dirty' money from around the world that it started requiring real estate agents to track the identities of purchasers.[57]

---

54 Cited in ibid., p. 403.

55 Sam Pizzigati, 'The Dark Shadows Grand Fortune Casts', *Too Much* (blog entry), 2 June 2014, available at toomuchonline.org.

56 Louise Story and Stephanie Saul, 'Towers of Secrecy: Stream of Foreign Wealth Flows to Elite New York Real Estate', *New York Times*, 7 February 2015.

57 Louise Story, 'US Will Track Secret Buyers of Luxury Real Estate', *New York Times*, 13 January 2016.

Indeed, the towers are only the most visible sign of a much broader shift. This has involved the loosening of social obligations or regulations in housing and planning; the withdrawal of long-standing rent controls; the eviction of lower-income tenants; the privatisation of public space; aggressively race-based 'zero tolerance' policing and other social controls; and the deepening power of finance and real estate capital over urban planning. These forces have combined powerfully in the explicit repackaging of Manhattan as a luxury brand for the world's super-rich, a process that has led directly to the rapid growth of New York's increasingly dispersed homeless population (from 23,000 in 1993 to more than 60,000 in 2014).

By 2014, a housing analyst calculated that 'a minimum-wage earner would have to work 139 hours per week to be able to afford the average apartment' in New York.[58] At the same time, over $8 billion is spent each year in New York on residences that cost more than $5 million each. And in 2013, Mayor Michael R. Bloomberg admitted that all this was the direct result of policy. 'If we could get every billionaire around the world to move here', he said. 'It would be a godsend.'[59]

After a century and a half during which commercial skyscrapers drove the development of the world's most famous urban skyline, the elite take-over of the urban skies means that Manhattan's skyline is now being reshaped by eyrie-like refuges for the world's super-rich. With the new towers crowding out the classic skyscraper icons of Midtown Manhattan such as the Empire State Building and the Chrysler Building, critics argue that street levels are being pushed into shadow while the classic iconography of Manhattan is being irreversibly changed.[60] Referring to the long history of vertical segregation between servant classes and socio-economic elites in nineteenth-century London and Paris, the *Guardian*'s Fred Bernstein urges us to understand the new phenomenon of super-tall elite towers by thinking 'of it as the new *Upstairs, Downstairs*, but on an urban scale.'

Housing towers for small numbers of wealthy occupants or investors require fewer elevators than corporate towers and so create more

---

58   Samuel Stein, 'DeBlasio's Doomed Housing Plan', *Jacobin* 15/16, Fall 2014, pp. 14–16.

59   Storey and Saul, 'Towers of Secrecy'.

60   Fred A. Bernstein, 'Supersizing Manhattan: New Yorkers Rage Against the Dying of the Light', *Guardian*, 16 January 2015.

lettable space. The reorganisation of business practices to reduce corporate demands for central office space has also meant that elite residential demand has also become the most profitable to serve in many global cities. Developers in New York, as in other global cities, have thus started building towers exclusively to house the world's tiny class of the itinerant überwealthy, people who 'live in the Middle East or China or Latin America and travel between London and Shanghai and São Paulo and Moscow as if they were going from Brooklyn to Manhattan.' Designed to access stunning views, especially in Midtown Manhattan and adjacent to Central Park, these towers are best understood, as *Vanity Fair*'s Paul Goldberger suggests, as places 'not for full-time residents but for the top 1 per cent of the 1 per cent to touch down in when the mood strikes.'[61]

The best known of New York's slender new towers is the eighty-nine-floor tower at 432 Park Avenue. At 150 feet taller than the Empire State Building, 432 Park Avenue is the second highest tower in Manhattan and the highest residential block in the Western world. Measured to roof height, it is actually the tallest building in Manhattan (until it is surpassed by the 1,770-foot Nordstrom tower under construction just next door).

Rather than the incorporating tightly packed and compact condos – the previous norm in Manhattan – the building elevates small numbers of residents within extraordinarily spacious and low-density living. Within its $95 million suites, which reach a height of up to 1,396 feet, the sensation is of flying in the sky, of soaring far above the streets and landmarks of Manhattan, with incredible views in all directions – from every room. 'From the 90th floor, you feel as connected to the sky as to the ground', Paul Golberger writes:

> The city is laid out like a map, and the enormous windows are less like frames for the view than wide-open portals to it. And inside, the high ceilings and large rooms make the place feel even less like a conventional apartment. The layout leaves an open vista through the apartment, so you can see north to the Tappan Zee Bridge and south to the new 1 World Trade Center tower.[62]

---

61   Goldberger, 'Too Rich, Too Thin, Too Tall'.
62   Ibid.

432 Park Avenue, the second highest tower in Manhattan after the new One World Trade Center tower, under construction, 2013

The view south towards the Empire State Building and One World Trade Center from a bathroom in a $95 million penthouse suite in the 432 Park Avenue tower

Essentially, the building is a stack of 104 super-luxury apartments superimposed on each other within a tiny 96-foot-by-96-foot (30-metre-by-30-metre) floor plate. As with most of New York's new super-tall and super-thin housing towers, each apartment – they range in price between $60 million and $95 million, or up to $11,500 per square foot – covers the entire floor-plate of the building.

Each of the several bathrooms in the tower's apartments is larger than the average Manhattan apartment. 'Let's stop this fantasy that building density and height are by their nature green', architect Lloyd Alter stresses. 'This stuff is some of the least dense housing that has ever been built in the city, inefficient tiny floor plates with single-family floor plans costing tens of millions of dollars.'[63]

Remarkably, 432 Park Avenue didn't even need full planning permission from the city. As the municipality only limits the ratio of floor area to plot size and has no limits on height, the tower can effectively go as high as developers want once they purchase 'air rights' – the legal right to occupy high-up space – from adjacent occupiers. The only official permission required to build so high was that of the Federal Aviation Administration.[64]

Dead Windows: Planning as Social Cleansing in London

Given London's status as the site of the largest concentration for 'ultra-high net worth individuals' on the planet,[65] it is no surprise that developers there are similarly focusing overwhelmingly on building super-high-end, and increasingly super-tall, £2 million-plus properties for the global überwealthy.

As in Manhattan, many of them are holding properties for large investments, and these sites will rarely, if ever, be inhabited by people at all. Such properties, the *Observer*'s Alex Preston argues, 'have become lavishly upholstered safety deposit boxes'[66] – buildings that consume

---

63   Alter, 'Time to Dump the Tired Argument'.

64   Bernstein, 'Supersizing Manhattan'.

65   These are defined as people with $30 million (£21 million) or more in assets (excluding their main home). See Danny Dorling, 'How the Super Rich Got Richer: 10 Shocking Facts about Inequality', *Guardian*, 15 September 2014.

66   Alex Preston, 'Room at the Top: London's Super-Prime Housing Market', *Observer*, 6 April, 2014.

iconic views for largely absentee owners while appreciating vast speculative profits. As in Vancouver and New York, many will remain unoccupied, their darkened façades and empty rooms looming arrogantly and absurdly over a population experiencing its worst housing crisis in living memory. London also provides a classic example of the ways in which simplistic critiques and representations of the supposed failures of vertically built mass social housing have paved the way for the proliferation of towers for the super-rich. Speaking of one of the forty-three-floor elite housing towers in Stratford, one legacy of London's Olympics-based 'regeneration' in 2012, architecture critic Juston McGuirk ponders that the building is the 'sort of high-rise that was supposed to be unpopular in this country [the UK], discredited architecturally and politically, at least when it was called council [social] housing.'[67]

In 2013, 85 per cent of all housing purchases in inner London – largely those in the higher and 'super-high' price brackets – were being snapped up by non-UK nationals (mainly nationals from China, Singapore, Malaysia, Russia and Hong Kong, places where London real estate agents hold lavish prebuild sales events).[68] Such frenzied speculation, often as a means of anonymously recycling money derived from corruption in a city now widely regarded as the world capital of money laundering,[69] is pushing already-astronomical prices further 'into the stratosphere'.[70]

Startlingly, as in New York, the numbers of residential super-high towers in London are rapidly overtaking the more traditional towers of corporate and banking headquarters. In the biggest reorganisation of London's urban form since the rebuilding after the Great Fire in 1666, over 250 towers of at least twenty storeys are now in the pipeline. The shift in profitability is such that office towers are also being converted to residential uses.

As in Vancouver, the vast majority of these towers, egged on by London's government for consolidating the skyscraper skyline of a

67   Justin McGuirk, 'Unreal Estate', *Domus*, 30 July 2012.

68   Ed Hammond, 'Foreigners Buy Nearly 75 per cent of Property in Inner London', *Financial Times*, 3 August 2013.

69   John Armitage, 'London Property Boom Built on Dirty Money', *Independent*, 4 March 2015.

70   Preston, 'Room at the Top'.

prominent 'world city', are being justified using vague platitudes about 'density' and 'sustainability' when in fact they are merely built as investment opportunities for global elites.[71] Indeed, the 6 per cent of demand within the £2 million-plus category of so-called 'new prime' market for the elite is currently receiving 50 per cent of all housing investment in London. This is almost equal to the entire investment going to house the 50 per cent of the city's population – fully 4 million people –who live on earnings of less than £50,000 per year.[72]

Such a situation is the direct result of an obsession among London's governing elite with sycophantically luring in the global super-rich. Such elites, Boris Johnson, London's mayor from May 2008 to May 2016, said in November 2013, echoing Mayor Bloomberg's comments in New York, 'deserve our humble and hearty thanks'. For if they didn't 'employ eau de cologne-dabbers', he added, ordinary families 'might otherwise find themselves without a breadwinner.'[73]

Real estate economics are also obviously pivotal. One market report in 2012 described the economics of marketising air, verticality and spectacular views in plain terms: 'In terms of height, the general rule is, "the higher the apartment, the greater the price premium". This not only reflects the enhanced views, but also the increased exclusivity of living towards the top of a tall tower.' The report estimated that, for every floor upwards in London, market values for elite residential apartments per square foot increase by 1.5 per cent.[74] Adding the name of a famous architect and fitting the unit out with balconies, exceptional space standards and super-high-end bathrooms, floors, kitchens and technology further compounds such increased profitability.

Meanwhile, the totally inadequate production of affordable or social housing means that London's poorer and middle-class populations are either displaced altogether or squeezed into ever more overcrowded

71   Duncan Bowie quoted in Dave Hill, 'Glistening Towers Can Beguile But Won't Provide the Homes London Most Needs', *Guardian*, 16 March 2014.

72   Hillary Osborne, 'New London Housing "Aimed at Wealthy" Creates Widening Affordability Gap', *Guardian*, 11 November 2013.

73   Sam Pizzigati, 'Can a Great City Overdose on Billionaires?', *Too Much*, 14 March 2014.

74   Knight Frank, 'Tall Towers', London, 2012. See knightfrank.co.uk/research/tall-towers-2012-1101.aspx.

and overpriced accommodation within the rest of London's housing stock. Between 2012 and 2015, over 50,000 low-income families were physically displaced from inner London because of the housing crisis combined unprecedented cuts in welfare funding.[75]

Many low-wage workers who remain are pivotal to the functioning of the city, but are crammed into tiny, illegally rented and often dangerous spaces in attics, basements, sheds and garages. Often highly overcrowded, with no provision for decent sanitation or fire escapes, and with no official record on maps and statistical registers, such improvised dwellings become extremely vulnerable to fires. 'It's a major concern if there's a fire', Anthony Bertuca, city attorney in the Chicago suburb of Berwyn, said about similar processes occurring there in 2010. 'And the firemen don't know that there's an apartment in the basement, or an apartment in the back, the attic, or that the first floor is separated.'[76]

In London, this situation has been dramatically compounded by the callous selling off and gentrification of public housing by local and central governments and the withdrawal of a wide range of welfare benefits for families, the disabled and other marginalised groups living in inner London. Worse still, the only way London's boroughs can now generate even tiny amounts of capital for 'affordable' housing – which still remains very expensive and out of reach of the genuinely poor – is through contributions from the developers of elite luxury towers in the form of 'planning gain'.[77] (Even this fig leaf now faces abolition from the Tory government.)

London's remaining estates of social and council housing – and the inherited legacies of modernist mass social housing such as the Heygate Estate in Southwark on the South Bank – meanwhile, are being 'regenerated' in ways that displace residents, re-engineer the areas as upper-middle-class or elite housing, and offer token units of affordable housing by way of camouflage. In such cases, the crumbling

75   Daniel Douglas, 'Over 50,000 Families Shipped Out of London Boroughs in the Past Three Years due to Welfare Cuts and Soaring Rents', *Independent*, 29 April 2015.

76   Antonio Olivo, 'Housing Crisis Drives Families into Overcrowded Living Conditions', *Chicago Tribune*, 28 March 2010.

77   Rowan Moore, 'London Is Being Transformed with 230 Towers: Why the Lack of Consultation?' *Observer*, 29 March 2014.

legacies of visions of mass social housing organised vertically with high levels of space, services and greenery are erased, to be directly replaced by new elite towers.

Controversially, many such towers are also being designed with separate, utilitarian 'poor doors' which shift the small number of lower-income tenants far away from the luxurious street-facing foyers reserved for affluent owner-occupiers. Prompting social conflicts reminiscent of Ballard's sci-fi novel *High Rise*, social or 'affordable' housing tenants of the blocks are also often denied access to collective gardens because they don't pay full maintenance charges. On other occasions, faults in water supplies have led the owners to supply temporary hosed water – but only to wealthy owner-occupiers. Social housing tenants also complain that their apartments are often not marked on entrance signs to developments.

'At Elephant and Castle in south London', the *Independent*'s Mira Bar-Hillel observes, referring to Heygate's regeneration-by-demolition, 'a council estate where over 1,500 families lived is to be replaced by developers Lend Lease with over 2,000 private homes, and it's rumoured that only 79 will be for social renting. Southwark Council describes this as "regeneration".'[78] Even single-bedroom apartments within the new development will sell for well over £400,000.

Worse still, while tenants have been scattered to the far (and cheaper corners) of London and beyond, scrutiny of the financial deals behind the scheme is all but impossible because of the secret deals between developers and the municipalities. 'Councils are pleased to turn a blind eye so they have higher rate payers within their boroughs', Ian Steadman of the *New Statesman* remarks. 'Developers getting … land at a fraction of its true value, on the promise of future profits that mysteriously never arrive; a revolving door between local authorities and regeneration consultancy and PR firms.'[79]

The impact of speculation on central land values, and the huge profits to be made from replacing the neglected remnants of social and municipal housing with elite housing towers, radically undermines

78   Mira Bar-Hillel, 'What Does the Skyrocketing Price of Property in the Capital Mean for Society?' *Independent,* 1 June 2014.

79   Ian Steadman, 'Look to the Heygate Estate for What's Wrong with London's Housing', *New Statesman,* 6 November 2013.

the chances that large-scale social housing will survive in London's core. Instead, as in New York, the super-elite is taking to the skies.

Sometimes, London's better-quality modernist towers – such as Ernö Goldfinger's Trellick Tower – have escaped the wrecking ball. Instead, exploiting Thatcher's 'right to buy' for council tenants, their apartments are now privatised and sold at high prices to design-conscious elites (often professional architects). The original social objectives of the towers – and the social and leftist orientations of their architects – have been quietly forgotten. In parallel with its protection from demolition through formal 'listing' as a building of historic importance, the Balfron Tower – lesser known twin of the Trellick – is now being sold off on the open market to wealthy purchasers by a housing association as a means of raising capital. There will be no 'social' or 'affordable' renting in the new regime. 'Design-centric living – which the architect envisaged for the everyday Londoner – will again be accessible only to the privileged few.'[80]

One artist who is about to be evicted from the tower notes how the community has moved from a mixed and cosmopolitan one to a homogenous white professional demographic. 'It's scandalous', he spits. 'If these flats are bought by overseas investors and then sit unoccupied, Ernö Goldfinger, a lifelong socialist, will be turning in his grave.'[81]

More perverse still, stylised images of Balfron and its sister tower Trellick are now widely used to adorn the chic modernist mugs, posters, cushions, crockery and even tea towels available in the designer shops that pepper London's hyper-gentrified neighbourhoods. In building up a cultural obsession with 'austerity chic' and firing up demand among an affluent, design-conscious clientele for the tower's now-private apartments, the image is used to sell off a great achievement of the socially universal welfare state. It therefore presides over what architecture critic Owen Hatherley calls 'the literal destruction of the thing it claims to love.'[82]

---

80   Eddy Frankel, 'The Changing Fortunes of the Balfron Tower', *Time Out*, 26 May 2015.

81   Ibid.

82   Owen Hatherley, 'Keep Calm and Carry On: The Sinister Message behind the Slogan That Seduced the Nation', *Guardian*, 8 January, 2016.

Global South Megacities: 'Heavenly Enclaves Surrounded by Slums'

Further startling examples of the elite domination of contemporary high-rise housing can be drawn from megacities in the Global South. The marketing of such towers is especially striking in Mumbai. 'Reach for it!' shouts the real estate billboard surrounding the new Indiabulls Sky Tower complex being built at the end of the new Bandra–Worli Sea Link sky bridge express way as it enters the city core. 'Consider it a blessing to share the same address as God.'[83]

The building offers a long list of luxury services, a suite of pools, spas and restaurants, all in the relatively cool air above the twelfth floor; below these is a tall podium of stacked, private parking garages. In addition, there is private rooftop helipad and a complex system of air-conditioning and pollution filtering. The Indiabulls Sky Tower's brochure is a panoply of exhortations that rising up is a direct indicator of status, power and exclusivity – the capsular aeriality of a Bond villain's lair. The brochure, moreover, plays on the deep linguistic tropes that reinforce such ideas. 'Way. Way above the rest!' it shouts. 'What it means to live in the sky!' 'Connected to the clouds and everything in the city!'

Next to the text are alluring images of executives dismounting from helicopters on the rooftop helipad or of a bikini-clad woman lounging next to building-edge 'infinity' swimming pools and looking over the Mumbai skyline beyond while sipping cocktails. 'When you have amenities like this up in the sky, you can expect your spirits to be continuously elevated!' the brochure exhorts. 'Possess your piece of the sky soon', it continues. 'And rise up to the City's most elite residences!'

Vicky Oberoi of Oberoi Constructions, developer of many of the most expensive vertical enclaves in Mumbai, points out that buildings like the Indiabulls Sky Tower are attractive because they bundle together a wide range of services, introduce access-control filters and walls against the perceived threats of the city outside, and deliver reliable, high-quality infrastructure services to residents on a club basis. 'I would call the [developments] in Mumbai vertical gated

---

83   As we see in chapter 10, the marketing for the tower also stresses that the higher residents live in the tower, the cooler the prevailing air temperature.

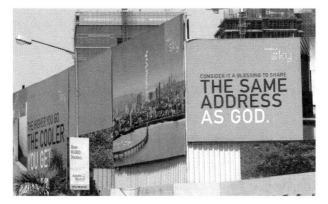

'Consider it a blessing to share the same address as God' and 'The higher you go the cooler you get' – advertising hoarding around the Indiabulls Sky Tower, Mumbai, 2013

communities', he recently said, because 'they take care of virtually all of [residents'] needs.' Mumbai historian Sharada Dwivedi characterises these enclaves as 'heavenly enclaves surrounded by slums'.[84] Their clear logic in creating a cosseted interior is to radically devalue the external street environment. 'As spaces are enclosed and turned inside' in the city, anthropologist Teresa Caldeira points out about similar structures in Brazil, 'the outside space is left for those who cannot afford to go in'.[85]

And yet even the Indiabulls Sky Tower is not the most extreme expression of the ascension of Mumbai's elites. An even more extraordinary example is the recent construction of a twenty-seven-storey, 400,000-square-foot tower which houses only one family – the Ambani family – of five. The $2 billion Antilla tower houses a six-storey vertical parking garage, three helipads, a mini-theatre, four floors on open-air gardens, six floors of parking, hundreds of servants, a series of airborne swimming pools and nine elevators.

A more powerful icon of hyper-inequality and the appropriation of central cities by elites – along with the related widespread collapse of modernist programmes of social and collective housing in towers – could hardly be imagined. Indeed, the realisation that this huge tower

---

84   Quoted in Nauzer K. Bharucha, 'Gated Societies Split City', *Times of India* (Mumbai), 3 March 2010.

85   Caldeira, *City of Walls*, p. 130.

Antilla: The Ambani single-family skyscraper, Mumbai.

was accommodation for a single family has reverberated through the labyrinthine politics of (in)justice in Mumbai. 'At some point the penny dropped for everyone', writes Indian journalist Vikram Doctor in the *Economic Times*,

> this whole structure was just for one family ... In part, this surprise could be for how the building subtly shifts the meaning that apartment blocks have come to acquire in Mumbai ... Because as a full apartment block, for just one family, it tears up the conventions of compactness: here, for all we know, each floor could be a room, a garden, or even a bathroom (more reasonably, a swimming pool), and none of it hidden away, but up in public view.[86]

New School anthropologist Vyjayanthi Rao stresses that the widespread sprouting of such secessionary towers across Mumbai 'has added a three-dimensional twist to the drama of hierarchy, exclusion

---

86   Vikram Doctor, 'Mukesh Ambani's Antilla: When Money Towers over a Wealth of Ideas', *Economic Times*, 20 October 2010, available at economictimes. indiatimes.com.

and dispossession' in the city.[87] The construction of this new archipel-ago of towers works to render concrete long-standing imaginations of futurity and globality that, in turn, are woven into complex land-scapes of displacement and predatory speculation against the dense informal cities that surround the new towers. 'This emerging vertical city', Rao writes, 'thus renders these landscapes [of surrounding, infor-mal urbanism] obsolete by the sheer force of juxtaposition against this fabric, now perceived as one of dereliction.' Crucially, however, the new elite towers rely on an army of cleaners, gardeners, nannies, chauffeurs and security guards, who often live in the ground-level horizontal informal communities that surround them.

Out of the City's Grasp: The Politics of Looking Down[88]

A final startling example of the ascension of urban elites into luxury towers can be drawn from Guatemala City. Here radical increases in levels of drug trade–related violence and insecurity have presaged a shift by elites from living in compounds beyond the fringe of the city to inhabiting a forest of new vertical towers right in the very centre. Within less than a decade, over 100 exclusive office and condo towers – replete with shops, pools, terraces, bars, gyms, and, of course, high-tech security – have punctuated the city's skyline. The towers, clad in glass and aluminium, are marketed with aspirational and globalised monikers.

This new verticality of elites in Guatemala City 'marks yet another strategy by which elites abandon public space', write anthropolo-gists Kevin Lewis O'Neill and Benjamin Fogarty-Valenzuela. They do this by 'lifting themselves above the poor, the marginalized, and the violent, they engage themselves or each other but not their fellow citizen below.'[89] With the vertical secession of the elites into the condo towers, practically the whole city is now residualised below the luxury towers whose names – 'Dubai Tower', 'Ivory Tower' and so on – hint

87 Vyjayanthi Rao, 'Proximate Distances: The Phenomenology of Density in Mumbai', *Built Environment* 33:2, 2007, p. 245.

88 The phrase 'out of the city's' comes from Michel de Certeau, *The Practice of Everyday Life*, Minneapolis: University of Minnesota Press, 1998.

89 O'Neill and Fogarty-Valenzuela, 'Verticality', p. 379.

at the aspirational cosmopolitanism of their residents. Many suspect that the capital to construct these towers is laundered through the violent drug trafficking that has made Guatemala City one of the world's most dangerous places.

Rather than being 'over there' in exurban secure enclaves, Guatemala City's elites are thus increasingly seen to be 'up there' from the perspective of the barrio dwellers living down below in the city's incised valleys. 'A new skyline indexes a new class of cosmopolitanism, one that floats above the city', O'Neill and Fogarty-Valenzuela explain. 'The experience of looking up at privilege, the experience of looking down on the masses, now defines Guatemala City.'[90] From the patios, pools, cocktail bars and penthouses on top of the towers and podiums, the violent landscapes of the city far below become an aesthetic spectacle to be consumed from afar. A troubling and gritty place is rendered instead as a tranquil spectacle, an aesthetic background. 'Here, you don't see gang members', admitted one condo resident to O'Neill and Fogarty-Valenzuela:

> Here you see only elites. And from this perspective, it's just so peaceful. You know, we're actually at the top of the tallest building in Guatemala! And these apartments are the most exclusive in all the country! And just think how relaxing it is to just sit up here with a drink and just unwind! This is simply the most luxurious place in the entire city.[91]

A stark politics of fear and demonisation defines this register. It is here that long-standing moral assessments linking height and depth to social worth begin to pool. 'Those people up there must think that those people down there are really at risk, that they are risky', one middle-class resident reflects. 'Those people who live down there must do bad things; they must be bad people. They are people who probably hurt other people.'[92] O'Neill and Fogarty-Valenzuela cite another who argues that a simple vertical register now exists in the city whereby 'the lower you go, the more dangerous it gets'.

People inhabiting the favelas compressed into Guatemala City's

---

90   Ibid.
91   Ibid., p. 386.
92   Ibid.

valleys, meanwhile, must ascend the 300 to 400 steps up to the higher city to work, get cellphone coverage, or call for emergency services (which will often decline in any case to descend to the barrios). They also experience the rubbish, waste and polluted water that is dumped down from the higher city above. The language of the favela splits urban life into *abajo* (below) or *arriba* (above). 'The police are *arriba* and would never dream of walking *abajo*', one favela resident laments.[93]

Beyond the case of Guatemala City, the politics of looking down on the rest of the city far below elite housing towers connects all the disparate cases where the super-rich are colonizing cocoon-like luxurious eyries far above in the urban skies. All resonate powerfully with the famous essay 'Walking in the City' first published in 1980 by French sociologist Michel de Certeau. From the top of Manhattan's World Trade Center, de Certeau pondered the contrast between the view from the skyscraper and the messy realities of the street-level city. 'To be lifted to the summit of the World Trade Center is to be lifted out of the city's grasp', de Certeau wrote:

> One's body is no longer clasped by the city's streets that turn and return it according to anonymous law; nor is it possessed, whether as player or played, by the rumble of so many differences and by the nervousness of New York traffic … When one goes up there [the viewer] leaves behind the mass that carries off and mixes up in itself any identity of authors or spectators … His elevation transfigures him into a voyeur. It puts him at a distance. It transforms the bewitching world into by which one 'was possessed' into a text that lies before ones eyes. It allows one to read it, to be a solar eye, looking down like a god.[94]

Several particularly revealing examples of the narcissistic processes through which the super-rich address the rest of the city from their new vertical cocoons have recently emerged. These expose the contradictions whereby they – and the developers who build their towers – tend to combine a peculiar and often fearful removal from the city's surface with a desire to inhabit it (or at least inhabit the spaces above

---

93 Ibid., p. 382.
94 De Certeau, *Practice of Everyday Life,* p. 92.

it). Another common trait is the overwhelming material power, sense of entitlement and crass arrogance of tower resident-owners.

In January 2015, in our first example, a video advert produced by London developer Redrow – already notorious as provider of some of London's most infamous 'poor door' towers – produced a video ad for their new luxury apartment complex in Aldgate. According to Redrow's website, the building 'towers twenty-one storeys above Aldgate East like a blade of light, its glass fin protruding dramatically to add a sculptural quality.'[95] It is located on the edge of both London's financial district and the district of Tower Hamlets, one of London's poorest, with 44 per cent of the population living in poverty. The advert provoked a political storm.[96]

Merging a wide range of metaphors equating physical ascent and height with masculine and bodily power, virility, superiority and domination, the advert, carefully shot in the style of the movie *American Psycho*, depicts the journey of an archetypal City financier on his 'rise' to power and dominance. This becomes apparent in his clear revulsion at experiencing the dense messiness of London's Tube; it culminates in an epiphany-like rise through ruthless ambition that allows him to ascend socially and physically to own a new £4 million-plus Redrow penthouse overlooking London's financial district.

Striding to his window, surrounded by designer trappings of extreme wealth, the banker gazes down at the streets far below. He then narrates in the first person with calm pride the fact that he can now 'look down on the city that could have swallowed you whole, and say "I did this!" To stand with the world at your feet!' A social media storm of dark satire quickly led Redrow to withdraw the advert from the web. Nevertheless, the ad, although far from unusual, quickly became a leitmotif of London's increasingly dystopian housing situation.

'It is a totally clear expression of the psychotic nature of housing in London at the moment', architect Sam Jacob said of the ad. To him, its

95   Redrow London, n.d., 'One Commercial Street', available at redrow.co.uk/london/en/developments/one-commercial-street.

96   Nell Frizzell, 'Tower Hamlets Psycho: A Symbol of Britain's Housing Crisis', *Guardian,* 15 January 2015.

narrative, which parallels the marketing of towers for the super-rich everywhere, 'plunges us back into the ultimate yuppie fantasy – the fact that the individual only exists in relation to the brands that they own, the things that they've bought. That property and housing is just about individual success, investment, money, achievement.' Jacob continues: 'It's all part of the same narrative. The separation of the individual from collectivity, the fact that you rise above the city, the idea that the city is a kind of beast that is there to be beaten or to beat you. That of course means you're separated from society and the things that really make a city exciting.'[97]

Such solipsism is symbolised further by the latest plans for über-wealthy housing in London's huge £15 billion Nine Elms development around Battersea. As ground-level and public swimming pools are closed and threatened across the city because of the UK government's extreme austerity drive, an entirely transparent thirty-metre-long 'sky pool' is being built as a bridge between two of the condo towers. From this, residents of the complex – where most apartments are well over £1 million and even a tiny studio costs £600,000 – will be able to take a dip while looking down on the adjacent Thames, London's streets, and the new castle-like US Embassy being built next door – through the transparent base of the 'sky pool'. Residents will also be able to swim between the complex's rooftop bar, spa and orangery, all of which are connected by limbs of the pool. 'The experience of the pool will be truly unique', Sean Mulryan, CEO of the developers, Ballymore, said in 2015. 'It will feel like floating through the air in central London.'[98]

The *Architizer* blog immediately lauded the Nine Elms 'skypool' as a rare example of a new private housing scheme 'providing an architectural landmark and tourist attraction for the wider public.' Others were less flattering. 'Tourist attraction?' one anonymous reader spat straight away. 'Finally we will now have a place to literally go and look up at the rich arseholes.'[99] The fact that Wandsworth, the local

---

97   Oliver Wainwright, '"American Psycho" Property Promo Pulled after Twitterstorm', *Guardian Architecture and Design Blog*, 5 January 2015.

98   Hilary Osborne, 'Would You Take a Dip 35 Metres Up in London's First "Sky Pool"?', *Guardian*, 20 August 2015.

99   Paul Keskeys, 'Arup Associates Is Engineering the World's First Sky Pool between Two Towers', *Architizer*, 21 August 2015.

council, is currently forcibly dispersing some of its neediest homeless communities hundreds of miles away to properties it has purchased in much cheaper locations, as a means of reducing its welfare budgets, only adds to local resentment of the spiralling inequality and injustice in the district.[100]

A third and final example comes from the rare insights into the lives of the wealthy elites who inhabit fortified luxury apartment complexes rising high above Rio, São Paulo and Recife contained within Gabriel Mascaro's superb 2009 documentary *Um Lugar ao Sol* ('A Place in the Sun'). Discussing the ways in which elites have abandoned ground-level living in Brazil's cities because of fears for their security, one interviewee in the film expresses her love of the feeling of 'always being closer to the sky' while 'seeing all the beauty of Rio, despite all the poverty'. She admires aesthetically the changing colours of an adjacent favela 'that looks like a load of little colourful dolls' houses'.

Commenting on the rapidly changing view of the city's geography and skyline, she even discusses with her husband the new sight of tracer bullets flying among the favela landscapes far below as warfare between rival drug gangs has intensified. 'They are beautiful!' she exclaims, laughing somewhat uncomfortably. 'We have a free fire-works display almost every day!' 'A penthouse is the same as an island', her partner continues. 'Except that it is above everything.'[101]

Beyond Luxified Skies

> Could a high-rise, high-density residential tower ever be a desirable place to live for anyone but the super-rich?
>
> – Goldhagen, 'On Architecture: Living High'

No area of the politics of the vertical dimension comes close in importance to that of housing. With urban populations mushrooming and 75 per cent of the world's population of 11 billion likely to be living in

---

100   Sophia Sleigh, 'Homeless Wandsworth Families to Be Housed as Far Away as Birmingham', *Your Local Guardian,* 16 January 2015.

101   Gabriel Mascaro, *Um Lugar ao Sol,* Rio de Janeiro: Vitrine Films, 2009. See pt.gabrielmascaro.com/Um-lugar-ao-Sol.

cities by 2050, the stacking of housing will inevitably, as Ed Glaeser argues, be a crucial factor in the future of humanity.

Equally clearly, the sprouting of towers for the super-rich that in many cities now constitutes de facto housing policy is a social catastrophe in the making. The parallel transformation of cities discussed here is the material and often dystopian embodiment of the ways in which the current neoliberal version of capitalism continues to concentrate ever more extreme amounts of wealth and resources into the hands of the very few, to be used to sustain speculative dynamics that accentuate this wealth further while severely damaging the lives and life chances of everyone else.

Far from unleashing market forces to build up cities in ways that provide affordable housing for all – as in Ed Glaeser's initially seductive vision – such processes of neoliberalisation are merely allowing cities to be reconstructed into forests of super-tall cocoons, owned and controlled by the super-rich, who might occasionally design to occasionally even inhabit the structures. A democratisation of urban housing it most certainly is not.

Combined with the way oversimplifying prejudices have led to the wholesale dismantling of mass social housing in many cases, the last few decades have seen a striking colonisation of the urban skies by the world's super-rich. The manufacturing of the myth that stacked and vertical housing can never work for people on low incomes has been a key factor working to clear the way for the elite take-over of the urban skies.

A further problem is that urban and planning debates centre almost totally on the four building façades while neglecting or forgetting what photographer Alex MacLean has called the 'fifth façade': the roofscape. This increasingly gilded and private world – which is absolutely pivotal to the luxification of the urban skies – is visible only from above. A potentially crucial urban and public resource in crowded cities, it enters planning debates all too rarely. MacLean, whose brilliant book *Up on the Roof* exposes New York's hidden rooftops, emphasises how rooftop private and semi-private restaurants and bars, pools, playgrounds and parks are proliferating across New York's roofscapes. Concealed from the dense and polluted city streets below by altitude, such facilities are captured by MacLean's startling photographs. 'The dramatic effect of this vertical separation is apparent in a[n aerial] photograph of poolside sunbathers', MacLean writes. 'Lying on deck chairs, they are oblivious to the traffic that appears to pass right next to them, but which actually flows twenty-odd floors below. These outdoor spaces float above the city like elevated islands.'[102]

As well as neglecting roofscapes, architectural and urban debates often miss the bigger, structural picture shaping housing and gentrification crises. Typically, they focus only on the details of designs for high-rise housing, and the ways in which they might be physically remade to be less like single-ended and dreary silos full of cordoned-off cells for 'dormitory-style' living.[103] However, in following the available money architects inevitably tend to focus on housing for wealthy groups, and such debates therefore miss a fundamental and much more important question: can high-rise housing ever be democratised again, in ways that learn the lessons of the often disastrous programmes of the 1950s and 1960s? Such a question is absolutely crucial to the possibility of democratic urbanism and of democratic societies in the early twenty-first century. For without controlling unrestrained financialised speculation in land and real estate – what Mike Davis calls the 'demarketization' of urban land[104] – these can be but pipe dreams.

A central goal of the social reform of the mechanisms of urban development must therefore centre on ways to control and limit the speculative power of finance capitalism that forces the extreme commodification of urban land and real estate as investment vehicles. At the same time, methods must be developed to channel a significant portion of the profits from land development into resources for creating accessible and high-quality housing for the urban masses based on regulated rents and abilities to pay.

Crucial here is a refocusing once again on the *occupants* of housing

---

102   Alex MacLean, *Up on the Roof: New York's Hidden Skyline Spaces*, Princeton, NJ: Princeton Architectural Press, 2012, p. 89.

103   OMA's 2013 'interlace' vertical village project in Singapore is an influential example of how towered housing blocks can be integrated together in imaginative ways that support public space, gardens and public services at many levels. See chapter 9.

104   Mike Davis, 'B-52 Bomber Radicalism: A Plan for Rational Improvements to the City of Los Angeles', *Jacobin* 15/16, Fall 2014, p. 28.

rather than the current fetish for the mere appearance of built structures. Far too much contemporary urban planning operates merely as a crass device to produce supposedly 'iconic' landscapes while radically ignoring of the ownership, control or occupation of those landscapes – and their contributions to addressing broader social goals or crises.

Only by addressing these linked imperatives will there ever be the possibility of breaking the poisonous nexus that grips so many contemporary cities. This forges deep, structural connections between neoliberal planning and city marketing; the hegemony of real estate interests organised to serve the wealthiest 1 per cent; globalised and often corrupt financialisation and land speculation; and ever-deepening housing crises. Only by forcibly unravelling these connections at the structural level might the real possibilities of creative design, of transparent and democratic engagements with communities about their futures, and of returning to a fully social vision of urban planning even begin to be imagined. Zoning and 'planning gain', to stipulate social and affordable housing obligations, offers merely a camouflage that allows developers to buy off planners and construct ever-more elite housing towers.[105] Instead, robust efforts are necessary to tax the capital gains from elite housing locally in order to finance nonmarket and affordable housing.

Creative experiments in designing quality social housing in dense urban contexts are clearly also important. The scale and extent of housing crises in many cities, however, mean that even these measures can only offer token, ameliorative gestures. Without more fundamental transformations at the structural level – changes that will inevitably mean important alterations in the political and economic dynamics of capitalism – little can be done to improve things.

The challenges here are immense and urgent. Social and political movements need to fully embrace ambitious agendas for remaking housing systems in toto. States must be remade and reclaimed so that they cease to be anti-democratic mechanisms for enforcing predatory privilege and the remaking of cities as 'luxury brands', camouflaged cynically behind discourses of 'regeneration', 'renaissance',

---

105   On the case of New York, see Sam Stein, *De Blasio's Doomed Housing Plan*.

'sustainability' – or, as in Ed Glaeser's arguments, some necessary or inevitable connection between building high and the supply of affordable housing.

Above all, truly public and fully regulated social housing must be rehabilitated as a pivotal idea.

Without such transformations, cities will continue to be remade to serve the interests of a super-affluent cabal, who often pay minimal taxes, or, worse still, are heavily subsidised through public budgets. The growing disconnect between housing and labour markets will inevitably continue to create larger and larger populations of evictees and homeless, and to drive out the poorer and middle classes who are fundamental to the continued economic and social vitality of cities. The social, economic and cultural vibrancy of cities will, in turn, inevitably wither and suburbanise further, testament to the skewed priorities of an age in thrall to money, luxury urban branding, the quick buck and narcissistic greed. Beyond this, any remaining notion of the always highly chimeric liberal political tenet that cities are organised through a public commons, organised for the many and not the few through systems of representative or insurgent democracy, will seem ever more like some mythic story from an increasingly distant age.[106]

The prospects are not promising. One unprecedented shift that will create further challenges involves the apparently inevitable introduction of suborbital space travel systems in the near to medium term. These systems will allow the world's überwealthy to tie together their distant properties with ever greater speed and ease. While the introduction of regular space tourism flights for the super-rich has been delayed by the crash of the Virgin Galactic in October 2014, regular low-orbit travel is likely to emerge in the medium term – for those who can afford it.

With the prospect of travel times between London and Sydney reduced to 2.2 hours, 'luxury' real estate agents are already foaming at the mouth. Such systems would probably compound the real estate pull of major cities like London and New York, which would suddenly become more accessible to a much wider population of ultra-wealthy

---

106   See Amin Ash, Doreen Massey and Nigel Thrift, *Cities for the Many Not the Few*, Bristol: Policy Press, 2000.

individuals within an acceptable travel time. Routine suborbital travel would thus encourage more multiple home ownership for the super-rich across the globe. Yolande Barnes of the Savills real estate agency reckons that 'when China and some other parts of Asia really discover how to develop good holiday resorts, there's huge potential for more Europeans to think about second home ownership there. It could quite easily become a much more global market.'[107]

---

107   Cited in John Sunyer, 'The New Market Space: Billionaire Investors Look Beyond Earth', *Financial Times*, 28 February 2014.

9.

Skywalk/Skytrain/Skydeck:
Multilevel Cities

From the science fiction cinema of Fritz Lang's 1927 classic *Metropolis* through the novels of H. G. Wells to the 1920s futurist architecture of Hugh Ferris, radically vertical cities laced by raised systems of walkways and transport connections were a staple of the Western urban imagination throughout the twentieth century.

The Italian Futurist Antonio Sant'Elia, who published his projection of the *Città Nuova* ('New City') in 1914, has been an especially influential figure here.[1] He urged the embrace of radical mechanisation within a dramatically extended vertical and three-dimensional imaginary of future cities. 'The houses of concrete, glass and iron', Sant'Elia urged, 'must rise on the edge of a tumultuous abyss'. Instead of ground-level streets stretching 'like a foot-mat level with the porter's lodge', future cities would instead 'be linked by metal walkways and immensely fast escalators.' 'Let us throw away sidewalks, arcades, steps!' he extolled. 'Let us raise the level of the city!'[2]

Like many futurists and modernists, Sant'Elia saw the ground-hugging city as an oppressive, polluted and desultory space which new technologies could completely obliterate and transcend. He believed that his vertical city of the future would 'pile up the cells which have for so long been crushed on the ground, and set them high above the earth, bathed in light and air.'[3]

---

1   See Antonio Sant'Elia, Luciano Caramel and Alberto Longatti, *Antonio Sant'Elia: The Complete Works*, Rome: Rizzoli International Publications, 1988.

2   Antonio Sant'Elia, *Architettura Futurista*, Milan: Galleria Fonte d'Abisso, 1984 [1914].

3   Ibid, p. 280.

Inevitably, the here-and-now futurism of the fast-growing forest of skyscrapers in Chicago and New York – cities that also possessed raised systems of elevated railroads and, for a short time, plans for airship docking stations on the tops of the tallest towers – loomed large in such imaginaries.[4] Countless journalists, magazine editors and architects projected the burgeoning skyscrapers of these two cities into a radically vertical global future where the buildings would be matched by comprehensive, vertically segregated systems for accommodating pedestrians, motor traffic, mass transit and other infrastructure. (See the 1928 example from New York planner Harvey Wiley Corbett on p. viii.)

The Great Depression prevented the widespread realisation of such imaginaries. It was not until the 1960s that vertically segregated circulation became a dominant theme of post-war urban planning. Influenced by architectural radicalism such as the 'plug-in' city from the Archigram group,[5] the huge raised megastructures proposed for Tokyo by a group of Japanese architectural futurists known as the Metabolists,[6] and the one-square-kilometre 'artificial platform city' imagined by the Obayashi Corporation in the same city,[7] vertically segregated circulation became an obsession in urbanism and urban planning.[8] 'It is only logical to conceive of multi-level cities', the Archigram group argued. 'The organisation of, say, New York, which

4   See Jean-Louis Cohen and Hubert Damisch, *Scenes of the World to Come: European Architecture and the American Challenge, 1893–1960*, Paris: Flammarion, 1995.

5   See Peter Cook and Michael Webb, *Archigram*, New York: Princeton Architectural Press, 1999.

6   Japanese architect Maki Fumihiko defined a 'megastructure' in 1964 as a 'large frame in which all the functions of a city are housed'. Megastructures had, he argued, 'been made possible by present day technology', Maki Fumihiko, *Investigations in Collective Form*, St Louis: Washington University Press, 1964, p. 1.

7   Hideo Obitsu and Nagase Ichirou, 'Japan's Urban Environment: The Potential of Technology in Future City Concepts', in Gideon Golany, Keisuke Hanaki and Osamu Koide, eds, *Japanese Urban Environment*, Oxford: Elsevier Science, 1988, pp. 324–36; and Zhong-Jie Lin, 'From Megastructure to Megalopolis: Formation and Transformation of Mega-Projects in Tokyo Bay', *Journal of Urban Design* 12:1, 2007, pp. 73–92.

8   Cook and Webb, *Archigram*. See Reyner Banham's definitive *Megastructure: Urban Futures of the Recent Past*, London: Harper Collins, 1976.

tolerates multi-level components, connected by only two horizontal levels (street and subway) and both of those at the base, is archaic'[9]

The widespread destruction of cities through strategic bombing in World War II created opportunities for planners to realise such dreams in practice. With large parts of central London smouldering in ruins following the Luftwaffe's bombing raids of 1940 and 1941, British architects and planners were gripped by visions of radical re-planning the city. Influenced by the anti-street screeds of the arch-modernist Congrès Internationaux d'Architecture Moderne (CIAM) organisation founded in 1928 by Le Corbusier, architects William and Aileen Tatton-Brown suggested the comprehensive redevelopment of London based on the idea of the vertically segregated city. Such programmes involved the complete rebuilding of cities as vertically stratified systems, separating motor traffic on one layer, pedestrian movement on another and high buildings above.

Suggesting the construction of massive podium buildings along London's streets – large, ground-level blocks providing the raised base for further building above – the Tatton-Browns' vision centred on 'a completely new ground level for pedestrians where city dwellers could roam freely with their cars parked on roadways below, their homes and jobs towering above'.[10] Lifting the pedestrian up onto a new artificial urban ground and away from noxious and lethal vehicular traffic would, like the vertical housing and office towers of Le Corbusier, bring them into a near-utopian world of light, air and freedom.

To do this, though, it was necessary to raze almost completely existing ground-level city centres and start afresh. The comprehensive redevelopment plan for central Newcastle – one of the most extreme plans of all – called for the need to 'prepare a fresh layout in three dimensions, and then to redevelop the areas as a whole in one continuous operation'.[11] The vision was of rebuilding central Newcastle as a 'layer-cake' city. This was partly achieved; the district of the city around the central motorway is an iconic – although rapidly

9   Ibid., p. 10.

10   Aileen Tatton-Brown, and William Tatton-Brown, 'Three-Dimensional Town Planning', *Architectural Review* 40, September 1941, p. 83.

11   Newcastle City Council, 'Central Area Redevelopment Plan', Newcastle, 1963, p. 12.

deteriorating – example of three-dimensional urban reconstruction from the post-war period.

At the same time, car and commercial traffic was be unleashed from the disturbance of intervening human bodies within an unconstrained world of free-flowing mobility below. Crucial here was the shift from one all-purpose system of roads to a labyrinth of single-purpose ones, organised three-dimensionally within the huge new concrete megastructures of the city. (Critics suspected from the outset that the dominating motivation behind the idea of raised walkways in the UK was simply to remove people from the accelerating momentum of proliferating vehicles.)

City centres would thus be progressively re-engineered into huge multifunctional and multilevel containers[12]: three-dimensional megastructures designed using the latest modernist and functionalist concepts to 'heap up' housing, commerce, retailing and leisure while providing enough space for the mass-automobile society. Vertical stacking would, the argument went, allow land to be used much more intensively than through the more traditional horizontal separation of land uses in cities.

One master plan for the comprehensive redevelopment of central Birmingham outlined the underlying ideas. 'A factor which is absolutely essential in any modern master plan is the principle of segregation', it suggested. 'No project for urban renewal, be it extensive or quite local, will match up to modern necessities unless it provides for proper segregation of operations.' Such a shift, it was argued, was 'essential for safety, for maximum concentration of use, and for amenity and comfort … The transport design should, therefore, aim at the segregation of pedestrians, city roads, service roads, and car park roads, leading to multi-level circulation of functions such as two-storey shopping.'[13]

Shaped by the thinking of the Tatton-Browns, between 1955 and 1970, the City of London embarked on an ambitious programme of

12 The quote comes from John Gold, 'The Making of a Megastructure: Architectural Modernism, Town Planning and Cumbernauld's Central Area, 1955–75', *Planning Perspectives* 21:2, 2006, p. 113.

13 Institution of Municipal Engineers, *Town Centre Redevelopment, Proceedings of the Institution's Convention*, London: Institution of Municipal Engineers, 1962.

vertical segregation. Raised walkways laced together modernist office blocks; megastructures like the Barbican operated through a series of vertical layers; and the gradual disentangling of systems of motorised and bodily movement were organised, project by project. Plans for a thirty-mile raised pedestrian network stipulated an entire 'city in the sky' criss-crossing the whole of the City of London and connecting to the rest of the metropolis. 'Here at last a vision will come true', the London County Council gushed in 1960. 'Right in the centre of the metropolis thousands of people will live near their jobs. They will not have to travel during the rush hour, they will be able to move in complete safety throughout the area, where there will be many shops, restaurants, etc. on elevated walkways away from the noise and fumes of motor cars.'[14]

These days London's raised walkways – where they survive, as in the area around London Wall and the Barbican – are commonly derided. Often windswept, poorly designed, barely used, inaccessible to disabled people, and a widespread source of fear or insecurity, the London public voted with their feet and chose to stay on terra firma. As a consequence, today, the City of London's upper-level system has quietly been abandoned.[15] Dismantling even the patchily realised system of walkways in the City has been a continual feature of policy and investment since the 1970s. A similar process of sporadic demolition is ongoing in Newcastle. In many places, only an urban geek or an urban explorer will notice the isolated sections of raised thoroughfare that remain along the bases of modern office blocks, forlornly waiting to be linked into a grand walkway system that never came.

Indeed, planning historian Michael Hebbert believes that London's walkways, along with other vertically segregated modernist projects across the UK – from Cumbernauld's town centre in Scotland through Birmingham's 'Motopia' to T. Dan Smith's 'Brasilia of the North' in Newcastle – to be some of the most loathed in the UK. 'Dismantling or disguising the legacy of deck access and walkway design', he argues, 'now absorbs a good share of the British government's "problem

14   London County Council, *The Administrative County of London: Development Plan First Review*, London: London County Council, 1960, p. 169. Cited in Michael Hebbert, 'The City of London Walkway Experiment', *Journal of the American Planning Association*, 59:4, 1993, p. 442.

15   Hebbert, 'City of London Walkway', p. 446.

estates" budget. Several recently built megastructures are being demolished and the original pattern of streets and sidewalks reinstated.'[16]

Internalising Downtown

Despite the general failure of raised walkways in the UK, vertically segregated systems of walkways, skywalks, skybridges and raised podiums, which draw to varying degrees on these genealogies, are still proliferating widely. While the occasional iconic success has occurred in Europe (notably with Richard Rogers's Centre Pompidou in Paris), it is in North America and Asia that the full realisation of the whole city-wide application of such planning has been realised.

The startling emergence of multilevel pedestrian systems in North America since the 1960s has occurred as planners and real estate interests in declining city cores struggled to compete with the suburbanisation of both urban populations and the norms of urban life. Impressed by both the musings of Leonardo da Vinci and the emerging modernist experiments in Europe, North American master planners in the 1960s also embraced the idea of the multilevel city as a radical means of renewing and decongesting decaying urban cores so they could accommodate mass automobile use and compete with the burgeoning malls in the suburbs. The 'planning principle which underlies the orderly and reasonable reorganization of the city center', Vincent Porte, the planner behind the interior subterranean city built in central Dallas, stressed in 1969, 'involves separating cars and pedestrians onto different levels – the so-called multi-level city.'[17]

---

16   Ibid, p. 433. As an aside, just as this book was completed, an urban walk which I regularly undertook for students, colleagues, friends and visitors through the 'layer cake' legacies of T. Dan Smith's Newcastle – a walk I had been doing since my childhood when the structures were built – unexpectedly became impossible. As all efforts to sell the city concentrated on its Roman, Norman, medieval, industrial and twenty-first century history, the access stairs to what remains of the city's 1960s modernist walkway system were quietly covered over with impenetrable steel covers. Modernist multi-level Newcastle, dismantled and unimagined, is no longer an officially sanctioned part of the city's history.

17   Vincent Ponte and Warren Travers, *Dallas Central Business District: A Report Prepared for the City of Dallas*, Dallas: Ponte-Travers Associates, August 1969, p. 15.

Commercial mall skybridges bypassing traditional streets in Minneapolis

The proliferation of vertically segregated interior cities in North America between the 1960s and the 1990s was such that urban design scholar Barry Maitland found by 1992 that seventeen North American cities had systems connecting at least twenty city blocks; thirty-four cities had smaller systems. 'Among the innovations which have transformed North American cities in the past 40 years', Maitland wrote, 'the development of discrete, grade-separated pedestrian networks in the downtown core areas is surely one of the most remarkable ... The idea of an interior city from which one might never need to step outdoors, is on the point of realization in a score of locations across the continent.'[18]

Unlike the case of London, these systems lace office plazas, parking garages, malls, entertainment districts and government buildings with miles of raised – and sometimes subterranean – walkways and tunnels which are entirely enclosed. This is the strategy of 'building cities in the sky' – a solution where 'the street is only for driving on, and parking under; where drivers and passengers move from house to office, shop or theatre without setting foot on the street.'[19]

Some of the largest interior cities have been built in cities with particularly extreme climates (Winnipeg, Montreal, Toronto, Houston, Minneapolis). Indeed, the eighteen-kilometre system of skywalks in

18 Barry Maitland, 'Hidden Cities: The Irresistible Rise of the North American Interior City', *Cities*, 9:3, 1992, p. 162.

19 Kerry Hamilton and Susan Hoyle, 'Moving Cities: Transport Connections', in John Allen, Doreen Massey and Michael Pryke, eds, *Unsettling Cities: Movement/Settlement*, London: Routledge, 1999, p. 58.

Minneapolis is so extensive that its various routes are coloured and named like subway lines to minimise confusion. Maitland's survey found, however, that climatic extremes were less significant a motivation for the lacing together of interior cities than were the advantages to real estate developers or the ability to connect large systems of multilevel car parking garages directly to major commercial or retail space.

As urbanist and photographer Sze Tsung Leong suggests, vertically segregated and interiorised downtowns are entirely different from the traditional world of the open surface-level street. 'The success and proliferation of interiorized activity', she writes, 'and the fact that its nodes can be placed anywhere as islands whose connective tissue is a sea of formlessness and nothingness, has left the outside amputated, mostly inhabitable, and quite often a space of threat.'[20] Such systems thus amount to the construction of privately controlled and surveilled archipelagos that secede from the street system, leaving it – metaphorically and, where the new system is raised up, physically – as a lower-status environment populated by those excluded from the new interior city.

Architectural historian Charissa Terranova criticises such systems for amounting to a parallel 'second-tier city'. Their hyperfunctional connectivity over a plane vertically separated above or below the traditional street, she argues, works to 'create an extreme form of stratification in a context better suited for mixture, the integration of people from all different races and classes.'[21] Poor urban minorities, Terranova writes, have often been relegated to residualised and exteriorised street levels 'where retail has tended to languish and reserving the walkway system for white-collar workers.'

Conversely, the world within the interior complexes is, at best, private/public space organised overwhelmingly around the imperatives of consumption. The move from outside to inside is a passage between worlds. 'Step from the wind and cold on the street outside into the new urban realm', invites architecture critic Trevor Boddy.

---

20   Sze Tsung Leong, 'Readings of the Attenuated Landscape', in Michael Bell, Michael and Sze Tsung Leong, eds, *Slow Space*, New York: Monacelli Press, 2008.

21   Charissa Terranova, 'Ultramodern Underground Dallas: Vincent Ponte's Pedestrian-Way as Systematic Solution to the Declining Downtown', *Urban History Review* 37:2, 2009, p. 27.

'As the glass doors firmly close, the mental realm changes. We are inside, contained, separate, part of the system, a consumer, a pursuer, a cruiser.'[22]

There is certainly strong evidence that interior cities in North America often 'accommod[ate] those activities (and people) that can be commercially exploited, expelling the rest.'[23] In many cities, the raised up (or subterranean) system has become the dominant means for pedestrians to move around the downtown area. While they inevitably offer complex ecologies of public, private and semi-private space which are not entirely exclusionary – and some are designed to link more favourably to public streets and transit systems – very often, the primacy of the interiorised city works to residualise the traditional street.

The residualised street can, in turn, all too easily become 'no more than a traffic sewer or refuge collection zone'[24] – a place inhabited by the marginalised groups excluded by the security guards and cameras that police the corporate, interior zone. As global temperatures rise, the growing frequency of urban heat crises, and the fact that the air-conditioned interior dumps its heat onto the street outside, mean that interior skywalk cities will also inevitably exaggerate the urban heat-island problems faced by their cities.

Such vertical environmental contrasts are compounded by the ways in which private, vertically segregated pedestrian systems can become progressively delinked from surrounding sidewalks. Actual access from the public street often becomes increasingly tenuous as the self-perpetuating logic of extending interiorised commercial walkway systems grow horizontally over time. Entrances to the walkway system from the street below are mediated by access to securitised corporate office buildings, elite condominiums or upmarket hotels. Commercial imperatives and a politics of fear, in other words, can result in pulling up the 'ladder' connecting the skywalk city to the street system. Linkages to the street, often already unsigned or inconspicuous, are closed, built over or replaced by connections through

22   Trevor Boddy, 'Underground and Overhead: Building the Analogous City', in Michael Sorkin, ed., *Variations on a Theme Park: The New American City and the End of Public Space*, New York: Macmillan, 1992, p. 123.

23   Ibid., p. 167.

24   Ibid., p. 168.

retailers or auto garages. Security guards and CCTV cameras provide intensified controls filtering flows between outside and inside.

Wider processes of social polarisation, moreover, have often worked to exaggerate the social separation of inside and outside within the downtowns of various North American cities. Urban critic Trevor Boddy notes, for example, how the widening social problems in 1980s Minneapolis meant that the city's then thirteen-kilometre (and now eighteen-kilometre) skyway system 'became something it was never intended to be: a fortress, a filter, a refuge'. The city's downtown street system – an increasingly residualised space for the poor, the mentally ill and the failed consumers externalised from the interior system – became a source of fear for those inside. As a result, numer- ous security guards worked to surveil the passage-points linking inside and outside in order to reassure the overwhelmingly white, middle-class and suburban shoppers and executives using the interior city. One of their duties was to dissuade 'the poor, infirm, black, native Indian, or mentally ill from entering the skyway system.'[25]

Undertaking a study of the social and economic classes of street users and the users of the vertically segregated interior cities, urban scholar Kent Robertson 'notes a striking difference between the typical skywalk user and the street-level pedestrian.' This suggests, he argues, 'the beginnings of a dual-level downtown society in which people are physically separated by class.'[26] Not surprisingly, those high-income residents who make their homes in the condominium developments that are increasingly connected to enclave complexes – develop- ments that are often now provided with customised and secured schools, health care, fitness suites, pools and commercial services – have been shown to 'have a lower level of civic concern than non- enclavers.'[27]

In a highly automobile-oriented society such as the United States, raised corporate plazas linked exclusively to freeways and parking garages can be almost completely inaccessible to pedestrians on the

25   Boddy, 'Underground and Overhead', p. 138.

26   Kent Robertson, 'Pedestrian Skywalks in Calgary, Canada: A Comparison with US Downtown Systems', *Cities* 4:3, 1987, p. 208.

27   Jason Bayne and David Freeman, 'The Effect of Residence in Enclaves on Civic Concern: An Initial Exploration', *Social Science Journal* 32:4, 1995, p. 419.

street. Geographer Steven Flusty, writing about the then-new Bunker Hill downtown complex of private elevated plazas, corporate sky-scrapers and lush greenery and water features in Los Angeles, relates how he tried to reach the complex from the streets below by foot. 'The Hill's designers are not too keen on pedestrians coming up from below (except janitors)', he concludes. 'The entire Hill is … separated from the adjacent city by an obstacle course of open freeway trenches, a palisade of concrete parking garages and a tangle of concrete bridges linking citadel to citadel high above the streets … We could attain the summit from the south, but only by climbing a narrow, heavily patrolled stair "plaza", studded with video cameras and clearly marked as private property.' [28]

Megacity Skytrains and Skywalks

Outside the United States, the elevation of elite pedestrian spaces across urban centres has also sometimes been accompanied by their interconnection with raised mass transit systems which are unasham-edly elitist and systematically exclude the urban poor.

Bangkok's Sky Train – a raised, 23-kilometre system which started operation in 1999 – is a powerful case here. Geared explicitly towards tourists and Thailand's wealthy and middle classes, the cleanness, coolness and quietness of the elevated train spaces provide a jarring contrast to Bangkok's notoriously congested and humid streets below. The system has been widely lauded by the media and government elites as the city's 'supreme symbol and icon of Bangkok's entrance into the realm of the super-modern.'[29] It has become a symbol of national arrival into a neoliberal world dominated by 'global cities' with glitzy, elitist, infrastructure. Indeed, Thai urban scholar Mark Isarangkun na Ayuthaya stresses that Skytrain has quickly 'attained a unique status as the icon of contemporary Bangkok. Its overwhelming presence is featured in every conceivable media – new music videos, movies or

28   Steven Flusty, 'Building Paranoia', in Nan Ellin, ed., *Architecture of Fear*, New York: Princeton Architectural Press, 1997, p. 57.

29   Tim Richardson and Ole Jensen, 'How Mobility Systems Produce Inequality: Making Mobile Subject Types on the Bangkok Sky Train', *Built Environment*, 34:2, 2008, p. 223.

Echoes of Fritz Lang's *Metropolis*: Bangkok's Skytrain system

advertisements. The Skytrain is an indispensable symbol of the new generation.'[30]

The Skytrain's physically raised status, on columns 12 metres above the city streets, resonates with its symbolic loading as an icon of modernity, superiority and futurity. Users who can afford the premium-level ticket price – monthly tickets cost over 10 per cent of average monthly wages in Thailand[31] – experience the city 'within an elevated urban realm of cool spaces, while being voyeurs of the relatively chaotic "other" realm below.'[32] Through providing radically improved levels of elevated mobility for Thailand's wealthier groups, the Skytrain has supported the emergence of an 'exclusive, elevated urban realm'. This is organised across the malls, hotels, offices and leisure spaces that are integrated seamlessly into real estate developments at the system's stations. 'Buying a Skytrain ticket – a passport to the world above – is a practice of

30   Mark Ayuthaya, 'Intense Multiplicity: Bangkok', *Architectural Design*, 75:6, 2005, p. 16.

31   Mike Jenks, 'Above and Below the Line: Globalization and Urban Form in Bangkok', *Annals of Regional Science* 37:3, 2003, pp. 547–57.

32   Richardson and Jensen, 'How Mobility Systems Produce Inequality', p. 224.

separation between mobile and immobile, rich and poor, modern and traditional.'[33]

As Skytrain reorganises the geographies of everyday life, Bangkok's elite are starting to live, work and entertain themselves within a raised archipelago city of enclaves, which offer new concentrations of premium services and spaces geared to their needs, laced together along the raised urban plane by Skytrain lines. The system thus integrates with customised real estate and branded leisure, retail and living space to constitute 'an organ of capital flow' which increasingly secedes as a whole complex from the lower echelons of Bangkok.[34]

'The upper middle classes and the rich people transport themselves and live, generally speaking, from third floor and up,' urban scholar Gitte Marling observes. 'They work in buildings with air conditioning; they shop in air conditioned shopping malls; go to cinemas and train in cool fitness centres. They even transport themselves in air conditioned cars on elevated high ways or in sky trains.'[35]

Bangkok's Skytrain symbolises broader processes of vertical segregation across many of Asia's burgeoning cities. Indeed, the contemporary growth of vertically raised walkway systems in Asian cities is even more spectacular than that which occurred in North America in the 1960s and 1970s. The thirty-six raised skywalks built in the last decade in Mumbai have generated the most controversy. As with the parallel network of flyovers being built for cars, these skywalks vertically bypass some of the most congested, and contested, ground-level streetscapes in the city.

Offering the possibility of uninterrupted progress, the new regulated walkway spaces again contrast markedly with the haphazard world rendered as an aesthetic backdrop below. British geographer Andrew Harris believes that many have 'been created to enable particular groups to move through the city without having to acknowledge and negotiate the widespread dispossession and poverty that remains the dominant and abiding experience for most people below.'[36]

---

33   Ibid., p. 226.

34   Ayuthaya, 'Intense Multiplicity', p. 16.

35   Gitte Marling, *Bangkok Songlines: Spaces, Territories, Mobility*, Aalborg: Aalborg University: Department of Architecture and Design, 2005, p. 34.

36   Andrew Harris, n.d., 'Aerial Visions and Grounded Realities', available at india-seminar.com/2012/636/636_andrew_harris.htm.

It is the dazzling system of walkways in Hong Kong, however, that is most internationally famous. The city – the densest and most verticalised in the world – offers a startling system of over 500 vertically raised walkways snaking between the huge, raised podium structures at the bases of upmarket hotels, residential blocks, malls and corporate enclaves. In many ways, the stacking of walkways in Hong Kong echoes the city's long history of pioneering innovations in using space extremely intensively and vertically in other domains. 'Like their counterparts, the double-decker bus, double-decker ferry and double-decker tram, the double-decker pedestrian movement system exemplifies [the] "sky city" concept.'[37] Hong Kong's raised walkways allow those who have access to begin to inhabit the kind of raised-up, premium accommodation and mobility systems so beloved of science-fiction writers. Anthropologist Tim Choy talks of a day spent in the company of an executive from the Tsingtao beer company as he 'wends his way expertly through Wanchai, a government and nightlife district on Hong Kong Island, without ever touching the ground.'[38]

Hong Kong is the first city on earth to have a three-dimensional urban guidebook devoted to it.[39] Titled *Cities Without Ground,* its authors highlight the fact that the reach and complexity of multilevel walkway systems – as well as a startling density of subterranean, highway and raised skyscraper housing, hotel, leisure and corporate developments – mean that, for the first time in human history, a major city no longer has to have any recognizable relationships with its actual ground level. 'Hong Kong enhances three-dimensional connectivity to such a degree', the they write, 'that it eliminates reference to the ground altogether. Hong Kong is a city without ground.'[40]

37   Stephen Lau, Jun Wang, Renganathan Giridharan and Sivaguru Ganesan, 'High-Density, High-Rise and Multiple and Intensive Land Use in Hong Kong: A Future City Form for the New Millennium', in Michael Jenks and Nicola Dempsey, eds, *Future Forms and Design for Sustainable Cities*, London: Routledge, 2005, p. 157.

38   Tim Choy, 'Air's Substantiations', paper for Berkeley Environmental Politics Colloquium, 2010, pp. 9–11, available at globetrotter.berkeley.edu.

39   Jonathan Solomon, Clara Wong and Adam Frampton, *Cities Without Ground: A Hong Kong Guidebook,* Hong Kong: Oro Editions, 2012.

40   Ibid., p. 3. As we shall see in chapter 11, this is perhaps ironic given that Hong Kong is also a city which rests increasingly on manufactured ground 'reclaimed' from the ocean.

Hong Kong has become, in effect, a connected complex of mega-structures. These construct accessibility and interconnection within a three-dimensional field that extends from deep subterranean space to several hundred metres above the ground. Such a development makes the city a global capital of innovation and building in esca-lators, elevators and people movers – as well as mass rapid transit, raised walkways, podium decks, vertical housing towers and multi-deck ferries.

In some parts of the city, these multiple grounds allow for an entirely interiorised existence. 'During unfavorable weather, pedes-trians can often complete their entire day of travel without leaving enclosed areas offered by skywalks and underground tunnels.'[41] To capture this, the guidebook's authors sought to build a new style of three-dimensional urban cartography designed to help the naviga-tion of a 'labyrinthine urbanism in which even locals are frequently lost'.[42] Entering a raised or sunken walkway, pedestrians in Hong Kong can be unknowingly sucked directly into apparently inescap-able lobbies of elite hotels, the elevator halls of corporate or banking headquarters, or the platforms of a subterranean MTR subway train or ferry terminal.

Cities Without Ground thus provides a unique style of urban cartography suited to this most three-dimensional of urban environ-ments. Here the cartographers intervene practically to address the widespread sense, in contemporary cities and societies, that humans are often unable to locate themselves and organise their surround-ings meaningfully through what geographers and psychologists call 'cognitive maps'.

Wandering around the confusing multiple layers, walkways and dead-ends of Los Angeles's Bonaventure Hotel in the late 1980s – a structure that mimics the multiple levels of Hong Kong in miniature – philosopher Fredric Jameson used that architectural experience as an allegory to describe the wider disorientations inherent within post-modern culture. 'The latest mutation in space', Jameson famously

---

41   Nathan Costa Ferreira, Stephanie Rose Lesage, Jordan Daniel Vishniac and Zibo Wang, 'Principles of Comprehensive Pedestrian Networks in a Multi-Layered City', report for Designing Hong Kong and the Harbour Business Forum, February 2013, p. 20,
42   Ibid., p. 28.

wrote, 'postmodern hyperspace – has finally succeeded in transcending the capacities of the individual human body to locate itself, to organise its immediate surroundings perceptually, and cognitively to map its position in a mappable external world.'[43] Jameson linked such disorientation to the wider problem of understanding our position in relation to processes of globalisation and urbanisation:

> It may now be suggested that this alarming disjunction point between the body and its built environment ... can itself stand as the symbol and analogue of that even sharper dilemma which is the incapacity of our minds, at least at present, to map the great global multinational and decentred communicational network in which we find ourselves caught as human subjects.[44]

In the cartography of *Cities Without Ground* the vertical axis of multitier Hong Kong is stretched to allow oblique views of the city's multiple layers, and their complex interconnections, to be rendered legible on a two-dimensional surface for the first time.

Here, then, is an urban cartographic revolution: a shift to a three-dimensional rendering of space and accessibility that is thoroughly in keeping with the shift towards vertically layered urban environments across the world. The innovation is being widely lauded across the design disciplines. Until now, traditional two-dimensional maps have been 'woefully inadequate at displaying these dense layers of information', writes a software engineer in the *Randomwire* blog. These new maps, by contrast, present 'a totally fresh perspective on Hong Kong and the result is frankly amazing.'[45]

---

43   Fredric Jameson, *Postmodernism: or, The Cultural Logic of Late Capitalism*. Durham, NC: Duke University Press, 1991, p. 44. Since Jameson wrote those famous lines, as we saw in the introduction, the sense of a disorientating loss of a stable ground and horizon has been a major feature of recent philosophical debates surrounding the links between urbanisation, globalisation and technological change within postmodern cultures. Combining multi-screened digital media, rapid transportation and vertical architectures, such cultures offer their viewers multiple and moving perspectives from many points simultaneously. See Nanna Verhoeff, *Mobile Screens: The Visual Regime of Navigation,* Amsterdam: Amsterdam University Press, 2012.

44   Jameson, *Postmodernism*, p. 44.

45   *Randomwire*, 'Hong Kong: Cities Without Ground', 27 August 2012, available at randomwire.com.

Hong Kong's complex labyrinth of pedestrian spaces are generally more open to the air and more loosely controlled than those in North America. In the absence of other spaces within the hyper-dense confines of Hong Kong, many are appropriated for street food vending, impromptu art exhibitions, community mobilisations, gatherings and picnics or meetings of the city's armies of domestic or migrant workers. Although prohibitions, CCTV surveillance and security guards are common, the complexity and redundancy of the systems means that contravening their efforts can often be successful. Even Hong Kong's Occupy protests in 2014 sought to make their presence felt within the city's complex of walkways. Advocates of the systems argue that pedestrian flows in Hong Kong are simply so large that ground-level sidewalks on the fringes of roads and highways are increasingly impossible.

In Hong Kong, complex combinations of sterile securitisation and vibrant public mixing tend to exist cheek-by-jowl within the network of raised walkways. Uses also exhibit much variation across a twenty-four-hour period. Urban designer Juliana Rotmeyer's research on the subject concluded that Hong Kong's 'elevated pedestrian walkways can be both places and non-places depending on the publicness of space and suggest how a transition of publicness can occur within such spaces.'[46]

Processes of social stratification, though more complex than in North America, still can arise in Hong Kong's layered city. Many walkways – especially in the Admiralty and Central districts on Hong Kong Island – work to elevate the relatively prosperous and powerful by linking directly between the podium level of luxury hotel lobbies, elite apartment blocks, corporate headquarters and elite shopping malls. At the same time, their connections to the ground level – with its dramatically inferior air quality and intense pollution – can be tenuous.

---

46 Juliana Rotmeyer, 'Publicness of Elevated Public Space in Central, Hong Kong: An Inquiry into the Publicness of Elevated Pedestrian Walkway Systems as Places and Non-Places', PhD thesis, University of Hong Kong, January 2010.

Spatial Dead-Ends: Beyond Vertical Sprawl?

As developers and city planners across the world create raised pedestrian and transit spaces, many are arguing, in keeping with the themes of this book, that a fully three-dimensional sense of the urban public realm is now necessary. Questions of physical accessibility and social inequality are now constructed within the complex volumes of urban built space both above and below the traditional ground level and can no longer adequately be represented on the two-dimensional maps traditionally used by urban geographers and transport planners.

Horizontal imaginations of urban space are clearly inadequate to understand the emerging urban labyrinths which seamlessly blend over-ground, ground-level and subterranean complexes and mega-structures and link them together unevenly through elevators, escalators, tunnels, skywalks, subways, walkways, bridges, stairways, people-movers and skytrains.[47] Without better ways of understanding and representing these emerging urban environments, planners, designers, social scientists and social movements alike will struggle to contest their designs and exclusions and address their palpable problems. As we saw with the *Cities Without Ground* project, this means, above all, a shift from two-dimensional to three-dimensional methods in mapping and cartography.

A further question emerges when we consider the politics of the dominant form of design in emerging vertical cities. Invariably, these spaces are being built through the serial reproduction of private, access-controlled, vertical 'silo' structures. Accommodating stacked housing, hotels, retail, leisure, sports and offices within ever more grandiose structures, such structures all too easily emerge as solipsistic and inward looking 'urban islands' which tend to 'residualise' the exterior city.[48]

Beyond the tiny traffic of elite helicopter movements,[49] such

---

47   Jean-Claude Thill, Thi Hong Diep Dao and Yuhong Zhou, 'Traveling in the Three-Dimensional City: Applications in Route Planning, Accessibility Assessment, Location Analysis and Beyond', *Journal of Transport Geography* 19:3, 2013, pp. 405–21.

48   Shelton Barrie, Justyna Karakiewicz and Thomas Kvan, *The Making of Hong Kong: From Vertical to Volumetric*, London: Routledge, 2013, pp. 124–6.

49   See chapter 4.

structures link to the wider city only at the ground and subterranean levels through various walkways, highways and transport systems. In many cases, even such limited connections are often highly fortified and surveilled and are oriented overwhelmingly towards relatively affluent auto drivers rather than pedestrians.[50] In the process, as we saw with the case of US skywalk cities, street levels can easily become residual – sterile and commercially dead, polluted canyons for those same auto drivers' vehicles. In fast-warming cities, heat and air-conditioning can easily add to this vicious circle.

The danger of such an inward-looking model of tower development, as Swiss architects Oke Hauseer and Max Schwitakka have recently argued, is that it results in 'the repetitive insular stacking of privatized space' and creates sterile and often elitist towers that 'ultimately dominate … the stagnant public ground.'[51] Many critics interpret the domination of contemporary urban landscapes by forests of privatised towers as systems of vertically sprawling gated communities or as secessionary cul-de-sacs pointing upwards.[52]

While towers tend to be tightly concentrated in more central locations, such critics suggest that they are no better than the horizontally spread gated enclaves that now dominate many suburban and resort cities in areas the world. Both work to separate their inhabitants beyond their securitised exterior; both rely heavily on forms of infrastructure technology – the automobile and elevator – to allow their inhabitants to participate selectively in the wider city from a safe distance.

Instead of leap-frog suburbs full of gated communities distributed within short horizontal distances from the urban centre, urban designer Iris Hwang wonders whether current models of urban growth in Asia, dominated by gated vertical silos, merely produce

---

50   See chapter 6 of the author's book with Simon Marvin, *Splintering Urbanism*, London: Routledge, 2001.

51   Oke Hauseer and Max Schwitakka, 'Core City – Unbalanced Ratios', in Davide Deriu and Josephine Kane, eds, 'Vertigo in the City: Conversations between the Sciences, Arts and Humanities', University of Westminster, 2015, available at westminster.ac.uk.

52   An important early example was offered by urban designer Ken Yeang. See Ken Yeang, *Reinventing the Skyscraper: A Vertical Theory of Urban Design*, New York: Academy Press, 2002.

what she calls a 'skyscraping suburb'. As a consequence, she thinks that 'instead of the automobile, people will be highly dependent on elevators and escalators' to connect to the wider city.[53] With many vertical enclaves internalizing a wide range of services and amenities for their elite owners, such projects are becoming more and more securitised and solipsistic, their relationship to the urban street ever more remote. The risk here is that such a radical 'emancipation from the ground',[54] which reaches its apogee with the phenomenon of elite helicopter commuting in São Paulo, works to residualise the urban street – a space already under intense pressures from congestion, pollution, building and reduced public space and light penetration.

In such a context, such critics wonder, why limit skybridges to the urban layers immediately above the surface? Why not push for systems of bridges or connecting public walkways and plazas organised at the middle and upper layers of tall buildings as well? 'Is it too far-fetched to believe', architect Anthony Wood wonders, 'that [with] drive and planning, what has started at 10m elevation in cities such as Hong Kong, Minneapolis or Calgary could not occur at 100m, or 200m, in those cities and others?'[55]

Such a question goes to the heart of the politics of vertical urbanism, which, as Dutch architect Darrel Ronald suggests, 'must represent a dynamic vertically integrated urban space of transportation, public space, landscape, infrastructure and interchanges.'[56] Japanese architect Hiroshi Hara offers an intervention here. He argues that 'rather than concentrating on the vertical aspect, which creates a spatial dead-end', a fully three-dimensional city should 'depend on sky passages that connect buildings together at certain levels. In the early twentieth century, each building had its own underground level; now

53   Iris Hwang, 'When Does Stacking Become Vertical Sprawl?' *WIT Transactions in Ecology and the Environment* 93, 2006, pp. 283–93.

54   Iris Hwang, 'Leapfrogging from Vertical Sprawl to Volumetric City: A Study of Compact, Viable 3D Future Model Using Hong Kong', *Proceedings of Ecocity World Summit*, 2006.

55   Antony Wood, 'Pavements in the Sky: The Skybridge in Tall Buildings', *Architectural Research Quarterly* 7:3/4, September 2003, p. 332.

56   Darrel Roland, 'When Towers Lean Together, a New Sky Is Found: The Vertical Urbanism of Generative Networks', M.Arch. final project, University of Montreal, 2005.

these are connected and became part of the city. The same thing could happen in the air.'[57]

Could not vital public and open space threatened on the surface be replaced by new public space, built in 'skycourts' high in the air? Shouldn't urban planners now work in three dimensions to calculate the needs for public space and other public facilities at various levels, rather than using only two-dimensional maps?[58]

Although some high-level skybridges have been built, they have so far been dominated by systems which link adjoining private and commonly owned skyscrapers like Kuala Lumpur's Petronas Towers. Fully public skybridge systems linking varieties of tall buildings across whole urban districts or even large areas – systems that resemble some of the imaginaries like those offered by the avant-garde architecture group Archigram of the 1960s and the more contemporary ideas of mile-high vertical cities laced by sky lobbies and bridges offered by architect Ken King[59] – have yet to emerge. Most cities instead develop new towers through logics of competitive and privatised verticality, where each iconic structure is designed to out-do, and be separated from, its adjacent competitors within fragmented and separated land and real estate markets.

Within single projects possible exemplars are already emerging here. The 2005 Mirador building in Madrid by the Dutch architects MVRDV, for example, is organised around a series of vertically stacked mini 'neighbourhoods' integrated around skyplaza spaces which successfully work as genuinely public spaces. The structure certainly offers as a 'counterpoint against the massive uniformity of the surrounding housing blocks'.[60]

Another MVRDV project – 'The Cloud' in Yongsan, Seoul – will consist of two 300-metre towers linked together halfway up, between the twenty-seventh and thirty-seventh floors, by a ten-floor 'plinth'

57   Cited in Wood, 'Pavements in the Sky', p. 329.

58   Jason Pomeroy, 'The Skycourt: A Viable Alternative Civic Space for the 21st Century', *CTBUH Journal* 3, 2007, pp. 14–19.

59   See, respectively, Hadras Steiner, *Beyond Archigram: the Structure of Circulation*, London: Routledge, 2013, and Kenneth King and Kellogg Wong, *Vertical City: A Solution For Sustainable Living*, Shanghai: China Social Sciences, 2015.

60   Mercedes Martty, 'Rethinking Urbanism Through Vertical Cities', 3 March 2014, available at sourceable.net.

structure. It will by filled with spaces for retail, parks and swimming pools; the exterior levels will house patios, decks, gardens and pools. The architects claim that the project is little less than a 'reinvention' of the skyscraper and that these spaces and facilities will be both private and public in nature. Although many have criticised the apparent resemblance of the Cloud towers to the image of the World Trade Center during the 9/11 attacks, few have questioned how genuinely 'public' these spaces and facilities will be in a development so obviously pitched at the elite end of the market.

Integrating a range of separate towers into 'vertical cities' which are genuinely open and public will inevitably be much more challenging. Only a powerfully coordinated approach to planning, engineering and design between emerging groups of tall buildings similar to the integrated engineering that currently plugs them into ground and sub-terranean-level infrastructures might allow raised skybridge systems to emerge in the future. Were such towers built and the new, raised-access bridges fully public in terms of their accessibility, UK architectural researcher Antony Wood, for one, believes that there is considerable potential for addressing the overwhelmingly private cultures of vertical urban sprawl. 'Could some of the retail, arts and leisure facilities that normally occur at ground level within the city', he wonders, 'be lifted up into the sky to occupy a new "public zone" at height?'[61]

Given the barriers to the successful implementation of a fully vertical and public skybridge system within vertically growing cities dominated by private real estate development, however, the sci-fi urban visions discussed at the start of this chapter will have readers waiting for a considerable while yet. Such is the elite domination of urban heights these days that it is questionable whether even a successful mobilisation on behalf of such a vision could really open such spaces up to the less wealthy or less powerful. Indeed, where the latest high-level bridges and decks between towers are being constructed, they are much more likely to house private swimming pools for the upper middle classes and überwealthy than anything remotely accessible to the general public.[62]

---

61   Wood, 'Pavements in the Sky', p. 329.

62   See also the 'sky-pool' currently under development at Nine Elms in London discussed in chapter 8.

The super-luxury answer to 'vertical sprawl' and 'spatial dead ends', a 'sky park' atop the three towers of the fifty-five-storey five-star Marina Bay Sands Hotel in Singapore. The world's largest cantilevered platform, built on manufactured land, it was opened in 2010 by the Las Vegas Sands Corporation. It is a 340-metre long deck, 190 metres above ground, and features a 150-metre-long pool for guests with a 'vanishing edge' designed so that, for swimmers, the water blends seamlessly into the cityscape below. According to the *Skyscraper Dictionary*, 'The image of people dipping their toes against the backdrop of the Singapore skyline has become something of an icon image for the city.'

The most startling example here is 190-metre 'skydeck' filled with luxury bars and a full-length 'infinity' pool which connects the two towers of the $600-a-night Marina Bay Sands Hotel in Singapore. Itself built, as we discuss in chapter 11, on manufactured ground vertically built up from sand sucked from the sea floor or horizontally appropriated from nearby poorer countries, the hotel's advert strapline is a simple one: 'Even the sky is not the limit!'

Beyond such luxified skies, the power of the public sector to shape high-rise public housing design in Singapore also allows for more democratic 'sky park' possibilities that seem all but impossible in contemporary London, Vancouver, Mumbai or New York. Singapore's Housing Development Board, which houses 80 per cent of the city-state's population, is now fully embracing the idea of designing high-quality and well-maintained 'sky parks', 'mini parks' and a wide range of other public and community facilities concepts located at mid-height or on the roofscapes of its new housing tower complexes. One of its projects – the 'Pinnacle at Duxton' – programmes such facilities throughout the levels of seven linked towers in an especially imaginative way.[63]

63   See Yuri Hadi, Tim Heath and Philip Oldfield, 'Vertical Public Realms: Creating Urban Spaces in the Sky', Council for Tall Buildings and Urban Habitat Conference, Shanghai, 2014, available at global.ctbuh.org.

10.

Air: Lethal Domes

Air ... from Johannesburg to Tehran, to Delhi to Jakarta, isn't about aesthetics, or even possible climate change at some point in the future: it's about life and death now
> – Timothy Doyle and Melissa Risely, *Crucible for Survival*, 2008

Humans, increasingly, manufacture their own air. For a species which expires without breathable oxygen within two or three minutes, this human manufacture of air is of incalculable importance.[1] Human existence comes only after breath.[2]

The process of the machinic manufacture of air happens in a variety of related ways. On a planetary scale, three centuries of rampant urban-industrial growth mean that the earth's atmospheric composition is radically different from what it was in the mid eighteenth century. Greenhouse gas data provides the most startling examples here: CO_2 levels in 2011 were 40 per cent higher than those in 1750; nitrous dioxide levels were 20 per cent higher; atmospheric methane rates were 150 per cent higher.

While the processes are complex, and nonhuman factors obviously remain important, there is little doubt that such changes, along with wider transformations in the earth's ecological systems, are central to rising global temperatures. Climate change is in fact the result of a planet-wide and centuries-old vertical process. It involves the extraction of trillions of tonnes of fossil fuels – mainly coal, oil

---

1   Memorably, Elias Canetti, the Italian philosopher, labeled this the 'defenselessness of breathing'. See Elias Canetti, *The Conscience of Words: Essays,* London: Picador, 1987. See Marijn Nieuwenhuis, 'On One Breath All Depend', *Journal of Narrative Politics* 1:2, Spring 2015, available at journalofnarrativepolitics.com.

2   Peter Sloterdijk, *Terror from the Air,* trans. Amy Patton and Steve Corcoran, Los Angeles: Semiotext(e), 2009.

and gas – from reserves found deeper and deeper down in the earth's crust. These are then burnt to sustain urban and industrial societies. Their embodied carbon is then released into the earth's air and atmosphere – carbon which derived from countless decayed life forms sedimented deep into geological formations tens or hundreds of millions of years ago.

Geologically speaking, this mass 'liberation' of deeply buried carbon from the subterranean sphere to the air is happening in the merest blink of an eye. 'The end of pre-history appears on the horizon', philosopher McKenzie Wark argues, 'as carbon bound within the earth becomes scarce, and liberated carbon pushes the climate into the red zone'.[3] The results of this vertical 'carbon liberation' are already startling. Global mean temperatures rose 0.7°C between 1951 and 2012. Projections of average temperature levels for 2081–2100 suggest further rises of anything between 0.3°C and 4.8°C, depending on changing concentrations of greenhouse gases.[4]

Crucially, between 70 per cent and 80 per cent of all greenhouse gasses emanate from the world's urban areas – or the intensive agricultural, transport and energy systems built to sustain them.[5] Obviously, the human manufacture of air reaches particular levels of intensity in and around the three-dimensional aerial environments within and above big cities. Crucially, from our perspective, such processes are marked by strong vertical patterns. Major urban areas create giant, warmed-up domes or 'heat islands'. These are warmed by the city's release of energy; the extra-high concentration of greenhouse gases (and other pollutants) that linger above cities; and the tendency of concrete and asphalt to absorb the sun's heat quickly (a process which creates strong vertical and horizontal gradations in temperature).

Urban heat islands are, in turn, systematically filled with complex 'cocktails' of pollutants from all the energy-intensive activities that

---

3   Wark calls this process the 'carbon liberation front'. Quote from McKenzie Wark, *Molecular Red: Theory for the Anthropocene,* London: Verso, 2015, p. xv.

4   All data from Working Group I, 'Contribution to the Fifth Assessment Report of the Intergovernmental Panel on Climate Change', in Intergovernmental Panel of Climate Change, *Climate Change 2013: The Physical Science Basis,* Cambridge: Cambridge University Press, p. 161.

5   Mike Hodson and Simon Marvin, *World Cities and Climate Change: Producing Urban Ecological Security,* Oxford: Oxford University Press, 2010.

concentrate in and around cities: power generation, industry, oil-based transportation, building use, construction, and so on. As urbanisation intensifies and spreads, a wide range of global health organisations are asserting that these polluted and warmed urban domes of air are becoming one of humanity's greatest killers.

By 2100, the UN estimates that the world's population will be between 11 billion and 15 billion, and that fully 65 per cent to 85 per cent of that population will inhabit cities located primarily in hot, tropical or semitropical locations. The future threat of major urban heat and pollution emergencies thus seems an especially daunting one.

Recent climate models for the impact of global warming in the Gulf region – an area where political elites routinely frustrate climate change negotiations and preside over the greatest per-capita greenhouse gas emissions on earth – suggest that parts of it will become entirely uninhabitable during heat emergencies after around 2070.[6]

Despite the growing public discourses addressing air-quality emergencies in and around the world's big cities, the political nature of the human manufacture of air in and around cities remains poorly explored. Academic debates on the subject tend still to de dominated by technical, medicalised and public health debates which fail to underline the essential environmental politics characterising urban heat and pollution crises. Political ecologist Raymond Bryant diagnosed over fifteen years ago that 'the existing literature [on changing air quality] is largely devoid of political analysis.' This problem, he said, inevitably works to obfuscate the ways in which 'unequal power relations are … "inscribed" in the air.'[7] Remarkably, his comments retain their power today. [8]

One reason for this neglect is that, while air enables our existence and permeates our bodies, its very transparency and ubiquity makes

6   Jeremy Pal and Elfatih Eltahir, 'Future Temperature in Southwest Asia Projected to Exceed a Threshold for Human Adaptability', *Nature Climate Change*, 26 October 2015.

7   Raymond Bryant, 'Power, Knowledge and Political Ecology in the Third World: A Review', *Progress in Physical Geography* 22:1, 1998, p. 89.

8   It must be noted, though, that more progress has been made exposing the environmental injustices and the complex epidemiologies of ill-health in cities related to air pollution.

it easy to forget – until it is removed or compromised. Because it is the most forgettable aspect of nature, modern thinking and modernist design have tended to assume that air and the atmosphere would always be there to support human existence. 'This element that incontrovertibly constitutes everything', French philosopher Luce Irigaray writes, 'does not impose itself on our perception nor on our conscience. While permanently present, it allows itself to be forgotten'.[9]

Even though the situation is changing fast, air appears in social and political thinking all too rarely. 'Air matters too little in social theory', anthropologist Tim Choy asserts. 'Aside from signifying a loss of grounding, air is as taken for granted in theory as it is in most of our daily breaths … Air is left to drift … neither theorized nor examined, taken simply as solidity's lack. There seems at first to be no reason not to let it.'[10]

Much work thus remains to be done to explicate the political aspects of manufactured urban air in the context of rapid urbanisation, rising social inequality and global climate change. Such a project needs to work to make explicit the political nature of the anthropogenic and machinic manufacture and material conditioning of both 'good' and 'bad' air, through design, technology, capitalist industrialism, militarism, warfare, commodification, consumerism and so forth.

Air, in other words, needs to be wrenched finally and fully from any lingering post-Enlightenment categories of its givenness as a 'public' good within a 'Nature' that is external to the processes of urban, industrial and social life. Emergencies surrounding bad or hot air, in other words, need to be viewed as social rather than natural disasters. Influential anthropologist Bruno Latour, building on the work of German philosopher Peter Sloterdijk on the use of manufactured air in war, engineering and urbanism,[11] stresses the essential politics of air and its oxygen in the context where humans, who expire without it in two minutes, increasingly inhabit urban environments where air is manufactured. 'You are on life support', he writes:

---

9   Luce Irigaray, *L'Oubli de l'Air*, Paris: Minuit, p. 15. Cited in Ruud Kaulingfreks and René Ten Bos, 'Learning to Fly: Inspiration and Togetherness', *Electronic Journal of Radical Organization Theory* 7:2, 2001, pp. 1–13.

10   Tim, 'Air's Substantiations', Paper for Berkeley Environmental Politics Colloquium, 2010, pp. 9–11, available at globetrotter.berkeley.edu.

11   See Sloterdijk, *Terror from the Air*.

It's fragile, it's technical, it's public, it's political, it could break down – it is breaking down – it's being fixed, you are not too confident of those who fix it. Our current condition merely relies on our more explicit understanding that this tentative technological system, this 'life support', entails the whole planet – even its atmosphere.[12]

Killer Heat Waves, Toxic Domes

The 'urban heat island' effect means that the raised ambient air temperatures at the core of large urban areas are usually at their highest during clear, still nights. These commonly reach temperatures which are between 3°C and 10°C higher than those in surrounding areas.[13] Such effects are important contributors to global warming as a whole. Although their precise contribution remains controversial among climatologists, the best recent evidence suggests that the extra heat given off by urban areas, because they absorb the sun's energy so effectively, has contributed 15 to 21 per cent of global warming as a whole over the past 150 years (as opposed to greenhouse gas emissions and other factors).[14]

Recent research using satellites shows that urban heat islands can have even greater effects: one major study in the United States in 2010 showed that summer temperatures in the main cities on the Northeast – Boston, New York, Philadelphia and Washington, D.C. – were on average 7°C to 9°C (13°F to 16°F) warmer than surrounding rural areas over a three-year period.[15]

As well as ameliorating cold winters, urban heat islands can dramatically accentuate the lethal effects of hot summers within the context of a warming planetary climate. Medical studies demonstrate

---

12 Bruno Latour, 'Air-Condition', in Caroline Jones, ed., *Sensorium: Embodied Experience, Technology, and Contemporary Art,* Cambridge, MA: MIT Press, 2005, p. 104.

13 Lisa Gartland, *Heat Islands: Understanding and Mitigating Heat in Urban Areas,* Routledge: London, 2010.

14 Zeke Hausfather and Matthew Menne, 'Urban Heat Islands and US Temperature Trends', *Real Climate,* 13 February 2013, available at realclimate.org.

15 NASA, 'Satellites Pinpoint Drivers of Urban Heat Islands in the Northeast', December 2013, available at nasa.gov.

that there is a 'significantly increased risk of hospitalisation for multiple diseases, including cardiovascular disease, ischemic heart disease, ischemic stroke, respiratory disease, pneumonia, dehydration, heat stroke, diabetes, and acute renal failure due to urban heat waves.[16] Indeed, the US Environmental Protection Agency has estimated that, between 1979 and 2003, heat exposure caused more premature deaths in the United States than hurricanes, lightning, tornadoes, floods and earthquakes combined.[17]

Emergencies such as the Chicago heat wave in 1995 and the European heat wave of 2003 have dramatically revealed the ways in which systematic inequality, housing policies, poor urban design and hopelessly inadequate emergency response arrangements can combine to allow urban heat waves to become mass killers of the poor, the lonely, the old, the weak and the vulnerable.

In the 1995 heat wave in Chicago, after a forty-eight-hour period of daytime temperatures between 41°C and 43°C, those without air conditioning living near the black asphalt roofs of the city's notorious public housing projects on the South Side quite literally baked. Many were too worried about the possibilities of crime to open their windows. Often, people who did have air conditioning could not afford to turn it on because of high electricity costs (power outages caused by the peak in demand were also a major problem).

By Friday, 14 July, severe heat-related illnesses were afflicting thousands in the city. Chicago's emergency services were completely overwhelmed by calls. Hospitals, soon full to capacity and beyond, refused entry to additional patients. People began to die so fast that emergency morgues were set up in freezer trucks.[18] By the end of the week, 739 excess deaths had occurred because of the extreme heat (and especially the lack of cooling at night). The pattern related closely to the geography of poverty: most victims were old, poor, isolated and male – they died alone. African American neighbourhoods, struggling with decades of abandonment, disinvestment and fear,

---

16   Bart Ostro, Stephen Rauch, Rochelle Green, Brian Malig and Rupa Basu, 'The Effects of Temperature and Use of Air Conditioning on Hospitalizations', *American Journal of Epidemiology* 172:9, 2010, p. 1053.

17   NASA, 'Satellites Pinpoint Drivers'.

18   Eric Klinenberg, *Heat Wave: A Social Autopsy of Disaster in Chicago*, Chicago: University of Chicago Press, 2002.

suffered levels of isolation that made them especially vulnerable to heat wave deaths.

The heat catastrophe across Europe in 2003, which prematurely killed around 70,000 people, similarly affected the old, the ill and the lonely living isolated lives in major cities like Paris (where at least 4,800 such people, labelled the 'Forgotten' in the French media, prematurely lost their lives).[19] As in Chicago, the most lethal spaces were marginal, poor-quality apartments high up in the tenements beneath the dark, baking slate and asphalt roofs. (Similarly, the crisis was worsened by widespread use of air conditioning, as we shall see shortly.)

'Many of these forgotten victims lived in *chambres de bonne*', historian Richard Keller writes, 'the former domestic servants' quarters under the roofs of many of Paris's buildings that are a legacy of Prefect Georges-Eugène Haussmann's reconstruction of the city in the nineteenth century'.[20] Indeed, the deaths of the isolated, poor and old helped to expose the Janus-faced vertical architectures and geographies of central Paris: a sumptuous and burnished street level for the bourgeoisie hiding an invisible, decrepit (and dangerous) world of attic-living for the poor.

Keller explored the personal residences of the isolated and elderly people who died in the heat wave (many of whom were buried, like victims of the Chicago heat wave, in unattended funerals). Entering the street-level front door of the apparently wealthy Haussmannian block where one of the heat wave's victims had lived, he discovered that 'it is actually two buildings in one. A marble-lined entryway gives access to the building concierge's apartment, the elevator, a wide staircase leading to the main building's apartments, and the courtyard.' The rear side of the block, Keller found, was, in stark contrast, 'accessible only by a serpentine and decrepit service staircase. This side of the building houses the *chambres de bonne*, seven or eight such apartments with a communal toilet and sink at one end of the hall.'[21] These apartments, hidden away high up from view and raised up to the

---

19 See Richard Keller, *Fatal Isolation: The Devastating Paris Heat Wave of 2003*, Chicago: University of Chicago Press, 2015.

20 Richard Keller, 'Place Matters: Mortality, Space, and Urban Form in the 2003 Paris Heat Wave Disaster', *French Historical Studies* 36:2, 2013, p. 302.

21 Ibid., p. 307.

sun, were the killing zones in Paris's 2003 heat wave. These dwellings illustrated profoundly how heightening social inequalities, manifest in vertical patterns that are easy to overlook, can dramatically affect the vulnerabilities of marginalised populations during urban heat emergencies.

Urban heat islands have a further, much more neglected effect: they dramatically increase the local meteorological energy available for violent weather events within and around cities. Indeed, as cities sprawl into megalopolitan urban regions, so weather events which derive from such energy are becoming apparent. A spate of violent tornadoes on the fringes of Istanbul in the hot summer of 2014, for example, were judged by meteorologists to be the direct results of rapid urbanisation. Virtually unknown previously in the region, they were generated by flows of hot air surrounding Istanbul's extending and intensifying heat island. Startlingly, it seems that the urbanisation of the Istanbul region has reached such a scale that the radical thermal changes involved have created entirely new meteorological processes.

'What weird old gods of weather have Istanbul's architects accidentally awoken?' architecture critic Geoff Manaugh wonders. 'This conjures up frankly outrageous images of a city so sprawling – and so thermally ill-conceived – that huge masses of air at different temperatures are now rising into the sky to do battle, violently colliding like mythological titans above the city to generate the surreal tornadoes now ripping through the neighborhoods below.'[22] To Manaugh, it is clear than one future focus of urban design on a urbanising and warming planet should be the weather itself.

As well as unliveable heat, processes of urban industrialisation systematically manufacture whole environments where the ambient air itself becomes a toxic element which kills millions of people a year. Such domes of lethal air sit more or less permanently above many major cities, effectively blocking urban populations from the fresher air above or around. As urban populations in many fast-growing cities have gained access to the material fruits of modernity, so they have progressively been denied access to life-giving air.

22 Geoff Manaugh, 'Weather Is the Future of Urban Design', *BldgBlog*, August 2014, available at bldgblog.blogspot.co.uk.

Le Corbusier called the air of industrial cities 'devil's air' – and for good reason.[23] The statistics here are even more startling than those for urban heat emergencies: urban air is killing city dwellers at alarming rates. This is not new, of course. Indeed, deadly air in a myriad of variations has been a basic feature of urban and industrial life since their advent.[24] In 1952, in one famous episode in London, for example, 13,000 people died in a three-month smog episode in the city, an event caused largely by coal smoke trapped by temperature inversions above the city.

Recent scientific studies estimate, however, that global death rates from air pollution are rising exponentially. Toxic air is now generating the world's biggest public health crisis. In 2014, following new evidence that the stresses of polluted air are responsible for many deaths through strokes and heart diseases among physiologically stressed urbanites, the World Health Organization (WHO) estimated that fully 7 million people were killed by air pollution across the globe in 2012. 'The risks from air pollution are now far greater than previously thought or understood, particularly for heart disease and strokes', argued the WHO's Maria Neira. 'Few risks have a greater impact on global health today than air pollution; the evidence signals the need for concerted action to clean up the air we all breathe.'[25]

The WHO estimated that 4.3 million of total deaths were due to indoor air pollution (mainly from lit stoves), and 3.7 million were due to bad external air tainted by fossil fuel combustion. The most lethal aspects of the latter involves sulphur and nitrogen dioxide (major causes of chronic respiratory and cardiovascular ailments); poisonous ozone (formed when sunlight reacts with pollutants); carbon monoxide (which prevents the blood from transporting oxygen properly); various forms of airborne particulate matter (from diesel engines and coal fired power stations); carcinogens such as benzene and lead; and airborne dust created by construction work.

---

23   Le Corbusier, *The Radiant City*, trans. Pamela Knight, New York: Art, Architecture and Engineering Library, 1930.

24   For a superb history of air pollution in London, see Peter Brimblecombe, *The Big Smoke: A History of Air Pollution in London since Medieval Times*, London: Routledge, 2011.

25   World Health Organization, '7 Million Premature Deaths Annually Linked to Air Pollution', 2014, available at who.int.

When analysis takes into account the secondary deaths through cardiovascular and pulmonary mortalities (especially emphysema and chronic bronchitis), fully one in eight of all human deaths were caused by bad air inside and outside. Children, the elderly, the poor and those with respiratory and heart problems are dramatically over-represented in this annual figure. And such figures don't even begin to communicate the psychological, social and economic costs of toxic urban air.

In China alone, air pollution, largely from cars and industries within cities, is estimated to kill over 1.2 million people prematurely per year. The combination of the growth of mass car use, extreme reliance on dirty forms of coal, and rapid industrialisation make Chinese cities the most polluted in the world. The situation is so bad that average life expectancy for the 500 million people living in northern China is now declining since people are in effect being poisoned throughout their lives. The latest research suggests that this population will collectively lose more than 2.5 billion life-years of life expectancy – an average of five years each – due to toxic urban air.[26]

In India, meanwhile, a conservative estimate suggests that 620,000 people die prematurely each year through the effects of urban air pollution.[27] This figure is also growing rapidly as the country urbanises at very fast rates and the middle classes switch to car use. Of 180 Indian cities monitored for sulphur dioxide, nitrogen dioxide and suspended particulate matter, only two, Malappuram and Pathanamthitta in Kerala, met the World Health Organization's rather generous criteria for 'acceptable' pollution in 2012.[28]

---

26   Edward Wong, 'Pollution Leads to Drop in Life Span in Northern China, Research Finds', *New York Times*, 8 July 2013.

27   'Air Pollution Fifth Leading Cause of Death in India: Study', *Economic Times*, 14 February 2013.

28   These standards are as follows: for sulphur dioxide – 20 micrograms per cubic metre of air on average over 24 hours, or 500 micrograms per cubic metre of air on average over a 10-minute period; for nitrogen dioxide – 40 micrograms per cubic metre of air on average over a year, or 200 micrograms per cubic metre of air on average over a 1-hour period; for 2.5-micron-diameter suspended particle matter – 10 micrograms per cubic metre of air on average over a year, or 25 micrograms per cubic metre of air on average over a 24-hour period; and for 10-micron-diameter suspended particle matter – 20 micrograms per cubic metre of air on average over a year, or 55 micrograms per cubic metre of air on average

Particulate dust thrown up by diesel engines, coal-burning power stations, construction projects and industry is the single biggest killer within the toxic domes above cities. Such dust literally asphyxiates people through cancers, lung diseases and asthma. By 2050, there could be 3.6 million premature deaths a year from exposure to particulate matter, most of them in China and India, a recent report by the OECD estimates.[29] Chilling epidemiological records and surprises are continually emerging here: in November 2013 an eight-year-old girl living adjacent to one of Beijing's massive flyovers became the youngest person ever to be diagnosed with lung cancer.

Toxic urban atmospheres are especially lethal in cities that are hemmed in by mountains or other natural features; where concentrations of particularly dirty polluters are most intense; and during stable anticyclonic episodes where air fails to rise or get blown away and lingers for days and even weeks. It is now common for health authorities in major cities – Beijing, Lagos, Santiago, Mexico City, Kathmandu, São Paulo, Cairo, Jakarta and Athens are only some of the most notorious examples – to declare states of emergency during such situations. Millions of vehicles are forced off the roads; the most polluting industries are shut down; people, especially the most vulnerable, are urged to stay indoors until the smog clears.

Rice University architect Albert Pope, invoking Peter Sloterdijk's work on the weaponisation of air through lethal gas attacks in war, policing and terrorism, wonders if such crises in effect work as what Sloterdijk calls 'airquakes'. He asks: 'Can a set of ontological rights[30] – such as breathing – actually challenge or even displace economic hegemony?' To him, the unbearable urban air within many Chinese cities 'brings the elements of our life-world out of a background of neglect and foregrounds them as the ontological preconditions of human existence.'[31]

---

over a 24-hour period. See World Health Organization, *Air Quality Guidelines for Particulate Matter, Ozone, Nitrogen Dioxide and Sulfur Dioxide*, Geneva: WHO, 2005.

29 *OECD Environmental Outlook to 2050: The Consequences of Inaction*, Paris: OECD, 2014.

30 That is, rights to do with being or existence as humans.

31 Albert Pope, 'An Airquake in China', *Zonereseaerch.org*, 29 November 2013, available at zoneresearch.org.

Toxic urban air radically interrupts the entrepreneurial efforts of city agencies to brand and market their cities as blue-skied and fragrant-aired destinations for tourists, conferences, film locations, investment flows and, above all, sporting mega-events. In the run-up to the 2008 Olympics, for example, the authoritarian regime in Beijing – a city that pumps out more particulate matter than the country of Portugal and adds 400,000 cars to its roads every year – worked to re-engineer temporarily the city's air for the duration of the event by forcing traffic off the road and closing factories. While the population's health dramatically improved, the reversion to previous levels of transport, energy generation and industrial production immediately after the games quickly reinstated the city's catastrophic pollution problems.

By the end of 2013, the extreme pollution in Beijing and other big Chinese cities meant that airline pilots had to be given detailed training in how to land in smog. The crisis was so bad that the country's official media was reduced to releasing bizarre platitudes that the pollution meant that the people's 'knowledge of meteorology, geography, physics, chemistry and history [had] progressed.' Stranger still, blankets of killer smog were invoked as a geopolitical, defensive shield against the prying weapons of unknown enemies. 'Smog may affect people's health and daily lives', the announcer admitted. 'But on the battlefield it can serve as a defensive advantage in military operations.'[32]

There were limits to the regime's tolerance for Chinese citizens understanding the horrors of their urban pollution crises, however. In March 2015, state censors took Chai Jing's remarkable film on the subject – tellingly titled *Under the Dome* – off the Internet in China after it had drawn hundreds of millions of viewers and galvanised huge pressures on the government.[33]

Pollution crises sometimes interrupt apparently inexorable logics of urban warming. In a particularly prolonged smog event in February 2014, Chinese scientists warned that the smog blanketing the Beijing

---

32 Jonathan Kalman, 'Chinese Media Find Silver Linings in Smog Clouds, *Guardian*, 10 December 2013.

33 See, for example, 'Chai Jing's Review: Under the Dome – Investigating China's Smog', youtube.com, 1 March 2015.

'Airpocalypse': Everyday life in pollution-plagued Beijing

region was becoming so bad that its effects were starting to resemble those of a nuclear winter, creating a city almost 'uninhabitable for human beings'. Densities of suspended particles hit concentrations over twenty times maximum limits recommended by the World Health Organization. Photosynthesis rates in agricultural crops in the greenhouse-based systems within Beijing's hinterland were halved.[34]

In Hong Kong, meanwhile, authorities made a move in the year 2000 to tempt the Walt Disney Corporation to build a theme park there. They were nearly unsuccessful because the corporation felt that the city's notoriously bad winter air pollution 'did not mesh particularly well with the family image that Disney so prided itself on cultivating.'[35] Deep ironies lurk here of course: Los Angeles, the location of Disney's headquarters, has suffered episodes of catastrophic smog for decades. The contrast between Hong Kong's noxious and opaque air and the image promulgated by tourist managers is now so striking that plastic screens depicting blue-skied panoramas are routinely erected next to the iconic city viewpoints when pollution episodes obscure the skyline.[36]

34   Kalman, 'Chinese Media Find Silver Linings'.

35   Tim Choy, 'Air's Substantiations', unpublished paper, University of California, Davis, p. 6.

36   Michelle FlorCruz, 'Hong Kong Tourists Use Fake Skyline Backdrop during High Pollution Days', *International Business Times*, 22 August 2013.

Smog and simulation: A fake skyline erected for tourists in Hong Kong, 2013

For obvious reasons, tourist-based economies are especially vulnerable to toxic urban air. Urban pollution crises in China in late 2013 saw domestic and international visitor numbers to iconic sites such as Beijing's Forbidden City drop by 75 per cent. To bolster bookings, Chinese insurance companies even introduced travel insurance packages covering smog events.[37]

In Asian megacities such as Shanghai, the combination of rising vertical towers and the worsening state of city air creates its own aesthetic connection: the view of the smog-filled lower atmospheres for tower residents above. Giuditta Vendrame, an Italian who lived for eleven months on the seventeenth floor of a gleaming new tower in central Shanghai, recalls that the thickening haze of the city's polluted air 'often imbue[d] the city with a particular sense of lightness, suspension and fragility.' The foggy air, in turn, softened her view of the city's burgeoning forest of skyscraping towers. 'The city gains visual and architectural qualities', she writes. 'The light of the sunbeams penetrates this foggy layer, giving the city a magic and fairy-tale color. However, this "magical haze" is harmful. It is smog, air pollution.'[38]

---

37 Will Coldwell, 'Chinese Smog Insurance: Travel Agency Offers Air Pollution Policies', *Guardian*, 19 March 2014.

38 Giuditta Vendrame, 'Shanghai, Air and Other Stories: Casual Dissemination for a Biological Transformation', paper presented at Ambiances in Action /

The uneven distribution of bad air works horizontally as well. Less urbanised areas downwind of major metropolitan formations breathe the filth of a city they may never visit. Such downwind vulnerabilities are especially lethal after chemical spills – as with the release of toxic gas at the Union Carbide plant in Bhopal, India, in 1984 which has killed up to 16,000 people, or when they become radioactive due to atmospheric nuclear testing or nuclear catastrophes like those at Chernobyl and Fukushima.

Less often, it is cities that are downwind from bad air generated by rural conflagrations (or at least, changes in rural places driven by efforts to serve urban markets). The national pollution crises in the summers of 2013 and 2015 in Singapore and other parts of Southeast Asia, for example, were caused by Sumatran slash-and-burn forest fires in Indonesian rain forests to create space for palm oil plantations.[39] In 2015, Indonesian fires created such smoke problems in Singapore, Malaysia and Thailand that states of emergency were declared and half a million acute respiratory tract infections were reported in these countries.

At first sight the airscapes above European, Japanese and North American cities appear to be cleaner and less deadly than those in Asia. On a planetary scale, this has been achieved partly through a massive geo-economic shift across the horizontal terrain of the earth's surface. The huge and filthy extractive and manufacturing complexes that sustain consumption in North American and European cities is now largely offshored – strung out across China, East and Southeast Asia, Africa, Latin America and even Australia.

A major report of the Intergovernmental Panel on Climate Change in 2013 concluded that such wholesale offshoring from the West to East Asia was a key reason that global emissions of carbon dioxide and the other greenhouse gases increased twice as fast between 2000 and 2010 as they had during the previous three decades. This was because of the huge growth of manufacturing and logistics capacity powered by electricity generated from dirty, coal-burning power

---

Ambiances en Acte(s)/International Congress on Ambiances, Montreal, September 2012.

39   Peter Adey, 'Air/Atmospheres of the Megacity', *Theory, Culture and Society* 30:7, December 2013.

stations, particularly around Chinese cities. 'A growing share of CO_2 emissions from fossil fuel combustion in developing countries', the report concluded, 'is released in the production of goods and services exported, notably from upper-middle-income countries to high-income countries.'[40]

The circulation patterns of the global atmosphere, however, mean that even the horizontal outsourcing and offshoring of bad air across transcontinental scales fails to offer a complete insulation from bad air: a recent study finds that between 12 and 24 per cent of the sulphur pollutants in the western United States had been blown there from industrial and urban sites on China.[41]

Despite the global offshoring of some highly polluting industries, the air in European, Japanese and North American cities, moreover, remains far more deadly than might first appear. Smog events and resulting ozone remain major hazards; electricity generation is often still hugely dependent on fossil fuels; many cities remain clustered around hugely polluting industries; and auto transport, dependent increasingly on diesel fuel – with its lethal output of particulate matter, nitrogen oxide and carbon monoxide – is a major cause of premature death.[42] (The latter shift, justified because diesel engines release less carbon dioxide and are more economical than petrol ones, has been systematically covered up by decades of corporate corruption by the major car manufacturers who have deliberately altered the data that their cars' engines transmit during government pollution tests.) It is not surprising, therefore, that even conservative estimates by environmental scientists suggest that lethal domes of urban air kill 200,000 people a year in the United States and 500,000 across the European Union (40,000 of whom are in the UK).[43]

40   Cited in Suzanne Goldenberg, 'CO_2 Emissions Are Being "Outsourced" by Rich Countries to Rising Economies', *Guardian*, 19 January 2014.

41   Tim Walker, 'Made in China: LA's Smog Is the Latest Product from the Asian Superpower Exported to America', *Independent*, 21 January 2014.

42   See Jonathan Samet et al., 'Fine Particulate Air Pollution and Mortality in 20 US Cities, 1987–1994', *New England Journal of Medicine* 343:24, 2000, pp. 1742–9.

43   Jennifer Chu, 'Study: Air pollution causes 200,000 early deaths each year in the U.S.', *MIT News*, 29 August 2013; Michelle Roberts, 'UK air pollution "linked to 40,000 early deaths a year,"' *BBC News*, 23 February 2016; European Environment Agency, 'Premature deaths attributable to air pollution', 21 April 2016.

Contested Immunities

In all cities, the impacts of toxic and warmed-up air domes are distributed extremely unevenly and unjustly. While atmospheric pollution can be a great leveller in terms of wealth and class, elite groups are generally able to insulate themselves from its effects more effectively than the poor or marginalised. Here a three-dimensional cat-and-mouse game of environmental injustice is fought out as systems of linked, 'capsular' spaces such as condominiums and penthouses, malls, office complexes and upmarket cars are constructed that offer air conditioning (while pumping their heat and pollution straight to those immediately outside).[44] Air-conditioned cars, often flitting across the cityscape on raised flyovers, dump their heat, noise and carcinogens straight onto the relatively impoverished communities that such structures tend to bisect. Adjacent communities have been shown to suffer dramatically higher death rates from asthma and other pollution-related diseases than those further away from the highways. 'Residential proximity to freeways is associated with uncontrolled asthma.'[45]

In Los Angeles, for example, recent research has shown that largely Hispanic, Asian and African American neighbourhoods bisected by freeways and flyovers carrying the cars of largely white commuters between suburban neighbourhoods and downtown breathe by far the highest concentrations of deeply poisonous and carcinogenic substances such as vanadium, nitrates and zinc in the metropolitan area.[46]

The damaging impacts of auto exhaust emissions were one of the motivations of modernist architects in advocating the destruction of traditional streets and the mass housing of urban populations in raised towers. Cars would traverse the city on freeways surrounded

---

44   See Lieven De Cauter, *The Capsular Civilization: On the City in the Age of Fear*, Rotterdam: NAI, 2005.

45   Peter Huynh, Muhammad Salam, Tricia Morphew, Kenny Kwong and Lyne Scott, 'Residential Proximity to Freeways is Associated with Uncontrolled Asthma in Inner-City Hispanic Children and Adolescents', *Allergy*, 13 June 2010, available at ncbi.nlm.nih.gov.

46   John Steppling. 'Hollywood, the Police and the Poor', *TruthOut*, 21 December 2014, available at truth-out.org.

by buffer zones of pollution-absorbing greenery. These days, however, mass modernist housing programmes have mostly been abandoned, with occasional exceptions such as Singapore. The colonisation of (air-conditioned) vertical space has been reconstructed as an overwhelmingly elite programme – a three-dimensional elevation of the powerful bound up with the re-engineering of entire cityscapes largely to cater to their needs. As elites in many cities become concentrated in gated, air-conditioned, vertical communities and tall, climate-controlled workplace towers, they work to escape both the din of urban life and the pressing heat and pollution of the hotter urban surface.

Such vertical geographies of environmental injustice tend to be exaggerated where cities are built on mountainous terrain. Ascending up the proliferating skyscrapers in the world's most vertical city – Hong Kong – anthropologist Tim Choy is struck that 'the rich have access to good air, while the poor are relegated to the dregs, to the smog and dust under flyovers or on the streets.'[47] Elites, for example, can seek refuge from bad air, noise, heat and humidity by colonizing what Choy calls Hong Kong's 'airy refuges' – in skyscraper penthouses located in the topographic heights of the Peak or Mid-Levels and the extensive raised walkway systems in the central city on Hong Kong island.

Because the city's deep, canyon-like streets and the long so-called 'podium' structures at the base of towers act to channel and contain relatively heavy polluted air, meanwhile, this has crucial impacts on relative health of the vertically stratified population. 'In the typical street canyons of Hong Kong, air pollutants tend to be trapped in the bottom 15 m.'[48] Moreover, the massive podium blocks between the streets and the raised walkways in Hong Kong 'not only block most of the wind to pedestrians (affecting comfort and air quality), but also minimize the "air volume" near the pedestrian level (affecting air quality).'[49]

---

47   Choy, 'Air's Substantiations', p. 29.

48   Kam-Sing Wong, Edward Ng, and Raymond Yau, 'Urban Ventilation as a Countermeasure for Heat Islands toward Quality and Sustainable City Planning in Hong Kong', *Journal of Heat Island Institute International* 7:2, 2012, pp. 11–17.

49   Edward Ng, 'Air Ventilation Assessment for High Density City: An Experience from Hong Kong', paper at Seventh International Conference on Urban Climate, 29 June–3 July 2009, Yokohama, Japan, available at ide.titech.ac.jp.

The layered politics of urban atmospheres are not lost on the real estate agents and developers who build, design and market the world's vertical gated communities. As we saw in Chapter 8, elite towers in India are now marketed on the basis that living higher is a cooler experience than ground-level inhabitation. Such towers thus offer what Sloterdijk has termed 'spatialized immune systems',[50] lifting elites above the bad air and heat of the grounded city below – as well as above the dense populations of poorer people.

Also pivotal to the fragmentation of atmospheres is the global boom in the air-conditioning industry. Expected to almost double between 2012 and 2018 – from $98.2 billion to $178.4 billion in 2018 – the global air-conditioning industry is in bonanza mode.[51] In 2013, air-con accounted for 10 per cent of global electricity demand – a figure that, with thirty-eight of the world's fifty biggest cities located in the tropics, is rising fast.[52] Dutch scholars Morna Isaac and Detlef van Vuuren calculate that global power use for air-con will multiple fortyfold during this century. It is likely to outstrip that used for heating around 2065 and by 2100 exceed it by two-thirds. Global energy demand for air-con use is expected to multiply thirty-three-fold by 2100 as middle-class urbanites struggle to cool their spaces amidst severe heat crises and rising temperatures caused by global warming and intensifying urban heat islands.[53] The fashion for huge, glass-walled towers in elite housing projects in hot countries only adds to need for air-con because they trap so much energy from the sun's rays. Statistics of air-con growth are remarkable. For example, fully 50 million domestic air-con units were purchased in China alone in 2010. In cities like Mumbai, air-con already accounts for 40 per cent of power demand.[54]

Urbanisation, urban heat-island effects and the very warming of the planet, combined with the ubiquity of consumer capitalism,

---

50   Sloterdijk, *Terror from the Air*.

51   Transparency Market Research, 'Global Air Conditioning Systems Industry Is Expected to Reach USD 178.4 Billion in 2018', 2013, available at prnewswire.com.

52   Cited in Henry Grabar, 'Dream City: Air Conditioning Is a Public Good', *Salon*, 10 August 2013.

53   Cited in 'No Sweat', *Economist*, 5 January 2013.

54   Jon Henley, 'How Desire for Cold Drives Global Warming', *Guardian*, 27 October 2015.

provide a perfect market environment for an industry which offers the promise of manufacturing what Sloterdijk has called 'thematized' or 'designed air'.[55] 'The breaking up of the social world into spaces of moral interdependence inaccessible to one another', he suggests, 'is analogous to the micro-climatic fragmenting of the atmosphere'.[56]

The growing normalisation of air-con urbanism in hot climates like the southern US has been paralleled by major architectural, social and geographic shifts. The first air-con unit was invented in 1914. By 1960, 20 per cent of homes in the US South owned an air conditioner; by 1973, 80 per cent of US cars had air-con. Such shifts helped precipitate a massive geographic shift in population in the post-war period: population densities in the southern states of the US 'Sunbelt' almost doubled between 1930 and 1980. The 1970 Census was dubbed the 'air-conditioned census' by the *New York Times* because its data revealed the way the technology was helping to reorient US geography, allowing comfortable living in the South even in the summer.[57] Between 1945 and 2013, air conditioning was a pivotal factor in the population of the US Gulf Coast rising from less than 500,000 to over 20 million.[58] By 2015, 90 per cent of US homes were air conditioned; US power uses for air-con equalled power used by the whole of Africa for everything.[59]

Many other nations have followed the US path towards mass air-con use. Overwhelmingly, such processes are organised through individualised market forces distributing personal machines as consumer durables or increasingly taken for granted add-ons to personal vehicles. Such transformations are reflected strikingly in urban landscapes in many megacities where large buildings gradually become strewn with walls of individual air conditioners. This trend is especially noticeable in China, where mass individual air-con units in their millions poke out of vast towers, built without central air-con, across major cities. One tower in Fuzhou is such a spectacular example that it has been dubbed the 'new Great Wall of China' and is now a tourist attraction.

---

55 Sloterdijk, *Terror from the Air*, p. 94.
56 Ibid., p. 99.
57 Peter Adey, *Air: Nature and Culture*, London: Reaktion, 2015, p. 156.
58 Cited in *Economist*, 'No Sweat'.
59 Cooling burgeoning Internet data centres is particularly power-intensive.

Such a triumph of individualised solutions to a collective problem is highly problematic. This is because air-conditioning units are essentially selfish devices. The laws of physics inevitably mean that heat removed from the cooled, bubble-like, air-conditioned enclosures cannot disappear. It must, instead, be dumped outside the walls. Indeed, the proliferation of air-conditioned interiors leads to greater amounts of expelled heat via the heat exchangers on the frontages and roofs of the buildings.[60] Such external dumping of removed heat further exacerbates both urban heat-island effects and the intolerable temperatures of the wider street environment. This, in turn, adds to the increasingly urge by those who can afford it to find refuge within an air-conditioned environment, which further increases air-con use, greenhouse gas emissions and so on.

Research on the 2003 heat emergency in Paris by Cécile de Munck of the French Centre for Meteorological Research suggests that increased air-con use in the city exacerbated the problem. The amount of heat removed from building interiors to Paris's streets was sufficient to significantly worsen the city's overall heat crisis (and increase the temperature differences between the street and cooled building interiors). Following detailed modelling of the impacts of air-conditioning heat dumping on the 2003 crisis, de Munck and her colleagues concluded that 'the classic means to meet the cooling needs of the buildings in Paris during a heat wave event similar to that of 2003 are likely to increase street air temperatures and, consequently, the amplitude of the heat island, with the most intense impacts near the greatest AC waste heat releases'.

Notably, this exacerbation of heat-island effects is most powerful in the densely built and largely affluent districts such as the centre of Paris – places where air-con has been the most widely installed and where running costs tend not to be a problem. Moreover, while temperatures are currently increased by about 0.5°C by air-con heat dumping in the most urbanised parts of the city, the widespread use of so-called 'dry' air-con, which dumps more heat, and widening

---

60   Anyone who has stood next to the extracted air-con outlet of a major mall, hotel or office complex in a hot city can testify to the oven fan–like experience. See Emily Williams, 'From *kang* (炕) to *kongtiao* (空): China's Twentieth-Century Cooling', *Journal of Chinese Humanities* 1:1, 2014, p. 196.

air-con use have disturbing implications for future heat crises. A doubling of air-con use in Paris – likely with current trends, and the use of dry systems throughout the city, within a decade or so – would, the researchers predict, quadruple the effect of air-con on Paris's heat island. This would involve a 2°C increase in temperature at the time when the city's population not living in air-con environments are most vulnerable to 'thermal stress' – during the night.[61] (Research on similar impacts in Phoenix, Arizona – a city with much more widespread air-con use than Paris, has concluded that air-con increases the temperature of the urban heat island by 1°C –1.5°C.)[62]

A second vicious circle for air-con cities involves pressure from the peaks of electricity demand created by urban air-con systems. Such peaks have been proven to lead to major power blackouts.[63] Behind the unprecedented blackout across the megalopolitan Northeastern US on 14 August 2003 – the most powerful example thus far – lay an overstretched electricity system that was particularly overburdened with demands from air-conditioning systems.[64] The extraordinary rates of growth in air-con use force the use of extra fossil fuels for electricity generation, increase related threats to energy security, lead to the release of more particulate matter and greenhouse gasses, and increase the risk of major power outages. The vicious circle here seems unbreakable: more air conditioning; exaggerated climate change–related temperature rises; increasingly intolerable urban heat-islands; further demands for air-con environments; and so on. Stan Cox pinpoints the spirals clearly: 'Turning buildings into refrigerators burns fossil fuels, which emits greenhouse gases, which raises global temperatures, which creates a need for – you guessed it – more air-conditioning.'[65]

61 Cécile de Munck et al., 'How Much Can Air Conditioning Increase Air Temperatures for a City Like Paris, France?' *International Journal of Climatology* 33:1, 2013, p. 224.

62 Francisco Salamanca, Matei Georgescu, Alex Mahalov and M. Wang, 'Anthropogenic Heating of the Urban Environment due to Air Conditioning', *Journal of Geophysical Research: Atmospheres* 119:10, 2014, pp. 5949–65.

63 See Stephen Graham, ed., *Disrupted Cities: When Infrastructure Fails*, Routledge: New York, 2009.

64 Grabar, 'Air Conditioning Is a Public Good!'

65 Stan Cox, 'In the Heat Wave, the Case against Air Conditioning', *Washington Post*, 11 July 2010.

Such feedback loops add further to the vulnerabilities faced by marginalised urban groups, who have no choice but to endure urban heat-islands without air conditioning. Detailed research on heat emergencies demonstrates clearly that 'ownership and usage of air-conditioners significantly reduce[s] the effects of temperature' on the wide range of conditions, diseases and ailments that can become killers during urban heat waves.[66] The lessons of the killer heat emergencies in Chicago in 1995, across Europe in 2003, in India in 2014 and elsewhere are again deeply relevant here. There remains a startling absence of public policies to systematically organise the delivery of adequately cool environments for the urban poor within rapidly warming cities faced by dramatic rises in consumer electricity costs.

In such a situation, market-based distribution of life-saving bubbles of coolness can only work to kill increasing numbers of the old, the poor, the weak and the ill – many of whom are made even more vulnerable because of the physiological stresses caused by polluted air. Many public health commentators are now arguing that the inevitable failure of markets to deliver cooling to those who need it most mirrors the failure of markets for many other 'public' goods. Learning from cities like Hartford, Connecticut, for example, urban writer Henry Grabar argues that public municipal infrastructures for cooling air are essential to tackle both urban heat crises and the contribution of individualised air-con markets to toxic air (after all, many North American cities have long traditions of organising collective heat, steam and electricity infrastructures).[67]

Apartheid Atmospheres

Importantly, air conditioning is increasingly being applied to much bigger environments than single office, housing or mall buildings. Upscaled use of air-conditioned interiors has been central, for example, to Dubai's spectacular emergence as the ultimate dreamworld of neoliberalism, with an archipelago of air-conditioned interior 'experiences', each of which enjoys a wholly manufactured climate. This trend, which is even leading to the air conditioning of whole

---

66 Ostro et al., 'Effects of Temperature and Use of Air Conditioning', p. 1053.
67 Grabar, 'Air Conditioning Is a Public Good!'

beaches, perhaps reaches its extreme with Ski-Dubai, the conceit of a complete indoor skiing environment with real snow in the middle of one of the world's hottest deserts, one that regularly reaches 50°C beyond the walls. In 2015, Dubai planners announced the construction of an entire indoor ski resort, complete with a 1.2 km slope.

Like some bad sci-fi movie, air pollution crises are also driving urban elites to engineer a wide range of domes and capsules which benefit from filtered, good-quality air and temperature control and which are removed from the wider urban environment. In one of the most powerful examples so far, governors of Beijing's International School for elite, expat children have spent $5 million housing their previously outdoor playgrounds and sports spaces within a giant plastic dome. This allows the air breathed by the school's children to be filtered to very high standard by powerful US-made industrial air filters that control the interior's relationship to the urban outside.[68] 'It's a bit of a change having to go through an airlock on the way to class', Travis Washko, director of sports at the school, admits. 'But the kids love it, and parents can now rest assured their children are playing in a safe environment.'[69]

As well as being a staple of urban comics and science fiction, much larger urban domes have also been proposed as ways to create climate-controlled urban air spaces within Dubai's huge, 4.5 million square metre 'mall of the world' project. In Houston, a group of local engineers proposed in 2010 a mile-wide dome to cover the entire business district – a means of confronting increasingly frequent and intensifying hurricanes and worsening heat and pollution crises. The only way to save Houston, an apocalyptic *Discovery Channel* documentary intoned, 'is to move it indoors'.[70] Although only a speculative

---

68   According to its manufacturers, the system 'targets [particulate matter] PM2.5 contamination and harmful outdoor gaseous pollutants including ozone, to keep the Chinese Air Quality Index (AQI) below 50 at all times', however bad the air is outside the membrane. 'International School of Beijing Installs Air Cleaning Equipment Designed and Manufactured in California', Ultraviolet Devices, Inc., 5 February 2013.

69   Oliver Wainwright, 'Inside Beijing's Airpocalypse: A City Made "Almost Uninhabitable" by Pollution', *Guardian*, 16 December 2014.

70   Discovery Channel, 'Saving Houston with a Dome', 2010, available at discovery.com.

project, the idea sparked fierce debate in Houston's media. Residents in the zones just outside the city's business district wondered if they could benefit from an extended project or even of a second dome was possible.[71]

Designers in Beijing are meanwhile looking to upscale the International School's ideas to a much larger dome enclosing a major new privatised urban park in the city.[72] Architects have also suggested burying copper coils under parks to create electrostatic fields which attract smog particles from the immediate atmosphere.[73]

These examples of the growing interiorisation of 'nature' powerfully echo Buckminster Fuller's influential ruminations between the 1940s and 1960s on the possibilities of dome-like constructions at various scales within which urban air could be precisely controlled. Famously, in 1960 Fuller suggested a giant, 400-tonne glass geodesic dome encompassing Midtown Manhattan which would permanently sustain what he called a 'Garden of Eden' climate.[74] Fuller claimed that 'the cost of snow removal in New York City would pay for the dome in 10 years.'[75]

Today's 'bubbles' for the precise manipulation of urban air contrast sharply, however, with Fuller's urban planning ideas in one crucial respect. His projects were rooted in an ethos of the democratic manipulation of urban air for cities and urban districts as public goods and public spaces to be experienced by all. Examples like Dubai's giant malls and ski resorts, Beijing's expat school and a myriad of privatised corporate plazas and überwealthy residence towers, by contrast, are organised carefully to allow powerful elites to cordon themselves off from the worst effects of a deteriorating urban life outside. They are

71   See Simon Marvin, '"Volumetric Urbanism: Artificial "Outsides" Reassembled "Inside"', in Olivier Coutard and Jon Rutherford, eds, *Beyond the Networked City*, London: Routledge, 2015, pp. 227–41.

72   See Kimberly Mok, '"Bubbles" Biome in Beijing Could Let Residents Breathe Clean Air', *Treehugger*, 8 March 2014, available at treehugger.com.

73   See, for example, studioroosegaarde.net/project/smog-free-project/.

74   See Krausse and Kichtenstein, *Your Private Sky*. Le Corbusier was also preoccupied with ideas for conditioning perfect urban climates. 'But where is Utopia, where the weather is 64.4°F?' he wondered. Le Corbusier, *Radiant City*, p. 42.

75   Quoted in Lloyd Alter, 'A Look at Bucky Fuller's Dome over New York City', *Treehugger*, 10 March 2014, available at treehugger.com.

exemplars of a widening range of efforts, at a variety of scales, to try and make good air privately available to those who can afford it, amid an increasingly lethal exterior.[76]

Crucial questions surround such an incremental and haphazard privatisation of urban air through the spread of air-conditioned spaces and enclaves designed against a deteriorating exterior. Clearly, such projects inevitably become self-defeating at the urban and planetary scales. Beyond their sometimes negative impacts on those inside – who can succumb to poor health through problems such as 'sick-building syndrome' – these interiorised capsules of privatised air contribute disproportionately to the deterioration of the planetary climate outside their engineered bubbles. The sheer contradiction between the mass and density of the inevitably public city and dreams of controlled, hermetic microclimates shaping the inherently mobile air around mobile individuals inevitable breaks down.[77]

'People feel very strongly that their private constructions of immunity are endangered by the presence of too many constructions of immune spheres', Sloterdijk writes.[78] Such bubble-like worlds are 'pressed against each other and destroy each other.'[79] Thus, city-dwellers increasingly feel compressed and crowded within and between archipelagos of privatised interiors and deteriorating exteriors organised based on principles of extreme inequality. Italian design scholar Giudetta Vendrame, reflecting on living in Shanghai, does indeed get the sense that the city's residents seem to 'feel suffocated' by the proliferation of air-conned interiors separated off from the deteriorating exterior city of ground-level toxic air. It's 'as if there isn't enough space', she continues. 'As if there isn't enough air for us. On one side the fear of suffocation, of no-breath. On the other (out)side the fear of the unknown, the invisible [hazards of urban air pollution].'[80]

---

76   See Sandra Kaji-O'Grady, 'Privatized Atmospheres, Personal Bubbles', *Architecture and Culture* 3:2. 2015, 175–95.

77   Some itinerant billionaires reportedly travel the world with their own private air supplies, which pump clean, cool and filtered air into whatever home they're staying in at the time.

78   Peter Sloterdijk, 'Something in the Air: An Interview with Erik Morse', *Frieze* 127, November/December 2009, available at frieze.com.

79   Ibid.

80   Vendrame, 'Shanghai, Air and Other Stories'.

Beyond the private and elitist nature of contemporary domes of relatively good or cool air, their construction is often sustained by sacrificing the bodies of unknowable labourers who expire through heat exhaustion while working to construct the spectacular façade. If the increasingly hot urban world can be starkly divided between those who are inside air-con environments and those who are outside, the construction of a whole suite of vast air-conditioned hotels, malls, leisure attractions and even football stadia by armies of near-slave labourers within the 50°C temperatures of the UAE, Saudi Arabia and Qatar is the lethal apogee of such injustice.

In Qatar, 2 million indentured labourers from Nepal, Pakistan, India and the rest of South and South-East Asia are constructing these edifices in a $140 billion programme to ready the enclave for the 2022 World Cup. The International Trade Union Confederation has warned that 4,000 construction workers are likely to die before the start of the tournament; at least 185 Nepalis – who make up a sixth of the migrant work force – died in 2013 alone.[81] Over 500 Indian workers – between 20 and 30 a month – died between 2012 and 2014.[82] 'As things stand', the Play Fair Qatar campaign calculates, 'more than 62 workers will die for each game played during the 2022 tournament.'[83] That's one for every 90 seconds of football that will be played in the tournament. Most death certificates of workers in Qatar are marked with the catch-all attribution of 'natural' 'cardiac arrest' by Qatari doctors. This deflects attention from the lethal working environment that is the real cause of such huge death rates. The dark irony is that, when opened, the entire archipelago of bubble-like visitor spaces – including, the Qatari government claim, the World Cup stadiums – will be air-conditioned.

Just down the coast in the UAE, bonded South Asian labourers are also dying in great numbers to construct air-con megacities for locals, expats and tourists. 'During the summer, temperatures soar above 45°C (113°F), and visitors are advised to walk outdoors only in

81   Owen Gibson and Pete Pattison, 'Qatar World Cup: 185 Nepalese Died in 2013 – Official Records', *Guardian*, 24 January 2014.

82   Owen Gibson, 'More Than 500 Indian Workers Have Died in Qatar since 2012, Figures Show', *Guardian*, 18 February 2014.

83   Quoted in Marina Hyde, 'How Many Slave Deaths for the Qatar World Cup Can Fifa Put Up With?' *Guardian*, 20 May 2015.

the evening, and drink water continually', writes Richard Abernethy. 'Heat stroke is a killer for workers doing heavy physical labour for shifts of 12 hours or longer.'[84]

Human Rights Watch cite a report from the journal *Construction Week* which found that 880 migrant construction workers died in the UAE in 2004 alone.[85] The Indian consulate registered the deaths of 971 Indian citizens in 2005; 61 of these were registered as site accidents, many from heat stroke and heat exhaustion. The report found that 'as many as 5,000 construction workers per month were brought into the accident and emergency department of Rashid Hospital in Dubai during July and August 2004.' The Indian government say that at least 60 Indian citizens died building the Burj Khalifa alone, but Emirati employers of bonded labourers on the site have regularly been exonerated for brutal violence against workers in UAE courts.[86]

Extreme racism, isolation, brutal working conditions, alienation and failure to be paid have also created an epidemic of worker suicides. Indeed, some workers leap to their deaths from the very skyscrapers they have helped construct. In May 2010, journalist Nesrine Malik heard about the first worker suicide off the Burj Khalifa. 'Gossip about the suicide was horrifyingly callous', she noted. '"It only took 10 months" [after the opening of the hotel], one person said. "He's inaugurated the building", another almost laughed. "Why did he jump?" I asked. People shrugged. He's probably an expatriate worker, I was told – it's usually them.'[87]

With even darker irony, the very construction of Dubai that these workers sacrifice so much for is actually worsening the heat crises and urban heat-island effects that are so dangerous to their lives. 'What could be hotter than the desert?' Emirates journalist Nick Leech asks.

---

84   Richard Abernethy, 'Dubai: In a Playground of the Super-Rich, Workers Confront a Bonded Labour System', *International Marxist-Humanist*, 16 August 2010, available at internationalmarxisthumanist.org.

85   Human Rights Watch, *Building Towers, Cheating Workers: Exploitation of Migrant Construction Workers in the United Arab Emirates*, Washington DC: HRW, 2006.

86   Rafia Zakaria, 'The Burj Khalifa: Behind the Glitz', *Patheos.com*, 15 January 2010, available at patheos.com.

87   Nesrine Malik, 'Dubai's Skyscrapers: Stained by the Blood of Migrant Workers', *Guardian*, 27 May 2011.

'The answer is a city in the desert.'[88] Dubai's huge growth produces ever more hectares of asphalt and concrete, which absorb more of the sun's heat and become even hotter, creating a dome of super-hot, polluted air that lingers above the city.

Startlingly, official discussions of how to deal with Dubai's heat crises fail even to mention its effects on the vulnerable construction workers who are exposed to it all day long. Instead, the concern is for the small parts of the Emiratis', expats' or tourists' urban experience that is not already absorbed within chains of linked and mobile air-con bubbles. 'We've all felt that unbearable blast from the asphalt while walking the final few metres to our cars', one article in the UAE *National* relates. 'But few realise how damaging the effect of this can be.'[89]

Qatar and the UAE represent stark examples of the wider construction what Mike Davis and Dan Monk termed the 'dreamworlds of neoliberalism'[90] – cities sustaining fantasy lifestyles for the wealthy built at the expense of unknowable numbers of heat-related deaths among near-slave migrant workers. After the UK's then shadow sports minister Clive Efford expressed revulsion at the latest revelations of worker deaths in Qatar in 2013, Australian journalist Maher Mughrabi wondered,

> Where exactly has this man been? Dubai, Qatar and Bahrain have been hosting the stars of golf, tennis, snooker, formula one and, of course, horse racing for decades now. And all those holidaymakers in Dubai who have sampled the shopping festival, the mall with the indoor ski slope or zooming up in the lift of the world's tallest building should also know that all this was built through the same system of labour that is suddenly so appalling.[91]

---

88 Nick Leech 'Overheating Cities "Can Cause Us More Than Discomfort"', *National*, 7 May 2012.

89 Ibid.

90 Mike Davis and Dan Monk, *Evil Paradises: Dreamworlds of Neoliberalism*, New York: New Press, 2009.

91 Maher Mughrab, 'Shocking News of "Slave" Deaths in Qatar No Surprise', *Sydney Morning Herald*, 3 October 2013.

Atmo-Terror, Weather-War

It is important, finally, to remember that the creation of spaces of bad or lethal air is often deliberate rather than unintentional: the main objective rather than the by-product of other activity. As already noted, Sloterdijk has done much to excavate the political history of what he calls 'atmo-terror': the deliberate manipulation of air, weather and climate as an ultimate means destroying an enemy or an Other.[92] Sloterdijk's work explicates powerfully how such ideas shaped the gas attacks of World War I; the gas chambers of the Holocaust; techniques of strategic fire and atomic bombing; the use of hot and cold conditions as means of inflicting pain on detainees; and Cold War experiments in military weather modification and biological and chemical warfare.

All such techniques, notes Sloterdijk, involve the up-scaling of ideas of air-conditioning of small, local 'bubbles' around individual bodies, rooms or buildings to larger urban, regional or even planetary scales. Indeed, political scientists Brad Evans and Julian Reid remind us that 'it is no coincidence that we may trace the origin of climatic conditioning to warfare.'[93] It is inevitable, then, that debates about weaponising weather overlap with those concerned with using geo-engineering techniques to address crises of climate change, intensifying extreme weather events, and resource exhaustion.

In addressing this overlap, however, we must overcome the long-standing myth that meteorology and climate are entirely 'natural', drawing only on other-than-human forces. 'So long as meteorology presents itself as a natural science and nothing else', Sloterdijk stresses, 'it can pass in silence over the question of the weather's possible author.'[94] While the International Panel on Climate Change is coming fully to grips with unintentional effects of urban-industrialism on the earth's atmosphere, it has so far failed completely to address real or potential acts of climatic warfare.[95]

---

92 Sloterdijk, *Terror from the Air*.

93 Brad Evans and Julian Reid, *Resilient Life*, Cambridge: Polity Press, 2013, p. 126.

94 Sloterdijk, *Terror from the Air*, pp. 86–7.

95 See Jacob Darwin Hamblin, *Arming Mother Nature: The Birth of Catastrophic Environmentalism*, Oxford: Oxford University Press, 2013.

Such a shift is long overdue. 'In the United States', one major US military study in 1996 predicted, 'weather-modification will likely become a part of national security policy with both domestic and international applications.'[96] Intensifying storms, shaping cloud cover, denying rain and water, instigating severe heat waves: the authors predicted that a deeply hubristic military menu might be available by 2025 whereby controllable weather systems might be deployed mechanically against 'future adversaries'. They suggest that, like the plot from a bad sci-fi film, US global meteorological stations and research centres simply be reprogrammed to help control such events. Indeed, the US military already has a history of deliberate weather modification. Between 1967 and 1972, for example, the US deployed secret chemical cloud-seeding techniques in Vietnam in an attempt to extend the monsoon over the crucial Ho Chi Minh trail and so bog down the Viet Cong.[97]

In China, meanwhile, major efforts are being put into cloud-seeding infrastructures in an effort to create artificial rain to wash way deadly clouds of urban pollution. China already has an army of 50,000 'weather-warriors' trained to man 7,000 cloud-seeding artillery guns; an equivalent number of rockets bearing cloud-seeding chemicals; and over 50 cloud-seeding aircraft.[98] Unlike such 'weather warfare', environmental writer Jamais Cascio reports, 'geoengineering would be subtle and long term, more a strategic project than a tactical weapon.'[99]

Future offensive geo-engineering – linked closely to civilian research on geo-engineering to tackle climate change, in which the CIA is taking a leading role[100] – could take a wide variety of terrifying, and deeply unpredictable, forms. 'Over-productive algae blooms can actually sterilize large stretches of ocean over time, effectively

---

96   Tamzy House et al., 'Weather as a Force Multiplier: Owning the Weather in 2025', US Air Force, 1996, available at csat.au.af.mil/2025/volume3/vol3ch15.pdf.

97   See James Fleming, 'The Climate Engineers', *Wilson Quarterly*, 2007, pp. 46–60.

98   Wainwright, 'Inside Beijing's Airpocalypse'.

99   Jamais Cascio 'Battlefield Earth', *Foreign Policy*, 28 January 2008.

100   Alan Robock, 'The CIA Asked Me about Controlling the Climate – This Is Why We Should Worry', *Guardian*, 17 February 2015.

destroying fisheries and local ecosystems', Jamais Cascio stresses. 'Sulfur dioxide carries health risks when it cycles out of the stratosphere. One proposal would pull cooler water from the deep oceans to the surface in an explicit attempt to shift the trajectories of hurricanes.'[101]

At a smaller scale, state efforts to weaponise air have long been central within innumerable contemporary confrontations between state security forces and a wide spectrum of activists and social and political protestors. Indeed, 'atmospheric policing'[102] – using tear gas attacks to create temporary toxic atmospheres above urban streets – is now so ubiquitous and banal that such attacks go unremarked. Across the world, Occupy protests, demonstrations against climate change, political summits or mega-events, marches against evictions and gentrification, protests against police brutality – all succumb amid clouds of state-sponsored toxic air supplied within a booming market for lethal air by the so-called security industry.

Here a century-long history of tear gas emerges which again connects us through deep genealogies to the gas attacks on the Somme and elsewhere in the early twentieth century and the many chemical attacks since. As communications scholar Anna Feigenbaum has shown, the standard practice of tear-gassing protestors on city streets involved transmuting chemical weaponry from war to routine pacification (with consequences that are fatal far more commonly than is usually recognised). So widespread are images of tear-gassed protestors in contemporary news reports, she writes, that, 'desensitized to these images, people often forget that tear gas is a chemical weapon, designed for physical and psychological torture.'[103]

As urban police forces become more militarised, so they deploy counter-insurgency weapons and doctrine against domestic urban populations in which pacification through exploiting the defencelessness of breathing mutates into a major industry in its own right (known, in typical deceitful parlance, as 'non-lethal' or 'less-lethal' weaponry).

---

101   Ibid.
102   This term comes from Anna Feigenbaum and Anja Kanngieser, 'For a Politics of Atmospheric Governance', *Dialogues in Human Geography* 5:1, 2015, pp. 80–84.
103   Anna Feigenbaum, '100 Years of Tear Gas', *Atlantic*, 16 August 2014.

Here, within the hybrid category of peace/war, we confront the most insistent moments where the right to air and the right to the city are one and the same. 'While tear gas remains banned from warfare under the Chemical Weapons Convention', Feigenbaum emphasises, 'its use in civilian policing grows. Tear gas remains as effective today at demoralizing and dispersing crowds as it was a century ago, turning the street from a place of protest into toxic chaos.' Tear gas, she continues, 'clogs the air, the one communication channel that even the most powerless can use to voice their grievances ... As those who signed declarations at The Hague back in 1899 knew, peace cannot be made through poison.'

With airspaces deliberately reengineered into toxic and lethal devices as a standard atmo-terrorist means to undermine protest against the extremes of urban neoliberalism, we confront perhaps the most insistent example of the politics of urban life in and around the urban street becoming a politics of air. Warwick politics professor Marijn Nieuwenhuis, observing the mass tear-gassing of 2013 protests against the commercial redevelopment of public parks in Istanbul, argues that 'the ongoing struggle over Gezi Park and other spaces around Turkey (and beyond) are no longer primarily being fought on the ground. They are instead increasingly taking place in the air.'[104] As in the trenches of 1915, the gas mask becomes a primary instrument of survival – and resistance.[105] 'Means of air conditioning (e.g. gas masks) have instead turned into the primary instruments of resilience', Nieuwenhuis continues. 'Any form of effective resistance against atmo-terrorism should, therefore, start by securing the air from which life springs.'[106]

---

104   Marijn Nieuwenhuis, 'Terror in the Air in Istanbul', *Society and Space*, 2013, available at societyandspace.com.

105   In China a wide range of high-tech pollution masks are available linked to smartphone apps which give wearers real-time data on local pollution concentrations.

106   Nieuwenhuis, 'Terror in the Air in Istanbul'.

Part Two: Below

Imagine grabbing Manhattan by the Empire State Building and pulling the entire island up by its roots. Imagine shaking it. Imagine millions of wires and hundreds of thousands of cables freeing themselves from the great hunks of rock and tons of musty and polluted dirt. Imagine a sewer system and a set of water lines three times as long as the Hudson River. Picture mysterious little vaults just beneath the crust of the sidewalk, a sweaty grid of steam pipes 103 miles long, a turn-of-the-eighteenth-century merchant ship buried under Front Street, rusty old gas lines that could be wrapped twenty-three times around Manhattan, and huge, bomb-proof concrete tubes that descend almost eighty storeys into the ground.

– Robert Sullivan, *Underneath New York*

The cover of the 1991 reprint of Harry Granick's classic *Underneath New York*

11.

Ground: Making Geology

The talent the geological sciences have for placing humans on unfathomable time lines – in which human history appears as little more than a gracious footnote to forces too powerful to measure and too slow to watch – seems to be exercised less and less as images of melting glaciers and exponential curves produce a very different kind of feeling … The image of the city, in particular, as a thing that is *made of geology* or on geology, increasingly has to contend with the idea of *the city as a thing that makes geology.*

> – Seth Denizen, 'Three Holes: In the Geological Present' (author's emphasis)

From the wooded summit, large swathes of the pancake-flat East European plain stretch out to a hazy horizon. The glitzy new landmarks of post–Cold War Berlin stud the distant panorama; the needle-like TV tower of Alexanderplatz is slightly farther away. The Teufelsberg hill, at a height of 120 metres, is comfortably the highest spot in Berlin. A large, verdant summit, it might easily be mistaken for a geological feature with a history stretching back millions of years or, perhaps instead, as the remnant of moraine shunted here by some long-gone ice sheet.

And yet, as it stands today, Teufelsberg is barely fifty years old. Beneath its soils lie not a complex geological stratigraphy but the dark secrets of verticalised total war. Between the summit and the original, flat land surface lies one-seventh of all the rubble removed from the bombed-out cities of the whole of Germany in the vast post-war clearing and reconstruction operations that went on between 1945 and 1972.

The position of this newly constructed peak was so dominating that in 1973 the US National Security Agency built one of their largest electronic listening posts on the hill: the tattered ruins of it can still be seen today. Much of the remains of a third of all pre-war Berlin, which totalled 50,000 burnt and bombed-out buildings – sixteen square kilometres of the city, yielding about 75 million tonnes of rubble – are piled high beneath the hill's surface. Pushed together into a rising mound, a dead city rests below the deceptively pastoral surface: the result of a systematic techno-industrial process of aerial annihilation and war. As novelist W. G. Sebald recorded, by the end of the war in many bombed-out German cities, there were over 20 cubic metres of rubble for every person left alive.[1] Vast, near-deserted ruin-scapes were all that was left.

It's no wonder, then, that Berliners call Teufelsberg the 'devil's mountain'. More powerfully than perhaps any other, this huge feature hints at the often-overlooked ability of humans to forge the very ground beneath their feet. Teufelsberg is also a perfect reminder that a good place to begin any exploration of the political aspects of the vertical dimension – whether 'up' from the ground or 'down' beneath it – is to remember that the very ground and geology beneath our feet is itself increasingly manufactured.

The Ground Beneath Our Feet

Of all things, modern humans tend to naturalise the ground, seeing the terrestrial platform beneath their feet as some immutable and natural product of geological processes working over unimaginable time horizons. Such an understandable tendency leads to an over-whelming sense of ground as an inherently *horizontal* phenomenon – the very surface of the earth stretching to and beyond the horizon.

Such a perspective radically underplays the importance of the *vertical* accumulation and composition of ground. For, increasingly, the terrestrial material beneath the feet of our fast-urbanising species is anything but 'natural' geology: it is the vertically accumulated phenomenon of *manufactured* ground. The making of such artificial ground is a neglected feature of the mass shift of humankind to urban

---

1 Cited in Isabel Sutton, 'W. G. Sebald's Apocalyptic Vision: The World Will End in 2013', *New Statesman*, 4 June 2013.

living; it is also a key by-product of the industrialisation of construction, mining, war and agriculture.

Geologists now estimate that the deliberate shift of material by humans through construction, mining, agriculture and the generation and the movement of materials deemed to be waste now amounts to around 59 billion tonnes a year.[2] Startlingly, this total now exceeds the transport of material by the world's rivers and oceans (22 billion tonnes) by almost 300 per cent.[3] Rising levels of urbanisation, extraction, industrial agriculture and construction around the world mean that this figure is growing fast. Little wonder that geologists are on the verge of formally re-labelling our geological epoch – currently the post-glacial Holocene – as the Anthropocene: the age in which human agency shapes land, soil and the very geology of the earth – as well as air, atmosphere, biosphere and ocean – more powerfully than any other 'natural' force.

Globally, it was estimated that by the year 2000 around 21 tonnes of rock and soil were moved for every one of the planet's then 6.5 billion humans through agriculture and construction. (This does not even include the unintentional movement of material, for example, through the stimulation of erosion through deforestation.)[4] Similarly, mining and soil erosion induced by human activity have now been estimated to move ten times as much material globally as glaciers (around 42 billion tonnes of rock and soil per year).[5]

Geologists call human-generated geological features like the Teufelsberg hill 'artificial' or 'manufactured ground'. Not surprisingly, such ground is densest in ancient cities that have been continuously inhabited, rebuilt and redeveloped over thousands of years. It is also particularly thick beneath old industrial cities which have

---

2   Pascal Peduzzi, 'Sand, Rarer Than One Thinks', *Environmental Development* 11, 2014, p. 208.

3   Simon Price, Jonathan Ford, Anthony Cooper and Catherine Neal, 'Humans as Major Geological and Geomorphological Agents in the Anthropocene: The Significance of Artificial Ground in Great Britain', *Philosophical Transactions of the Royal Society A: Mathematical, Physical and Engineering Sciences* 369:1938, 2011, pp. 1056–84.

4   Roger Hooke, 'On the History of Humans as Geomorphic Agents', *Geology* 28:9, 2000, pp. 843–6.

5   Gavin Bridge, 'Material Worlds: Natural Resources, Resource Geography and the Material Economy', *Geography Compass*, 3:3, 2009, pp. 1217–44.

experienced many cycles of construction and destruction. The cycle here is as old as urbanisation itself, although the scale of the processes involved has multiplied massively in the last two centuries. Fire, disaster, war, replanning, obsolescence, ruination or simply the desire for improvement leads to the demolition or destruction of buildings or infrastructure, or simply to their absorption into a higher level of ground, aided by gravity. New urban soils are gradually created from 'trash, construction debris, coal ash, dredged sediments, petro-chemical contamination, green lawns, decomposing bodies, and rock ballast.'[6] Such accretions, in turn, are flattened to create a new, raised, surface level, which then becomes the building surface and the new 'ground' level.

Over centuries, large cities thus literally rise up on ground of their own making. They build their own geology and move up to levels considerably beyond that created by 'natural' stratigraphy. This level, in turn, tends to sink under the accumulated weight of the city and its continually growing manufactured ground. In other words, the 'city on the hill' – the deeply symbolic assertion of the power of cities to transform human fortunes – is often, quite literally, built on a hill of its own making.

Studies have shown, for example, that the 20 per cent of Manchester classified as 'artificial ground' can easily reach depths of 10 metres. The ancient city of York, meanwhile, is based on at least 8 metres of human-made geology. The surface of Rome, which hides many complete ancient worlds, has been built up as much as 15 metres (50 feet) in the last 2,000 years.

Given that in nearly all urban cultures, burials take place below ground, these deep urban geologies are also the spaces housing incalculable numbers of previous urban populations. (It has been estimated that fully 6 million dead are housed with the extraordinary 200-mile network of tunnels, old quarries and caves that form the Parisian catacombs, for example). Invariably, such remains are redis-covered in ancient cities whenever the ground is disturbed though deep construction.

---

6   Seth Denizen, 'Three Holes: In the Geological Present', in Etienne Turpin, ed., *Architecture in the Anthropocene: Encounters among Design, Deep Time, Science and Philosophy*, New York: Anexact, 2013, p. 40.

In artificial ground, then – as in most other geological formations – depth down can normally be equated with temporal distance 'back' into history. However, the processes of modern redevelopment, based on deep excavation, the driving of piles into the rock, and the construction of huge complexes requiring subterranean infrastructure, means that the layering of successive artificial ground in big cities does not produce a simple series of strata.

'Successive phases of development', geologists Simon Price and his colleagues stress, 'have added to, or in some cases re-used and recycled, this artificial ground, leaving a complex "stratigraphy" of deposits, including drains, middens, pits, cellars, foundations and trenches among other features.'[7] Urban archaeologists have done much to understand this complex patterning of human-made ground, especially in European cities occupied more or less continuously since Roman times.[8] While occasionally entire street surfaces or historic ground levels are revealed during archaeological or construction projects, it is very rare for artificial ground to be simply made up through the simple accretion of historic layers, piled one over the other in vertical accretion *in situ*. Manufacturing ground also involves the levelling and filling of natural or geological cavities, valleys or low-lying areas to create a flatter landscape ready for urbanisation and industrial development.

While the street level of major cities thus tends to be naturalised, urban history is replete with extraordinary examples of the vast geologic work necessary to create it. Mexico City, for example, which has sunk 10 metres in the last century, was built on the bed of a huge drained lake on the site of the Aztec capital of Tenochtitlan. Downtown Chicago, meanwhile, is the product of a nineteenth-century engineering project to raise the city's ground level above the swamps where it was located. In Manhattan, meanwhile, the vast grid-scape that was constructed across the whole island between the eighteenth and twentieth centuries involved more than just the surveying and laying out of the grid and its subsequent development. Right across

---

7   Price, 'Humans as Geomorphic Agents'.

8   Matt Edgeworth, "The Relationship between Archaeological Stratigraphy and Artificial Ground and Its Significance in the Anthropocene', Geological Society, London, Special Publications 395:1, 2014, pp. 91–108.

the island, huge engineering works and earthworks were necessary to erase Manhattan's naturally hilly landscape by gnawing away at the uplands and using the material thus created to fill in the lowlands and valleys. Manhattan is not naturally flat – indeed, its name was coined by the island's original inhabitants, the Lenni Lenape nation and means 'island of many hills'. Like everything else in this apogee of modernity, Manhattan's flatness was manufactured through wild cycles of speculation and creative destruction.[9]

Like all major 'world cities', in fact, New York can be viewed as a 'geological hot spot' – a crucial node in the historic and contemporary human manufacture of local, regional, national and international geology. As an indicator of the 'geologic turn' under way in the arts, social sciences and humanities, New York's Smudge Studio have published a guidebook illustrating how the city is a geologic force of truly global importance within the contemporary Anthropocene period. They trace the distant origins of the materials that make up the city's pivotal supplies of concrete, steel, road salt, gold reserves, food, energy, water and fossil fuels. They also map the new geologies and landscapes created by the city's construction industries, demolitions and waste outputs.

Most remarkable here is the analysis of how cities like New York which face cold winters create their own huge 'terminal moraine' landscapes by bulldozing millions of tonnes of dirty, salty snow – full of worn brake linings, tyre dust, exhaust pipe chips and other detritus – into huge urban 'glaciers' (urban ice and snow stores). These then melt in the summer months, dumping their 'moraines' – just like 'natural' glaciers – as new geologic formations in the process.[10]

Finally, Smudge Studio provide an insight into the usually hidden ways in which cities work to metabolise nature in a myriad of ways. In New York, they write, 'humans channel and reshuffle earth materials on a scale and with consequences that rival major geologic events.' They then draw parallels between the geologic processes of city life and natural geological events. 'Like an island-building volcano or a

9   Eric Sanderson, *Mannahatta: A Natural History of New York City*, New York: Abrams, 2013.

10   See Christian Neal MilNeil, 'Inner-City Glaciers', in Elizabeth Ellsworth, Jamie Kruse and Reg Beatty, eds, *Making the Geologic Now: Responses to Material Conditions of Contemporary Life*, New York: Punctum Books, 2013, pp. 79–81.

river-diverting fault shift', they write, 'the City instantly transforms materials that took slow and powerful earth forces vast spans of time to create. In the process, the City unleashes utterly new geo-dynamics that will play out for thousands – and in some cases millions – of years to come'.[11]

Indeed, such urban geological processes work through generations, drawing precious metals and resources from mines and pits at the ends and depths of the earth to be refined, processed, manufactured, and dug into the city in the form of vast concentrations of subterranean pipes, wires and conduits. Here a stark irony presents itself. World urbanisation and economic growth regularly create spikes in commodity prices as even the frenzied extension of mining (largely in the Global South) fails to meet demand. The so-called 'commodities super cycle' between 2000 and 2014 is a powerful example. Thus, as metals become more expensive and valuable, the very manufactured geology under the world's cities becomes a lucrative 'mine' itself. Authorities in Scandinavian cities are already exploring techniques that will allow them to dig into their manufactured ground to pull out the valuable metals within unused, obsolescent or previously forgotten 'hibernating' infrastructure – old tram lines, disused district heating pipes, abandoned power and telephone wires, forgotten nineteenth-century gas networks and so on – as resources to sustain contemporary economic development.

In the manufactured ground found underlying the industrial city of Norrköping (population 120,000), for example, Swedish technology scholar Björn Wallsten estimates that there are fully 5,000 tonnes of iron, copper and aluminium waiting to be 'mined'.[12] Globally, such is the vast scale of the abandonment of metals in the artificial ground underpinning the world's cities – what he calls 'urks' in Swedish – that humans are currently using only 50 per cent of all the metals they have ever extracted from the earth. The rest lie abandoned and unused in old infrastructure and redundant artefacts embedded in the dense sediments beneath cities. Indeed, the metals embodied into human

---

11   Jamie Kruse and Elizabeth Ellsworth, *Geologic City: A Field Guide to the Geoarchitecture of New York*, New York: Smudge Studio, 2011.

12   See Björn Wallsten, *The Urk World: Hibernating Infrastructures and the Quest for Urban Mining*, Linköping: Linköping University, 2015.

infrastructures are starting to outweigh those left in the ground to mine. Wallsten estimates that there is as much copper embedded in the wires within Swedish telecom and electricity grids as there is left in the vast Aitik complex – Sweden's, and one of Europe's, largest copper mines.[13]

Exported Ground

Artificial ground, far from being static, is also quite literally exported on ever-greater scales. As at Teufelsberg, major excavations of material in mining, construction, post-war reconstruction, and mega-engineering projects lead to the movement of huge amounts of material which necessitates new ground to be manufactured elsewhere. Boston's famous 'Big Dig', for example – a massive 1990s project to sink the city centre's raised 1950s flyover system into huge new tunnels bored beneath the city's downtown – meant that over 12 million square metres of material had to be disposed of. It was 'distributed to many different locations in the Boston area, ranging from construction sites, to landfills in need of caps, to a deep ocean disposal site.' Spectacle Island, off the city's shore, gained 16 hectares in size due to additional dumping.[14] Meanwhile, in the UK, at Samphire Hoe on the Kent coast in South East England, a 40-hectare piece of new coastal land was created through the dumping of the 20 million tonnes of material excavated to build the Channel Tunnel. Currently, at Wallasea on the Thames estuary, an island the size of the City of London is being created as a bird reserve out of the material excavated in London's mammoth Crossrail subterranean train project.

Simon Price and colleagues from the British Geological Survey estimate that mining in the UK over the past four centuries has led to the removal, dumping, or use of nearly 20 cubic kilometres of (often badly polluted) material. This amounts to four times the volume of Ben Nevis, the UK's tallest mountain. Many of the apparently 'natural'

---

13 Björn Wallsten, 'Urks and the Urban Underworld as Geosocial Formation', *Science, Technology and Human Values,* forthcoming.

14 James McCarthy and Kate Driscoll Derickson, 'Manufacturing Consent for Engineering Earth: Social Dynamics in Boston's Big Dig', in Stan Brunn, ed., *Engineering Earth*, Rotterdam: Springer, 2011, pp. 697–713.

landscapes of mining regions are almost entirely manufactured as the legacy of these processes. For example, the 200 hills which dot the landscapes of Johannesburg – the very foundations of the city– are actually ground manufactured from the often highly polluted tailings of the 130 years of gold mining that led to the building the city. 'I don't think many residents even think of [the hills] as being made by hand', photographer Jason Larkin writes. 'They see them as just part of the "natural" backdrop to the city.'[15] Some of the 6 billion tonnes of material – laced with naturally occurring uranium and heavy metals, cyanide and acids used in the processing of ores – is now being re-mined using new technology to remove traces of gold left in the initial process. And so the artificial ground of the 'City of Gold' is remade again.[16]

Catacomb-like networks of excavated space and abandoned mining infrastructure riddle mining landscapes for kilometres downwards. No wonder that the surface levels of such regions are constantly adjusting as the gravitational settling of subsidence gradually lowers the ground level back down towards the level it was before the energetic frenzy of urban-industrialism manufactured it anew.

In the current period, wholesale open-cast mining environments, developed to allow large-scale machinery to remove much bigger volumes of the sought material, involves the systematic removal of the natural geological surface of whole districts to extract resources underneath. The notorious oil sands landscapes of Alberta are a powerful example here. In what activists have called a 'toxic sacrifice zone' – a pristine boreal forest the size of England – the very geology itself is being deeply excavated en masse by giant machines to be processed at huge environmental cost to produce hydrocarbon products.[17]

Open-cast coal mining in Kentucky, West Virginia, Virginia and Tennessee, meanwhile, is being transformed radically to centre on the low-cost removal of entire coal-bearing mountains. The highly polluted material produced as a by-product – often eighteen to twenty

15   Cited in Pete Brook, 'The Toxic Landscape of Johannesburg's Gold Mines', *Wired*, 18 June 2014.

16   See Martin J. Murray, *City of Extremes: The Spatial Politics of Johannesburg*, Durham, NC: Duke University Press, 2011.

17   See Andrew Nikiforuk, *Tar Sands: Dirty Oil and the Future of a Continent*, Vancouver: Greystone Books, 2010.

Sacrifice Zone: Helicopter view of mountaintop removal coalmining in the Appalachians in the US

times more bulky than the removed coal – is then simply dumped to fill adjacent valleys. The result, in short order, is the replacement of mountain ranges and complex ecosystems by an eerily flat, toxic landscape too poisonous to ever be used for agriculture.[18]

Port cities are also often partially built on manufactured ground that has been imported over centuries in the form of ships' ballast progressively dumped onshore to allow arriving ships to take on cargo. The famous quaysides of Newcastle in North East England – the author's home city – are actually built on 'ballast hills' created through the dumping of ballast brought in by coal ships returning repeatedly to the Tyne over a period of 300 years or more to export coal. Many port cities on the eastern seaboard of the United States also have manufactured shorelines that owe much to the dumping of ballast by fleets of European ships over centuries of trade. Archaeologists in New York find coral and flint deep in the foundations of Manhattan, brought there from the Caribbean and England, respectively. Unknown to most of their citizens, cities thus even export geology to each other. In such cases the ground is, quite literally, testament to centuries of the reverse movement of excavated sediment and other materials, used

---

18   See Julia Fox, 'Mountaintop Removal in West Virginia: An Environmental Sacrifice Zone', *Organization and Environment* 12:2, 1999, pp. 163–83.

to add weight to unknowable numbers of the ship movements that connected the strung-out geographies of capitalism.

Flows of the wastes of capitalism, usually from rich to poor places, sustain the manufacturing of new ground in contemporary times in similar ways. For example, accelerating cycles of built-in obsolescence in global electronics industries mean that the volume of discarded mobile phones, DVD players, computers and other 'e-wastes' will rise from 50 million tonnes to 65 million tonnes a year between 2012 and 2017. By this date, a body of material weighing 200 times as much as the Empire State Building – that's 9 kg for very person on Earth – will be dumped on the fringes of coastal cities, largely in China, Latin America, the Caribbean and Africa, to be dismantled and processed by hand, by armies of poor labourers, often in appalling conditions. Once the valuable metals and parts are removed the rest will sediment itself into new urban ground.[19]

The 'Archaeosphere'

The science of geology has evolved to study the stratigraphic accumulation of rocks and materials through 'natural' processes. Archaeology, by contrast, developed to understand the evolution of human societies through their preserved material legacies in the ground. Is manufactured ground the preserve, then, of the geologist or the archaeologist?

Well, both: the proliferation of artificial ground is drawing the two disciplines into unprecedented collaboration. Increasingly, both work closely to explore and understand the human-made land on which so much of our civilisation is built. Leicester University archaeologist Matt Edgeworth has recently suggested that the artificial ground created by humans should be considered neither as mere archaeology or geology but as a hybrid domain, formed through complex mixtures of natural and cultural forces. This he labels the 'archaeosphere'.[20] Historic streets, tunnels, ports, industrial sites, foundations and religious and commercial buildings – the stuff of urban archaeology – are thus layered within and through the complex stratigraphy of waste,

19 'E-Waste up a Third by 2017: UN', *Melbourne Age*, 17 December 2013.
20 Edgeworth, 'Archaeological Stratigraphy'.

human remains, rubble, ballast and soil. To him the archaeosphere is best understood as

> a kind of giant carpet covering large areas, on which the furniture of the human world (its buildings, bridges, monuments, pylons, oil-rigs, telegraph poles, roads, railway viaducts, cities, shanty towns, parks, airports) stands and is supported, and into which it will eventually crumble. Deep-layered in places, threadbare and patchy in others, this carpet of near-global extent provides the surface on which people carry out their lives. Like a carpet, it is so well-used it is taken almost totally for granted.[21]

The extreme cycles of creation, destruction and uneven development that characterise contemporary capitalist urbanism necessarily mean that rates of ruination and the manufacture of geology are especially high. Contemporary cities are radically provisional; their built and infrastructural forms are prone within capitalism to extremely rapid destruction, obsolescence, ruination or replacement.[22] Booms, bubbles, slumps, depressions, wars, demolitions and violent ideological shifts tend to add to these waves of erasure and ground-making. Whole swathes of the urban-industrial core of modern capitalism in Europe and North America are currently experiencing at least partial ruination; many industrial cities in the world's 'rust-belts' are shrinking rapidly in population; central Detroit, once the beacon of industrial modernity, is a powerful demonstration of such a process: what was once the fourth-largest US city is now an experiment in vast, partially inhabited, ruination.

Around 40 per cent of central Detroit has now been abandoned, its urban structures gradually collapsing through arson, demolition and removal into the (artificial) ground. This process is aiding vegetational succession that is turning parts of the central area of Detroit green once more. Culminating sometimes in groves of silver birch trees, this is the same process that reclaimed the land denuded by the retreat of the ice sheets some 12,000 years ago.[23]

---

21 Ibid.

22 Max Page, *The Creative Destruction of Manhattan, 1900–1940*, Chicago: University of Chicago Press, 2001.

23 Peter Del Tredici, 'The Flora of the Future', *Places Journal*, April 2014, available at placesjournal.org.

Revelations of the content of manufactured ground can offer unexpected moments of urban time travel. In New York and San Francisco, for example, several complete new shorelines were created to add to developable land during the urban booms of the eighteenth and nineteenth centuries. In a process now being repeated at much bigger scales in Dubai, Hong Kong, the Netherlands, and other centres of land 'reclamation', the gaps between the old piers of the cities' harbours were simply filled in with whatever landfill was at hand until new ground extended to entirely new wharves beyond.

Most extraordinarily, fleets of derelict ships, obsolescent at the time, were often used to help fill the space between the old wharves. New York archaeologists excavating a site at 175 Water Street in 1982 discovered what they thought was just another in a long series of wooden wharves. But its curved shape, pitch coating and the tropical shipworms embedded in the wood revealed the structure to be a 35-metre-long ship dubbed the 'Ronson'. The ship had spent many years in the eighteenth century transporting food south from New York to the Caribbean slave plantations, returning with the fruits of their labours: sugar, fruit and molasses.[24] Additional eighteenth-century ships have been unearthed under the collapsed World Trade Center during construction of the new One World Trade Center Tower, built between 2006 and 2014 on the same site.

A series of ships found beneath the modern streets of San Francisco were similarly embedded in the city's new ground because they were surplus to requirements after having transported some of the gold speculators who converged on the city en masse in the mid nineteenth century. In fact, hundreds of abandoned nineteenth-century ships form part of the landfill upon which San Francisco's modern downtown is built. Rotting and obsolescent, they never went back to their original ports; instead, they were subsumed into the city's subnature. In the 1920s, Amelia Ransome Neville, an ageing San Franciscan, recalls her amazement at seeing the ships being interred as a child in 1856. 'We went, one day, down to Long Wharf', she recalled, 'now part of the filled-in land that extended the city's waterfront ... It was

---

24   Anne-Marie Cantwell and Diana diZerega Wall, *Unearthing Gotham: The Archaeology of New York City*, New Haven, Conn.: Yale University Press, 2003, p. 234.

strange to see old ships built into the city streets; derelicts that had been left where they lay in the mud flats when the land was filled in, waves and lapping water forever lost to them.'[25]

In a complex process of vertical subsumption, modern cities thus literally tend to swallow the complex material cultures of their earlier systems of transportation, industry and trade. In the process, the surface levels of contemporary cities inevitably end up perched atop deep archaeospheres. These are inevitably contested and politicised: struggles focus on which elements within the palimpsests of buried structures, artefacts and narratives are to be excavated, researched, or memorialised – and which, conversely, are to be destroyed, neglected or forgotten.

In ancient 'global' cities such as London, Rome or Paris, such struggles are dominated by the challenges of 'rescue' archaeology – gaining windows of time during real estate projects to dig downwards before sites are again sealed off by bitumen, basements and concrete piles. The inevitability that digging down to excavate one layer of history will destroy the residues of others also inevitably results in contentious problems. In places dominated by powerful religious and ideological conflicts, competing archaeological projects and discourses struggle to enrol stones and artefacts into historical imaginations which bolster contemporary claims on the land. 'National imaginations require signature of the visible', Dutch archaeologist Maja Gori contends. 'And archaeology as a practice is about signatures of the visible.'[26]

In Palestine/Israel, a notable case, archaeological exploration has been central to Zionist efforts to link contemporary Israel to the Biblical foundation narratives of Judaism. Architectural writer Eyal Weizman argues that the unfamiliar surface landscape of Palestine that confronted Zionist colonisers on their arrival in the new state of Israel in the mid twentieth century 'was transformed … [in their] minds into a protective wrap, under which the historical longed-for landscape was hidden.' Zionist archaeology thus 'attempted to

25   Quoted in Alex Marshall, *Beneath the Metropolis: The Secret Lives of Cities*, New York: Carroll & Graf, 2006, p. 56.

26   Maja Gori, 'The Stones of Contention: The Role of Archaeological Heritage in the Israeli–Palestinian Conflict', *Archaeologies* 9:1, 2013, p. 223.

peel this visible layer and expose the historical landscape concealed underneath.'[27]

Prime Minister Benjamin Netanyahu, justifying such a strategy in 2010, argued that 'our existence depends not only on the Israeli Defense Force or our economic resilience – it is anchored in … the national sentiment that we will bestow upon the coming generations and in our ability to justify our connection to the land'.[28] As a result, the surface and above-surface violence, war against and eviction of Arabs and Palestinians that has permeated Israel's evolution have had their subterranean parallels in efforts by the Israeli state Antiquities Authority to misrepresent one of the world's deepest and most complex archaeospheres as overwhelmingly or exclusively Jewish.

This effort has been used to bolster claims that the new national identity of Zionist Israel can be directly linked with the idea of 'inheriting' material Biblical foundations and so creating a continuum of Jewish inhabitation. Such thinking supports the notion that Palestinians are merely temporary 'trespassers' on land ordained by God for the Jewish people. Here efforts have focused on excavating deep structures to render the progression from ancient Israel to contemporary Israel as a self-evident and naturalised process ordained by scripture. 'There was a continuous effort to anchor new claims to ancient ones', Weizman writes, 'as a series of settlements were constructed adjacent to or over sites suspected of having a Hebrew past.'[29]

Thus, acts of surface colonisation in the ongoing appropriation of space from Palestinians have often been directly shaped to bolster subsurface claims. The names of new Israeli settlements are often taken from the Bible and located very closely to sites of ancient Jewish archaeological settlements. The new Jewish-only settlement of Tel Rumeida, carved since 1999 out of the middle of a Palestinian neighbourhood in the ancient city of Hebron on the West Bank, has even been built on stilts within a protective wall as a means of protecting Bronze Age excavations beneath it that are used to bolster historical

---

27   Eyal Weizman, 'The Politics of Verticality: Excavating Sacredness', *Open Democracy*, 28 April 2002, available at opendemocracy.net.

28   Cited in Gori, 'Stones of Contention', p. 226.

29   Weizman, 'Politics of Verticality'.

Jewish claims that the area was the original 'City of David'. To sustain this situation, and to support the settlement of Tel Rumeida by groups of ultra-nationalistic and often violent Jewish fundamentalists, much of the old centre of Hebron has been violently remodelled as a sterile and highly militarised security landscape.[30]

Terraforming; Making Ground

> The old adage, 'Buy land – they're not making it any more' is no longer true!
>
> – René Kolman, 'New Land in the Water'

Artificial ground – and its attendant archaeospheres – does not just accumulate over time; it is, as already noted, increasingly manufactured and on remarkably large scales. Echoing the remarkable land drainage and reclamation projects in medieval Holland and England, or the dreams of using controlled nuclear explosions to reengineer the earth's surface in the 1950s and 1960s,[31] the manufacturing of large amounts of new 'reclaimed' land is now as central to the extension of coastal megacities as is their more celebrated vertical extension through skyscraper and other high-rise construction.[32]

The port of Rotterdam was a key laboratory of mass land reclamation in the 1970s. Here, the manufacture of new geology around the mouth of the Rhine allowed the development of the city's Europort, still one of the largest container ports in the world. The practice is now so central to urban growth in Hong Kong, Tokyo, Singapore and elsewhere that its advocates argue that '"buying" new land by "making" it through reclamation is turning out to be less expensive than developing old land.'[33]

---

30   See Chiara De Cesari, 'Hebron, or Heritage as Technology of Life', *Jerusalem Quarterly* 41, 2010, pp. 6–28.

31   Scott Kirsch, *Proving Grounds: Project Plowshare and the Unrealized Dream of Nuclear Earthmoving*, New York: Rutgers University Press, 2005.

32   See Brian Hudson, *Cities on the Shore: The Urban Littoral Frontier*, London: Pinter, 1996.

33   Réné Kolman, 'New Land in the Water: Economically and Socially, Land Reclamation Pays', *Terra et Aqua* 128, September 2012.

In 'reclaiming' land on bigger and bigger scales new dredging technologies allow sand and gravel to be sucked from 100 metres or more down in adjacent seas, estuaries, islands, coasts and oceans to fill the required volume with sediment. This allows ever-more grandiose land construction projects to be funded, planned and engineered in coastal cities and ports. Indeed, the Netherlands, as a nation, is largely a construct of several centuries of such activity: new islands alike IJburg, just north-east of Amsterdam, represent the state of the art in the engineering of new ground. In other major global cities – notably Tokyo and Mumbai – manufacturing new ground has radically remade the city's ground. Tokyo has added 25,000 hectares of land to its harbour; since the seventeenth century, Mumbai has gradually been remade from an archipelago of seven islands into a single peninsula.

In Hong Kong, 6 per cent of the territory's land had been reclaimed as of 2011. Controversial plans are in place to reclaim 1,500 more hectares at twenty-five sites by 2039. As in Singapore, many of Hong Kong's most famous recent skyscrapers are actually built on manufactured ground. Across the ex-border in China proper, meanwhile, the massive infrastructural and urban growth along the country's east coast in the last forty years has involved one of the greatest manufactures of new land ever seen. In total, this new land amounts to fully 12,000 square kilometres – twelve times the area of the whole of Hong Kong.

Less visibly, dredging based 'reclamation' is also intrinsic to a myriad of beach 'nourishment' efforts in tourist resorts. As sea levels rise, storms become more frequent, offshore sand reserves are dredged, and coasts are increasingly sealed up within hard concrete shorelines, beach erosion is coinciding with huge global shortages in sand. Many authorities in beachy tourist areas, where a lack of sand means simple, immediate economic collapse, spend the whole winter rebuilding deceptively pristine beaches with sand imported from wherever it can be sourced. The crisis is so bad in Florida that authorities have even considered grinding up recycled glass to produce the all-important sand.[34]

---

34 Lizette Alvarez, 'Where Sand Is Gold, the Reserves Are Running Dry', *New York Times*, 24 August 2013.

Such land 'reclamation' involves the vertical capture of more than adjacent sand: as these reserves are exhausted, and as projects become larger, sand is increasingly brought – legally and illegally – across growing distances to the sites of land-making.[35] In effect, this means that land itself is now flowing from poor to rich countries and from rural areas to cities. 'Less obvious than the increased capital flows across territories is the flow of territory itself', architect and geographer Joshua Comaroff writes. It is a form of appropriation, he notes, 'that differs rather dramatically from traditional seizures of territory, through war or colonial expansion'.[36]

In Singapore, radical extensions of territory through the importing of sands and aggregate – as well as foreign labour – have long been prerequisites for the country's dramatic programme of high-rise construction. To keep pace with population growth – from 1.6 million in 1960 to 4.8 million in 2010 – extending the small city-state through making new land is central to national strategy.[37] Between 2004 and 2014, 120 square kilometres was added to the country – 20 per cent of its size at independence in 1965. A further 100 square kilometres of new land is planned by 2030.[38] To facilitate this process, huge guarded stockpiles of imported sand are held in the city's Seletar and Tampines districts, ready to be distributed to the next reclamation projects. The volumes required are enormous: just 0.6 of a square mile of new ground requires 37.5 million cubic metres of fill – the capacity of nearly 1.5 million dump trucks.[39]

Malaysia, Indonesia, Cambodia and Vietnam, noticing that entire beaches and sandy islands were simply disappearing overnight as legal and illegal miners cashed in on Singapore's sand-import drive, have now banned sand exports. As territory itself becomes a tradeable and moveable commodity, diplomats now speak of 'sand

---

35   Sand is also necessary to produce glass, the concrete used in vertical construction, and in high-tech industries.

36   Joshua Comaroff, 'Built on Sand: Singapore and the New State of Risk', *Harvard Design Magazine* 39, 2014, p. 138.

37   Peduzzi, 'Sand, Rarer Than One Thinks'.

38   Maria Franke, 'When One Country's Land Gain Is Another Country's Land Loss', Working Paper No. 36, Institute for International Political Economy, Berlin, 2014, available at ideas.repec.org.

39   Comaroff, 'Built on Sand'.

Losing ground: Poster from India's Awaaz Foundation, fighting to stop illegal sand mining for urban construction in Mumbai

wars'[40] as local communities struggle to retain fishing and tourism industries, environmentalists fight the devastation of coastal and aquatic ecosystems and politicians worry that national sovereignty claims are literally being stolen as material is used to bolster the claims of wealthy states and city-states elsewhere.[41] Many local groups and NGOs are now struggling to protect local coastlines – for example, the campaign organised by India's Awaaz Foundation against illegal mining of beaches in Maharashtra around Mumbai to support land-making and construction in that city.

Few places in the world match the scale of land manufacture in the Gulf. Here, the availability of land inland has been ignored in a rush to engineer a series of enormous and often deeply troubled projects designed to maximise the real estate premiums of coastal properties while being instantly recognisable through the satellite-mediated gaze of Google Earth (see chapter 1).

The huge land manufacturing projects built thus far in Dubai – the two 'Palms' and the 'World' archipelago – have already multiplied Dubai's natural coastline over twenty times from 70 kilometres to 1,500 kilometres. Future, as yet unbuilt, megaprojects like the 'Universe'

40   See Denis Deletrac's 2012 documentary at sand-wars.com.
41   See Fazlin Abdullah and Goh Ann Tat, 'The Dirty Business of Sand: Sand Dredging in Cambodia', Lee Kuan Yew School of Public Policy, National University of Singapore, 2012, available at http://lkyspp.nus.edu.sg.

The terrestrial surface as Google Earth brandscape: The view of Dubai's 'World' and one of the two 'Palm' developments from the International Space Station

Dredgers constructing the 'World' artificial archipelago off the coast of Dubai through a technique known as 'rainbowing'

and the 'Waterfront' would add further to this multiplication. Dubai 'World' is a 34 million tonne rock and asphalt megastructure constructed on a platform of compacted, manufactured land made of 450 million tonnes of dredged sand. This has literally been sucked up and out of the seabeds around Dubai through fleets of 'rainbowing' dredgers.

Marketed as an opportunity to provide the ultimate solipsism – one's own private island – the marketing spiel for the project asks potential investors and inhabitants to dream of their 'very own blank canvas in the azure waters of the Arabian Gulf', where 'orchestrating your own version of paradise … is a much needed inoculation against the ordinary, and where you'll discover that The World really can revolve around you'. Plagued by huge financial problems,[42] a lack of demand, erosion by storms, rises in sea level and complaints by residents that the environment is unliveably hot and poorly serviced, Dubai's World project has so far been a massive failure. 'Instead of a millionaire's playground', the UK's *Daily Mail* reported in 2010, 'there are 299 mounds of bare sand sweltering in the 40+ degrees centigrade heat'.[43] Indeed, like a plot from a Ballardian sci-fi novel, the anti-gravitational hubris of the World is collapsing into entropy: the islands are gradually falling back into the sea and a litigation storm of huge proportions is gathering.

Despite their problems, the Dubai projects have created a new bandwagon as urban marketers across the globe rush to imitate them. Artificial islands shaped as urban brandscapes for vertical, as well as terrestrial, consumption are proliferating as the basis for upscale real estate and tourism projects. Zoran Island in Thailand, the 3,000 hectare chain of forty-one islands in the Khazar archipelago 25 km south of Baku in Azerbaijan (planned to house a million people), and Valencia's Isla Luna are only a selection of the most important projects.

Other examples follow Dubai in shaping new islands into local and national symbols that are easily recognizable through the Google

---

42   The $60 billion debt the project created for the developer, Dubai World, was a major reason that forced Dubai to go to its rich Emirati neighbour, Abu Dhabi, for a $10 billion bailout in 2008.

43   Adam Luck, 'How Dubai's $14bn Dream to Build The World Is Falling Apart', *Daily Mail*, 11 April 2010.

Earth–equipped laptops or smartphones of potential viewers, investors or consumers. A range of examples emerge here: a pearl island in
Qatar; Russia's Federation Island – in the geographic shape of Russia
itself – at Sochi in the Black Sea; a wave-shaped island in Oman; one
shaped like folded silk off Kuwait; crescent- and star-shaped islands
off Karachi; and an elaborate archipelago of fish and crescent-shaped
islands off Bahrain.[44] 'One curiously geographical form through
which [the] circulation of new globalising, cultural spatialities takes
place is the artificial island,' geographers Mark Jackson and Veronica
della Dora write. 'The worldwide phenomenon of the artificial island
has become a key defining imaginary and material form of 21st-cen-
tury development visions clamouring to "ornamentalise" and reinvent,
their urbanising coastlines.'[45]

Agitation by local artists, journalists and researchers about the
catastrophic social and environmental impact of corrupt, elite-led
land-manufacturing programmes in Bahrain were a key spark of the
pro-democracy uprisings there that were brutally suppressed by local
and Saudi forces in 2011. The activists mourned the replacement of
Bahrain's coastal fishing and pearling communities – now distant
from the sea – with miles of deluxe high-rise hotels and condos on
manufactured land owned by the local dictatorship and distant elites
in developments presided over by big Western architecture and planning firms.

'An island nation once completely dependent on the sea, through
its fishing and pearling activities', the activists wrote, 'has today nearly
turned its back on it. Nearly: all [except] for the high-rises competing
for a postcard view of the sea and a few disseminated fishermen's huts
searching for a slice of sea along the temporary coastline.'

Worse still, 65 square kilometres of public land has been parcelled
off to private developers by corrupt local elites at no or only notional
cost. The destruction of natural water channels traditionally used for
drinking water also means that Bahrain, now totally dependent on

---

44   Mark Jackson and Veronica Della Dora, '"Dreams So Big Only the Sea
Can Hold Them": Man-Made Islands as Cultural Icons, Travelling Visions, and
Anxious Spaces', *Environment and Planning A* 41:9, 2009, p. 2092.

45   Jacks and della Dora '"Dreams so big only the sea can hold them"',
p. 2088.

Huge land reclamation projects reshaping the geography of Bahrain, 2015

desalinisation, is the most 'water stressed' country on earth.[46] And the Bahraini public has access to less than 10 per cent of the new privatised coastlines.

In the context of global warming and rises in sea levels, the shipping of scarce beach materials from poor to rich places for land-making has crucial implications for the geographies of current and future vulnerability. At sites of construction, the material can be vertically built up to manufacture bastions against ongoing sea-level rises; at sites of removal, its loss can radically expose communities to increased risks.

The entirely new island-city of Eko Atlantic, currently being built using material dredged up from the Atlantic floor off the coast of Lagos, Nigeria, is a powerful example here. A private and deliberately elitist enclave of soaring towers and green parks built to house 250,000 people, the city evokes the offshoring of elites so commonly evoked in science-fiction films (think *Blade Runner* or *Elysium*). The World Bank's man in Africa calls Eko Atlantic the 'future Hong Kong of Africa'. Away from the dangers and violence of Lagos, and beneath the camouflage of some unconvincing greenwash, the city will be a particularly welcome home to the corporate elites who service the disastrously destructive oil exploitation in and around the Niger Delta.

One key rationale for the new city is its relative vertical elevation above the low spits, creeks and islands of Lagos, with their stilt-built

---

46 Dia Saleh, 'Bahrain: An Island without Sea', *Arteast*, Fall 2013, available at arteeast.org.

informal cities, which are extremely vulnerable to intensifying storm surges and rising sea levels. To defend against coastal erosion and flooding, Eko Atlantic island is being surrounded by what the *Guardian*'s Martin Lukacs has called the 'Great Wall of Lagos' – a sea defence barrier made of 100,000 five-tonne concrete blocks. A powerful example of the exploitation of the risks of disaster by capitalist elites, the new corporately built island promises to insulate Nigeria's wealthy elites from the miseries that Lagos's urban poor are experiencing in the face of global sea-level rises.

The project can only be interpreted, writes Lukacs, as 'an architectural insult to the daily circumstances of ordinary Nigerians. The criminalised poor abandoned outside their walls may once have served as sufficient justification for their flight and fortification – but now they have the very real threat of climate change as well.'[47] The case of Eko Atlantic shows that the world's real estate and reclamation industries increasingly sell the manufacturing of land as a miraculous solution to problems of congestion, population growth and urban development.

In a final important example of the politics of dredging material up from the seabed to make land, China's terraforming of a string of 'fake' islands in the Spratly Archipelago in the South China Sea since December 2013 demonstrates that 'reclaiming' land through dredging can also work to bolster major national geopolitical claims to subsea resources and maritime and air space in contested zones. By July 2015, 810 hectares (2,000 acres) of land had been created through China's terraforming programme in a remote but strategically vital area fully 500 miles from mainland China.[48] Crucially, by being 'habitable' to humans – unlike the atolls and reefs at their root – these new islands can be the formal basis for China's sovereignty claims at the UN in the hotly contested South China Sea. Moreover, in a strategy similar to that which allowed the US military to 'island hop' across the Pacific in World War II, these islands are now being surmounted by three brand-new military-length runways as a means

---

47   Martin Lukacs, 'New, Privatized African City Heralds Climate Apartheid', *Guardian*, 21 January 2014.

48   Asian Maritime Transparency Initiative, *Mischief Reef*, January 2015, at amti.csis.org/mischief-reef/.

to allow China to project its military power both vertically and horizontally.

The ecological impacts of these terraforming projects are often catastrophic. At a stroke, they wipe away complete maritime, sea floor and shoreline ecosystems, sometimes manufacturing a simulacrum of 'nature' while presiding over its devastation.[49] Migratory wading and sea birds, in particular, are suffering a steep global decline as the estuaries and mudflats that they rely on in and around the world's major coastal cities are increasingly replaced by airports, container ports, malls, esplanades and resorts constructed on reclaimed land. In mid-migration, hungry for food, such birds are literally left with no place to land. In East Asia, 'routine destruction of inter-tidal habitats at a massive scale and the disturbance at key sites are lowering populations of coastal waterbirds, pushing some to threatened status and others to near extinction', according to Roger Jaensch, chief executive of the Partnership for the East Asian–Australasian Flyway group, which lobbies to protect migrating birds.[50]

Meanwhile, by literally sucking new ground from adjacent sea floors, marine ecosystems are literally wiped away as well – albeit out of sight. Added to these problems, the re-engineering of coasts strips away crucial 'buffer' ecosystems like mangrove forests. As was demonstrated during the flooding of New Orleans by the storm surge which accompanied Hurricane Katrina in 2005, this deforestation leaves upstream cities perilously vulnerable to floods, especially as typhoons and hurricanes become more violent due to global warming.

Waste Ground

It is in the more prosaic worlds of urban waste production that the contemporary manufacture of artificial ground reaches its greatest overall scale. The growing amount of new ground manufactured out

---

49 See John Burt, 'The Environmental Costs of Coastal Urbanization in the Arabian Gulf', *City* 18:6, 2014, pp. 760–70; Paul Erftemeijer et al., 'Environmental Impacts of Dredging and Other Sediment Disturbances on Corals: A Review', *Marine Pollution Bulletin* 64:9, 2012, pp. 1737–65.

50 'No Place to Land: Loss of Natural Habitats Threatens Migratory Birds Globally', New York: United Nations Environment Programme, 2011.

of disposed waste is the product of a global economy where, as historian Susan Strasser puts it, 'The growth of markets for new products came to depend in part on the continuous disposal of old things.'[51] In many ways, landfills, as prime sites for the manufacture of artificial ground within contemporary urbanism, must therefore be considered 'the true archaeological sites of late modernity.'[52]

In 2002 there were around 3 billion urban residents in the world, each of which threw away, on average, 0.6 kg of municipal waste (a total of 700 million tonnes per year). Only a decade later, the volume of landfill had almost doubled: the world's 3.7 billion city-dwellers were creating fully 1.3 billion tonnes of landfill globally per year. By 2025, moreover, the World Bank has estimated that the globe's likely population of 4.3 billion urban residents will generate about 1.4 kg of municipal solid waste per person per day, amounting to over 2.2 billion tonnes of landfill globally per year.[53] In the most wasteful 'throw-away' societies, per capita waste generation reaches particular extremes. Each urban American is estimated to produce 2500 pounds (1133 kg) of solid waste per year, over half of which is still piled high into landfill sites.[54]

Urban landfills are vast concentrations of the effluvia of consumerism and capitalism on their way to becoming new, highly toxic, geology. Landfills are also a massive source of greenhouse gas emissions. (In the more advanced sites, these emissions are captured and used as fuel.) They also offer startling opportunities for the burgeoning field of contemporary archaeology; urban waste mountains quickly become, after all, the modern archaeospheres of artificial ground.[55]

The world's biggest urban landfills these days are waste mountains – as much above ground as below. Some now reach heights of 200 or

51   Susan Strasser, *Waste and Want: A Social History of Trash*, New York: Macmillan, 1999, p. 15.

52   Cinzia Scarpino, 'Ground Zero/Fresh Kills: Cataloguing Ruins, Garbage, and Memory', *Altre Modernità*, 2011, pp. 237–53.

53   Daniel Hoornweg and Perinaz Bhada-Tata, 'What a Waste: A Global Review', *Urban Development Series 2012*, no. 15, Washington, DC: World Bank, March 2012.

54   Thelma Gutierrez and George Webster, 'Trash City: Inside America's Largest Landfill Site', *CNN*, Atlanta, 2012.

55   See Rodney Harrison and John Schofield, *After Modernity: Archaeological Approaches to the Contemporary Past*, Oxford: Oxford University Press, 2010.

300 metres. Indeed, in the still largely horizontal landscape of western Los Angeles, the Puente Hills landfill, at 150 metres tall, is one of the city's largest anthropogenic features – quite fitting in a city famous for its profligate consumption. 'This used to be a dairy farm; a valley filled with cows producing milk,' trash researcher Edward Humes said of Puente Hills in 2012. 'And now it's a geological feature made out of trash.'[56]

In the megacities of the Global South landfills have an even greater significance: they are places of mass inhabitation by the poor and marginalised. India alone is home to at least 1.7 million so-called 'rag pickers'. Overwhelmingly made up of women and children from India's deeply marginalised 'lower' castes of landless labourers and children (note the vertical metaphor), rag pickers search the wastes produced by the urban habits of the more wealthy for material that can be recycled and resold to sustain a perilous existence. In a nation with a pitifully low level of formal waste recycling their remarkable innovations take waste materials and remanufacture them into some-times high-end items sold in upscale shops.

Rag-pickers, though, are prone to diseases caused by the toxicity of their environments; death and injury through collisions with waste machinery; mortality and disease due to drug, alcohol and solvent abuse; and predatory sexual violence in and around their work and living places. The edges of many Indian landfills are also sites where the most marginalised or recent in-migrants attempt to stake a first claim in a city by building new and extremely precarious shanty communities.

New Delhi alone has over 350,000 rag-pickers – 3.5 per cent of the entire population. Arising at dawn, the rag picker children sometimes travel over 20 km a day to and from the dumps. Carrying heavy loads on bare feet they are prey to many physiological conditions and dis-eases, risks exacerbated in bad weather. In addition to the risks from competing with packs of dogs and with cattle for the best of the day's pickings, they are vulnerable as well to sexual violence.[57]

As rates of urbanisation and consumerism intensify, especially in

---

56 Quoted in Thelma Gutierrez 'Trash City: Inside America's Largest Landfill Site', available at cnn.com, 28 April 2012.

57 'Street Children, India', 2006, available at gvnet.com.

the Global South, so the vertical growth of landfills brings a startling new peril: gravity itself. Poorly supported, inadequately engineered and often located on sloping, undevelopable and badly drained sites, rising landfill mountains are extremely vulnerable to slides and collapses caused by storms, earthquakes or even lightning strikes. Since these slopes are often immediately surrounded by shanty communities, the dangers are obvious.

Waste-slides often kill the urban poor below in sudden collapses of the piled-up rubbish of the rich far above. Indeed, lethal waste-slides work to reveal the ways in which the piling up of waste in densely settled spaces necessarily leads to the production of highly unnatural, indeed manufactured, disasters. Such events go largely unnoticed, unreported and unrecorded, however – especially in the Global North. Even academic specialists on landslides barely ever register waste-slides, tending instead to focus their efforts on more 'natural' landslides in rural and mountainous areas and earthquake zones.

Undertaking a detailed search, Dave Petley, one of the world's authorities on landslides, found that 'not a single [academic research paper] exists on garbage landslides'.[58] Rarer, larger, events are at least recorded. A waste-slide in Guatemala City in June 2008, for example, killed at least 50 shanty dwellers and rag pickers. It prompted Petley to explore records from similar disasters in the first international survey of its kind, covering 2,620 fatal waste landslides between 2004 and 2010.[59] These, he found, buried alive and killed 32,322 people: an average of 4,617 people a year.[60]

One of the most notorious waste landslides occurred in the Philippines on the edge of a large dump on the periphery of Payatas, a suburb of Manila, in July 2000. After a major storm the entire waste mountain collapsed down onto an adjacent shanty community of 800 families, organised to support rag pickers. The sliding mass caught fire in the process as the flammable gases within the waste touched lit stoves and power lines. At least 216 people died, and 200, possibly

---

58   Dave Petley, 'Garbage Dump Landslides', *American Geophysical Union Blog*, 22 June 2008, available at blogs.agu.org.

59   Quoted in Petley, 'Garbage Dump Landslides'.

60   Karl Mathiesen, 'Is the Shenzhen Landslide the First of Many More?' *Guardian*, 23 December 2015.

many more, were missing and presumed dead. Most of the bodies were simply left subsumed within the ocean of waste.

Following the disaster, Romeo Capulong, a leading Filipino human rights lawyer, assisted local communities and victims' relatives in the preparation of a lawsuit. To Capulong, the culpability of local state, private waste contractors and municipal policy makers was clear. 'We want justice for the victims', Capulong said in July 2000. 'We want to highlight the criminal neglect of the government … as well as public officials when it comes to the plight of the poor people. The immediate cause of the tragedy was the height, weight and the condition of the structure that they kept dumping garbage on.'[61]

Slips of artificial ground during massive bursts of urban construction and mining add another set of fast-growing risks. Two cases at the end of 2015 provide powerful examples. In the first, at least 200 itinerant miners died as they slept as mining waste from one of Myanmar's largest jade mines slipped over their adjacent shack community in Hpakant. In the second example, at least 74 people were killed when construction waste accumulated over two years on a hillside slipped after heavy rain to bury thirty-three buildings in the sprawling megacity of Shenzen, China. One of the first such examples recorded by landslide experts, the Shenzen case demonstrates the risks involved in vertically shifting vast chunks of geology in the often corrupt construction of urban megaprojects. Officials responsible for the waste pile were quickly arrested.

Landfill to Landfill

> The relationship between skyscraper and pit has taken on new implications.
>
> – Lucy Lippard

Disasters like landfill slides involving the movement of waste ground in and around the world's megacities are obscured by an almost complete absence of media coverage; by contrast other movements of

---

61   Angela Pagano, '"Promised Land" Garbage Landslide Kills at Least 200 in the Philippines', *World Socialist Website*, 21 July 2000, available at wsws.org.

waste and rubble spark long periods of total media saturation. Because it interred the remains of 2,753 people who died in the attacks, the removal of the vast mound of material created by the vertical collapse of New York's World Trade Center, following the terrorist attacks of 11 September 2001, provoked particularly intense debate. The huge project to clear the 1.6 million tonnes of smoking debris from the site of the collapse – our final example of the politics of manufactured ground – raises important but neglected questions about the links between vertical architecture and the waste ground it creates after it is removed.

Carefully excavated and moved across New York's harbour to the city's largest landfill site – Fresh Kills on Staten Island – a complex politics has surrounded this most sensitive and controversial of projects. Given that the sites for the Twin Towers were originally created through the manufacture through centuries of areas of waterlogged landfill, the eventual interment of their remains on Staten Island underlines the radical circularity of processes linking urban ruination and the manufacturing of ground. (The 92-acre site for Battery Park City, just to the east of the towers, was manufactured in the 1970s using sand dredged up from the Atlantic Ocean.)[62]

To cultural analyst Jani Sandura, the building of the world's tallest structures, at least partly on manufactured ('reclaimed') ground, suggests 'both the spectacular heights to which garbage may be raised and the less popular vision of capital built upon the foundations of its own refuse.'[63] Of course, the removal process was much more complicated than is usual in projects incorporating the shifting of rubble from collapsed buildings away from city cores. The recovery operations were strongly inscribed with both nationalist and more personal calls for sanctity and care in dealing with the human remains of the victims and their resting places. So strong was this pressure that the entire volume of material was raked through by hand on a series of plastic-walled 'disassembly' lines before the material could be interred.

---

62 Phillip Lopate, *Waterfront: A Journey around Manhattan*, New York: Crown, 2004.

63 Jani Scandura, *Down in the Dumps: Place, Modernity, American Depression*, Durham, NC: Duke University Press, 2008, p. 3.

The barge loads of material shipped from Lower Manhattan to Staten Island consisted of rubble made up of crushed and broken concrete, asphalt millings and pulverised and broken steel in various sizes. But personal effects, mixed with body parts, inevitably peppered the remains. Among the material sifted and deposit, were '4,100 body parts, 1,350 crushed vehicles, clumps of human hair, the engine from one of the hijacked planes, dozens of Gap bags and Fossil wristwatches ... Blue Cross/Blue Shield insurance cards ... diamond engagement rings ... sets of keys ... baseball memorabilia.'[64]

The Fresh Kills site thus bears painful witness to the devastating destruction of the two symbolic vertical towers after the 9/11 attacks. From across the harbour, *Vanity Fair* journalist William Langewiesche observed the barges carrying the Twin Towers debris gliding from the tip of Manhattan to be unloaded at Fresh Kills. 'The hilltop was of course part of America', he reflected. 'And by geographic measures it was not far removed from Manhattan: on a clear day from there you could even count the monuments of the [New York] skyline, minus two. But it was isolated and exotic nonetheless.'[65]

For decades the principal landfill of New York, Fresh Kills was for much of the latter part of the twentieth century the world's largest landfill. Indeed, the 900-hectare, 75-metre-high Fresh Kills mound was one of the largest human-made structures in the world. For decades, the site had stood as a startling physical proxy for the extraordinary levels of waste generated by American urban consumerism. The dumping of the World Trade Center debris was Fresh Kills' last interment. Months after the closure of the Fresh Kills landfill to municipal waste, the debris from the sixteen-storey-high 'pile' at Ground Zero was the last to be interred in the Fresh Kills site before it was sealed for rehabilitation and reuse.

One of the largest programmes of landscape architecture ever attempted – so big, in fact that it is deemed to herald a new phenomenon of 'landscape urbanism'[66] – the 'Lifescape' project aims to create a large park out of the closed Fresh Kills landfill, the first large new

---

64   Ibid.

65   William Langewiesche, *American Ground: Unbuilding the World Trade Center*, New York: Macmillan, 2002, p. 195.

66   See Charles Waldheim, ed., *The Landscape Urbanism Reader*, New York: Princeton Architectural Press, 2006.

park built in New York for a hundred years. It the largest of many emerging plans in the world's more affluent cities designed to turn waste ground into a new urban order of green landscape. Such is the scale of the transformation that it will not be complete for thirty years.

Lifescape's designers, Field Operations, James Corner's landscape architecture practice, have integrated a huge pair of horizontal earthworks into the project as a 9/11 memorial. These twin horizontal earthworks will directly mimic the vertical doppelgängers of the Twin Towers, memorializing their bloody incarceration into the ground. In this way, the designers seek to explicitly relate the horizontality of the emerging leisure landscape being inscribed atop the Fresh Kills landfill with the extreme verticality of the architectural remains that they inter.[67]

The monument itself is 'formed by two inclining landforms that mirror the exact width and height of each tower laid on its side.'[68] From the top of the earthwork visitors will be carefully integrated into a horizontal vista, with New York's remodelled vertical skyline puncturing the horizon. The monument will thus be shaped to allow visitors to experience a distant absence while standing atop the memorialised remains of the World Trade Center (and the forgotten remains of decades of municipal waste).

Visitors will look out on an iconic vertical view that no longer exists. The absent towers before them, interred in an 'afterlife' in the green ground below their feet, emerge as one ultimate symbol, perhaps, of the ways in which all vertical structures erected against the force of gravity must eventually be remade into manufactured ground.[69]

---

67 Lifescape's lakes, habitats and waterways will also work across another dimension of vertical politics: they have been designed as a major buffer to protect New York from the rising sea levels and increasingly violent storm surges associated with global climate change.

68 Christopher Lindner, 'New York Undead: Globalization, Landscape Urbanism, and the Afterlife of the Twin Towers', *Athens Biennial*, 2013, available at athensbiennale.org.

69 The afterlife idea comes from Christopher Lindner, 'New York Undead'.

12.

Basement/Cellar: Urban Undergrounds

> Wander the streets of central London and it can seem that everyone
> aspires to live like hobbits.
> > – Charlie Ellingworth, 'In a Hole? It's Time to Stop Digging'

Like the clichéd arch-villains of a James Bond movie, the super-rich moguls, oligarchs, plutocrats and sheikhs who occasionally inhabit London's Kensington and Chelsea now crave their own solipsistic subterranean lairs. Beneath the pristine stucco of the lines of Regency terraces burrows an unknowable labyrinth of deeply excavated super-luxury cocoons.

In the years between 2008 and 2012, permission was granted for over 800 such subterranean excavations in Kensington and Chelsea – the epicentre of the elite burrowing phenomenon that is connected to the London's remarkable 'plutocratisation'. As the trend spread, so reports emerged that similar underground cocoons are being constructed in other emerging super-rich or fast-gentrifying neighbourhoods in London, notably Highgate and Islington.

Like the sprouting of hundreds of elite housing towers discussed in Chapter 8, this trend is fuelled by the massive influx of elite capital buying safe 'trophy assets', a trend that has reshaped London in the wake of the global financial collapse. The *Guardian*'s Will Hutton raged 'at the phenomenon of young people, unable to afford sky-high London rents, cramped into one shared room, while the super-rich dig down under their homes or buy the house next door to expand their living space.'[1]

The London Basement Company, a UK-based company specialising in basement excavation and conversion, reported in 2008 that they

---

1 Will Hutton, 'Britain Is Scared to Face the Real Issue – It's All About Inequality', *Observer*, 19 January 2014.

were experiencing a 30 per cent year-on-year increase in basement projects. Between 2001 and 2014, applications for major residential basements in Kensington and Chelsea rose from 46 to 450. In addition, such projects were becoming more gargantuan: the average new floor space created in 2004 was 400 square feet (37.2 m²); by 2008 this had grown to 700 square feet (65 m²).[2]

In these 'iceberg houses', the subterranean volume can exceed the volume of housing space above the surface by a factor of three or more. Some take gargantuan proportions. A response to the illegality of vertical or lateral expansion in tightly regulated historic parts of London's West End, the largest are replete with private bowling alleys, swimming pools (whose depth can be changed automatically via a remote control), billiard rooms, gun rooms, multiple bedrooms, servants' and nannies' rooms, playrooms, car parks, and even, in one notorious – and so far unbuilt – example, a tennis court and vintage car museum complete with car lift.[3]

Like most things associated with the underground of cities, London's 'iceberg house' phenomenon has quickly generated its own urban myths. Some believe that fleets of mechanical diggers await future archaeologists – entombed deep in the clay following the completion of projects because it was the easier and cheaper option than bringing them back to the surface.

'We're selling [London] as a forward-looking metropolis', argues Ademir Volic, architect of the major schemes for estate agent Jon Hunt. 'And yet we can't change a single window in a conservation area. Everything has to be hidden underground.' Thus, the architects exploited a loophole in the treatment of subterranean space in UK planning law. They 'analysed the planning laws and realised that they cover everything above the surface of the ground, but nothing beneath it. There was nothing whatsoever that could stop us from drilling all the way down to the South Pole.'[4]

---

2   Cited in John McCarthy and Ross Kilgour, 'Planning for Subterranean Residential Development in the UK', *Planning Practice and Research*, 26:1, 2011, pp. 71–94.

3   These details are drawn from Oliver Wainwright, '"Billionaires' Basements": The Luxury Bunkers Making Holes in London Streets', *Guardian*, 9 November 2012.

4   Quoted in Wainwright, 'Billionaires' Basements'.

Excavating these spaces is extremely expensive. The burrowed space needs to be three-dimensionally engineered into the complex networks of pipes, tunnels and conduits that saturate London's sub-surface. Large conveyor belts raise the rubble, rock and soil to the surface into hoarded-off skips for removal (at a collective rate of 10,000 tonnes a day in 2014). Such projects inevitably damage or kill surface-level trees and accentuate the risk of serious flooding (especially when they burrow beneath rear gardens). They also raise vociferous opposition and lead to legal disputes because of the extended disruption and the destabilizing effects on neighbouring properties and the street. Such opposition pits global celebrity against global celebrity: anti-basement neighbours Jimmy Page and Joan Collins have apparently opposed the building plans of Robbie Williams and Andrew Lloyd Webber.

And yet, like manufactured 'reclaimed' land on the coasts of booming megacities discussed in chapter 12, the newly created space is a relative snip. In London's overheated property market, costs in 2012 for newly excavated space ran to £500 per square foot compared to around £2,500 per square foot to buy above-ground space in the same neighbourhoods.

As elites colonise the coveted neighbourhoods of the world's so-called 'global' cities, so, in the small number of such cities where accommodation is organised as houses rather than flats, subterranean excavation operates as the shadow of the more familiar and obvious vertical extension of super-luxury penthouses, condominiums and skyscraper complexes. In London, this has necessitated the development of new planning policies to control the subterranean volume below the surface. At least in Kensington and Chelsea, such regulations have allowed the borough to prohibit the very largest basements, prevent basement construction beneath listed and conserved buildings, and tightly control the smaller basements that remained permissible.

Basement Underworlds

The recent colonisation of selected subterranean spaces by the super-rich in cities like London contrasts strikingly with the long-standing association of such spaces with poverty, disease, insurrection and the 'lower' orders or classes inhabiting a literal metropolitan 'underworld'. It has always been easy for dark, enclosed and damp basements and cellars to become associated with the social underground or underworlds within starkly hierarchical societies. Not uncommonly, pejorative discourses about cellar-dwellers and other inhabitants of the physically low or subterranean spaces of cities have worked to stigmatise or dehumanise them. This is not just because of their putatively ill-kempt appearance, disease, poverty or potential political threat: it is also because of the very subterranean nature of their existence. In imagery they were closer to nonhuman beasts and imaginary underworlds, or to fiery depths of hell itself.

Cellars have also long been likened to caves, and thus their occupants to the primitive ancestors of modern humans, who were long imagined, in the linear narrative of human 'progress', to be 'cavemen'. Beyond large cities, there is, in fact, a long history of troglodytic living, often in response to persecution. From Shanidar in Iraq to Andalucia in Spain and Cappadocia in Turkey, subterranean human settlements have a long history. Within modern cities, of course, systems of basements and cellars – where they have existed – have also been widely deployed as the last desperate spaces of protection during periods of strategic bombing and total war.

In Europe in the nineteenth century, the long-standing linguistic tropes used to demarcate 'high' or 'upper' parts of society from 'low' or 'lower' orders or classes were powerfully reinforced by the realisation that the vertical geographies of the city itself were physically stratifying according to conventional representations of goodness, fitness or morality. Providing the least-costly spaces because of their darkness, dampness and appalling conditions, basements and cellars accommodated the most desperate people at the very highest densities. In some British examples, high-density housing for the working classes was deliberately built along ditches and ravines so that extra cellar space could be created to house them without the costs of excavation.

Basements not surprisingly figure heavily in the history of industrial urbanism as sites of extreme poverty, overcrowding, malnutrition, disease and illegal housing – and of elite fears of the resulting moral decay and political threat from the urban 'underclasses'. A shocked

Jacob Riis's photograph of officials from the New York City Tenement House Department inspecting a basement accommodation in New York, c. 1900

German traveller to London at the end of the eighteenth century noted that 'a third of the inhabitants of London live underground' in 'cellar dwellings' entered by steps leading down from the streets.[5]

A century later, American social reformer Jabob Riis's famous exposé of the lives of New York's very poor, *How the Other Half Lives* (1890),[6] focused particularly on how, as in many great cities then and now, 'much of New York's so-called ethnic underworld lived and slept in underground spaces.'[7] Riis found that many of the most recent immigrant families crowded into fetid, lightless and filthy basements deep below the city's tenement blocks. Such spaces, many below water table and tide levels, were prime sites for the spread of diseases like cholera. Riis deemed these basement inhabitants to be 'cave dwellers'[8] whose physical descent into the city's subsurface

---

5 Cited in Peter Ackroyd, *London Under: The Secret History Beneath the Streets*, London: Random House, 2011, p. 7.

6 Jabob Riis, *How the Other Half Lives*, New York: Dover, 1971(1901).

7 Thomas Heise, *Urban Underworlds: A Geography of Twentieth-Century American Literature and Culture*, New York: Rutgers University Press, 2011, p. 61.

8 Riis, *How the Other Half Lives*, p. 17.

paralleled a complete moral collapse to a point where, as geographer Thomas Heise puts it, 'they were hardly worthy of life on the surface'.[9]

Cellar-occupants also feature widely in Marxist and radical critiques of the extreme inequalities inherent within capitalist urban industrialisation. Friedrich Engels, horrified at the living conditions of the workers in 1880s Manchester, emphasised how the process of forcing the poor into teeming cellars worked to render them increasingly invisible to above surface lives of the city's mercantile bourgeoisie. Token reforms merely redistributed the crisis spatially. 'In reality', Engels wrote, 'the bourgeoisie has only one method of solving the housing question after its fashion – that is to say, of solving it in such a way that the solution continually reproduces the question anew.' Without structural reorganisation of labour and housing markets, Engels argued, the destruction of notorious slum areas merely meant that slum housing would 'appear again immediately somewhere else and often in the immediate neighbourhood! The breeding places of disease, the infamous holes and cellars in which the capitalist mode of production confines our workers night after night, are not abolished; they are merely shifted elsewhere!'[10]

Such critiques find their more contemporary resonances in housing crises in cities over the past half-century. Worsening crises in London, Toronto, New York, Vancouver and elsewhere are forcing larger and larger populations of poorer tenants into illegal units and overcrowded basements. These offer a startling contrast both to the excavated lairs and the rising housing towers of the super-rich in those same cities.

By 2012, for example, the fast-growing Toronto suburb of Brampton had fully 30,000 illegal, unregulated and often dangerous basement apartments occupied by new Canadian migrants. As in many cities, these have been cheaply converted to lettable housing as owners sought to cash in on the lucrative possibilities their cellars offered in an extremely expensive housing market. In 2015 in Newham, east London, meanwhile, the local council discovered one small house in

---

9   Heise, *Urban Underworlds*, p. 63.

10   Friedrich Engels, *The Housing Question*, New York: International Publishers, 1935, pp. 74–7.

the district inhabited by twenty-six recent migrants from Romania, seven of whom were living in its tiny basement.

Long-standing traditions of demonising the inhabitants of base-ments – or using the idea of basements pejoratively as social metaphor or allegory – find their counterparts in the way many discussions of the social, political or cultural 'underworlds' and 'undergrounds' of cities also gravitate to various forms of 'basements' terminology. In 1965, for example, Swedish sociologist Gunnar Myrdal coined the controversial term 'underclass' by directly invoking the allegory of the basement and the 'basement class' as the lowest of the low within a broader society. In a notorious book filled with clashing vertical met-aphors and allegories, Myrdal argued that there was 'an ugly smell rising from the basement of the stately mansion.' This was caused, he argued, by the concentration in certain areas of 'unemployed, and gradually unemployable persons' who threatened to become 'a useless and miserable sub-stratum' of American society – the 'underclass'.[11]

Other discourses have long equated the physical depth of basement space with underground and underworld cultures in cities, discourses that threaten and titillate in equal measure. The idea of 'underground' film, publishing, music, activism or other forms of culture has long connected subversion and bohemian living with the occupation of subterranean spaces. French 1960s activists the Situationists, working to undermine corporate capitalism 'from below', likened their work and that of similar movements to that of an 'old mole' burrowing through the foundations of bourgeois life 'above'. 'An irreducible dis-satisfaction spreads subterraneanly, undermining the edifice of the affluent society', they noted in 1962, stressing that the 'old mole' was 'still digging away'.[12]

New York's lively gay, lesbian, transvestite and drugs scenes between the 1910s and 1930s centred on a range of illicit basement nightclubs

---

11   Gunnar Myrdal, *Challenge to Affluence*, New York: Random House, 1963, pp. 40–41 and 53.

12   The 'old mole' phrase derives originally from Marx. Cited in Christoph Lindner, and Andrew Hussey, eds, *Paris-Amsterdam Underground: Essays on Cultural Resistance, Subversion, and Diversion*, Amsterdam: Amsterdam University Press, 2014, p. 8. American novelist and 'beatnik' poet Jack Kerouac, a luminary in the 1950s and the 1960s counterculture, similarly titled one of his books *The Subterraneans* (1958).

in districts like Greenwich Village, set up partly to escape the constraints of Prohibition (1919–1933). This led many commentators to connect basements per se with illicit, exotic, and, for the political right, degenerate sexual and drug subcultures. 'In the basement is all that is naughty,' novelist and journalist Djuna Barnes – notorious for immersing herself in New York's bohemian scenes – wrote in 1918: 'Spicy girls in gay smocks.' Hinting at further sexual intrigue at another club located still further down into the district's cellars, Barnes calls it 'the real unknown. Even a basement has its basement', she notes. 'And this one is the basement of Bohemia.'[13]

In Praise of the Basement

Cellars and their occupants also featured as poster children of modernist architectural movements aimed at bringing light and air to the metropolis and its inhabitants. In his dreams of rational and machinic cities filled with light and air, Le Corbusier effectively banished the basement or cellar from his architecture: he boasted that breaking the earth was not necessary with his modernist constructions because they were raised up towards the sun and air on columns and stilts. 'My ground is intact, unbroken', Le Corbusier gushed proudly. 'I draw an automobile on this regained ground [for parking], and I let air and vegetation go through.'[14] In the process, as historian David Gissen points out, 'the clean-up of the modern sewer and the banishment of the cellar from modernity represented a victory of the rhetoric of light and air over the dark, the tepid and the dank.'[15]

However, basements have also had their advocates. Some philosophers, as part of the wider backlash against the steamroller of modernist urban renewal, have been keen to point out the psychosocial

13   Djuna Barnes, *Nightwood*, New York: New Directions, 1961, p. 240, cited in Heise, *Urban Underworlds*, p. 99. See also Scott Herring, *Queering the Underworld: Slumming, Literature, and the Undoing of Lesbian and Gay History*, Chicago: University of Chicago Press, 2009.

14   Le Corbusier, *Precisions: On the Present State of Architecture and City Planning*, Cambridge, MA: MIT Press, 1991, pp. 38–40.

15   David Gissen, *Subnature: Architecture's Other Environments*, New York: Princeton Architectural Press, 2009, p. 34.

importance of cellars and basements. French phenomenologist Gaston Bachelard, for example, argued passionately that housing provided more than technologically modern and sanitised 'machines for living' (in Le Corbusier's infamous phrase).

Housing architecture, Bachelard countered, also needed to address primordial psychological human needs for spaces within which dreamlike experiences could link with subconscious cultures of nature. Indeed, he defended the need to maintain both the vertical limits of the traditional house – the attic and the basement – for these reasons. (Both were to be completely eradicated from the city under Corbusian paradigms). The cellar, Bachelard wrote, 'is first and foremost the dark entity of the house, the one that partakes of subterranean forces. When we dream there, we are in harmony with the irrationality of its depths.'[16]

Such psychoanalytic celebrations of the power of basements to link positively to subconscious and primordial worlds of fear, madness, hell and haunting, however, are likely to ring decidedly hollow to those forced to inhabit inadequate basements because of poverty and the rampant housing crises which afflict so many of the world's major cities.

---

16   Gaston Bachelard, *The Poetics of Space*, Boston: Beacon Press, 1992, p. 23.

13.

Sewer: Sociology and Shit

A good sewer was a far nobler and a far holier thing ... than the most admired Madonna ever printed.

– John Ruskin

To place anything in the sewer is to define it as a waste product of the world above it.

– David L. Park

In the late 1830s London, the largest urban area in the world with 2 million people, was a city wracked by cholera epidemics caused by inadequate sanitation systems. Huge numbers of London's urban poor were, quite literally, living in human excrement. London's rivers were massive open sewers. The haphazard and ancient series of small and incomplete sewers that had existed since the sixteenth century simply provided conduits for excrement to flow more effectively into the rivers. Newly installed water pipes merely added to the problem: fashionable flushing water closets now discharged into the sewers human waste that previously would have been buried.

In such a context, social reformer Edwin Chadwick, a London civil servant who had worked previously on the social regulation of London's poor, began to investigate the effects of poor sanitation on the moral and physical health of London's urban poor. The result was Chadwick's famous 1842 report *The Sanitary Condition of the Labouring Population*.[1] As a great utilitarian reformer, Chadwick argued that engineering new sewage systems was necessary to reduce

---

1   Edwin Chadwick, *The Sanitary Condition of the Labouring Population of Great Britain, 1842*, ed. Michael W. Flinn. Edinburgh: Edinburgh University Press, 1965 [1842].

the mortality of the poor and to integrate them as fit and healthy working bodies into the productive economy of London. 'The annual loss of life from filth and bad ventilation,' Chadwick argued, 'are greater than the loss from death or wounds in any wars in which the country has been engaged in modern times.'[2]

A vital intervention, Chadwick's report mapped the surface and subsurface topography of London in unprecedented detail and analysed the gradients that would allow gravity to pull waste through the new sewer system. The imperative, Chadwick argued, was 'the use of water and self-acting means of removal by improved and cheaper sewers and drains ... Refuse when thus held in suspension in water may be most cheaply and innoxiously conveyed to any distance out of towns'[3] In 1847, Chadwick's report led directly to the formation of the Metropolitan Commission of Sewers, the first body in the history of London tasked with organising a unified and universal network of sewers for the city.[4]

Laying the intellectual foundations for the building a universal system of 1,400 miles of sewers under London over the next half-century or so, Chadwick, like other Victorian moralists and reformers, scripted hierarchical social relations and vertical moral geographies in parallel.[5] As is common in the history of the relationships between people, waste and social class, distance downwards towards and into the earth was widely constructed as a proxy of increasing inhuman abjection.[6] Distances upwards, by contrast, were the source of moral and social quality and – literally – uprightness and civilisation – in the face of nature's gravitational degradations. 'Elevation' thus carried with it parallel notions of moral, economic, social, theological and bodily superiority.[7] 'Cleanliness', John Wesley,

---

2   Like most commentators in London in the 1840s, Chadwick believed that diseases like cholera were transmitted by 'miasma', fetid gases and odours, rather than being waterborne. Chadwick, *Sanitary Condition*, p. 369.

3   Ibid., p. 370.

4   Paul Dobraszczyk, *London's Sewers*, London: Shire, 2014, pp. 15–17.

5   See Martin V. Melosi, *Sanitary City: Urban Infrastructure in America from Colonial Times to the Present*, Baltimore: Johns Hopkins University Press, 2008, chapter 2.

6   See Rosalind Williams, *Notes on the Underground: An Essay on Technology, Society, and the Imagination*, Cambridge, Mass.: MIT Press, 1990, chapter 5.

7   See David L. Pike, 'Sewage Treatments: Vertical Space and Waste in

Construction of new sewers above the Fleet River in London, 1870s

co-founder of Methodism, famously preached in 1778, was 'next to Godliness.'

Thus, London's slums, with their heavily packed basements and cellars – and their dirt, smell, prostitution and pestilence – Chadwick deemed to be the 'lowest districts of the metropolis', places both topographically and morally 'lower' than the burgeoning suburbs and their bourgeois homes for the rich and middle classes.[8] Chadwick suggested that conditions in such places directly created 'an adult population short-lived, improvident, reckless, and intemperate, and with habitual avidity for sensual gratifications.'

To understand and regulate such public health geographies, Chadwick and a small army of other reformers relied on a 'top-down'

Nineteenth-Century Paris and London', in William A. Cohen and Ryan Johnson, eds, *Filth: Dirt, Disgust, and Modern Life*, Minneapolis: University of Minnesota Press, 2005, pp. 51–77.

8   'The undrained clay beneath the slums oozed with cesspits and sweated with fever', historian Harold Dyos said about 1880s London. 'The gravelly heights of the suburbs were dotted with springs and bloomed with health.' Dyos, *The Victorian City: Images and Realities*, vol. 1, London: Routledge, 1999, p. 370.

survey and mapping of the location of the city's 'lower orders' – and their immoral or transgressive bodies – from 'some high window' or superior position. Mappings and surveys of populations, in parallel with sanitary engineering, were an important part of the huge growth in bureaucratic and physical *inspections* of the Victorian city.[9] As cultural analysts Peter Stallybrass and Allon White suggest, Chadwick, the great utilitarian, was adamant that the poor and their abject bodies needed to be regulated 'from above' by their social superiors using the latest techniques of top-down cartography and social surveys. This was necessary so that the urban barriers which separated them from inspection, observation and regulation by their superiors could be overcome. [10]

Here empirical observation was tantamount to a literal and metaphorical enlightenment to expose the 'dark underworlds' of the metropolis to scrutiny and control. Combined with the new sanitary and police sciences, the god's-eye view of new innovations in mapping could work to re-moralise the poor, integrating them productively into the wider metropolis and improving the lives of the 'upper class' bourgeoisie in the process.[11]

Sewer as Refuge, Sewer as Rationality

> Hygiene is the modern project's supreme act.
> – Nadir Laiji, *Plumbing: Sounding Modern Architecture*

It was in such a context that the great urban rationalisation plans of the mid and late nineteenth century were pushed through to forcibly re-engineer large Western cities with great systems of open thoroughfares

---

9   Geographer Chris Otter calls the Victorian age the 'age of inspectability'. See Otter, *Victorian Eye: A Political History of Light and Vision in Britain, 1800–1910*, Chicago: University of Chicago Press, 2008, chapter 3.

10   Peter Stallybrass and Allon White, *The Politics and Poetics of Transgression*, Ithaca, NY: Cornell University Press, 1986, p. 194.

11   We must not forget, of course, the visceral reality of verticality and gravity in unsewered cities. The gravitational dropping of 'night soil' from higher windows had its own terrible notoriety for those unfortunates below who got in the way. Jan-Andrew Henderson tells of the experience of visitors to Edinburgh's notorious Old Town. 'If you didn't live in Edinburgh and you heard a cry from

which would expose the poor to light, scrutiny and (if necessary) the efficient mobilisations of the army. Most famous here are the radical projects of Baron Haussmann – working with his engineer, Eugène Belgrand, in the Second Empire Paris of Napoleon III in the 1850s.

In response to the revolutionary insurrections in 1848, Haussmann sought to use the process of ploughing a citywide system of boulevards through the labyrinthine fabric of Parisian alleyways to deliberately expel or carve up many of the most notorious poorer districts that were deemed to be centres of insurrection. Boulevards were designed to the width of one cavalry squadron; vistas were opened up so that the streets would be extremely hard to block with barricades and could be swept by artillery. In addition, troublesome populations were forcibly decanted away from the city core.

Meanwhile, below ground, a 350-mile network of state-of-the-art mechanically cleaned sewers provided a subterranean parallel to the construction of Paris's boulevards. Under the supervision of Belgrand, as in London, the city's limited and poorly constructed medieval sewers were systematically superseded. In the process, social and political cleansing and ordering was to be accompanied with moral and physical cleansing and ordering. Again, the project was represented by elites as the imposition of rationality and order over a complex of what was deemed to be dirty, dangerous and chaotic 'cloaques' (or middens – a word also used to mean 'dens of iniquity').[12] The new sewers were so celebrated (and relatively clean) that a special vehicle was constructed to shepherd VIPs around the system on subterranean tours.

Initially Haussmann and Belgrand baulked at the dropping of faecal matter into their new sewers. The collection and selling of 'night-soil' was, after all, still a lucrative industry. Once they relented, however, the carefully engineered sewers of Paris – and, in turn, other cities – emerged as symbolic and metaphysical realms. They were seen as parts of the body politic – whether a mechanic or an organic intestine for

---

above', he relates, 'you were quite likely to look up and see who was calling to you – which didn't do much for the tourist trade.' Jan-Andrew Henderson, *The Town Below the Ground*, London: Mainstream, 1999, p. 30.

12   Steve Duncan, 'The Historiography of Urban Sewerage in the Transition from Early Modern to Modern Cities', unpublished paper, n.d., available at academia.edu.

Parisian sewer workers in a newly built sewer below the Boulevard de Sébastopol, 1872

the city – for expunging shit down away from the civilised, cleansed and purified bourgeois surface realm above.

Before Belgrand's rationalisation of Paris's old, inadequate and haphazard sewers, they were very different realms. Spaces in which society's outcasts could gather, the sewers were refuges from which to challenge the bourgeois order above. Because they were so accessible, Victor Hugo, author or *Les Misérables*, argued that they unveiled the city's excretions and made visible what he called 'the sincerity of filth'.[13] Hugo saw the pre-Haussmann sewers as little less the 'conscience of the city'.[14] In *Les Misérables* the sewer is a place where the poor and the outcasts of society gather together as a collective population which can erupt upwards at any moment to threaten the world above ground.[15]

Jean Valjean, protagonist in *Les Misérables*, escapes down through a street grating into the democratic otherworld of the sewer. Proclaiming their honesty compared to the conceits of bourgeois urban life just a few metres above, he reflects that there 'are no more false appearances, no possible plastering, the filth takes off its shirt,

13   Quoted in Stallybrass and White, *Politics and Poetics*, p. 204.

14   Victor Hugo, *Les Misérables,* New York: Modern Library, 1992 [1862], p. 1090.

15   Matthew Gandy, 'The Paris Sewers and the Rationalization of Urban Space', *Transactions of the Institute of British Geographers* 24:1, 1999, p. 24.

absolute nakedness, rout of illusions and of mirages, nothing more but what it is ... The last veil is rent. A sewer is a cynic. It tells all.'[16] As so often in urban history, the sewer offered refuge and respite to all those who struggled against the violence and repressive injustice of the bourgeois urbanism above. 'Crime, intelligence, social protest, liberty of conscience', Valjean continues, 'theft, all that human laws pursue or have pursued, have hidden in this hole.'[17]

Belgrand's vast engineering project meant, however, that Paris's sewers were increasingly rationalised. They became much less haphazard and more vertically segregated from the boulevards above. They were also more heavily controlled and policed and more respectable as a rationally engineered system for gravitationally discharging the city's filth in a modern manner. 'What is arguably the most exciting sequence in the whole of nineteenth-century French fiction', writes historian Christopher Prendergast of *Les Misérables*, 'is utterly unimaginable in the sanitised and regimented sewers of the Second Empire.'[18]

Sewers thus became central to a powerfully technocratic ideology of managing the city's flows and circulations through a series of scientifically constructed infrastructural edifices. By carrying filth as well as water, they helped sustain new ideas of the orderly, mobile and fragrant city; new concepts of bodily and urban hygiene; new styles of household consumption; and new disciplines of urban engineering.

Hiding the Excretory City

> Plumbing, with every sanitary flush, with every gleaming knob and valve, every glint of the surface of the porcelain, is meant to allow you efficiently to forget about the fact of your personal self. One quick flush and you're gone.
>
> – Margaret Morgan, 'The Plumbing of Modern Life'

Above all, by completing a universal system of engineered sewers – a process not fully completed in Paris by 1930 – cities became radically

---

16   Hugo, *Les Misérables*, p. 1058.

17   Jean Valjean, in Hugo, *Les Misérables,* ibid.

18   Christopher Prendergast, *Paris and the Nineteenth Century*, Oxford: Blackwell, 1992, pp. 88–9.

Porthole to filth: Sewer workers, Manchester, 1912

deodorised. As the odour of human excrement was removed from the urban surface, its associations changed radically. As 'the smell of human excrement began to lose the last semblance of its rural associations with fertility: from now on it was to be indicative of disorder, decay and physical repulsion.'[19]

In the process, where they have been universalised, modern sewers have tended to vertically distance urbanites from their connections with the metabolised nature of both water and their solid wastes. In the process, 'shit' was culturally transformed into 'sewage'; the emptying of the bowels was remade as a vertical passage down from bowel to the ceramic bowl of the toilet to the sewer.[20] With the metabolism of human waste removed below ground, the excretory city became veiled and removed from the deodorised surface within the systems of subterranean sewers.

19   Gandy, 'Paris Sewers', p. 32.

20   Ian Roderick, 'Household Sanitation and the Flow of Domestic Space', *Space and Culture* 1, 1997, p. 122.

Once the initial celebrations of completing the awesome task of extending huge subterranean sewer and water systems to large cities abated, these systems, too, subsided in visibility at the city scale. The ornate and highly visible sewage treatment plants built in the high Victorian age as memorials to their technical mastery of 'Nature' are now either forgotten or reused for other purposes; they have largely been replaced by huge modern exurban facilities. 'The success of city sanitation', journalist Rose George emphasises, 'is evidenced by its removal from conversation.'[21]

Completing urban sewers laid the foundations for the widespread modern obsession with the fantasy of entirely odourless cities.[22] Such idealisations of completely clean, orderly and odourless cities reached their peak with the modernist urban ideals of the twentieth century with their fetish for perfectly clean and white buildings, rooms and cities – accommodating perfectly clean and deodorised bodies. At the very time when modernist architects were obsessed with the use of glass to project the value of transparency through a building's form, it is notable that both the toilet within the building and the sewer below it retreated radically far from view.[23]

Fantasies of perfectly odourless and clean cities have also been central to the rise of the concept of the modern home – a capsule both connected seamlessly through plumbing and other technologies to the many circulations and natures that sustain it, and yet at the same time aloof and autonomous.[24] Plumbing and sewers, ever more sophisticated and universal, underpinned such visions while they themselves were increasingly rendered as the largely invisible and taken-for-granted substrate of the city (until they fail or break down, of course).

---

21   Rose George, 'The Blue Girl: Dirt in the City', in Rosie Cox et al., eds, *Dirt: The Filthy Reality of Everyday Life*, London: Profile Books, 2011, p. 159.

22   Ivan Illich, 'The Dirt of Cities, the Aura of Cities, the Smell of the Dead, Utopia of an Odorless City', in Malcolm Miles, Tim Hall and Ian Borden, eds, *The City Cultures Reader*, London: Routledge, 2004; Prendergast, *Paris*, p. 79.

23   Michael Dutton, Sanjay Seth and Leela Gandhi, 'Plumbing the Depths: Toilets, Transparency and Modernity', *Postcolonial Studies* 5:2, 2002, pp. 137–42.

24   See Maria Kaika, 'Interrogating the Geographies of the Familiar: Domesticating Nature and Constructing the Autonomy of the Modern Home', *International Journal of Urban and Regional Research* 28:2, 2004, pp. 265–86.

In the process, in many cities the human act of exploiting gravity by defecating vertically down into the sanitised toilet in the modern home becomes strangely disconnected from the sewers that lie immediately below.[25] The act of defecating in a modern private toilet thus becomes delinked from other places or processes.[26] Modern bathroom plumbing and design further isolates the excreting body from the uncanny world of the sewer to which it invisibly connects. It also signifies the uprightness and civilisation of using a modern toilet while being removed from its natures.[27]

Huge efforts are made in contemporary urban life to construct this myth of the complete separation of individual intimacy from the vast collective sewer infrastructures just below the porcelain. Hotel cleaners encase toilets in plastic for each new guest; Japanese manufacturers construct high-tech toilets with complex control panels and a wide range of futuristic devices; any hint that individualised toilet experiences in high-end places might in any way overlap with the previous ablutions of others becomes a source of great protest and revulsion.

The wider social and ecological worlds of manufactured nature at the same time become systematically denied and ignored: water appears as if by magic from the tap; energy sparks from the socket; throwing garbage into a hole in a wall makes it miraculously disappear, and so on.

Such relations have been turned into bureaucracies and commodities – contracts within oligopolistic markets with distant water and waste transnationals operating with global reach. The huge work necessary to continually bring water to the city while removing its shit – the very metabolism of urban life – goes on continually, underground as well as beyond the city. But it now operates in the

---

25 In the process, attention is also removed from what happens horizontally downstream as the waste is processed, removed and often dumped elsewhere, 'back' into the wider biosphere – with often devastating consequences. See Marvin Macaraig and Anders Sandberg, 'The Politics of Sewerage: Contested Narratives on Growth, Science, and Nature', *Society and Natural Resources* 22:5, 2009, pp. 448–63.

26 Maria Kaika, *City of Flows: Modernity, Nature, and the City*, London: Routledge, 2012, p. 47.

27 Lahija and Friedman, *Plumbing*, p. 41.

background, beyond and beneath the privatised water closets and the secret fall of fecal matter and other human wastes on porcelain.

This metabolism, though, rears its head when sewers fail or when their content remains or becomes visible on the surface. Ageing infrastructure and the corroding effects of vibrating roads above, along with legions of rats, accumulations of fat and noxious gases below, have rendered many nineteenth-century sewers in need of urgent and massive repairs. Huge interceptor sewers, in particular, have often been essential as city authorities redirect sewage that was initially discharged into rivers into large chemical treatment plants established in the far suburbs or exurbs.

The Sewer Uncanny and Its Limits

Conventional interpretations of the ways in which sewers have been used to obscure the excretory nature underlying the city often invoke Sigmund Freud's 1919 psychoanalytic ideas of the uncanny (*unheimlich* in German) to underline how sewers are a key focus of dreaming within contemporary life.[28] In these speculations, Freud overlaid conventional vertical ideas about the 'higher' and 'lower' body onto the notion that the linkage between human bodily functions and a city's infrastructures for dealing with excrement were both powerfully familiar but also strangely mysterious and incongruous. For Freud, 'the uncanny is that class of the frightening which leads back to what is known of old and [is] long familiar … which has become alienated from it only through the process of repression.'[29]

With the sewer rejected and pushed away from the contemporary imagination, so the argument goes, the boundary between the surface of the city and the subterranean sewer becomes marked as the horizontal boundary between 'the irrational and rational, culture and nature, the invisible and visible.'[30] Sewers thus become secret sites for marginality, haunting, tyranny and monstrous mythology.[31]

---

28 Sigmund Freud, *The Uncanny*, London: Penguin, 2003 [1919].
29 Freud, *Uncanny*, pp. 220, 241.
30 Gandy, 'Paris Sewers', p. 34.
31 Pike, 'Sewage Treatments'.

As marginalised spaces, they lurk threateningly in opposition to the rationalised and ordered spaces of the urban surface. This boundary, of course, is extremely permeable: at any time what's down below can rear up and challenge the clean, rational, bourgeois city above.

Arthur, a sewer worker in Christopher Smith's 2004 subterranean London horror film *Creep*, points out that the shit, tampons, condoms and all the things that can be flushed down the toilet can, once the sewer becomes blocked, suddenly push back to the sinks of what he calls the 'people upstairs'.[32] (Fears about 'fatbergs' blocking sewers beneath fast-food restaurant districts and hence pushing sewage to the urban surface are an excellent contemporary example here.[33])

Sewer failures and blockages not only lead to sewage in the streets; rat populations can move to the surface, too. Two-thirds of Hamburg's estimated population of 800,000 rats, it is estimated, live in the city's sewer system, gnawing repeatedly through its walls.[34] As long as the rats remain below, they are left to stalk collective fears. Once unleashed above, fear turns to revulsion and terror – as discussed widely within Freudian psychoanalysis – when they emerge from the subterranean realm as the ultimate demonised Other.[35]

Exploiting and perpetuating such fears is a whole sector of popular culture. In a huge spectrum of films, novels, cartoons, urban myths and science fiction representations, sewers become absent but uncanny spaces prone to housing uncontrollable and unknowable infestations of rats and monsters, octopuses and crocodiles, even aliens and unknown civilisations. Whether they focus on cat-sized rats, alligators in Manhattan, dog-sized pigs in London, the monstrous mythology of sewers has persistent themes. The creatures

---

32   Chang, 'City of Rats, City of Swallows'.

33   Such blockages are an especially serious problem underneath fast-food districts because the discharged liquid fat solidifies, blocking the sewer in the process. Bodily sclerosis can quickly translate into urban sclerosis. See Simon Marvin and Will Medd, 'Clogged Cities: Sclerotic Infrastructure', in Stephen Graham, ed., *Disrupted Cities: When Infrastructure Fails*, New York: Routledge, 2010, pp. 85–96. See also Rebecca Ratcliffe, '10-Tonne Fatberg Removed from West London Sewer', *Guardian*, 21 April 2015.

34   Manfred Sack, 'Messages from the Bowels of the Earth', in Peter Seidel, ed., *Underworld: Sites of Concealment*, Berlin: Hennessey & Ingalls, 1997, p. 9.

35   Stallybrass and White, *Politics and Poetics*, p. 207.

'have not only been removed from the world above but transformed by that removal', David Pike emphasises. 'Bloated by the sewage on which they feed, their excess size reveals the paradoxical fecundity of waste.'[36]

Examples, in addition to *Creep*, include John Sayles's 1980 horror film *Alligator* about sewer alligators in Chicago and Andrew Bonime's 1984 film *CHUD* about cannibalistic 'humanoids' living in sewers beneath New York's streets.[37] In such movies and novels, literary academic David Pike argues, sewers become 'personifications of the powerful and alien qualities of the modern city for which the world above can find no place.'[38]

While such works are influential and entertaining, the use of psychoanalytical ideas suggesting a simple analogy between the psychological experience of the vertical human body and the vertically structured metropolis is deeply problematic. Such thinking works to obscure the social relations of capitalism and urbanism under which such environments are manufactured, maintained and restructured. As we will see in the next chapter, this in turn leads to the widespread demonisation of the homeless people who live in the tunnels below ground as semi-animalistic so-called 'mole people', often depicted as a threatening presence to urban civilisation above.[39] Similarly, the 3,000 street children in Ulan Bator, Mongolia's capital, are often vilified by the nation's elites for sheltering from that city's bitter cold by inhabiting its sewer and tunnel systems.

Ideas of the subterranean uncanny also often work to subtly replicate misogynistic traditions of thinking which demonise the processes of the female body by linking them in an essential way with the anxieties linked to the urban subterranean. The history of linking the representation of women – especially the demonised figure of the prostitute – in analogous ways to the threats of contaminated water is especially important here.[40]

---

36   Pike, 'Sewage Treatments', p. 53.
37   For a full list, see 'Subterranean Horror: A List', available at imdb.com.
38   Pike, 'Sewage Treatments'.
39   Jennifer Toth, *The Mole People: Life in the Tunnels beneath New York City*, Chicago: Chicago Review Press, 1993.
40   See Morgan, 'Plumbing of Modern Life'.

Many misogynistic traditions of Western thought construct women as abject, threatening or inferior by emphasising how essentially they are associated, through menstruation and female sexuality, with dirt and filth. Historian Christopher E. Forth stresses that women's bodily life has widely been inscribed 'as a mode of seepage' that is inherently threatening to civilisation, order and male power and which requires paternalistic or violent control (or both) to ensure both physical and social hygiene (as well as controlled sexuality and reproduction).[41]

Freudian ideas of urban psychoanalysis have also repeatedly invoked enclosed spaces – subterranean pits, cavities, hollows and so on – as symbolically connected to female genitals or to the uterus and menstruation. Such ideas essentialise the uncertain flows of messy and threatening fluids within bodies and cities as somehow intrinsically 'female'. These are then widely opposed to the 'masculine' and solid world of rational engineering, which heroically over-comes and dominates such threats with hard science and new sewer technologies.[42]

Vertically structured ideas of the uncanny work also to support bourgeois and conservative ideas about the huge challenges of democ-ratizing sewers and sanitation in Global South megacities, where often only the elites have access to frequently inadequate systems. In filling the 'lower' city with an endless array of demons, monsters and urban myths, these ideas work to make the lives of the people whose working lives involve the movement of the city's shit even less visible and even more marginal than they would otherwise be.

Even in cities where sewers are comprehensive and well engi-neered, a workforce of 'flushers', using pretty much the same manual techniques as they have for centuries, is essential to maintaining flow. New York has around 300; Paris, 284; London, only 40.[43] While there is little doubt that their work has reduced child mortality in cities more than even modern medicine, these workers remain unseen and unrecognised.[44]

---

41 Forth, 'Health, Hygiene, and the Phallic Body', p. 109.
42 See Roderick, 'Household Sanitation', pp. 124–5.
43 George, 'The Blue Girl', p. 158.
44 Ibid., p. 159.

Sewer Work, Sewer Apartheid

When sewers do not exist, or are partially or poorly maintained, much larger workforces face extremely perilous lives continually moving the city's shit. This is the case in many Global South megacities where the legacy of colonial systems of sewerage still persist only in elite enclaves. The provision of piped sanitation and water supply remain minimal for the urban majorities, for example, in cities like Mumbai and Delhi, communities that live in self-built informal housing. This reflects a broader global situation where fully 1.7 million people are killed every year by diseases caused by poor water and sanitation (88 per cent of which are caused by infectious diarrheal diseases).[45]

In such contexts, state policy often proscribes the building of proper sewers to self-built settlements as a supposed deterrent to their construction. In Mumbai, for example, any shanty town constructed since 2006 is deemed to be illegal and is thus deemed to have no right to formal sewerage or mains water provision. State and city police, meanwhile, are often complicit in criminal rackets that import water into desperately dehydrated communities in tankers to sell at extortionate prices. They are also under pressure from elites who lobby to have their cities violently purged of the poor to produce what they see as an orderly and clean environment.[46]

Public defecation in parks, roadsides or creeks is thus now criminalised in many Indian cities, even though millions of people have little choice but to practice it. Within neoliberal megacities with utterly inadequate sanitation, rather than a matter of public politics or municipal action, the act of shitting is all too easily reconstructed as an individual, private matter within a bourgeois notion of order, cleanliness and criminality.[47]

---

45 Annette Prüss-Üstün, David Kay, Lorna Fewtrell and Jamie Bartram, 'Unsafe Water, Sanitation and Hygiene', chapter 16 in Majid Ezzati et al., eds, *Comparative Quantification of Health Risks: Global and Regional Burden of Disease due to Selected Major Risk Factors,* vol. 2, Washington, DC: World Heath Organization, 2004.

46 See Stephen Graham, Renu Desai and Colin McFarlane, 'Water Wars in Mumbai', *Public Culture* 25:169, 2013.

47 See Renu Desai, Colin McFarlane and Stephen Graham, 'The Politics of Open Defecation: Informality, Body, and Infrastructure in Mumbai', *Antipode* 47:1, (2015), pp. 98–120.

In the absence of elite-driven efforts to engineer comprehensive and universal urban sewers, many shanty-dwellers struggle with improvised toilets, most of which simply empty into holes in the ground, watercourses or the sea, with terrible consequences for public health. In such a context a few impressive but poorly resourced NGOs struggle to provide tiny numbers of public latrines to tens of thousands of people at a time. In Mumbai – a wealthy city pumping billions of dollars into infrastructure projects designed entirely for elites to sustain the image of a 'global' city – fully 40 per cent of all deaths in the city's huge shanty areas are directly attributable to infestations and parasitic diseases arising from the catastrophic sanitation situation. Death rates in such places are 50 per cent higher than in adjoining, sewered districts.[48]

Such is the lack of modern sewerage systems that many Indian cities still rely on large numbers of people to physically move human waste. In 2005, fully 800,000 people – the so-called 'manual scavengers' – had such jobs in India, even though legislation has notionally banned many of the jobs. All day, every day, they physically sweep up and move the shit in public latrines that are unconnected to sewers for removal elsewhere.[49]

As we have seen in many other cases in this book, extreme notions of social, class and religious hierarchy work here to sustain and link with vertical distinctions of moral or social worth within wider notions of a theologically stratified city or even cosmos. Added to this, many of the workers have no option but to carry their loads on their heads. 'In the rainy season,' Naravanamma, one toilet cleaner, relates,

> it is really bad. Water mixes with the shit and when we carry it [on our heads] it drips from the baskets, onto our clothes, our bodies, our faces. When I return home I find it difficult to eat food sometimes. The smell never gets out of my clothes, my hair. But this is our fate. To feed my children I have no option but to do this work.[50]

48   Colin McFarlane, 'Governing the Contaminated City: Infrastructure and Sanitation in Colonial and Post-colonial Bombay', *International Journal of Urban and Regional Research* 32:2, 2008, 415–35.

49   See Tam Stephanie, 'Sewerage's Reproduction of Caste: The Politics of Coprology in Ahmedabad, India', *Radical History Review* 116, 2013, pp. 5–30.

50   Cited in Mari Marcel Thekaekara, 'Combatting Caste', *New Internationalist,* July 2005.

Forty-three-year-old Devi Lal, a 'sewer diver' in Delhi, 2012

'Never again!' is the mobilising slogan of India's 'manual scavenger' communities. 'Never again clean other people's shit … Never again allow your children to live in shame and fear.'[51]

The entire population of toilet cleaners in India are 'Dalits', the people previously labelled with the ultimate pejorative 'untouchables'. Through extreme religious and social demonisation, they are confined to the 'lowest' category within India's complex caste system. The system itself derives from a 4,000-year-old set of Hindu laws that manufacture metaphorical connections between the vertical aspects of theological, social and bodily realms more powerfully than any other discussed in this book. The part of the Creator's body deemed to be the origin of each caste has been used ever since to systematically structure that caste's opportunities, status and power:

> From the head came the Brahmins, a priestly class, who are the most pure. From the arms came the Kshatriyas, the warriors and rulers. From the lower limbs were born the Vaishyas, the traders. And from the feet the Sudras, the lowest caste, destined to serve the other three.[52]

Dalits were deemed to be so abject that they were not even deemed to originate from the 'lower' body of the Creator. The result has been complete demonisation, extreme violent domination and a process of often unremarked exclusion.

---

51   Mari Marcel Thekaekara, 'The End for Hands-on Toilet Cleaning in India?' *New Internationalist*, 29 November 2012, available at newint.org.

52   Thekaekara, 'Combatting Caste'.

Dalits also work as 'sewer divers' to physically unblock overworked and inadequate subterranean sewers in India. They wear no safety gear, and their death and illness rates are shocking. In July 2013, in one example, three men died unblocking a sewer under a Delhi arts centre; in April of the same year two more men died doing the same work under a private hospital in Chennai. Because the men who die are Dalits, often no prosecutions or criminal convictions ensue.[53]

As part of the wider project of improving the life of the Dalits, a major social mobilisation is now under way across India to abolish 'manual scavenging'. The Indian state has made repeated promises to this end. Progress, at last, is now being made to eradicate the whole range of jobs involving the human movement of excrement in India. Decades of legal challenges, protests, strikes and mass mobilisations are gaining such purchase that national prohibition was passed by the government in 2013. Fully eradicating the jobs in practice, however, will be a major challenge.

---

53   Agrima Bhasin, 'No Exits from These Tunnels of Death', *The Hindu*, 29 July 2013.

14.

Bunker/Tunnel: Subsurface Sanctuaries

As we have noted throughout this book, the urban subterranean has long been imagined by elites as a literal 'underworld' of criminality and lurking political threats. In the latest incarnation of this tradition, national military-industrial elites are increasingly (re)imagining the spaces below ground as sites beyond the reach of the vertical surveillance by the drones, helicopters and satellites they have developed so expensively over the last few decades.

Some military and security commentators even see a powerful *causal* connection between the contemporary proliferation of spy planes, drones and spy satellites and the tendency for the militants and states who fight against those who control them to burrow – and burrow deep. 'The visual capabilities and capacities of the unblinking eyes in the skies have driven those being watched underground', cultural theorist Ryan Bishop suggests.[1] He argues that digging underground bunkers is now a main challenge to US military technology and hegemony. No matter how powerful the arrays of technological eyes ranged above the ground, the continued physical opacity of the ground to their gaze – what Bishop calls the 'triumph of the surface' – remains (for now at least).

Such vertical axes of surveillance, targeting and burrowing are far from new, however. Rather, current incarnations echo and intensify centuries of burrowing against attack from above – in medieval siege warfare, in the trenches of World War I, in the vast concrete bunkers of World War II, and in the preparations for 'mutually assured destruction' of the Cold War. (American journalist Albert Kahn memorably

---

1   Ryan Bishop, 'Project "Transparent Earth" and the Autoscopy of Aerial Targeting the Visual Geopolitics of the Underground', *Theory, Culture and Society* 28:7/8, 2011, pp. 270–86.

quoted one child's fear when researching the psychological effects of the latter. 'Please mother!' the child pleaded. 'Can't we go some place where there isn't any sky?'[2])

All of these outbursts of bunkering have repeatedly reworked prevailing notions of the use of warfare from above to try to destroy defensive and military architectures on or below ground. Collectively, such transformations have also repeatedly reworked traditional horizontal thinking about the 'fronts' and 'backs' of military conflicts laid out maplike across territory. Such concepts have given way instead to a world of aerial military weapons systems based on the use of gravity and ballistics to destroy huge reinforced bunkers.

In *Bunker Archaeology*, his hugely influential reflection on the ruined bunkers of Hitler's Atlantic Wall, French philosopher Paul Virilio reflected in the 1970s on the prevailing tendency for Cold War bunkers to get both bigger and deeper. He predicted that subterranean burrowing would progress 'to such an extent that burial would be accomplished definitively, and the earth [would become] nothing more than an immense glacis exposed to nuclear fire.'[3] Future urbanism, he had argued nine years earlier, would 'have much more to do with ballistics than with the partition of territories.'[4]

Military and security forces, especially in the United States, are indeed becoming more and more obsessed about the implications of the deep burrowing of their adversaries for their abilities to destroy from above. One influential paper produced by the US Air Force's Air University in 2000, for example, stressed that the various enemies of the United States were building ever deeper and more elaborate subterranean complexes as a deliberate attempt to 'thwart America's probing eyes'[5] of drones, aircraft and – especially – satellites circling and loitering at various heights overhead.

---

2 Albert Kahn, *The Game of Death: Effects of the Cold War on Our Children*, New York: Cameron & Kahn, 1953, p. 23.

3 Paul Virilio, *Bunker Archeology*, trans. George Collins, New York: Princeton Architectural Press, 2004 [1975], p. 46.

4 Claude Parenti and Paul Virilio, *The Function of the Oblique*, London: Architecture Association, 1966.

5 Eric Sepp, 'Deeply Buried Facilities: Implications for Military Operations', Occasional Paper No. 14, Center for Strategy and Technology, Air War College, Air University, Maxwell-Gunter Air Force Base, Montgomery, Alabama, 2000.

Donald Heilig, a theorist with the US Air Force, further links this burrowing with advances in the accuracy of US ordnance based on the use of GPS satellites for targeting. In 2000, he predicted that ever more 'precise' bombing will mean that 'our enemies will be forced deeper and deeper into the earth, possibly presenting overwhelming challenges to US Air Force strategists.'[6]

Rather than the mass, mutual urban burrowing of the two main strategic blocs during the Cold War,[7] contemporary so-called 'asymmetric' conflict between states and nonstate adversaries renders the burrowing of the adversary as inherently problematic. Al-Qaeda's famous caves and tunnels at Tora Bora in Afghanistan, which allowed Bin Laden to escape a savage bombing campaign by the US Air Force in late 2001, have become a key example of how a tiny, ill-equipped force can thwart a global superpower and its aerial and space-based hegemony by simply digging deep into geological formations.

But the United States' adversary states are burrowing as well. John Norgard and his colleagues of the US Air Force Academy talk of a 'proliferation of strategic subsurface sanctuaries'.[8] Located deep within the geologic terrain of US adversary states, these are geared towards the production and storage of weapons of mass destruction, the covert development of military capabilities and the protection of leaders.

The idea of untargetable targets brings an almost existential crisis to a US military culture long based on the idea that it is possible to lob or drop high-explosive or nuclear ordnance anywhere onto any target on the earth quickly and with impunity. The US Department of Defense estimates that there are 10,000 'deeply buried faculties' in existence globally – a possibly propagandist estimate. Whatever the real total, there is little doubt though that it is growing rapidly as both nation-states and nonstate insurgencies embrace sophisticated

6   Donald Heilig, 'Subterranean Warfare: A Counter to US Airpower', Air University, Maxwell-Gunter Air Force Base, Montgomery, Alabama, 2000.

7   See Tom Vanderbilt, *Survival City: Adventures Among the Ruins of Atomic America*, New York: Princeton Architectural Press, 2002.

8   John Norgard, Michael Wicks and Randy Musselman, 'Deep Ground Penetrating Radar (GPR) WIPD-D Models of Buried Sub-Surface Radiators', paper presented at Wireless Communication and Applied Computational Electromagnetics, IEEE/ACES International Conference, Honolulu, 2005.

new burrowing and tunnelling technologies in reaction to the ever-increasing reach and power of vertical surveillance and bombing.

'Without having the ability to hold those [underground bunker] targets at risk', US Assistant Secretary of Defense Jack Dyer Crouch argued in 2002, 'we essentially provide sanctuary.'[9] Michael Dudas, a subterranean warfare specialist from the US Navy, urges that extending the geopolitics of conflict deep into the earth's subterranean sphere constitutes a domain of struggle for continued US hegemony that is every bit as important as the more familiar ground, air, space, oceanic and cyberspace domains. 'Today, with advanced mining and construction methodologies', Dundas writes, 'tunnels can be pushed through bedrock, lined with high-strength, high-performance concrete at depths significantly greater than ever before.' He even reasons that high-tech tunnelling technologies used to burrow tunnels beneath global cities should be internationally regulated and proscribed in the same way as chemical, biological or nuclear weapons.[10]

Today's deeply buried facilities can be gargantuan. They range from underground cities beneath thousands of feet of quartz in the Russian Urals; a complete underground city near Moscow that can apparently accommodate 120,000 officials, replete with cinemas, theatres, apartments and a subterranean railway into the city centre; a 3,100-mile network of subterranean tunnels and command bunkers in China; a vast subterranean archipelago with underground rail networks beneath the Demilitarised Zone in North Korea; and underground nuclear and chemical warfare facilities in Iran. Not to be forgotten, of course, the entire command complex of the US military and state itself is deeply buried within a series of massive, high-tech bunker complexes buried deep into the bedrock.[11]

---

9   Quoted in Tom Squitieri, 'Bush Pushes for Next Generation of Nukes', *USA Today*, 7 June 2003.

10   Michael Dudas, 'Bedrock Prime: How Can the United States Best Address the Need to Achieve Dominance within the Subterranean Domain?', thesis, US Army Command and General Staff College, Fort Leavenworth, Kans., 2012.

11   This situation also brings to mind the legendary 'mine-shaft gap' scene in Stanley Kubrick's superb Cold War satire *Dr Strangelove* (1964). In this scene, US generals, deep in their control room bunker, fantasise about living blissfully in deep mine-shafts after a global nuclear holocaust, procreating a new society with beautiful women. The mood changes, though, when General Buck Turgidson (played by George Scott) starts worrying that the Soviets – doing the same in their

Bunker-Busting Delusions

Goaded by the invulnerability and invisibility of deep bunkers, the Pentagon is investing heavily in a new generation of sensors designed to radically reduce the opacity of the ground. One programme, named 'Transparent Earth', aims to offer a Google Earth-like 3D interface that would be able to display the physical, chemical and geological properties of Earth to a depth of five kilometres.[12] Mark Smith of the Geospatial Corporation, the company undertaking part of the project, reflects that 'underground is truly the final frontier'.[13] His hope is that, when complete, Transparent Earth will mean that 'for enemies of America, going underground may no longer be an option'.[14]

This effort to make the global subterranean legible uses probes that are sent down thousands of miles of existing, as well as new, pipelines, boreholes and mine systems (the Homestake Mine in South Dakota is a prime centre for these investigations). Harnessing the latest advances in geophysical science from both oil and mining exploration and earthquake research, these programmes are exploring a wide range of sensors – magnetometers, gravimeters, sound- and radio-wave sensors, vibration and seismometers, and the use of various parts of the electromagnetic spectrum – to build up full-scale monitoring of the subterranean domain. The generation of artificial lightening, through the highly controversial HAARP (High Frequency Auroral Research Program) facility in Alaska, is also being envisaged as means of locating deeply buried facilities by using the radio and sound waves produced by bolts of electricity.

These disparate systems are envisaged to be so sensitive that, as well as detecting earthquakes and subterranean explosions, they could monitor strains caused by the earth's tides, barometric pressure, natural disasters and global construction activity – as well as, of course, deep excavations to build bunkers and tunnels by US

---

own bunkers – would keep some nuclear weapons after Armageddon to attack US mine-shafts: the so-called 'mine shaft gap'.

12   Katie Drummond, 'With DARPA's "Transparent Earth", Underground Doesn't Mean out of Sight', *Wired*, 2 September, 2010.

13   Cited in Drummond, 'Underground Doesn't Mean out of Sight'.

14   Clay Dillow, 'On DARPA's List: A Real-Time, 3D Picture of the Earth beneath Our Feet', *Popular Science*, 2 September 2010.

Boeing's 30,000-pound Massive Ordnance Penetrator (MOP) 'bunker-busting' bomb – and the team who built it

adversaries. 'It is time to harness these technologies for military purposes and use them to find and map the caves and tunnels used by our adversaries', says Greg Duckworth of the Special Projects Office of DARPA, the Pentagon's high-tech research agency.[15]

The US military are also developing new weapons designed to destroy such bunkers once they have been detected. Most important here is a whole suite of conventional and nuclear 'bunker busting' bombs. These have startlingly phallic names such as 'Deep Digger', or the largest and newest, the 7-metre-long, 30,000-pound Massive Ordnance Penetrator – 'MOP' to its friends – produced by Boeing.

Advocates of the MOP, the most powerful non-nuclear 'bunker buster' in the current US arsenal, argue that it can get through 60 metres of reinforced concrete to destroy a bunker or tunnel complex beneath. The MOP bomb has recently been redesigned after an urgent Pentagon request to give it more capability to destroy Iran's deeply buried nuclear enrichment facilities at Fordo.[16] These are buried so deeply that several MOPs would be required, each penetrating down below the craters left by the previous weapons.[17]

---

15   Greg Duckworth, 'The Enemy Beneath: Finding and Monitoring Unimproved Underground Facilities', Special Projects Office, Defense Advanced Research Projects Agency, Washington, DC, 2005.

16   Michel Chossudovsky, '"The Mother of All Bombs" (MOAB) Slated to Be Used against Iran', *Global Research*, 3 May 2013, available at globalresearch.ca.

17   Julian Borger, 'The Truth about Israel's Secret Nuclear Arsenal', *Guardian*, 15 January 2014.

Despite repeated requests, the United States has so far denied the Israelis – who are keen to acquire the means to destroy the Fordo bunkers on their own – access to the MOP as part of its $3 billion a year arms shipments to the country. Following the nuclear agreement between the United Nations and Iran in July 2015, hawkish opponents of a negotiated settlement to the Iranian nuclear question continued to argue that the United States should export both MOPs, and the B-52 strategic bombers necessary to carry them to Israel.

The development of bunker-busting weapons has not been limited to conventional explosives. We have already seen how some military theorists have suggested that free-fall tungsten rods could be dropped from satellites as a means to destroy them. Several specialised nuclear weapons have also been designed to explode below the surface of the earth as a means to destroy subterranean facilities. One so-called nuclear Earth Penetrator Weapon (EPW) is the United State's twelve-foot-long, javelin-like B61-11 'mini-nuke'. This weapon is the first US nuclear device to be fielded since the global testing ban; between 60 and 150 have been deployed.

Ronald Reagan seriously considered using B61-11s to destroy alleged chemical weapons complexes at Tarhunah as part of the wider US bombing campaign against Libya in 1996. Harold Smith, assistant secretary of defence at the time, asserted that B-2 stealth bombers would use the weapon if asked by Reagan. 'We could not take [Tarhunah] out of commission using strictly conventional weapons', Smith said. The B61-11 'would be the nuclear weapon of choice'.[18]

But even the B61-11 is widely seen by Republicans and Pentagon specialists as only an interim step towards the goal of being able to take out even very deeply buried bunker complexes at will and at very short notice – whatever their depth. George Bush's 'Nuclear Posture Review' of 2002/3 argued that the B61-11 'has a very limited ground penetration capability' and 'cannot survive penetration into many types of terrain in which hardened underground facilities are located.'[19]

---

18   Cited in Hans M. Kristensen, 'The Birth of a Nuclear Bomb: B61-11', 2005, Nuclear Information Project, Federation of American Scientists, available at nukestrat.com.

19   Dudas, 'Bedrock Prime'.

In response, development funds were pushed in 2003 towards a 'Robust Nuclear Earth Penetrator' (RNEP; note once again the sexualised masculine terminology) – a weapon allegedly able to penetrate deep into the earth to use a nuclear explosion to destroy much deeper bunkers. Advocates of a new range of nuclear bunker busters even argue that nuclear explosions are a good way of dealing with buried chemical or biological warfare facilities. 'The extreme heat generated from a nuclear weapon', one research study argued in 1999, 'can vaporize chemical or biological hazards that may be aerosolized by a conventional bomb.'[20]

Although funding for the RNEP was cut in 2005, the B61-11 is undergoing a major redesign that, critics say, will make its use far more tempting to US military and political leaders. Driven by fear of deepening bunkers in North Korea, designers have now made the weapon steerable to make it more accurate. It is also equipped with a new nuclear warhead that can be varied in size – supposedly to minimise 'collateral damage' when used. Retired Gen. James E. Cartwright, once one of Obama's chief nuclear strategists, has admitted that the changes to the bomb makes its use 'more thinkable'.[21]

The continued deployment of weapons like the B61-11, and the doctrine surrounding their imagined first or 'pre-emptive' use, bring nightmarish dangers.[22] Such increasingly 'thinkable' weapons are dangerous delusions. The strategic danger is, of course, that first use of a nuclear weapon would prompt nuclear retaliation by target adversaries or their allies. Scientific journalist Ben Phelan has also suggested that the inevitable limits on the material strength of the weapons, combined with the huge force of impact, mean that – even when dropped from great heights – they would penetrate to nothing like the depths advertised by the US defense industry. In one trial, Phelan

---

20   Thomas Moore, 'Does the United States Need to Develop a New Nuclear Earth Penetrating Weapon?', MA thesis, University of Phoenix, Oahu, Hawaii, 1999.

21   Cited in William Broad and David Sanger, 'As US Modernizes Nuclear Weapons, "Smaller" Leaves Some Uneasy', *New York Times,* 11 January 2006.

22   The B61-11 has a 400-kiloton nuclear warhead. See Sidney Drell, James Goodby, Raymond Jeanloz and Robert Peurifoy, 'A Strategic Choice: New Bunker Busters Versus Nonproliferation', Arms Control Association, Washington, DC, 2003 available at armscontrol.org.

notes that 'when dropped from a height of 40,000 feet, the B61-11 was able to penetrate three meters at most into the Alaskan tundra, and not at all into hard rock (that is, without self-destructing).'[23]

Even if it *was* exploded deep underground, a nuclear bunker-buster bomb would do much more than destroy the deeply buried bunker. A 100-kiloton nuclear weapon, for example, would also release at least 1.5 million tonnes of radioactive fallout into the atmosphere. This would have a capacity to kill or devastate a huge population through radiation poisoning once it was shifted around by wind patterns. 'Supposing that the missile's point of entry were miraculously neat', Phelan continues, 'a nuclear blast at the depths a real missile could attain would invariably breach the surface of the earth, expelling a hot fallout cloud in what is known as a "base surge". Such base surges are even more deadly than the fallout clouds of nuclear weapons that explode on or above the surface. They carry large plumes of highly irradiated soil and bedrock particles which spread quickly in all directions. Moreover, because bunkers are usually built in or near urban areas, such fallout would undoubtedly cause many thousands of deaths through radiation poisoning.[24]

Subterranean Insurgencies

At a more prosaic level, the greatest effort and research addressing the subterranean realm among national security states involves the targeting of less elaborate tunnel systems. These are the tunnels that are now routinely constructed to allow surreptitious or proscribed movements, migrations and economies to flourish, despite intensifying surface and above-surface level surveillance and the proliferation of heavily militarised and walled or fenced surface-level borders.[25]

It is no coincidence that illicit cross-border tunnels proliferate most when surface-level borders are walled and militarised. 'Just as every wall casts a shadow', architect Bryan Finoki writes, 'so too does

---

23 Ben Phelan, 'Buried Truths: Debunking the Nuclear "Bunker Buster"', *Harper's*, December 2004.

24 Ibid.

25 Bryan Finoki, 'Tunnelizing Migration 1: The Border Tunnel Capital of North America', *Subtopia* (blog), 2009, available at subtopia.blogspot.co.uk.

each inspire its own mechanism of subversion … The wall is an object that inadvertently designs its own negation', in the form of tunnel systems.[26]

Motivations of those building tunnels beneath fenced or walled borders vary – from illicit drugs smuggling, people trafficking and what has been termed the 'tunnelization of migration',[27] to sustaining basic economic flows or full-scale subterranean insurgencies. Nevertheless, broadly similar cartel-controlled and ever more elaborate subterranean complexes are emerging in a wide range of varied cases: beneath the Gaza–Egypt border (with almost 1,000 tunnels); the 140 or so tunnels constructed beneath the US–Mexico border over the last twenty years (especially around Tijuana and Nogales, Arizona); and even a smaller set beneath the US–Canada border.

Where they function, cross-border tunnels work to render the above-ground discourses of perfect, militarised control as little less than a post 9/11 'security theatre'. They radically undermine the way militarised and patrolled borders are brought into being through a series of architectural fallacies asserting perfect administrative control. They thus work to challenge lucrative military-industrial fantasies, organised by politicians and contractors to symbolise projects deemed to 'protect' vulnerable national identities against some demonised, external or racialised other.[28]

Because the lethal security theatre of the above-ground walls relies on demonising all that it forces both beyond and below ground, by definition it very often also disguises the real nature of what flows in the tunnels. Tunnel worlds are invariably represented by national militaries and governments as being essentially criminal and nefarious even though very often – as in Gaza – they merely sustain the basic needs of human sustenance in places where the militarisation of surface borders and above-surface airspaces make doing so at ground level all but impossible.

Tunnels thus grow in parallel with the criminalisation of migration, deepening trade blockages, foreign occupation or colonisation

---

26 Bryan Finoki, 'Tunnelling Borders', *Open Democracy*, 26 November 2013, available at opendemocracy.net.

27 Finoki, 'Tunnelizing Migration'.

28 The term comes from Finoki, 'Tunnelling Borders'.

and binational corruption. 'The more we try to iron out folded surfaces, and flatten terrains', through the brutal Manichean world of militarised surface-level border walls, political researcher Brodie McGhie-Fraser argues, 'the more hybrid, fractured, contested, and contradictory those spaces become.'[29]

Once again, as so often in history, the deep linguistic and theological constructs of verticality mean that those circulations and people driven into subterranean realms are easy to demonise, animalise or dehumanise, and to project as targets requiring violent destruction. 'By driving the world's labor/refugee overflow underground, it becomes easier to perceive such a superfluous population as less human and through a wider lens of "ferality".'[30] Gaza again provides the most extraordinary example here. The brutal targeting and destruction that the Israeli military regularly throw down from above on a prison-city of 1.5 million trapped within the militarised walls have forced the entire economy into what is in effect a nationalised system of tunnels run by Hamas, the government of the Gaza Strip.

In so doing, however, Israeli elites are able to cast the tunnels – which are used to smuggle livestock, goods, money, workers, NGO and medical employees, hospital patients, fuel and a wide range of commodities essential for maintaining even basic health and life – as purely terroristic devices requiring repeated destruction and closure.[31] Tunnels are thus represented as 'terror tunnels', 'attack tunnels' or 'smuggling tunnels', but never as 'baby medicine tunnels', 'economic lifeline tunnels' or 'child survival tunnels'. Nor do we hear of the often traumatising and lethal experience of those having to negotiate the dangerous tunnels to maintain even rudimentary living standards.[32]

---

29 Brodie McGhie-Fraser, 'Gazan Tunnels and a Politics of Verticality', E-International Relations Students, 3 October 2015, available at e-ir.info.

30 Finoki 'Tunnelizing Migration'.

31 'Hamas Has Lately Regulated the Flourishing Tunnel Industry in the Gaza Strip', Meir Amit Intelligence and Terrorism Information Center, Gelilot, Israel, 29 October, 2008.

32 One Palestinian student commented in 2014 of the experience of being dragged through a Gazan–Egyptian tunnel in a plastic sheath: 'I was between life and death – the slides are just large coffins.' Cited in Eado Hecht, 'Gaza: How Hamas Tunnel Network Grew', BBC News, 22 July 2014.

A Palestinian being lowered to work on one of the tunnels linking the Gaza strip with Egypt

In another example, the perceived strategic importance of further illicit tunnel complexes beneath the US–Mexico – and, to a lesser extent, the US–Canadian – border is such that NORTHCOM, the US strategic command for North America, has set up a special task force to address them. In 2006 the US Congress also passed a special law to criminalise transborder tunnels, adding momentum to the development of specialist sensors that could detect them. Specialised military tunnel warfare training facilities are now also proliferating, designed to resurrect the skills of subterranean warfare last practised widely by US forces against the labyrinth tunnel systems of the Viet Cong or in the al-Qaeda and Taliban caves in Afghanistan. In addition, full-scale military exercises also now take place in the vast subterranean realms beneath US cities. One occurred beneath Chicago in 2004, motivated by then-current efforts to control the elaborate bunkers and tunnels beneath Baghdad as well as perceived threats via subterranean infrastructures from urban terrorists (as well as wider clandestine activities such as those of urban explorers).[33]

---

33   David Noble and James Allen, 'Operation Tunnel: Confined-Space Operations within the Tunnels of Chicago', *Engineer*, July–September 2004.

Urban Underworlds, Urban Crises

Although freshly dug labyrinths of tunnels and bunkers are charged sites of insurgency, transgression, surveillance and (attempted) targeting on the world's borderlands, venerable ones beneath the cores of old cities are also increasingly contested. Here, once again, the invisibility of the complex worlds of tunnels beneath major urban areas plays out in a complex series of political, cultural and geographic struggles. In these, worlds of fantasy and imagination blur and blend with those of policy, prescription and – as with the Chicago tunnel exercise – attempted state control.

During the deep urban crises of the 1980s it was estimated that up to 5,000 people were living in the vast and growing complex of transportation, subway and other tunnels under Manhattan. The attractions of such a strategy, especially in cities with extreme climates, are obvious: heat, (relative) security, the possibility of some personal space, and shelter from wet and extreme weather. 'Living [homeless] on the street is very physical', Marc Singer, one New York tunnel dweller, said in 2014. 'If it rains, you get wet, and you only have as much as you can carry. But in the tunnels, you can build yourself a house.'[34]

The life of New York's tunnel dwellers was most famously described in Jennifer Toth's rather sensationalist 1993 book, *Mole People*.[35] Her book tapped into wider fantasies of a post-apocalyptic urban underworld so widely depicted during that decade in fiction, cartoons, video games and, most powerfully, film. Mixing concern and voyeurism, fascination with horror, mythology with social reportage, the animalistic metaphors central to Toth's book have been widely criticised for depoliticising the subterranean fate of the vulnerable and poor in contemporary America, since they literally sediment down into the artificial ground and tunnel spaces of the underground city, away from what she calls the 'topside world'.

Mole People revealed the lives of people like Seville Williams, a recovering drug addict who inhabited self-built houses in the tunnels

---

34   Marc Singer, cited in Sukhdev Sandhu, 'Dark Days: Going Underground with New York's Tunnel-Dwellers', *Guardian*, 26 January 2014.

35   Jennifer Toth, *The Mole People: Life in the Tunnels Beneath New York City*, Chicago: Review Press, 1993.

A picture from Andrea Star Reese's 'urban cave' project: Chuck, one of Manhattan's thousands of tunnel residents, settles down for the night deep below the street level

under the tracks fully 100 metres below the bustling hub of Grand Central Station in Midtown Manhattan. 'It's the decade of crack and homelessness ... It's the decade of the tunnels,' Seville lamented. 'People've been down and out since the beginning of time, but we's the first to actually live in tunnels. There's been nowhere else to go.'[36]

Such processes of vertical layering offer a startling mimicry of the vertically stratified city spaces that have long been the staple in science fiction. As the above-surface city of Manhattan becomes

---

36   Cited in Thomas Heise, *Urban Underworlds: A Geography of Twentieth-Century American Literature and Culture*, Rutgers University Press: New York, 2011, p. 213

hypergentrified and organised for the needs of the rich and super-rich, so the deep subterranean worlds below increasingly house the very poorest. German filmmaker Thomas Heise reflected in 2011 that New York's very poor had apparently 'exchanged their lightless tenement cellars for the toxic, rat-infested environments of dripping catwalks and electrocuting rails in the modern city's circulatory system.'[37] Such a shift has even led the *Guardian*'s Sukhdev Sandhu to wonder whether the archetypical American road trip – a profoundly horizontal and often desperate foray into the rural expanses of the American frontier in search of an alternative world – now has its vertical counterpart in forays within such subterranean communities.[38]

The urban subterranean is not immune from the pressures of the surface, however. Threats of urban terrorism are often leading security forces to seal up and patrol underground spaces. Security services are thus increasingly in conflict with fast-growing communities of self-styled illicit 'urban explorers', who are delving deep into the tunnel complexes below cities for recreation, entertainment, activism and research.

Meanwhile, within the officially sanctioned spaces, burgeoning interest in the dark and other-worldly spaces below the city offers many opportunities for repackaging it as a tourist attraction or commodity. Such pressures inevitably heighten social and political struggles over the urban subterranean. The extraordinary 177-mile complex of quarries and tunnels beneath Paris, to take one powerful example, houses a palimpsest of history and material culture that has long since been erased from much of the surface. Fully inhabited by a wide spectrum of clandestine visitors – from those organising subterranean cinema or music clubs to artists, photographers, urban explorers, graffiti artists, writers and homeless people – their outputs add to an accumulation of 300 years of cultural expression that, like the dust, dirt, bodies and collective unconscious of the city itself, merely accumulate without ever being removed (in stark contrast to the surface domain).[39]

37   Heise, *Urban Underworlds*.

38   Sandhu, 'Dark Days'.

39   Caroline Archer and Alexandre Parré, *Paris Underground*, London: Mark Batty Publishers, 2005.

In their classic book *Paris Underground,* Caroline Archer and Alexandre Parré call these spaces the 'Hidden Art Gallery of Paris'. They estimate that these complexes are visited by at least 80,000 Parisian 'catophiles' per year. Such densities of clandestine exploration – as with those discussed by Victor Hugo 170 years before – have led to responses from security elites and police understandably concerned about recent terrorist atrocities in Paris and the possible use of subterranean spaces for future attacks. As a result, Paris now has its own dedicated subterranean police force.

As well as increased subterranean policing, the urban politics of fear reconfigures bunkers, silos and tunnels in other ways. Cold War bunkers – engineered to be protected against the blast effects of megaton-level thermonuclear blasts – offer perfect places for housing the most valuable products of global, informational capitalism – data (resources that were also widely destroyed by the 9/11 attacks). In this vein, both ballistic missile silos and nuclear shelters have been repackaged as ultra-secure backup data storage centres. Both a vast subterranean Cold War bunker system beneath an Alpine mountain in Switzerland and an ex-anti-aircraft artillery installation built off the coast of Essex in England during World War II have recently been redeveloped as ultra-secure data centres.[40]

Meanwhile, the Strategic Data Services Group in Albuquerque, New Mexico, have taken over two former Atlas intercontinental nuclear missile silos near the city, comprising 1.2 million cubic feet of usable space. These have been converted into twenty-two-floor installations with a hundred servers placed on each floor. They market their services by arguing that deep installations, 'built to withstand most natural disasters and the perils of mankind', offer radical security for the backup data of digital capitalism in a world of routine infrastructure collapses, power outages and infrastructural terror attacks.[41]

---

40   See Ian Daly, 'Nuclear Bunker Houses World's Toughest Server Farm', *Wired*, 5 October 2010; Simson Garfinkel, 'Welcome to Sealand. Now Bugger Off', *Wired*, July 2000.

41   Cited in Andrew Webb, 'Roswell Missile Silo Reborn as Data Storage Center', *Albuquerque Business First*, 30 March 2003. Another silo, this one in Kansas, has been redeveloped as a $2 million subterranean condominium.

Bunker Tourism

As the surface environments of many cities become burnished with the identikit accoutrements of stage-managed spectacles, homogenised corporate consumption and gentrified stone-blasted 'heritage', so, as part of the wider growth of so-called 'dark tourism',[42] urban tourists now flock in increasing numbers to subterranean 'shadow architectures' of bunkers, tunnels and subterranean spaces packaged as 'authentic' tourist sites.[43]

'Bunkers throughout the world have become ready-made tourist attractions since the end of the Cold War', cultural theorist John Beck writes. He notes a huge proliferation of illustrated guides, websites and handbooks in the past twenty years.[44] The very incongruity of these material remains, amid spruced-up urban neighbourhoods or pastoral landscapes, no doubt adds to their attraction.

Whatever dark tourists' motivations, Don DeLillo stresses in his novel *Underworld* (1997) that these days a considerable number of them 'travel somewhere not for museums and sunsets but for ruins, bombed-out terrain, for the moss-grown memory of torture and war'.[45] The end of the Cold War, in particular, has left the subsurface of cities and the interstices between them pitted with a 'dismantled landscape' of hugely expensive tunnels and bunkers.[46] These spark a particularly deep and troubling fascination – a technological sublime. Their brute, immovable materiality strongly evokes collective and personal memories of what archaeologist Graham Fairclough has called 'a remembered past'.

---

42   John Lennon and Malcolm Foley, *Dark Tourism: The Attraction of Death and Disaster,* London: Continuum, 2000.

43   Simon Guy, 'Shadow Architectures: War, Memories, and Berlin's Futures', in Stephen Graham, ed., *Cities, War, and Terrorism: Towards an Urban Geopolitics,* Oxford: Blackwell, pp. 75–92.

44   John Beck, 'Concrete Ambivalence: Inside the Bunker Complex', *Cultural Politics,* 7:1, 2011, p. 94. Feeding this process, popular science and history TV channels pump out a stream of up-beat documentaries exposing the deep histories of the subterranean worlds beneath the planet's major cities. Most notable here have been the three series of the History Channel's *Cities of the Underworld* (2007–9).

45   Don DeLillo, *Underworld,* London: Picador, 1997, p. 248, cited in Beck 'Concrete Ambivalence', p. 95.

46   This term comes from Frank Watson, *Cold War Sites in England,* London: Hush House Publishers, 2004.

Here emerges a powerful series of resonances with the way the excavation of bunkers linked seamlessly in the Cold War with constructions of modernist Brutalism above the surface[47] within an all-powerful rhetoric of mutually assured destruction or 'exterminism'.[48] Such complexes – 'ruins of the twentieth century, of ideologies, conflicts, and dreams of mastery through reinforced concrete'[49] – lie ready for exploration by a spectrum of groups, from conspiracy theorists, archaeologists, architects, place marketers, to photographers and developers.

In parallel, the worlds of professional archaeology are now seriously engaged in researching, preserving and opening up Cold War tunnels and bunkers to public visitation.[50] Just as Brutalist architecture, built in Western cities between the 1950s and 1970s to directly imitate the functionalist and aggressive concrete of World War II military bunkers, is blasted away and demolished because of its current unpopularity,[51] so some of those military bunkers, woven into the very geology, are being revalorised as tourist sites.

As a result, major Cold War command bunkers in Cheshire and Kent are thus now accompanied by tourist signs on local road junctions un-ironically directing motorists the way to the nearby 'secret Cold War nuclear bunker'. Daily tourist trips operate around the vast archaeologies and architectures of thermonuclear war that are sedimented within and through the Nevada Proving Ground north of Los Angeles or the nuclear weapons test sites in Australia.[52]

47 See Owen Hatherley, 'Fossils of Time Future: Bunkers and Buildings from the Atlantic Wall to the South Bank', in Robin Mackay, ed., *Collapse: Geo/ Philosophy*, vol. 6, Oxford: Urbanomic, 2010.

48 See Vanderbilt, *Survival City*; Joseph Masco, '"Survival Is Your Business": Engineering Ruins and Affect in Nuclear America', *Cultural Anthropology* 23:2, 2008, pp. 361–98.

49 Beck, 'Concrete Ambivalence', p. 82.

50 Wayne Cocroft and John Schofield, eds, *A Fearsome Heritage: Diverse Legacies of the Cold War*, Walnut Creek, CA: Left Coast, 2007; Wayne Cocroft and Roger Thomas, *Cold War: Building for Nuclear Confrontation 1946–89*, Swindon, UK: English Heritage, 2003.

51 See David Monteyne, *Fallout Shelter: Designing for Civil Defense in the Cold War*, Minneapolis: University of Minnesota Press, 2011.

52 See Hugh Gusterson, 'Nuclear Tourism', *Journal for Cultural Research*

Meanwhile, vertical nuclear missile silos, buried deep beneath the pool-table-flat prairies of the US West and Midwest and designed to lob parabolas of mass extermination via inner space towards Soviet cities within minutes, have become unlikely public museums.[53] 'Able to launch from its underground silo in just 58 seconds', the website for one of these in Sahuarita, Arizona, states, 'the Titan II Missile was capable of delivering a 9-megaton nuclear warhead to targets more than 6300 miles (10,000 km) away in about 30 minutes. Nowhere else in the world can visitors get this close to an intercontinental ballistic missile in its operational environment.'[54] After exploring the silo, the website exhorts that 'you'll want to browse the Museum Store!' Here can be purchased 'Titan II, Civil Defense and other memorabilia', including 'pocket dosimeters used to detect radiation, rebar salvaged from Titan II missile sites, and replicas of an actual Titan II launch key'.

Perhaps most impressive, however, is the wide range of Cold War and Nazi-era tunnels and bunkers that are the focus of a thriving research, museum, publishing and excavation programme organised by the volunteer-led Berliner Unterwelten (Berlin Underworlds Association).[55] This programme now shepherds thousands of tourists and visitors around the collapsed flak-towers, deep air-raid bunkers in the bowels of S-Bahn stations, and networks of Cold War spy and escape tunnels that burrow within and below the rapidly gentrifying landscapes of central Berlin. Elsewhere in Germany, wartime bunkers, which are often so obdurate they literally cannot be demolished, have been creatively recycled as the bases for housing blocks, office complexes, art spaces, paintballing facilities and trendy nightclubs.[56]

The complexities of developing dark tourism in this most iconic city of twentieth-century history, though, means that some of the

8:1, 2004, pp. 23–31; Sue Roff, 'The Glass Bead Game: Nuclear Tourism at the Australian Weapon Test Sites', *Medicine, Conflict and Survival* 14:4, 1998, pp. 290–302.

53   See Gretchen Heefner, *The Missile Next Door: The Minuteman in the American Heartland*, Cambridge, MA: Harvard University Press, 2012.

54   Titan Missiles Museum, at titanmissilemuseum.org.

55   See the Berliner Unterwelten website at berliner-unterwelten.de.

56   Disused bunkers built during the Cold War deep into the Alps in Switzerland, meanwhile, are now used as residences, hotels, museums and even mushroom farms.

Berlin's almost limitless array of bunkers must remain hidden beneath tons of rubble and dirt. When part of Hitler's Führerbunker complex was discovered beneath the newly opened 'death-strip' of the Berlin Wall in the 1990s, complete with elaborate SS graffiti, it was quickly filled in to prevent it from becoming a site of pilgrimage for neo-Nazi and other far-right groups.

Such tensions hint at the wider risk that the rapid growth of bunker tourism denies the origins of these sites in periods of deep ideological violence, ruination and trauma. The dangers here are that their presentation as tourist attractions fails to communicate what 1960s avant gardists Situationist International called the 'urbanism of despair' that sustained their construction in the first place.[57] Instead, their presentation often wallows in a nostalgic form of what design historian Brian Dillon has called 'military-industrial sublime' where the techno-science of mass destruction becomes a mere ahistorical and aestheticised fetish.[58]

Urban Exploration: Beyond the Controlled Surface

> One of the things that's really interesting about that idea of exploring …
> is opening up the vertical dimension of the city.
>
> – Bradley Garrett, 'Urban Explorers'

Despite the growing efforts of some police and security forces and the selective translation of bunkers and tunnels into 'visitor destinations', the urban uncanny of the subterranean and other 'off-limits' sites – industrial ruins, infrastructural spaces, disused tunnels, unfinished stadiums and skyscrapers – remains a major pull for clandestine visits.

Most important here is the loose global affiliation of 'urban explorers' (UE): a diverse range of individuals, clans, tribes and communities. UE communities encompass a wide spectrum of people who explore

---

57   Situationist International, 'The Geopolitics of Hibernation', in Ken Knabb, ed. and trans., *Situationist International Anthology,* Berkeley: University of California Press, 1981, pp. 78–9.

58   Brian Dillon, 'Decline and Fall', *Frieze Magazine* 130, April 2010, cited in Beck, 'Concrete Ambivalence', p. 87.

and navigate proscribed parts of cities for adventure, entertainment, activism, comradeship, notoriety or research, then post the results of their efforts online or in books. Sometimes, as in Berlin, UE groups overlap heavily with the voluntary research and subterranean tourism groups discussed earlier.

Almost by definition, urban explorers direct most of their efforts at transgressing the liminal boundaries of 'normal' life that tend to confine urbanites to the surface-city (with limited, shepherded movements, of course, down into subway tunnels, along subterranean highways, or up through elevators to residences, hotels, offices or tourist viewing platforms). Of course, the familiar, surface city – well-maintained, mapped, surveyed, policed and packaged – offers the 'portals' to vertical transgression. But only in areas of substantial ruination or dereliction do surface-level sites offer significant attractions to UE communities.

As with bunker and tunnel tourism, the slippery quality of 'authenticity' is a driver here. The 'authentic' sites are the decayed, surreal and often startlingly beautiful spaces of the subterranean and above-surface cities that are normally off-limits to a city's citizens. With the planet mapped by globe-surveilling satellites, and every square centimetre of its surface territory imageable from the vertical gaze of a Google Earth, perhaps, the movement suggests, the real domains for exploration now lie just above and just below the extending landscapes of the world's cities.

One of the most influential UE writers and practitioners is US geographer Bradley Garrett. As part of his Ph.D. project collaborating with a group of twenty or so urban explorers in London, Garrett was pictured in newspapers around the world climbing London's Shard well before it was officially open or descending deep to explore London's hidden subterranean tunnels. Like many of his UE colleagues, Garrett draws on Italian philosopher Italo Calvino's book *Invisible Cities*, as well as on the legacies of Situationist International (SI).[59] The latter developed powerful vertical metaphors for their critique of the 'society of the spectacle' through meandering, unplanned walks or *derives* through mundane and overlooked places in cities. By

---

59   See Italo Calvino, *Invisible Cities,* London: Random House, 2010; Knabb, *Situationist International.*

An urban explorer navigating a sewer tunnel deep below central London

linking literal undergrounds with cultural undergrounds, SI sought to 'undermine' or 'dig away at' capitalist society by amplifying what they called the 'irreducible dissatisfaction [which] spreads subterraneanly, undermining the edifice of the affluent society.'[60] Their famous mantra? 'Beneath the street, the beach!'[61]

Garrett himself interprets UE – a practice he calls 'place hacking' – through a specifically vertical lens. To him, escaping the controlling power of capitalist discipline, commodification and spectacle, and their tendencies to construct passive, docile subjects, increasingly involves active, vertical exploration above and below the urban surface. UE journeys, Garrett writes, deliberately work to escape 'global urbanising forces which render the city increasing clean, "secure" and mundane.'[62] In opposition, they make places out of the abandoned, unfamiliar or unknown spaces of the city. The experience

---

60   Situationist International, 'The Bad Days Will End', in Knabb, *Situationist International*, p. 197.

61   See McKenzie Wark, *The Beach Beneath the Street: The Everyday Life and Glorious Times of the Situationist International*, London: Verso, 2011.

62   Bradley Garrett, 'Urban Exploration as Heritage Placemaking', in Hilary Orange, ed., *Reanimating Industrial Spaces: Conducting Memory Work in Post-industrial Societies*, Oakland: Left Coast Press, 2013.

of increasingly vertical movement above and below the street-level city, he continues, 'become[s] an extravagant passage of surreal encounter and discovery through the city in an attempt to discover and remake it in an image not mediated by corporate sponsors and bureaucrats but by bands of friends doing epic shit together.'[63]

Not surprisingly, urban exploring means that protagonists' imagination of what a 'city' might actually be tends to undergo a radical verticalisation.[64] Major new towers, puncturing the urban sky by day, become 'nocturnal playgrounds'. Deep and mysterious sewer systems, tunnels, forgotten subway stations, bunkers and caverns become familiar sites of daily infiltration and navigation. The city, in other words, becomes fully open as a volumetric experience.

Navigating the vertical axis so openly and frequently thus works to expose the ways in which both the subterranean and the above-surface domains of the city have long been socially, ideologically and imaginatively constructed in relation to the city surface. UE underlines how vertically circumscribed most people's experience of major cities really is as they navigate officially sanctioned spaces and infrastructures within increasingly privatised landscapes of consumption and leisure. It also helps to expose both the functioning and derelict 'backstage' machinery of globalised urban life – the dank conduits and caves established over centuries for moving data, water, people, energy and waste – that tend to remain hidden in the interstices and backgrounds of the city.[65]

Many urban explorers stress that their work challenges the accepted scripting of history within cities' official, often sanitised, worlds of 'heritage' tourism. In exploring and reusing the 'contemporary ruins' of cities, those who create books and films from their activities also

---

63   Bradley Garrett, 'Security Breach: The London Mail Rail', 24 April 2011, available at placehacking.co.uk. See also Bradley Garrett, *Explore Everything: Place-Hacking the City*, London: Verso, 2013.

64   Bradley Garrett, 'Undertaking Recreational Trespass: Urban Exploration and Infiltration', *Transactions of the Institute of British Geographers* 39:1, 2014, pp. 1–13.

65   The UE movement has also been criticised as being overly dominated, not by ideas of resistance, but by an exclusionary notion of 'exploration' based on old notions of the heroic male conqueror. See Carrie Mott and Susan Roberts, 'Not Everyone Has (the) Balls: Urban Exploration and the Persistence of Masculinist Geography', *Antipode* 46:1, 2014, pp. 229–45.

emphasise that they see their work as little less than an 'autopsy' of the way the rapid restructuring of capitalist societies quickly abandons vast urban and industrial landscapes to ruination.[66]

Like the tunnel-dwellers living under New York, however, cultures of urban exploration are threatened by growing efforts by police and security forces to securitise the urban subterranean. In a softer parallel to the targeting or destruction of clandestine subterraneanism beneath Gaza or the US–Mexico border, many police forces in global cities are cracking down on urban explorers, arguing that they aid potential terrorists by publishing photographs of the critical infrastructures of a city.[67]

The rapid expansion of underground construction, and the increasingly colossal scale of underground transport and utility projects – what novelist Will Self memorably called 'big, phallic-shaped [tunneling] machines banging into Mother Earth'[68] – work to further challenge the possibilities of urban exploration. In London, Garrett's Ph.D. thesis was appropriated by the British Transport Police as part of the evidence used to support charges against twelve urban explorers of 'conspiring to commit criminal damage' – a clear attempt to criminalise the whole movement.

Such trends make it ever more difficult to gain access to basic information about the geography of underground facilities. 'There are maps of gas facilities, of telecommunications, of cables and of sewers', writer Peter Ackroyd notes about London. 'But they are not available for public perusal. The dangers of sabotage are considered to be too great. So the underworld is doubly unknowable. It is a sequestered and forbidden zone.'[69]

In New York, meanwhile, a systematic agenda of securitising the subterranean within US metropolitan cores is going on as part of the wider Homeland Security programme.[70] Here, the most vertical

---

66 See Matthew Christopher, *Abandoned America: The Age of Consequences*, Paris: Jonglez, 2014.

67 In their defence, UE communities respond by saying they increase the security of a city by exposing weaknesses and loopholes.

68 Will Self, 'Will Self on Crossrail', *Guardian*, 2 September 2014.

69 Peter Ackroyd, *London Under*, London: Random House, 2011, p. 2.

70 We have already encountered these efforts in the case of US military exercises within the tunnels beneath Chicago.

and elevated acts of mass terrorist violence – using civilian aircraft to destroy, through eventual gravitational collapse, two of the world's most iconic skyscrapers – have had powerful repercussions deep beneath the urban surface.

Among many other creative engagements with, and explorations of, the tunnel worlds beneath Manhattan's street, Julia Solis's photographic and writing project published in her stunning book *New York Underground* became virtually impossible to continue after its publication in 2005.[71] Culverts were progressively welded shut; access points were closed off. 'The shadow of the terror attacks on 9/11', Solis wrote, 'spread into all manner of subterranean spaces'. As a result:

> the creative anarchy of earlier times … largely dissipated as security has tightened. The attacks have had a profound effect on New York's underworld, an area that now seems rife with threats. Here in an uninhabited realm, dark and unfamiliar to most New Yorkers, the city appears particularly vulnerable.[72]

The large and diverse homeless communities that have long inhabited the tunnels of Manhattan certainly face much greater challenges in settling in than was the case in the 1980s and 1990s. Those living there for many years have been removed at gunpoint as part of the subterranean security drive that happened as part of the city's 'war on terror'.

In 2011, Marc Singer, whose celebrated year 2000 documentary *Dark Days* was made in partnership with subterranean communities living in an abandoned section of the city's subway system, revisited the tunnels that he had lived in. 'It was quite surreal', he recalls. 'Amtrak [the US passenger train operating authority] had hollowed out the space. There used to be actual paintings and amazing art there, but they'd painted it grey. There was no graffiti, no rats, no semblance that anyone had ever lived there. It was quite sanitised and heavily patrolled.'[73]

---

71   Julia Solis, *New York Underground: The Anatomy of a City*, New York: Psychology Press, 2005.

72   Ibid., p. 5.

73   Quoted in Sandhu, 'Dark Days'.

15.

Mine: Extractive Imperialism on the Deep Frontier

> Extraction sustains our society … [However], as the world population becomes more urban and more spatially removed from the landscapes that supply its raw materials and energy needs … our reliance on remotely extracted natural resources only continues to increase, while our relationship to the landscapes of extraction recedes ever further from daily view.
>
> – Stephanie Carlisle and Nicholas Pevzner

Like so many of the themes addressed in this book, critical discussions of colonialism and imperialism have traditionally maintained an overwhelmingly horizontal frame. As we stressed in the introduction, books and atlases of exploration have long used a bird's-eye view from nowhere to mark colonial conquests as sequences of coloured-in shapes on globes or flat cartography. The maps of the resulting horizontal extent of empires that result are, in turn, clichés of imperial propaganda and school geography classes.

By startling contrast, only very rarely have the subterranean resources that have so often driven colonialist and imperial campaigns been mapped for popular attention. Beyond the professional worlds of geologists or mining engineers, vertical sections or diagrams of colonists' and imperialists' efforts to reach deep-lying minerals and fossil fuels are remarkably rare.

The wider extractive economy, meanwhile, remains neglected in many political and ecological debates. These, too, often display what has been called a 'surface bias' stemming from the dominant use of flat cartography as the key means of illustration, visualisation and imagination.[1] As we have seen throughout this book, such a situa-

---

1   Edward Said called this Western colonialism's 'cartographic impulse': its

tion is the result of a much broader 'flat' bias that has long existed in debates about the politics of geography. 'Geographical engagements with the relations between power and space have consistently focused on "surface imaginaries" of horizontal space at the expense of "vertical" inquiries into power over subterranean matter', US geographers Jody Emel, Matthew Huber and Madoshi Makene emphasise. 'Given the role of mining in the history of colonialism, this is a substantial oversight.'[2]

As they try to connect mining and extraction to the cities that depend on them within a context of 'planetary urbanisation', geographers and urbanists are now working hard to rectify this neglect by analysing the history, politics and contemporary manifestations of the 'colonial' or postcolonial underground.[3] This is important because, as our planet urbanises, the extraction of commodities is inevitably becoming ever more central to global capitalism.

With the boom – and bust – at the end of the twentieth and the start of the twenty-first centuries shaped heavily by planetwide resource grabs for nonrenewable primary commodities by the powerful against the (generally) less powerful – within a context of massive urbanisation (especially in Asia) – corporate investment in mining is growing rapidly. Globally, the uranium, diamond and metals mining industries were worth $80 billion in 1995; by 2008, they were worth $463 billion.[4]

---

tendency to use cartographic surveying techniques to fuel processes of imperial control and domination. Edward Said, *Culture and Imperialism*, London: Vintage, 1994, p. 272. See Anthony Bebbington and Jeffrey Bury, *Subterranean Struggles: New Dynamics of Mining, Oil, and Gas in Latin America*, Austin: University of Texas Press, 2013, p. 1.

2   Jody Emel, Matthew Huber and Madoshi Makene, 'Extracting Sovereignty: Capital, Territory, and Gold Mining in Tanzania', *Political Geography* 30:2, February 2011, p. 72.

3   The latter two terms come from Heidi Scott, 'Colonialism, Landscape and the Subterranean', *Geography Compass* 2:6, 2008, pp. 1853–69. See Martín Arboleda, 'Spaces of Extraction, Metropolitan Explosions: Planetary Urbanization and the Commodity Boom in Latin America', *International Journal of Urban and Regional Research*, October 2015.

4   Björn Surborg, 'The Production of the World City: Extractive Industries in a Global Urban Economy', PhD thesis, University of British Columbia, 2015, p. 89.

Canadian sociologist Henry Veltmeyer has described this rapid growth as based on a new model of 'extractive imperialism' – a form of primitive capital accumulation which has stark similarities to the 'old' styles of colonial extraction organised by European empires in the nineteenth century.[5] 'The modern notion of "development", backed by the World Bank, IMF and UN', mining activists Samarendra Das and Miriam Rose write, 'suggests that the evolution of the human race is directly linked to their consumption of mined resources.'[6] The figures here are startling. Production of mined cobalt grew by 165 per cent between 2003 and 2013; iron ore exploitation rose by 180 per cent in the same period; and there was a 50 per cent increase in nonferrous metals exploration between 2010 and 2011. Within only ten years, from 1995 to 2005, worldwide production of iron increased by 50 per cent, that of aluminium increased by 64 per cent, and that of copper increased by 42 per cent.[7]

All these increases in production involve deepening the vertical reach of mining, which involves digging further and further down, whether in open mines or shaft pits, to reach remaining, and increasingly scarce, reserves. (Remarkably, it is estimated that humans have already mined more copper than is left in the surface layers of the earth's crust.[8])

---

5 Drawing on Marx's original idea, in the case of mining 'primitive' capital accumulation involves the forcible removal of direct agricultural producers or indigenous people from land, their conversion into wage labourers, and the exploitation of the profits of mining to accumulate capital. Over the past two decades, as a challenge to such logics, many populist governments in Latin America have sought to renationalise mining and minerals extraction in an effort to derive more benefit from their exploitation and reduce negative environmental and social impacts. Figures are cited in Henry Veltmeyer, 'The Political Economy of Natural Resource Extraction: A New Model or Extractive Imperialism?' *Canadian Journal of Development Studies/Revue Canadienne d'Etudes du Développement* 34:1, 2013, pp. 79–95.

6 Samarendra Das and Miriam Rose, 'Prosperity or Plunder? The Real Story Behind the Global Mining Industry', *Foil Vedanta*, 12 August 2015, available at foilvedanta.org.

7 Figures from George Monbiot, 'So You Need That Smart Cuckoo Clock for Christmas, Do You?' *Guardian*, 25 November 2013; and Arboleda, 'Spaces of Extraction', p. 2.

8 Björn Wallsten, 'The Norrköping Iron and Copper Mine', Linköping University, 2013, available at iei.liu.se.

In Latin America and Africa, the two largest concentrations of mining frenzy, this shift has been called the 're-primarisation' of global capitalism. Remarkably, it means that exports of extracted and mined resources are becoming more important to the wider economic fortunes of such places (not less, as traditional models of development would have it). From a figure of 7 per cent of overall GDP in 1970, for example, commodity exports from Latin America had risen to 10 per cent by 2010.[9] Fully 76 per cent of Latin America's exports in 2011 were made up of agricultural, mineral and commodity raw materials (compared to only 34 per cent of those of the world as a whole).[10]

Such a transformation centres on a renewed form of primitive accumulation focused on huge growths in foreign corporate investment to extract mined commodities and raw materials. In the process, more and more of the subsurface domains within and beyond the surface-level borders of Latin American states have been handed to overseas extraction corporations as concessions to exploit. The undergrounds of countries and continents are thus being remade as volumes of postcolonial sovereignty, based on legal agreements that parcel them out to global mining firms under the armed protection of state security and paramilitary forces. To take just two powerful examples, between 2004 and 2008, the area of the national territory of Peru given over to exploration and exploitation by oil corporations grew from 14 per cent to 72 per cent. Between 2002 and 2009, the area of Colombia allocated to mining companies increased by over 450 per cent, from 1.05 million hectares to 4.77 million hectares.[11]

Such imperial resource grabs are pivotal but neglected elements within a neoliberalised version of capitalism which produces an increasingly savage sorting of a small cabal of überwealthy winners centred on a few global cities – and a mass of losers.[12]

---

9   Arboleda, 'Spaces of Extraction', p. 5.

10   Maristella Svampa, 'Commodities Consensus: Neoextractivism and Enclosure of the Commons in Latin America', *South Atlantic Quarterly* 114:1, 2015, pp. 65–82.

11   Figures cited in Arboleda, 'Spaces of Extraction', p. 6.

12   See Saskia Sassen, 'A Savage Sorting of Winners and Losers: Contemporary Versions of Primitive Accumulation', *Globalizations* 7:1/2, 2010, pp. 23–50.

Skyscrapers as 'Inverted Minescapes'

One effect of the flatness of prevailing discussions about exploration, colonialism and empire is the assumption that the transport, infrastructure and mobilities that sustain them rest entirely on or above the earth's surface. And yet, just as shipping, railways, roads, telecommunications and aircraft have been the basis for extending empires horizontally and aerially beyond current 'frontiers', so colonial penetrations deep below the earth's surface have relied on their own transport system. This technological key to extending mining vertically downwards has been the shadow of that already discussed which makes tall buildings possible: the lift or elevator. One reason the two systems are rarely discussed together, however, is that it is conventional to label mining elevators with a different moniker: the 'cage'.

While even more rarely discussed than the politics of above-surface elevators, the politics of subterranean elevator travel – subsumed within the crucial but usually invisible worlds of mining – are even more startling than those above ground. It is also rarely realised that the technologies of building massive vertical mining structures deeper and deeper into the ground have fundamentally co-evolved

Belgian coalminers reemerging at the surface
in a miners' cage after their shift, 1920s

with those for building the growing forests of taller and taller skyscrapers into the sky.

Corporate skyscrapers, located at the cores of the world's 'global' and wannabe global cities, house the corporate executives, stock markets and super-rich financiers who draw portions of their vast wealth from neocolonial deep excavation of scarce and valuable metals and ores in the world's peripheries. We have already explored the extraordinary global obsession with the race to build ever-higher skyscrapers – and ever-longer elevator tracks – over the past 150 years or so. The parallel excavation of ultra-deep mines deeper and deeper into the earth, by contrast, is scarcely noticed at all.

It remains rare indeed for popular graphs showing the rising heights of skyscrapers and elevators over the last 150 years to also show the parallel, but actually far more extraordinary and dangerous, excavations downwards in mines. The only example of such a diagram known to this author accompanied architect Rem Koolhaas's exploration of architectural fundamentals at the 2014 Architecture Biennale in Venice.[13] Such a perspective reveals that mining cages have been plummeting miners over a kilometre vertically down into the earth for nearly a 150 years (since 1875). It also shows that the world's deepest mines currently are around 4 km deep – at least four times deeper than that other, much more familiar icon of modernity, the super-tall skyscraper.

In his pioneering work on the imperial resource grabs that sustained the explosive growth of San Francisco in the nineteenth century, Berkeley geographer Gray Brechin has explored the deep but neglected historic connections between mining and skyscrapers in unprecedented detail.[14] He shows how many of the technologies that were key to the building of corporate skyscrapers in North American downtowns from the late nineteenth century onwards emerged first in deep mines.

The deepening gold mines of the Californian Gold Rush in the 1850s, in particular, provided the sites where the ventilators, multilevel

---

13   Rem Koolhaas, 'Elevator', in Koolhaas, ed., *Fundamentals: 14th International Architecture Exhibition, La Biennale di Venezia*, Venice: Marsilio, 2014.

14   Gray Brechin, *Imperial San Francisco: Urban Power, Earthly Ruin*, University of California Press: Berkeley, 2003.

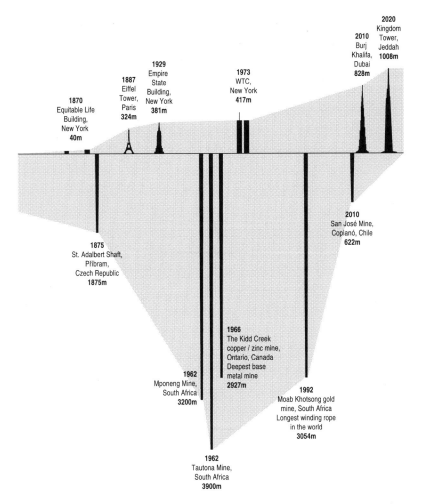

The parallel growth upwards and downwards of the world's highest skyscrapers and deepest mines between 1850 and the contemporary period (redrawn from Koolhass, 'Elevator')

telephones, early electric lighting and high-speed safety elevators that would later be pivotal to construction of the first downtown skyscrapers were first used systematically. 'All were demanded and paid for by the prodigious output and prospects of the gold mines of California', he writes.[15] In addition, the use of square supports, initially made of wood, to build large, multi-storey structures within mines to provide support as mined material was removed, later provided the basis for the famous steel girder structures of the first corporate towers.

_____

15   Ibid., p. 67.

The parallels between the processes of using these suites of technologies to dig down to provide the raw materials to construct skyscrapers were not lost on contemporary commentators. 'Imagine [the mine] hoisted out of the ground and left standing on the surface', reporter Dan De Quille wrote in 1877. The viewer 'would then see before him an immense structure, four or five times as large as the greatest hotels in America, about twice or three times as wide, and over 2000 feet high ... In a grand hotel communication between these floors would be by means of an elevator; in the mine would be in use the same contrivances, but instead of an "elevator" it would be called a "cage".'[16]

Brechin draws here on legendary American urban critic Lewis Mumford (1895–1990). Using Mumford's ideas of the capitalist 'mega machine' – where financial industries constitute an economic apex based ultimately on the exploitative and dangerous processes of mining, especially of gold and silver[17] – he stresses that De Quille's vision is even more evident in the contemporary context of super-tall 1 km towers, 3 to 4 km ultra-deep mines, and super-deep pits and quarries. Indeed, Brechin even suggests that the clusters of finance towers that have commonly signified the centres of 'global' cities for a century and a half should actually be seen economically and geographically as little more than 'inverted minescapes'.[18]

Such an idea forces us to consider how skyscrapers reach upwards from the staked territorial claims of real estate at the hearts of global cities or the cores of huge real estate projects: the tiny pieces of land at the heart of a tiny sample of metropolises from which global capitalism is directed.[19] Brechin addresses the unusual question of how such towers rely on both a wide range of mined materials for their

---

16   Dan De Quille, *History of the Big Bonanza: An Authentic Account of the Discovery, History and Working on the World-Renowned Comstock Silver Lode of Virginia City, Nevada*, Hartford, CN: American Publishing Co., 1877, p. 322.

17   From base to apex, Mumford's 'pyramid of mining' centres on mining, metallurgy, mechanisation, militarism and finance. See Lewis Mumford, *Technics and Civilization*, Berkeley: University of California, 2010 [1937].

18   See Gavin Bridge, 'The Hole World: Scales and Spaces of Extraction', *Scenario Journal 05: Extraction*, Fall 2015.

19   Brechin, *Imperial San Francisco*, p. 70.

construction and on speculative and commodified wealth that – ulti-mately –also heavily depends on mining.

It is worth looking in detail at contemporary but neglected exam-ples of the profound connections between deep mining and tall buildings. Doing so helps illustrate the enormous contemporary power of Brechin's critical but often overlooked insights. It seems especially appropriate, as we approach the end of *Vertical*, that we do this by returning to the ultra-thin pinnacle with which we started our narrative – a tower that has appeared since in various guises: Dubai's Burj Khalifa.

A crucial starting point for such a task is to realise, as sociologist Mimi Sheller has put it, that 'the … skyscrapers that serve today as the cathedrals of late modernity are grounded in the heavy (and dirty) industries of power generation, mining, refining, and smelting.'[20] To explore the Burj Khalifa's connections with extraction and mining, four related and overlapping processes need to be understood in par-allel. First, we need to look at the huge effort needed to provide the material for the tower. To construct the Burj Khalifa, 55,000 tonnes of steel, 250,000 tonnes (or 330,000 cubic metres) of high-performance concrete, 700 tonnes of aluminium and 85,000 square metres of glass were necessary. Such headline figures translate into a remarkable 79 tonnes of steel, 357 tonnes of concrete, a tonne of aluminium, and 121 square metres of glass for each of the 700 apartments in the building.[21]

Many other materials – Egyptian marble and Indian granite for flooring and upscale worktops and tables – were also necessary in smaller quantities to fit out the interior of the Burj with the required 'luxury' aesthetic.[22] Deeply mined gold, platinum, diamonds and other precious stones and metals were also required to fill the shelves

---

20 Mimi Sheller, *Aluminum Dreams: The Making of Light Modernity*, Cambridge, MA: MIT Press, p. 25.

21 It must be remembered, of course, that the Burj houses hotels, offices and restaurants as well as apartments. Apartments take up the bulk of the tower. However, fully 29 per cent, or 244 metres, of the Burj is totally unoccupied 'vanity height'. This makes the building's catastrophic environmental footprint even worse. If this 'vanity spire' were a free-standing building, it would be the eleventh tallest tower in Europe.

22 Remarkably for such a tiny nation the UAE is the third largest importer of marble in the world.

of the large indoor souk specialising in gold sales constructed in the enormous Dubai Mall at the base of the tower.

Even when such figures are considered, it is rarely emphasised that producing such extraordinary volumes of construction materials must, in turn, involve the mining, extraction and processing of countless tonnes of limestone, gypsum, bauxite (from India and Guinea), iron ore (from Australia and Brazil),[23] coal (to produce the steel and aluminium) and a wide range of other minerals, ores, aggregates and fuels across many locations. Crucially, the mining, manufacture and transport of most of these materials are very energy-intensive, require large amounts of scarce water resources, and produce large quantities of greenhouse gas emissions. 'In most projects in the UAE, however, materials are evaluated and selected based on aesthetics and cost and not on their energy and environmental performance.'[24]

Dubai, moreover, has so exhausted its own marine sand deposits through the vast dredging necessary to construct its various artificial island projects that – bizarrely for a desert nation – it had to import the sand necessary to produce the concrete for the Burj from Australia.[25]

Added to dependencies on coal, iron, aluminium and sand and aggregates are the vital roles both of other 'base' metals such as copper, nickel, zinc,[26] and of the rarer earth metals such as tantalum,

---

23   For each tonne of steel produced, about 1,400 kg of iron ore and 800 kg of coal are required. To produce each 1,000 kg of iron ore in a surface mine, between 2,000 kg and 8,000 kg of material must be extracted – a process with major pollution impacts on air, land and watercourses.

24   Hassan Radhi, 'On the Effect of Global Warming and the UAE Built Environment', in Stuart Arthur Harris, ed., *Global Warming*, SciYo, 2010, p. 98.

25   Desert sand is unsuitable for construction because of its high salt content and because its grains are very smooth and so do not adhere together. In 2012, nearby Qatar was the world's largest importer of sand and gravel, importing fully $6.5 billion worth of the material. With each tonne of cement needing around 7 tonnes of sand and gravel to manufacture, around 1.15 million tons must have been necessary to build the Burj tower. The UN notes that 'the world's use of aggregates for concrete can be estimated at 25.9 billion to 29.6 billion tonnes a year for 2012 alone. This represents enough concrete to build a wall 27 m high by 27 m wide around the equator'. Pascal Peduzzi, 'Sand, Rarer Than One Thinks', *Environmental Development* 11, 2014, p. 208.

26   From the perspective of this book, the use of the word 'base' – as in 'base metal' – to describe relatively common nonprecious and nonferrous metals – is telling. It stems from the old fourteenth-century French word 'bas' ('depth'), the

tin, tungsten and gold (collectively, '3TG'), in skyscraper construction and operation. This group– often labelled 'conflict minerals' – are crucial in furnishing buildings like the Burj, and global cities like Dubai, with functioning electrical and IT systems. They gain this name because they are the focus of resource wars that surround their extraction in some key conflict zones, notably Rwanda and the Democratic Republic of Congo.[27]

In the pivotal iron and steel sector, meanwhile, global growth in demand for iron ore, partly caused by the global proliferation of vertical and other massive architectural projects, has forced prices to rise dramatically. In 2008, alone, iron ore prices rose 50 to 60 per cent. Even with more recent price reductions due to the global economic slump, the three dominant iron ore companies – Brazil's Vale, Rio Tinto and BHP Billiton – are making huge investments to expand production, particularly in Brazil and Australia. (Qatar is rapidly building up an iron ore business in Brazil to provide for its own meteoric urban growth.)

David Robertson, business correspondent for the London *Times*, points out that the spectacular growth of steel-hungry skyscrapers, as well as the construction of huge factory landscapes in China, is so dependent on huge supplies of iron ore (as well as other metallic ores) that 'it seems inevitable that we will soon be talking about the strategic importance of these metals in the same way that we talk about oil.' As a consequence, Robertson argues – ironically, in an article read at 40,000 feet by passengers of the Emirates airline – that the epicentre of the global economy may no longer be the financial cores of London and Wall Street or even upstart global cities like Dubai. Instead, 'it is a vast expanse of red earth in the middle of nowhere': the iron-ore producing peripheries of rural China, Western Australia, northern Brazil and other mining areas.[28]

Architects Liam Young and Kate Davies further emphasise this point in their report about explorations of the pit and shaft mines that

key meaning, reflecting the metals' pivotal roles in modern industrial economies as the 'bottom, foundation, pedestal'.

27   Peter Eichstaedt, *Consuming the Congo: War and Conflict Minerals in the World's Deadliest Place*, Chicago: Chicago Review Press, 2011.

28   David Robertson, 'From Oil to Strategic Red Earth', *Emirates* 24:7, 4 February 2008, available at emirates247.com/.

sustain the world's cities. 'Here lies the shadow of those cities', they write as they venture to the bottom of deep iron ore pits in the desert interiors of Western Australia, 'the silent twin: the void where a land-form once was. These are the dislocated resource sites that support the world that we know'.[29]

The environmental and social impacts of each stage of the mining, transportation, processing and construction processes associated with all of these sectors need to be considered. All are controlled by a few giant and often esoteric multinationals; use vast amounts of scarce water and energy; are huge polluters; and are run and owned by tiny cabals of super-rich elites of financiers and predatory speculators, in often-corrupt alliances with states at various scales, and frequently backed by local security forces or their own violent militias.

Evidence of violations of human rights, labour rights and ideas of environmental justice by transnational mining companies is abun-dant.[30] Such companies often leave a wake of catastrophic social and environmental devastation in their wake. Indigenous and local people in the Global South are often displaced using violent mercenary and 'security' forces controlled by the mining companies themselves.[31] Trade unionists and community activists working against mining corporations are often targeted and killed. Toxic and polluted air, water and landscapes can leave a legacy of poverty and ill health for generations after the mining corporations have moved on. With crucial soil removed, dumped and heavily polluted, agriculture and foraging remain impossible long after the mining corporations have left (for this reason, activists call mining areas 'sacrifice zones').[32] The

---

29   Liam Young and Kate Davies, 'Unknown Fields Division', *Ground Up* 31, Spring 2012, pp. 6–14.

30   The best sources are the websites of NGO mining advocacy networks. See, for example, english.jatam.org.

31   This is the so-called 'resource curse': an initial stimulation of growth based on mining and commodity exports, followed by reduced wealth and deep-ening social, environmental and health problems caused by corporate mining and the haemorrhaging of profits to financiers in distant global cities. See Kenneth Hermele and Karin Gregow, *From Curse to Blessing? Africa and the Raw Materials Race*, Stockholm: Forum Syd, 2011.

32   See Lindsay Shade, 'Sustainable Development or Sacrifice Zone? Politics below the Surface in Post-Neoliberal Ecuador', *Extractive Industries and Society* 2:4, 2015, pp. 775–84

US Environmental Protection Agency ranks metal mining as the most toxic of all industries even when operating in the relatively well-regulated United States.[33]

In such a context, Cambridge criminologist Laura Gutiérrez Gómez has used her expertise to study abuses by gold mining corporations in Colombia. She characterises the criminal behaviour of many mining corporations as a form of accumulation by dispossession organised through systematic 'state-corporate' harm against the health, welfare and prosperity of local communities.[34]

A second process linking the Burj with mining involves the growing effort by UAE elites to diversify away from oil to mining and other forms of resource extraction. The wider engineering of sky-scrapers, infrastructure projects and huge islands has pushed Dubai and the UAE to the centre of global industries for mining, metal refin-ing, quarrying and aggregate extraction. Increasing efforts are being made to control, through ownership or joint ventures, the geographi-cally spread minerals, mining and extraction industries 'upstream' of the construction process in the UAE and Gulf.

Dubai companies, diversifying rapidly to deal with the future onset of reduced oil wealth, have become especially powerful as they gain control of new bauxite mines in Guinea in West Africa. This is an important factor given the importance of aluminium in skyscraper and infrastructure construction.[35] But refined aluminium is also Dubai's most important industrial export; the state-owned company Emirates Global Aluminium (EGA) is one of the biggest aluminium producers in the world.

'Dubai is the New York for Africans now', Mohammed Ali Alabbar, CEO of the Dubai real estate giant Emaar – developer of the Burj and a company fast diversifying into global mining – said in 2011. 'I really see that the link between Dubai, UAE and Africa is getting stronger and stronger.'[36] As well as gold, bauxite and iron ore in Guinea-

33   Brian Owens, 'Extreme Prospects', *Nature*, 20 March 2003, pp. S4–S7.

34   Laura Gutiérrez Gómez, *Accumulation by Dispossession Through State-Corporate Harm: The Case of AngloGold Ashanti in Colombia*, Utrecht: Wolf Legal Publishers, 2013.

35   James Wilson, 'UAE to Invest $5bn in Guinea Bauxite Project', *Financial Times*, 25 November 2013.

36   Simeon Kerr, 'Emaar Founder Eyes Africa's Commodity Riches', *Financial*

Conakry, his new company, Africa Middle East Resources (AMER), is taking control of major stakes in oil and gas concessions in Uganda, bauxite in Malaysia, oil and gas in Gabon, uranium and hydrocarbon interests in Niger, copper in the Democratic Republic of Congo, gold and coal deposits in Madagascar and phosphate concessions in Mauritania. 'The Burj was over', Alabbar said on another occasion, reflecting on the minerals strategy. 'I was thinking where to go, what to do next?'[37]

The rapid diversification of Gulf global cities like Dubai into extraction industries hints at the broader role a small group of global cities play in the geo-economics and geopolitics of global mining. These are the cities where major mining companies have their headquarters – especially Toronto, New York, Santiago, London, Los Angeles and Johannesburg[38] – and that gain much of the wealth and power that drives their increasingly vertiginous skylines through the wealth linked to mining.

Few people, for example, realise that the rising towers of Toronto's finance district and stock exchange ('TSX') now constitute by far the most important hub of the global mining industry. Following a period of aggressive recent expansion through acquisitions by Canadian mining capital in Latin and Central America and Africa, fully 75 per cent of global mining companies are now headquartered in Toronto. About 60 per cent are listed on TSX. In 2012, 70 per cent of the equity capital raised globally for mining was raised in Toronto. Canadian mining corporations, supported by recent national and local governments which have been exceptionally generous towards them, are now especially powerful in gold mining and extracting other precious metals.[39]

Moreover, lobbying and donations from Toronto's wealthy mining sector means that everything from hospitals, business schools and university chairs to art centres and museums now receive direct sponsorship from mining. Such 'philanthropy' has even allowed mining

Times, 4 March 2011.

37   Anil Bhoyrul, 'Emaar Chairman Alabbar Plots $10bn Mining Empire', *Arabian Business*, 4 May 2011.

38   Moscow, Rio, Sydney, Mexico City and Hong Kong are also important. See Surborg, *World City*, p. 74.

39   See Veltmayer, 'Extractive Imperialism'.

companies to influence primary education in the city's schools, so that any social or environmental criticism of their impacts on the extraction zones of the Global South can be removed from books and other teaching content. [40]

To explore the heart of this power, in 2013 local activist Niko Block went to the conference of the Prospectors and Developers Association of Canada (PDAC). The biggest conference in global mining, with 30,000 delegates from 100 countries, it's held annually in Toronto – reflecting the pivotal importance of the city, and Canada more generally, to global mining. Wandering the free bars around the convention centre, Block noted US Geological Survey stands showing off USGS research work detailing Afghanistan's deposits of gemstones, iron, magnesite, chromite, copper and lithium. He attended dozens of technical discussions on valuing the latest super-deep reserves and the challenges involved in using the latest 3D visualisation and radar systems to help improve prospecting for remaining deeply buried metals and minerals. [41] Late at night, Block saw echelons of chubby mining executives returning from nights on the town arm and arm with local sex workers.

Meanwhile, across town, a startlingly different conference was taking place: a small-scale NGO congress discussing efforts to resist the violent eviction of indigenous communities in remote regions of Guatemala, Congo and Mexico. Here the agenda was rather different. It focused on the burning of villages, environmental and health crises, the murder of activists and trade unionists, and intimidation of women in mining areas by mass rape – sometimes by proxy militia employed by the very same mining corporations whose executives were living it up at PDAC across town.

---

40 See Stuart Tannock, 'Mining Capital and the Corporatization of Public Education in Toronto: Building a Global City or Building a Globally Ignorant City?' *Burning Billboard*, 2009, available at http://burningbillboard.org.

41 'Corporate and state power in the natural resource sector', writes British geographer Gavin Bridge, 'is commonly constituted through volumetric practices, as those who live alongside resource extraction will know all too well. I mean this not in the simple sense that mining is about moving quantities of earth, but … that the exercise of power involves technologies of calculation, visualization and manipulation around volume', Gavin Bridge, 'Territory, Now in 3D!' *Political Geography* 34, 2013, p. 56.

'We are exploiting people and places that are otherwise made invisible to us', Block wrote. 'Mining is the business that built the skyscrapers at Bay [Street] and King [Street in central Toronto], which absorbs the money as it cascades into the city, as though from out of the clear blue sky, before rippling outward through downtown and toward [the financiers' neighbourhoods of] Ajax, Markham, Brampton, Burlington.'[42]

And, of course, we must attend to the extractive sources of the wealth needed to build the Burj and other Gulf towers, and especially the most important commodity chain underlying vertical construction in the Gulf: the speculative profits from oil extraction that have funded construction of megastructures like the Burj. 'Today the fantasy skylines of Houston or Dubai achieve a similar inversion' to the 'inverted minescapes' of San Francisco's towers in the late nineteenth century analysed by Gray Brechin, Durham geographer Gavin Bridge writes. 'Their thrusting towers and sprawling infrastructure embody the three-dimensional geographies of oil and gas fields in the Gulf of Mexico and the Middle East from which their wealth and power derives.'[43]

The final key linkage between mining and skyscrapers like the Burj Khalifa involves the flows of surplus capital from the extractive peripheries of the world into the burgeoning forests of elite housing towers in the world's global cities, which we discussed at length in chapter 8.

As often-corrupt extractive oligarchs search for low-tax and high-return safe havens for their bounties of excess capital in volatile economic times, invariably, as we have seen, the booming real estate markets of cities like London, New York, Miami, Vancouver, San Francisco and Singapore are at the tops of their lists. Many of the hard-to-trace shell companies that are buying the most expensive

---

42   Figures and discussion from Niko Block, 'On the Roots of Our Skyscrapers: The Cynicism and Depravity of Toronto's Extractive Economy', *Critical Utopias*, 23 July 2013, available at criticalutopias.net.

43   Even the (oil-generated) peak electricity consumption of the tower – 36 MW – is remarkably high, enough to power around 27,000 average Californian suburban homes. (The UAE has the largest per-capita environmental footprint on earth.) Quote is from Bridge, 'The Hole World'.

überwealth condos in the prestigious emerging towers we've already explored in New York and London are fronts for mining oligarchs.[44]

The Deepest Frontier: The Push for Deep Gold

> Gold value is a kind of fiction, embodied by a block of material wrung like blood from a stone from vast tracts of the earth to end up in a vault, in the earth.
>
> – Liam Young and Kate Davies, 'Unknown Fields Division'

To sustain the 'inverted minescapes' of today's burgeoning global cities and skyscrapers, deep mining must reach further and further into the earth's crust to reach the remaining reserves of a wide range of increasingly scarce ores and metals in the context of burgeoning demand, high prices, and the exhaustion of more accessible reserves.

It is the frenzy for gold – a sector where 40 per cent of global trade is now controlled by dealers in Dubai, the 'City of Gold' – that is driving the most extraordinary of all these deepening descents into the earth's crust. Although gold is no longer the basis for setting international exchange rates, this high demand continues because nation states still maintain some of their financial reserves in bullion; because global elites and middle classes still covet gold; and – most important – because, like real estate, investment demand for gold always benefits from its image as a 'safe haven' in times of economic turbulence.

Global demand for gold is increasingly difficult to meet, however. 'New shallow deposits [of gold], aren't easily being discovered around the world', Ray Durrheim, a South African seismologist, reported in 2007. 'The resources are at greater depths.'[45] Across the world, gold miners, just like miners for other precious and nonprecious metals,

---

44 Persistent research by the *New York Times* has identified examples here. One is mining magnate Anil Agarwal, who is notorious for the pollution near his mines in Zambia and the violation of indigenous land rights around proposed mines in his native India. Another is Russian oil magnate and politician Andrey Vavilov, who has long faced allegations of corruption. See Louise Story and Stephanie Saul, 'Towers of Secrecy', *New York Times,* 7 February 2015.

45 Quoted in Wadhams, 'World's Deepest Mines'.

are digging down to unprecedented depths as well as exploiting resources in more politically volatile places.

In South Africa – which, in 140 years, has produced 40,000 metric tonnes of gold, a figure which amounts fully to 50 per cent of all gold ever mined – the push to exploit the remaining ores is overwhelmingly a push for unprecedented depth in response to high demand and high prices.[46] The exhaustion of gold ores even 1 or 2 km below the surface, and the existence and mapping of super-deep ore fields, means that South Africa is seeing the deepest push for gold anywhere as companies and political elites seek to shore up rapidly waning production.

The Mponeng mine, 60 km from Johannesburg – along with the adjacent Tau Tona mine, currently the world's deepest – is a poster child for ultra-deep gold mining. In Mponeng, elevator descents reach over 3.5 km (2.2 miles) into the earth's crust at speeds approaching 60 km/hour. To put this in perspective, this descent is fully 10 per cent of the thickness of the earth's continental crust in South Africa. As architect Daniel Fernández Pascual puts it, 'As for today, the "deepest nation-state" in the world is South Africa.'[47]

Mponeng's huge vertical, three-deck elevators – perhaps they should more properly be called 'depressivators' or 'lowervators'? – take 120 miners at a time. Some 4,000 miners plummet down their shafts every day. The cages descend through the first leg of 2.5 km – a distance ten times farther than the elevators to the viewing deck of the Empire State Building ascend – in only six minutes. At such depths, the temperature of the rock, slightly closer to the radiation-based heat of the earth's core, reaches 60°C. To stop the miners from literally baking alive, and to bring the prevailing temperature to a still stifling 28–30°C, the entire mine has to be refrigerated using 6,000 tonnes of ice a day using special 'fridge shafts'. The object of such heroic and dangerous labour? A single extremely rich seam of gold only 30 to 50 cm thick laid down by ancient water flows in deltas and shallow seas some 3 billion years ago.[48]

---

46   The price per ounce of gold rose from $400 in 2003 to $1,700 at the end of 2012, then dipped to $1,060 in December 2015.

47   Daniel Fernández Pascual, 'The Clear-Blurry Line', *The Funambulist Papers 20*, available at thefunambulist.net.

48   All the gold on earth was manufactured in the unimaginably ancient

Producing 5,500 tonnes of rock a day, Mponeng's owners, Anglo-Gold Ashanti, obtain only 10 grams of gold per tonne. But this still amounts to 55 kg of gold per day – a weight worth over $2 million at September 2015 values.

Multi-level mines like Mponeng, whose galleries can stretch for many kilometres out from the cage shafts, are carefully designed using the latest geological sensing and visualizing technologies. (Mponeng has around 250 miles of tunnels, a total 36 miles longer than the entire New York subway system). In such mines, rock mechanics experts and specialist engineers use complex three-dimensional planning and modelling techniques to decide which rocks can be most safely and profitably excavated while minimising the risk of major seismic events or fractured rock.

Matthew Hart, a journalist for the *Wall Street Journal*, journeyed to the depths of the Mponeng mine in 2013. Echoing Gray Brechin's powerful idea of skyscrapers as 'inverted minescapes', his experience allowed him to compare the mine's cages/elevators with the elevators sustaining the world's tallest building. Hart reflects that, in the Burj Khalifa, a fleet of fifty-seven elevators move people up and down using 'sky lobbies' as staging posts between elevator journeys. By contrast, on reaching the base of Mponeng's first cage run, Hart and colleagues 'had traveled five times the distance covered by the Burj Khalifa's system, and had done it in a single drop.' They then walked through a vast subterranean 'lobby' to 'the cage that would take us deeper, to the active mining levels that lay far below. We stepped into the second cage and in two minutes dropped another mile into the furnace of the rock.'[49]

Just as they are central to higher skyscrapers, faster and bigger elevator systems are crucial in opening up deeper and deeper layers of gold and other metals and minerals to systematic exploitation. Echoing the debate on lighter cables in elevator lifts, *Mining Weekly* reports that 'with improved winder and rope technologies, cages can now be hoisted below 3000 m in a single drop.' To the mining industry

death-throes of stars. It is only water flows that accumulate scarce gold deposits into denser concentrations. See Sarah Zhnag, 'Terrifying Facts about the World's Deepest Gold Mine', *Gizmodo*, 16 December 2013, available at gizmodo.com.

49   Matthew Hart, 'A Journey into the World's Deepest Gold Mine', *Wall Street Journal*, 13 December 2013.

such a prospect offers 'great economic benefit in deep-level mines as it enables personnel to reach the rock face far sooner and thus have more productive time at the face.'[50]

In 2012, Mponeng alone produced $950 million worth of gold. Tempted by such extraordinary riches, gold mining corporations are already planning even deeper shafts to reach untapped ultra-deep resources. AngloGold Ashanti, for example, is planning to dig to 4.5 km by 2018, tempted by the estimated '100 million ounces of gold that cannot be mined conventionally' deep within South Africa's goldfields.[51]

As in skyscraper elevators, the weight of ropes is a pivotal constraint. Back in 1997 mining engineer David Diering admitted that 'if someone asked the question "what would stop us going to 5,000m today, assuming there was an ore body worth going to and enough money to pay for it?", the simplified answer would be "ropes!"'[52] Innovations like the carbon-fibre rope being launched for use in skyscraper elevators, and being developed in a disused mine shaft near Helsinki by the KONE elevator company, are thus likely to fuel the latest in a long line of technological crossovers over the next twenty years in the parallel push upwards for skyscrapers and downwards for mines.

Although they are nowhere near as deadly as the thousands of illegal, informal or artisanal mines that dot the mining regions of Latin America, Africa and parts of Asia, the elevators in relatively high-tech deep mines remain dangerous.[53] In May 1995, in the most notorious deep shaft disaster so far, the engine of an underground railcar in the Anglo-American Corporation's Vaal Reefs Mine near Orkney, South Africa, broke loose and fell down a 2 km (7,000-foot) elevator shaft, crushing a two-deck cage completely flat and instantly killing the 105 men within it.

---

50   Elizabeth Rebelo, 'World's Deepest Single-Lift Mine Ever', *Mining Weekly*, 29 September 2003. In addition, automated self-driving trucks are now widely used to move ore between the excavation galleries and the vertical cages.

51   Martin Creamer, 'AngloGold Ashanti Moving Closer to Ultra-Deep Mining Goal', *Mining Weekly*, 2 March 2013.

52   David Diering, 'Ultra-Deep Level Mining—Future Requirements', *Journal of the South African Institute of Mining and Metallurgy*, October 1997, pp. 249–56.

53   Mining accidents kill around 12,000 workers a year. Olivia Lang, 'The Dangers of Mining around the World', *BBC News,* 14 October 2010.

Like all major South African mines, Mponeng regularly reports deaths and injuries during normal operations. In South Africa, an average of five miners die each week.[54] At least six fatalities were reported in the mine by *Mining Weekly* during 2012/2013; the killers involved seismic collapses (which can reach Richter scale five in earthquake terms), heavy machinery malfunctions and electrocution.

Annual reviews of mine performance, along with detailed data on ore extraction, remaining reserves and costs, usually contain platitudes about such fatalities. 'There were regrettably eight fatalities at the West Wits operations during 2012,' one states. 'Three each at Mponeng and TauTona, and two at Savuka.' Under the subheading 'Sustainability Performance,' it continues, that 'the board and management of AngloGold Ashanti extend their sincere condolences to the family, friends and colleagues of the deceased.'[55]

'We would not generally oppose the idea of ultra-deep mining if our people were safe,' Lesiba Seshoka of South Africa's National Union of Mineworkers (NUM), told *National Geographic* in 2007. 'But we are opposing it on the basis that … we have already seen a significant rise of fatalities.'[56] Such resistance to ultra-deep mining fails, however, to address the gold industry's catastrophic record of fatalities and debilitating illness through degenerative and crippling diseases like silicosis, nor its appalling track record in legal denials for liability. South Africa's NUM – currently taking UK-owned gold firms to court in London along with 3,500 ex-miners to force recognition of the problem – calculates that there are at least 50,000 former gold miners in South Africa with the disease (which is often fatal through reduced resistance to TB). The class action suit started in October 2015.

What is especially striking is that, while huge investments go into deeper and deeper mines to keep miners alive while mining (and of course, to secure and protect the all-important gold), very little has been done about the air and ventilation problems that cause

54   Terry Bell, 'Miners Who Are Doing Dirty Work Deserve Better', *Business Report*, 6 October 2000.

55   AngloGold Ashanti, *Operation Profile: West Wits South Africa*, 2012, p. 4, available at aga-reports.com.

56   Wadhams, 'World's Deepest Mines'.

silicosis. 'It was always possible through ventilation and proper clothing to protect people from silica dust in [gold] mines', NUM president, Senzeni Zokwana said when interviewed about the case. 'But in the past men were down [the mines] just to break rocks and make money.'[57] Richard Spoor, an attorney representing some of London claimants, agrees. 'It was cheaper for the gold mining industry to cripple and maim workers by exposing them to excessive levels of dust', he says, 'than it was to take steps to protect their health'.[58]

As in many other extractive industries, gold miners face real dangers struggling to improve wages and conditions and often confront heavily armed state police working on behalf of mining corporations and political elites. In one of the worst such stand-offs in recent times, forty-four mine workers striking for improved pay were massacred by South African police in 2012 while protesting at the Marikana platinum mine, 20 km north of Mponeng; seventy-eight others received serious gunshot wounds.[59]

Finally, and once again in line with the broader geographies and politics of all metal mining, gold mining also has severe social and environmental impacts beyond the risks it creates for the miners themselves. The accumulation of toxic acids and cyanides used in the processing of gold ores can often result in devastating health and environmental spills. The physical movement and dumping of waste mine tailings, moreover, can be devastating for ecosystems that get in the way.

As we close our journey through the vertical geographies and politics of our world, such a point conveniently returns us the manufacturing of vertical ground by humans.[60] For it has been estimated

57   Cited in Tracy McVeigh, 'South Africa's Miners Take Lung Disease Fight to London', *Observer*, 27 April 2014.

58   Cited in Jennifer Schmidt, 'Gold Miners Breathe the Dust, Fall Ill: "They Did Not Give Me Nothing"', NPR, 22 October 2015.

59   See Crispen Chinguno, 'Marikana Massacre and Strike Violence Post-Apartheid', *Global Labour Journal* 4:2, 2013. Interestingly, public struggles over the meaning of the killings were sometimes played out through Google Earth satellite images. See Amanda du Preez, 'The Marikana Massacre: Seeing It All', *Safundi: The Journal of South African and American Studies* 16:4, 2015, pp. 419–42.

60   See chapter 11.

that, on average, fully twenty tonnes of toxic mining waste must be dredged out of the earth, processed and disposed of to produce the gold necessary to make a single, ten-gram, eighteen-carat gold ring.[61]

61   Owens, 'Extreme Prospects' p. S6.

Afterword

In his superb study of the importance of the vertical dimension in the history of western modernism, cultural theorist Paul Haacke finishes by stressing the transformative importance of the way contemporary societies are imagined. He reaffirms anthropologist Arjun Appadurai's crucial point that 'the imagination is today a staging ground for action, and not only for escape'.[1]

The preceding pages very much confirm such a view. In rendering the landscapes and geographies of our cities and planet more fully from a three-dimensional perspective, my aim in this book has been to reveal much more fully than has been achieved to date how the many vertical axes and dimensions of life and power in the contemporary world intersect with multiple layers of more familiar change within both geography and history.

Despite its achievements, however, what *Vertical* has not been able to do – beyond a few asides such as those in the 'Drone', 'Satellite' and 'Ground' chapters – is to address fully the myriad of social and political movements across the world that are working to *contest* our planet's extreme and intensifying vertical (and volumetric!) geographies.

In taking forward a politics that challenges the often disturbing vertical geographies explored in this book, it is useful to close by invoking Haacke's arguments about the importance of maintaining a *progressive* imagination of Appadurai's 'grounds for action' – one that is fully in tune with the startling, and often neglected, verticalities, strata and volumes of our world as laid out in this book.

'Instead of lying on a flat plane,' Haacke writes, 'this progressive idea of the imagination requires a higher vantage point from which to perceive the multiple horizons of the future, as well as the multiplicity of historical pasts, while at the same time acting in the time of the now.'[2]

---

1   Arjun Appadurai, *Modernity at Large: Cultural Dimensions of Globalization*, Minneapolis: University of Minnesota Press, 1996, p. 7.

2   Paul Haacke, *The Vertical Turn: Topographies of Metropolitan Modernism*, PhD thesis: University of California, Berkeley, 2011, p. 189.

Acknowledgements

From initial research to final publication, this book took the best part of a decade to complete. Without the extraordinary support of a wide range of people and institutions, *Vertical* would have been simply impossible. My debts are extraordinarily numerous, long-standing and extensive.

First, Newcastle University – and especially Charles Harvey, provost of my faculty between 2008 and 2014 – provided crucial financial support that was central to the research that led to this book.

Further crucial support came from the university's School of Architecture, Planning and Landscape – and especially Jill Mawson and John Pendlebury. Lucy Hewitt, now of Glasgow University, was a superb researcher whose tireless work over a period of two years was absolutely central to the successful emergence of the project. Thanks so much Lucy!

Also in the School, Karen Ritchie and Caroline Armstrong were inexhaustible in tracing and sourcing books. Cat Button and Konrad Miciukiewicz, (the latter now of UCL), gave amazing support through covering brilliantly for my teaching during my sabbatical and other absences. Mandy Carling provided much needed help in proofreading early drafts of chapters.

Second, the almost impossibly wide range of the book has necessitated great reliance on a range of friends and colleagues from across the social sciences and humanities. My debts here are far too numerous to detail completely. But thanks, especially, to Michiel Acuto, Pete Adey, Manuel Appert, Ash Amin, Louise Amoore, Ben Anderson, Manuel Appert, everyone at APL in Newcastle University, Rowland Atkinson, Kirstie Ball, Trevor Barnes, Yasminah Beebeejaun, Pierre Belanger, Chloe Billing, Ryan Bishop, John Beck, Trevor Boddy, Matthew Bolton, Lindsay Bremner, Neil Brenner, Richard Brook, Roger Burrows, Amy Butt, Cat Button, Igal Charney, Angharad Closs Stephens, Caren Kaplan, Bob Catterall, Richard Collier, Martin Coward, Jordan Crandall, Simon Dalby, Davide Deriu, Renu Desai,

Jago Dodson, Martin Dodge, Andrew Donaldson, Mark Dorrian, Stuart Elden, Saba Eslami, Rodrigo Firmino, Benjamin Fogarty-Valenzuela, Steven Flusty, Matthew Gandy, Bradley Garrett, Derek Gregory, Gaston Gordillo, Adam Grydehoj, Sheeraz Gulsher, Jeff Halper, Andrew Harris, Phil Hayward, Patsy Healey, Oke Hauser, everyone at ICRAC (the International Campaign for Robotic Arms Control), Ole B. Jensen, Craig Jones, Maria Kaika, Caren Kaplan, Nikos Katsikis, Francisco Klauser, Sara Koopman, Igor Krstic, Setha Low, Tim Luke, Mark Maguire, Hannah Marsden, Colin McFarlane, Simon Marvin, Michael Mulvihill, Deborah Natsios, Mark Neocleous, Bruce O'Neil, Kevin Lewis O'Neill, Nancy Odendaal, Trevor Paglen, Lisa Parks, Jamie Peck, Simon Parker, Lucas Pohl, Carolyn Prouse, Vyjayanthi Rao, Matthew Rech, Gillad Rosen, Steve Rowell, Mimi Sheller, Michael Sorkin, Wendy Steele, Daniel Swanton, Mikkel Thelle, Alessandro Vincentelli, Lauren Wagner, Eyal Weizman, Martin Wilmott, Alison Williams, Thomas Wolseley, Steve Wright and John Young.

Third, I also need to thank colleagues at Griffith University Urban Research Program, Brisbane, and at UBC's Peter Wall Institute and Geography Department in Vancouver for their warm hospitality during my stays in these places in September 2013 and November 2014, respectively.

Acknowledgements are due as well to colleagues and friends at the following places for helpful comments and feedback on presentations of some of the work in this book: Paris, European Urban Research Association, June 2014; Copenhagen 'Cosmopolitics' conference, 2014; Goldsmiths, London, 2014; UBC Geography, November 2014; 'The Vertical City' in Lyon, November 2015; 'Island Cities' in Hong Kong in March 2016; and 'Spaces of Security' at Maynooth, May, 2016.

Fourth, it is also important to stress that earlier versions of some of the essays in *Vertical* have already been published in journals: 'Air' in *City* 19:2/3, 2015, pp. 192–215; 'Housing' in *City* 19:5, 2015, pp. 618–45; 'Ground' in the *International Journal of Urban and Regioanl Research,* Debates and Development section (forthcoming); 'Elevator/Lift' in *Theory, Culture and Society* 31, 2014 and Malene Freudendal-Pedersen and Sven Kesselring's forthcoming edited book *Networked Urban Mobilities;* and parts of 'Bunker/Tunnel' in Paul Dobraczyk,

Carlos Lopez Galvis and Bradley L. Garrett, eds, *Global Undergrounds: Exploring Cities Within* (London: Reaktion, 2016).

Penultimately, I owe the production and editing staff at Verso an enormous amount of gratitude. Leo Hollis, especially, kept faith in *Vertical* through far too many ups and downs and seemingly endless delays. Leo also put in a huge amount of work thrashing the chapter drafts into a manageable and readable form that might actually cohere into something like a book. Mark Martin organised the production side of the book superbly; Steven Hiatt was a brilliantly effective copy editor; Michael Oswell did a fabulous cover design; and Sam Smith was tireless in tracing image permissions.

Finally, and above all, my love and grateful thanks go to Annette, Ben and Oliver, and to all my friends and colleagues, who have helped so massively in the production of this book.

Stephen Graham,
Newcastle, June 2016

Index